The Hidden People of North Korea

The Hidden People of North Korea

Everyday Life in the Hermit Kingdom

Ralph Hassig and Kongdan Oh

ROWMAN & LITTLEFIELD PUBLISHERS, INC.
Lanham • Boulder • New York • Toronto • Plymouth, UK

Published by Rowman & Littlefield Publishers, Inc.
A wholly owned subsidiary of The Rowman & Littlefield Publishing Group, Inc.
4501 Forbes Boulevard, Suite 200, Lanham, Maryland 20706
http://www.rowmanlittlefield.com

Estover Road, Plymouth PL6 7PY, United Kingdom

British Library Cataloguing in Publication Information Available

Library of Congress Cataloging-in-Publication Data

Hassig, Ralph C.
    The hidden people of North Korea : everyday life in the hermit kingdom / Ralph
Hassig and Kongdan Oh.
        p.   cm.
    Includes bibliographical references and index.
    ISBN 978-0-7425-6718-4 (cloth : alk. paper)—ISBN 978-0-7425-6720-7
(electronic)
    1. Korea (North)—Social life and customs.   2. Korea (North)—Social
conditions.   3. Korea (North)—Economic conditions.   4. Political culture—Korea
(North)   5. Korea (North)—Politics and government—1994–   6. Kim, Chong-il,
1942—Influence. I. Oh, Kong Dan.   II. Title.
DS932.7.H37   2009
951.9305—dc22
                                                                              2009029786

∞ ™ The paper used in this publication meets the minimum requirements of American
National Standard for Information Sciences—Permanence of Paper for Printed Library
Materials, ANSI/NISO Z39.48-1992.

Printed in the United States of America

We must envelop our environment in a dense fog to prevent our enemies from learning anything about us.

—Kim Jong-il

~

Contents

Preface

Kongdan (Katy) Oh's parents came from North Korea, although in the final years of the Japanese occupation they lived in China. As members of the educated class, her parents were understandably wary of the new communist "working-class" government being set up in the North, and with hundreds of thousands of other North Koreans, they fled to the South before the border was closed. Since coming to the South, they have not heard anything from their relatives who stayed behind.

Under a succession of South Korean authoritarian governments that viewed the North as an enemy state, school children had no opportunity to learn anything about North Korea except what the authorities permitted under the National Security Law—still in force today but greatly relaxed since the end of the Cold War. Nor was information about other communist states available. It was not until she enrolled in graduate study at the University of California, Berkeley, that Oh was able to begin an objective study of North Korea.

Upon graduation, she went to work for the RAND Corporation with a primary assignment to analyze how North Korea could threaten the national security of the United States. In practice, this meant that much of her work, first at RAND and then at the Institute for Defense Analyses, has been related to North Korea's weapons of mass destruction. A secondary field of study is the nature and stability of the Kim regime, which after the terrorist attacks of September 11, 2001, was dubbed one of the three "axis-of-evil" governments by the George W. Bush administration. Missing from this study, and from most studies of North Korea, is an analysis of how the ordinary people live; since they have absolutely no voice in formulating their government's policies, what happens to them is of little concern to foreign governments.

The book's first author, Ralph Hassig, developed an interest in North Korea after being asked to edit and coauthor reports and articles with Katy Oh, who happens to be his wife (they met while they were teaching for the University of Maryland University College in Seoul). Since the early 1990s, Hassig has devoted most of his research time to North Korean studies, doing much of the English-language writing and research and relying on Oh to do most of the presentations, Korean-language research, and networking with other North Korea watchers in South Korea and around the world.

After completing our first book on North Korea, which was published in 2000, we decided to write something about the North Korean people, a topic that up to that time had been extremely difficult to research because few North Koreans could get out of their country and few foreigners could get in. This situation began to change in the late 1990s as thousands of North Koreans escaped into China; by 2009, over fifteen thousand of these defectors had made their way to South Korea, where they provide valuable information about everyday life in the modern-day hermit kingdom they were forced to leave behind. By interviewing them and by talking with other interviewers and reading their reports, it is now possible to piece together what life is like in North Korea today.

Along the way we have become indebted to many people for information, insights, and materials pertaining to the North Korean people. We would particularly like to thank Dr. Seong Il Hyun, currently a senior research fellow at South Korea's Institute for National Security Strategy and formerly a North Korean diplomat, who was kind enough to read through our manuscript and give it his personal approval. Some of the defectors we interviewed wish to remain anonymous to protect their identity (most of them have relatives still living in the North), while others have gone public with their testimony, although sometimes they adopt new names in South Korea. These former North Koreans, along with numerous researchers from other countries who have directly contributed to this book, are listed here in alphabetical order: Amii Abe, Seungjoo Baek, Stephen Bradner, William Brown, Jin-Sung Chang, Seong-Ryoul Cho, Charles Hawkins, Takeshi Hidesada, Yoshi Imazato, Eun Chan Jeong, An-sook Jung, Chul Hwan Kang, Byeong-Uk Kim, Kap-Sik Kim, Koo Sub Kim, Kwang-Jin Kim, Kyung-Hie Kim, Sang-Ryol Kim, Seung-Chul Kim, Tae Hoon Kim, Taewoo Kim, Doowon Lee, Duk-Haeng Lee, In Ho Lee, Won-Woong Lee, Young-Hwan Lee, W. Keith Luse, Mitsuhiro Mimura, Marcus Noland, Seung-Yul Oh, Young-Ho Park, Scott Snyder, Jae Jean Suh, Ven. Pomnyun Sunim, Chang Seok Yang, and Yeosang Yoon.

~

About Korean Names
and Pronunciation

We'd like to say a few words about the romanization and pronunciation of Korean names. The Korean alphabet is a wonderfully transparent writing system, but when it comes to transliterating it into roman letters, there are several alternatives. Until 2000, the most common method was to use the McCune-Reischauer System, a version of which we use in this book because it is familiar to several generations of readers and because it is also used by North Koreans to translate their works into English. We have simplified the system by dispensing with apostrophes (used to indicate aspirated consonants) and diacritical marks above vowels. The resulting simplification will be admirably suited to the needs of most readers, and those who are familiar with Korean will be able to translate back into Korean. Since 2000, South Korea's Ministry of Culture and Tourism has put forward a somewhat different method of transliterating Korean into English. This method, the Revised Romanization, has met with some resistance, even from major South Korean newspapers, but now seems to have been adopted widely in South Korea. However, because it looks somewhat strange to many foreigners, ourselves included, we have chosen to stay with the older system.

In Korean names, the family name usually comes first, followed by one or two given names. Some Koreans hyphenate their two given names, others write them separately, and some even combine the two (for example, the book's second author). The official North Korean approach is to write them separately, as in Kim Il Sung and Kim Jong Il; however, to make it clear to foreign readers which are the family names and which are the given names, we have decided to use an equally popular approach and hyphenate the two names, hence, Kim Il-sung and Kim Jong-il. Throughout the book Korean names are presented in this manner except where Koreans (outside of North Korea) specifically use another form.

As for pronunciation, "Kim" (the most popular name in Korea) is pronounced just as it would be in English. "Il" is pronounced like "eel," and "sung" is pronounced much like the English word. "Jong" rhymes with "sung." In general, the vowels in romanized Korean names are pronounced more as they would be in romance languages than in English. For example, the letter *a* in Pyongyang, the capital city, is pronounced like the *a* in "almond," not the *a* in "salmon."

CHAPTER ONE

~

The Illusion of Unity

Unity of purpose and coordination of effort are important sources of strength for a nation, so it is not surprising that the Kim regime of North Korea (officially known as the Democratic People's Republic of Korea, or DPRK) has spent over half a century trying to unify the North Korean people socially and ideologically. The regime's unifying principle is not nationalism, however, but loyalty to the Kim family. Everyone is supposed to think the same thoughts—to be "dyed" with whatever the ideology of the moment is, whether it is Kim Il-sung thought, *Juche* theory, or military-first politics. The regime wants every citizen to be an obedient member of the Kim family. "Our people are a happy people who have an absolutely perfect guarantee for their destiny as a result of having joined their blood vessels of life with the great heart of the nerve center of the revolution."[1] That nerve center and "supreme brain of the revolution" is none other than Kim Jong-il. Nor are the people of South Korea (officially, the Republic of Korea, or ROK) excluded from this appeal: "The entire fellow countrymen uphold the respected and beloved General Kim Jong-il, the sun of the nation and outstanding military-first brilliant commander, as the center of national unity."[2]

But something has gone terribly wrong with the unity campaign. The regime's economic system of centrally controlled socialism collapsed in the 1990s, and at just that time, Kim Il-sung, the revered founder of the nation, died, leaving his son to address the nation's crippling economic problems. When the people discovered that the son was not up to the task, even though he had been running things behind the scenes for many years, they gave up on the regime and on socialism. It is difficult, after all, to unify around failure. Of course not everyone abandoned the regime: the political elites, including the top military officers, continued to support Kim Jong-il, and thanks to their support, North Korea remains in form much as it has been

1

since its founding in 1946. But a closer look reveals that the country is eroding on the inside. The North Korean people are no longer socialists; nor do they respect their leader. It is not easy to describe what their political and economic beliefs are or how they live from day to day.

In 2000 we wrote a book titled *North Korea through the Looking Glass*. As the title suggests, the book illustrates how different North Korea is in terms of ideology, politics, economy, and foreign policy from the kind of society that most of us are familiar with. Not just different, theirs is in many respects the complete *opposite* of our society. Instead of individualism, they have a collective lifestyle; instead of a regulated market economy, a regime-directed economy; instead of democracy, a dynastic dictatorship; and instead of a foreign policy of alliance and influence, isolation and belligerent contradiction. Even the Chinese, who are North Korea's strongest supporters and closest "friends," admit that their neighbor is backward and strange.

Kim Il-sung's social design is seriously flawed from the viewpoint of the millions of North Koreans who constitute the powerless "masses." The "great leader" so dominated North Korea that when he died in 1994, the central government practically closed down for three years, during which time 5 to 10 percent of the population died of starvation brought on by severe floods and worsened by the country's collapsed infrastructure. From the rubble of that economic collapse, a new North Korea is slowly taking shape, hidden behind the regime's façade of ideological unity.

Those who survived the great famine of the 1990s did so because they ignored what Kim had taught them. They looked out for themselves—the very opposite of what he had always told them to do. If you will, they walked back through the looking glass to our side. Their survival techniques were unofficial and even illegal, including growing crops on patches of appropriated land and trading goods in neighborhood marketplaces. And because their everyday activities were hidden from outsiders, and often from the regime itself, the emergence of this new North Korea only became apparent when defectors began streaming out of the country in the late 1990s. In our previous book we described North Koreans as "double-thinkers" who, like citizens of other totalitarian states, had learned how to mouth the teachings of the regime even while harboring quite different ideas in their minds. When Kim Il-sung died and the government stopped operating, North Korea's double-thinkers became double-doers.

A decade and a half after Kim's death, North Korea is still surpassingly strange—strange in the sense of being different, not irrational or bizarre. Almost everything about North Korean society is designed to strengthen the control and further the longevity of the Kim dynasty. This top-down view of North Korea constitutes the counterpoint theme of our book. Even as the people are beginning to take responsibility for their own lives, the regime is doing its best to preserve the original social design. These two social forces, change and conservatism, create a drama in North Korea today. It is not the drama of a glorious revolution but rather a kind of guerrilla economic warfare that pits the politically powerless masses against an increasingly demoralized ruling political class. Chronologically, this book takes up where the last one left off, around the turn of the present century. The society we described in the late 1990s, that is, the society as it was designed and built by the two Kims, was to some extent a façade, but now even the façade is cracking.

The two books take up parallel topics. The earlier book focused on the society and the system, whereas the present book looks more closely at how people live and work. Instead of a chapter on ideology, this book has chapters on the range of information available to North Koreans and how that information challenges and shapes their beliefs, although ideology is still discussed because it plays an important role in the information environment. The chapter on North Korea's economy has been updated and supplemented by an additional chapter on food, health, housing, and employment. The Kim regime's social-control measures, which were the topic of a chapter in the first book, are now viewed in terms of human rights, the law, and the experience of the defectors who choose to escape that control. Instead of a chapter on North Korea's military power, we now describe the life of North Korean soldiers. Both books devote a chapter to the North Korean leadership, but the present book focuses almost exclusively on Kim Jong-il. And finally, both books end with a brief chapter laying out our modest recommendations for American policy toward North Korea. Readers will find that these recommendations have not changed; nor, for that matter, have they been adopted with any conviction by Washington policy makers.

Social Regimentation

North Korea has not experienced anything like the political, economic, and social changes that swept through the former Soviet Union and Eastern Europe a decade ago or even the more gradual economic and social changes that have been transforming China since the early 1980s. North Korea remains the world's most regimented society. And it is also the most secretive. According to one defector, Kim Jong-il has told his people that if they wrap themselves in mystery, their enemies will be filled with uncertainty, and by "enemies," Kim means *all* foreigners.[3] For many centuries, Koreans jealously guarded their privacy, repulsing invasions from Japan and paying tribute to the distant imperial Chinese court in order to preserve a measure of Korean sovereignty—hence the nickname "hermit kingdom." Korea has never been the destination of waves of foreign immigrants; nor until South Korea industrialized in the latter part of the twentieth century have Koreans actively participated in the international community. Even today, North Korea, unlike its neighbor to the south, has established relatively few commercial, political, cultural, or social ties with other peoples.

Although North Korean society is largely hidden from view, in some respects, North Koreans are easier to describe than, say, Americans because they have preserved in large measure their cultural and racial homogeneity. There are ever so many Kims and Lees and Parks but hardly any families with foreign names. The Korean people, especially the North Korean people, are proud of their cultural purity, as is illustrated by a heated exchange that took place in May 2006 at a meeting between North and South Korean military officers. The two lead negotiators were engaged in small talk about farmers going out into their fields for the springtime planting, and the South Korean general noted that because the rural population in South Korea was declining, farmers sometimes took foreign brides (usually from Mongolia, Vietnam, or the Philippines). At this, the North Korean general snapped, "Our nation has always considered its pure lineage to be of great importance—and I'm concerned that our singularity will disappear." The South Korean replied that this influx of foreigners was "but a drop of ink in the Han River" (referring to the river that runs through Seoul), whereupon his North Korean counterpart yelled, "Not even one drop of ink must be allowed to fall into the Han River." And so another inter-Korean dialogue got off to a rocky start.[4]

Regimentation in North Korean society is most obvious when people are gathered in large groups. When the 687 deputies of the Supreme People's Assembly vote, they do so unanimously by all holding up their deputy cards. To do otherwise, especially if Kim Jong-il were in attendance holding up his card, would be counted as treason. North Korea is justly famous for its military parades and its special displays, like the Arirang Festival, where a hundred thousand students perform gymnastics in almost perfect synchronicity, backed up by a card section of twenty thousand students creating ever-changing pictures that look like a gigantic computer screen.[5]

Faced with such sameness, outside observers are often tempted to depersonalize the North Korean people, but of course individual differences, rooted in personality and the pursuit of self-interest, add variety to their private lives. Today, not only has the ideological dye faded throughout North Korean society, but people are becoming more individualistic in their appearances and lifestyles. Comfortable, Chinese-made, cotton clothing in bright colors is replacing drab clothing made out of the domestic synthetic fiber Vinalon and worn with a Kim Il-sung badge over the heart. Women experiment with a variety of hairstyles and have taken to wearing cosmetics. Young people are attracted to foreign music, dances, and consumer goods.

To the extent that the North Korean people have not accepted the idea of single-hearted unity around their leader, the Kim regime has imposed uniformity by employing an arsenal of social-control measures, although these measures are not as strong as they were before the 1990s because police officers and party officials are spending more time looking out for their own welfare and less time doing the bidding of the government and the party. One of the more effective means of controlling people is to group them together so that they can watch each other and feel accountable to the group for their behavior. School children often assemble in their neighborhoods and march to school like little soldiers. Workers in the same factory or office may be assigned to the same housing development. Before and after work hours, coworkers are required to attend political meetings and self-criticism sessions. At the local level, neighborhood committees (*inminban*) and cells of the Korean Workers' Party keep an eye on what people are doing, even in their homes. As *Minju Choson*, the government newspaper says, "There is not a person who is not affiliated with a neighborhood or people's unit. . . . When all people's units become a harmonious group in which the members help and lead one another, the strength of our society's single-hearted unity will be demonstrated even further."[6]

If the Kim family cult propaganda were totally effective in creating social unity, surveillance and punishment would not be needed to enforce loyalty. Kim has tried to put himself, his father, and his mother at the political, ideological, historical, and cultural center of North Korean life. The people are told that without the Kim family, there would be no North Korea. Yet it seems clear that most people have not taken this propaganda to heart. Like people everywhere, they gripe about their leaders—but in private, never in public. Thus, while North Korean society appears to be unified around the Kim regime, the disappearance of Kim Jong-il might expose the true sentiments of the elites and the masses.

A First Glimpse of the Hidden People

The Kim regime has thrown up many barriers to prevent outsiders from understanding the North Korean state and its people. It has tried to stage-manage everything—an extreme case of the sort of news spinning that all governments engage in to some degree. Sometimes North Korean officials tell the truth, but most of the time they either exaggerate to make themselves look good or they simply lie. A book authored by French visitors to North Korea is aptly titled *In the Country of the Great Lie* (*Au pays du grand mensonge*).[7]

The bare-faced lies are easily exposed because the general condition of the country is quite evident. To take an example at random, when *Korea Today*, a North Korean propaganda magazine published in several languages, informs its readers that "a well-regulated medical care system is in operation both in urban and rural areas, supported by well-equipped, comprehensive medical care centers and special preventive cure establishments, with the latest facilities," it does not take even a moment's thought to realize the claim is an outright lie.[8] However, it is harder to fathom the thoughts of the North Korean people. A German visitor to North Korea writes,

> Besides my photos, I have memories of the encounters I had on this trip. They are contradictory. I do not have the feeling I was truly able to look behind the façade. Is there such a thing as a normal life, and what does it look like? I may have been granted a few glimpses, but what was honest: the open and friendly curiosity, which is a true pleasure, or the silent, sometimes even hostile rejection of the stranger that shocked me? Was I "protected" for my own sake or the sake of the state from everything that otherwise constitutes traveling?[9]

The Kim regime allows only a small number of its citizens to travel outside the country and also places severe restrictions on those who would like to visit North Korea. Yet, not all foreigners are kept out. Thousands of diplomats, businessmen, and foreign aid workers have spent time in North Korea, although they rarely have the opportunity to meet ordinary North Koreans. A South Korean who spent a week in Pyongyang in 2003 described the experience as like taking a time machine back fifty years, and indeed many South Korean visitors see similarities between present-day North Korea and the South Korea of the 1950s and 1960s.[10] A Japanese tourist who joined a North Korean–Japanese bicycle tour from Pyongyang to Kaesong in 2002 likened the experience to cycling in a time warp and described the North Korean countryside as being "somewhere in the Middle Ages."[11] The cyclists were not permitted to take photographs of farmers or farm villages, and whenever they came to an area the North Koreans did not want them to see, they were loaded onto buses. Nicholas Bonner, who operates a tour agency in Beijing and has been arranging tours into North Korea since the early 1990s, explains, "To me, the difference is that North Korea went off on a tangent. It's not that it stayed behind, it just went off on a totally obtuse angle."[12]

Tourism is an important money earner for the Kim regime, which charges premium prices for ordinary accommodations. An estimated one hundred thousand tourists travel to North Korea each year, drawn largely by curiosity. By far the largest group of tourists includes the Chinese, with Japanese (including Japanese Koreans) in second place. Europeans can usually get visas, but on only a few occasions have American tourists been granted entry, for example, to view the summertime Arirang Festival. Individual tourists are rarely accepted. Visas are usually issued just before tourists board their flight or train for Pyongyang, and in cases where the visa is denied, the trip has to be cancelled at the last minute.

Foreigners are limited in where they can travel and what they can do. A Lonely Planet web page claiming, "You'll soon be zipping around like a local, thanks to this map of North Korea," is entirely off the mark: due to travel restrictions and ubiquitous checkpoints, not even locals "zip around" in North Korea. Cell phones are collected from foreign tourists at the border, and sometimes telephoto lenses are as well. Guides tell their charges what they can and cannot photograph, and it is forbidden to take pictures from the windows of moving vehicles, although some people sneak a few shots anyway. Guides have been known to scrutinize the digital photos in a tourist's camera and decide which ones can be kept and which must be erased.

Before entering North Korea, tourists are briefed by their tour guide on what they should and should not do. One group of Chinese tourists received the following instructions:

> While in the DPRK, do not move about as you please, nor ask questions or say things off the top of your head. You can joke about daily life, but never, never ask questions about how many wives Kim Il-sung had. Refer to the Republic of Korea as South Korea [the DPRK does not recognize the existence of a legitimate competing Korean government]. Don't openly take pictures of the people. Don't hand out food to children. Don't try to bring in cell phones; they will be held at the border and might be disassembled by the police and returned to you in pieces.[13]

Upon entry into North Korea, each tour group is assigned one or more minders and translators. Even when foreigners are able to slip away from their official escorts, they discover that ordinary citizens are often wary of having anything to do with them. One foreigner tells of sneaking away from his hotel and traveling around the neighborhood on a pair of roller skates he had brought with him, without seemingly attracting any attention from the inhabitants, who must surely have considered a roller-skating foreigner to be an unusual sight (no doubt they were watching him out of the corner of their eyes). Visitors wandering around town without an escort are likely to be intercepted by a plainclothes policeman who will gently but firmly lead the wanderer back to his hotel "for his own safety," with disagreeable consequences for whoever was assigned to watch over the visitor. Resident diplomats and staff members of foreign aid organizations also face restrictions on where they can travel and what they can do.

All tourists receive the same treatment and follow pretty much the same itinerary. They are typically taken first to the giant bronze statue of Kim Il-sung on Mansu Hill, where they are expected to bow and offer a bundle of flowers. Important foreign guests, including visiting government officials (among them, former U.S. secretary of state Madeleine Albright), are taken to the Kumsusan Memorial Palace, where Kim Il-sung's body lies in state. Other stops on the standard tour are Kim's birthplace at Mangyongdae on the outskirts of Pyongyang, the International Friendship Exhibition at Mt. Myohyang to view the tens of thousands of gifts that have been presented to the two Kims by visiting foreign delegations, the Arch of Triumph (nine meters taller than the one in Paris), the Tower of the Juche Idea (one meter taller than the Washington Monument), and the Pyongyang Metro (said to be the world's deepest). All these places represent North Korea's official ideology but say nothing about the lives of ordinary citizens.

Most visitors receive the impression that Pyongyang and its environs (almost the only part of North Korea they are permitted to see) are exceptionally clean, seemingly uninhabited except during commuting hours and on weekends, filled with monuments to Kim Il-sung and posters lauding Kim Jong-il, and dark at night except for the lighted monuments. The wide and empty streets bordered by tall apartment buildings give visitors an eerie feeling. Behind the main streets are acres of small homes crowded together on narrow, winding streets such as would be found in most Asian cities, but these neighborhoods are off-limits to foreigners. There are no advertisements other than billboards and banners with political slogans. There are few stores or restaurants. The recently constructed public markets and the semiauthorized open-air markets are hidden from view and generally off-limits to tourists. Visitors who take bus tours to nearby cities comment on the scarcity of traffic except for the occasional black government Mercedes and open trucks loaded with freight and people. The roadsides, even after dark, are lined with people walking from one town to another carrying all manner of goods on their backs. The phrase *dubal-cha* ("two-legged car") is used to refer to these people, who think nothing of walking twenty or thirty kilometers just to pick up a sack of potatoes.

A Russian visitor, frustrated at not being able to meet any ordinary North Koreans, satirically relates an incident that occurred one night as he looked out of his Pyongyang hotel window:

> A filthy-drunk man was reeling in the deserted street and muttering under his breath. "You lush," I shouted. The Korean looked up, said something in his own language that sounded like a "meow" [probably *muuh*, meaning "what?"], and ran away. I was proud of myself. A colleague who lives here had complained to me that he had never had a chance to talk with a local resident. This required permission from the Foreign Ministry for a meeting with a specific individual. Sometimes the authorities even granted the request. Of course, the Korean would afterwards disappear. Forever. For this reason, all attempts at official communication (the [North] Koreans have not had any unofficial communication with foreigners for about 60 years now) were abandoned for humane reasons. Now, however, I had heard an unofficial "meow." Even if it probably was a local obscenity, we had made contact![14]

American tourists are rarely granted visas. This travel ban is not unreasonable in light of the fact that most Americans are probably hostile toward the Kim regime (although not toward the North Korean people) and in that sense represent a threat to it. Those Americans who have the best chance of receiving a visa include staff members of aid organizations (although if they speak Korean their chances are significantly reduced because they might learn too much about the country) and entertainers. Notably, the New York Philharmonic played a concert in Pyongyang in 2008, and the American Christian band Casting Crowns played there in 2007. A handful of Americans who function as unofficial interlocutors between the North Korean and American governments and who are relatively sympathetic to the Kim regime (and, by the same token, critical of U.S. policies toward North Korea) are also welcomed in Pyongyang. The authors of the present book are not included in this sympathetic group.

The one hundred thousand tourists do not include visitors to the Mt. Kumgang tourist reservation built and financed by one of South Korea's Hyundai companies. By 2007, almost two million people, mostly South

Koreans, had visited Kumgang by boat, train, and private car. Kumgang tourists hardly get to see the real North Korea. A German visitor speaks of a "hail of prohibitions upon entry" and characterizes the resort area as a zoo where foreigners are separated from North Koreans by a fence, and she wonders what goes on in the minds of the North Koreans standing along the roadside and watching the tour buses pass by.[15] The only natives that most tourists come into contact with are tour guides and hotel staff. Many of the staff are actually Korean residents of China, and the authentic North Koreans are specially chosen members of the Korean Worker's Party who know better than to say anything other than what they have been instructed to say.

An intriguing account of the life of foreigners in Pyongyang has been provided by Michael Harrold, a Brit who went to North Korea in 1986 to work as an English-language editor for seven years. Being young and adventuresome, he often went to places that foreigners were not supposed to go and struck up acquaintances outside his approved circle of workmates. Yet, according to his account, in all that time he was never able to gain a satisfactory understanding of his immediate social environment, much less the society as a whole:

> For seven years I was shielded from North Korean reality. I learnt the language up to a point and I had friends, but still I barely scratched the surface of what North Korea was all about, what the people really thought. The explanation of how this could be achieved was simple enough. On the one hand, restrictions and surveillance were imposed, preventing me from meeting ordinary North Koreans. On the other hand, it was a privilege, one they were anxious not to jeopardize, for North Koreans to be in a position that brought them into contact with foreigners. . . . In a country where even living in the capital city was a privilege, everyone was careful about what they did and said, particularly around foreigners. The result was a population obsessed with casting themselves and their country in a faultless light. It was as if the propaganda became a part of their everyday life.[16]

Harrold made some good North Korean friends, or at least so he thought. But it sounds as though he could never be sure who was a friend and who was a spy (in many cases, they were probably one and the same). When he became involved in a brief physical altercation after a few drinks at one of the tourist hotels and was asked to leave the country (he declined a later invitation to return), he seemed to be in equal parts confused, ashamed, and angry as he replayed the fateful incident that ended his career in North Korea: "For once I felt grateful for the lies and deceit that were such a part of everyday life in North Korea. I'd learned the hard way not to believe or trust anyone, and now I could argue quite reasonably, to myself at least, that there was no particular reason why the Koreans should have been telling the truth in this any more than they had at any other time."[17]

Andrew Holloway, another Brit who went to Pyongyang as an English-language editor, in this case for a year in 1987, had even less opportunity to get to know the country. Holloway thought the North Koreans were the nicest people he had ever met but admitted that because of the controlled nature of the society, he was unable to form any close friendships. He believed the masses were "contented with their simple lives," almost child-like in fact, but for himself, he expected something more from life and could not wait to get out of the country. Most visitors to the country would almost certainly echo his matter-of-fact evaluation of North Korea: "It was not the type of society of which I would ever wish to be a member."[18]

On rare occasions, foreign media, including a couple of American television networks, have been allowed into North Korea, in addition to the press corps that accompany high-level foreign delegations. To their credit, a few foreign filmmakers have even managed to negotiate permission to make short documentaries. The documentary that comes closest to the subject matter of this book is titled *North Korea: A Day in the Life*. Directed by Dutch film-maker Pieter Fleury and released in coordination with the DPRK Ministry of Culture in 2004, the film is available in the United States for purchase or rental. Needless to say, the director had little freedom to choose whom, what, where, or when to shoot. The authorities provided him with what they claimed was a typical family living in Pyongyang and allowed him to follow its members around for a few days. To illustrate the difficulty of penetrating North Korean society, as well as to provide a further preview of the themes we will be presenting later in the book, some of the high points of the film are worth reviewing.

This model family consists of a husband and wife, their daughter, and two grandparents who share their apartment. The father seems to be studying English, the mother works at a small coat factory, and the daughter is in nursery school. The family lives in a gray apartment building on a street with other gray apartment buildings.

In the opening scene, the grandmother is preparing breakfast while the son carefully cleans the three framed photos of Kim Il-sung, his wife Kim Jong-suk, and Kim Jong-il that are required to be hung on the most prominent wall in every North Korean dwelling and workplace. The rooms are small and full of furniture. After a hearty breakfast of the sort most North Koreans could only dream of, the mother walks her daughter to kindergarten, first singing a children's song about trees and then urging the daughter to accompany her in a song that goes, "Our powerful people's army, that shakes heaven and earth, the pathetic Americans kneel on the ground, and beg for their lives" (actually, the lyrics translate to "the jackal-like American bastards"—but these words do not appear in the film's subtitles). Few cars are seen on the streets, just pedestrians and the occasional bicycle, but the camera does catch three large posters, two depicting North Korean soldiers ready for battle and the third depicting a large American and a small Japanese skewered on the end of a North Korean bayonet.

As the children file into the school, each child bows to a large painting of Kim Il-sung and Kim Jong-il surrounded by happy children. In the classroom the children sit on benches around the edge of the room as the teacher plays a taped morning message: "Flowers need the sun in order to blossom, and the children of our country need the love of our great general Kim Jong-il in order to grow." On the wall is a child's drawing of two North Korean fighter jets shooting down an American jet. In the hallway is a poster of little children dressed as soldiers attacking an American—or rather, an American's head, which seems to have been separated from his body.

A kindergarten lesson is presented in a room built around an elaborate model of the "secret camp" on Mt. Paektu where Kim Jong-il is supposed to have been born. A similar room has been described by a foreign tourist who was taken to Pyongyang's "model" kindergarten, suggesting that the film crew happens to be in this same school and raising the question of why this "typical" child in a city of three million would be attending such a prestigious school. The teacher tells the Story of the Returned Boots: "Sit up straight. Little comrades, when you have heard my story, you will know that our general is the most praiseworthy man on earth. When he was young, he was a child just like you. Comrades, do you know what boots are?" She holds up a pair of red-and-white rubber boots. "Have any of you ever played in the snow?" One child offers that he likes to throw "snow grenades." The teacher then explains that Kim Jong-il's mother gave him a pair of rubber boots. "The great leader was so happy with his boots he put them on right away, and he ran straight to his comrades. But suddenly our great leader Kim Jong-il stopped running. Do you know why?" One child, who has undoubtedly heard the story many times, answers, "Because he was sad?" "Yes, because he saw his friends were still wearing wet sneakers. That's why our thoughtful general ran right back home, and when he came back outside, he was wearing wet sneakers."

Meanwhile, the mother is on her way to the coat factory. Military music is playing on the subway public address system, and the obligatory photos of the two Kims are hanging in the subway car. At the factory entrance, the workers (all women) are greeted by a female agitprop team whose leader is praising Kim Jong-il while her half-dozen associates line up behind her waving red flags. As the workers prepare their sewing machines for the day's work, the factory manager announces that the factory has been assigned a quota of 150 coats for that day, although they made fewer than 100 the day before. Then the electricity goes out, and the women take out paperback books and read or talk to each other.

In a separate room the factory manager convenes a meeting at which he blames the power outage on "the American stranglehold and years of natural disasters" and predicts, "As long as imperialism continues, our energy problem will exist." Then he calls on the equipment manager to stand and give her report, which she reads in a monotone voice: "I am responsible for the equipment department. I am not a good manager. I did not prepare the equipment plan properly. It's my fault the machines are in bad shape and unreliable. I didn't train the workers well. That's why the whole department performs so poorly. I vow that I will improve the production lines." Everyone takes notes, and when she sits, there is a moment of silence. Then another manager reads his report: "Our comrades should know that the electrical shortage is caused by the isolationist policy of imperialist countries, above all, the U.S." The factory manager adds, "This problem will go on until our enemy is defeated."

At one point the "third broadcasting" speaker on the workroom wall comes alive with a "news flash": "Our great general Kim Jong-il has, on behalf of the people, received a letter from a Chinese delegation. The letter of thanks says, 'Pyongyang, we have seen the fantastic results of your socialist system and encountered a friendly tradition and warm atmosphere during our visit. We would like to express our thanks for the effort Korea has made to make our visit a success. DPRK, we wish you eternal life and happiness.'"

At the end of the day, the family gathers in its apartment and listens to the grandfather, dressed in a suit covered with war medals, tell Korean War stories about how the Americans bombed his school and his house, killing his father and older brother. When he enlisted and went to the front, "I shot at Americans. I was breathing fire. You can imagine how badly I wanted revenge." He proudly says, "Even my granddaughter says, 'Kill the American dogs.' I taught her that."

His daughter-in-law, smiling brightly, adds, "My father-in-law has often told us about the enemy and about his experiences during the war. So even though I wasn't in the war myself, his stories have shown me how bad and cruel those American dogs, our people's enemy, were to our people. We must ensure that our people never suffer at the hands of those American monsters again. I believe from the bottom of my heart that we must do everything to destroy all American monsters on our land [i.e., the Korean Peninsula]."

The Book Chapters

Following this brief preview of North Korea, we move in chapter 2 to a discussion of the ideas, leadership techniques, and lifestyle of Kim Jong-il and his father, who are the architects and builders of North Korea and the two people for whose benefit the country continues to exist separately from South Korea. Although they have governed much like other dictators, the two Kims stand out because they have had a much longer time to perfect their dictatorship.

The foundation of a society is its economy, which is the subject of chapter 3. The socialist command economy that Kim Il-sung adopted and that Kim Jong-il has embraced is more than an economy: it is a social-control mechanism. People who don't obey, don't eat. Although this economic model is admirably suited to keeping the Kim regime in power, it can only function as long as it receives foreign aid or allows the people to supplement their income by participating in a parallel economy. When the economy breaks down, as North Korea's has, survival becomes an individual rather than a collective effort, as is described in chapter 4, which takes a more detailed look at the health, welfare, and work of the people.

Chapter 5 begins with the self-evident proposition that people need information to make intelligent choices. In order to limit the choices available to its people, the Kim regime has severely restricted information. Predictably, the so-called mosquito net that the regime has drawn over the country to block outside influences has developed holes. By secretly listening to foreign radio and television broadcasts and watching smuggled videotapes and discs, North Koreans are learning about the outside world, and this unauthorized information is beginning to change their beliefs. However, beliefs, the topic of chapter 6, change slowly, and in North Korea any beliefs other than the officially sanctioned thought of the party must be carefully hidden. In fact, it appears that most North Koreans do not even think about politics but instead focus on economic survival.

Chapter 7 takes up the related topics of the law, political class, and human rights. It is not unusual for dictatorial governments to grant their citizens a long list of constitutional rights, but most of these rights exist only on paper. The more rights the people enjoy, the more constraints are placed on the leader. Since the late 1980s, millions of North Koreans have not even enjoyed the right to an adequate diet. If the Kim regime does eventually reform its political system, which is far from certain, granting its people more individual rights will probably be the last step it takes.

Chapter 8 recounts how hundreds of thousands of North Koreans have fled across the border into China and how, by 2009, over fifteen thousand of them had then made their way to South Korea. Severe economic hardships, loss of confidence in Kim Jong-il's leadership, and disillusionment and curiosity due to information about the outside world are the main reasons they leave their homeland. Their flight to China and their struggle to survive or move on to a more hospitable haven in South Korea provide clues about what North Koreans will face if the Kim regime collapses in the near future.

The material for these chapters has come to us from many sources. Because our writings have been uniformly critical of the Kim regime, we have not been permitted to visit North Korea; instead, we have let North Koreans come to us. Over two hundred defectors have been interviewed by Kongdan Oh in recent years. In addition, Koreans and Chinese who live on the Chinese side of the North Korean border have shared their observations. North Korean officials attending international conferences are usually eager to talk with Oh, whose family originally came from North Korea (although she was born in South Korea). We have also consulted many North Korea specialists in South Korea, China, and Japan and studied thousands of news reports, travelers' accounts, and direct transcriptions and translations of North Korean media reports and internal documents. We frequently quote from domestic North Korean sources as a means of illustrating the information environment in which the North Korean people live, and it must be admitted that a secondary motive for doing this is to convict the Kim regime with its own words.

North Korea is constantly changing, and in any case it is impossible to be entirely accurate when describing a population of twenty-three million people. We believe our conclusions about North Korea are substantially correct, although we would be the first to admit that a few of the details may not be entirely accurate or up-to-date. One of the defectors we have interviewed on several occasions has been kind enough to read through the entire manuscript and tells us that, based on his experience, our description is accurate in regard to not only the main themes but the details as well. We have done our best with what is at hand, and we encourage interested readers to consult other sources as well, because no two views of North Korea are identical. For a start, a short list of readings for further study may be found at the end of the book.

CHAPTER TWO

~

The Life of the Leader

To understand why the North Korean people live the way they do, it is necessary to understand the thinking and personality of their supreme leader, Kim Jong-il, who, along with his father, has shaped their lives and limited their chances. And just as the son continued his father's work, there is every reason to believe that whoever takes over for Kim Jong-il—most likely one of his sons—will govern in the style of the first two Kims.

The North Korean people are accustomed to being ruled by autocratic leaders. Since the end of World War II, the North Korean dictators have been Kim Il-sung and his son Kim Jong-il. Before that, it was the Japanese emperor and his colonial administrators, and before that, an assortment of Korean kings and queens stretching back for millennia. Almost inevitably, dictators use their powers to serve their own personal interests before those of their people, and this is certainly the case in North Korea, which is run for the benefit of Kim and his elite supporters.

Kim Jong-il is, by occupation, a dictator, and that job description limits his choices—and also the choices of his successor. It is no coincidence that his policies strikingly resemble those of other dictators, past and present. Thus, Kim is neither crazy nor strange; he is just doing his job. Ronald Winetrobe provides a good general description of dictators based on numerous case studies (not including North Korea) that fits Kim like a glove:

Such leaders tend to be paranoid, because they lack reliable information about what their people are really thinking about them. One of their chief concerns is staying in office, and to this end, they are engaged with more or less frequency (depending on the type of dictatorship) in buying loyalty and implementing repressive measures in order to do so. We know less about their subjects, but we do know that as long as they are at all numerous—and especially if they are unorganized—

the benefits to each one of overthrowing the dictator will be small compared with the potential costs. This free-rider problem helps dictators immensely in the task of staying in office, but it doesn't solve it completely, and under the right circumstances, they can be deposed, as dictators often are.[1]

Winetrobe would likely place Kim Jong-il in the category of most dangerous dictators: "Of all of the systems examined, dictatorship approaches the purest form in the role of a single individual, someone who is beholden to no interest group and who is not motivated by economic concerns. And as a dictatorship approaches this form, it becomes progressively more dangerous and more interested in controlling a wider fraction of the economy and society."[2]

Kim Il-sung's Legacy

When Kim Jong-il took over after his father's death, his official slogan was "Expect no change from me." From his father he inherited not only a country but a system of governance. Whether the son would like to make substantial changes is a moot question. Over a decade later, the only changes that have come to North Korea have occurred in spite of Kim.

By the time he died, the man known to North Koreans as the *suryong* ("great leader"), or more reverentially as *oboi suryongnim* ("fatherly great leader"), had taken his people down a dead-end road—although it would be equally true to say that the road led directly to the Kim family estate. Beginning life as a wandering young man with a limited education and no profession other than guerrilla fighter, he ended up virtually owning a country of twenty-two million people. Although he was able to hold on to power for almost half a century, he failed to achieve his oft-pronounced goals of seeing his people "eat soup with meat, wear silk clothes, and live in tiled-roof houses." He also failed to unite the two Koreas under communism. Yet he was, and still is, respected and even worshipped by most North Koreans. Kim enjoyed unparalleled power to shape his country, and as Adrian Buzo has perceptively written, North Korea in many respects reflects the outlook and experience of its founder.[3]

Lacking education and international experience, Kim and his comrades were unable to progress beyond the first and most obvious stages of nation building. When Deng Xiaoping and the ruling Chinese communist elites were authorizing significant changes in China's economic affairs, Kim could see nothing wrong with North Korea's Stalinist-style socialist economy. When the Soviet Union and Eastern Europe gave up on communism, Kim held firm. In the final two decades of his life, Kim gradually handed over the day-to-day affairs of state to his son and receded into semiretirement to over-see the writing of his autobiography. The book's title, *With the Century*, is misleading because rather than living *with* the century, Kim was stuck in the first half of it. His policies of the 1950s no longer worked in the 1980s and 1990s. And because his autobiography mixes personal reminiscences with the cult stories that party propagandists invented for him, it does more to confuse his life story than clarify it. For more accurate accounts of his life, one must rely on foreign biographers.[4]

Kim Il-sung was born on April 15, 1912, in the village of Mangyongdae, just north of Pyongyang. His name was Kim Song-ju, not Kim Il-sung—the name change did not occur until the early 1930s, when he took the name of a legendary guerrilla fighter about whom little is known. He had an ordinary, if somewhat difficult, childhood. His father, Kim Hyong-jik, was at various times a schoolteacher, a clerk, and an herbal pharmacist who had briefly attended an American missionary school and become a Christian, which was not unusual in Korea. Most Koreans bowed to the authority of the Japanese administrators and went on with their lives, but not the Kim family, which fled to regions of China that the Japanese had not yet occupied. Kim joined a youth league that harassed the Japanese troops who were gradually spread-ing out over China, and at the age of seventeen, he was arrested and sen-tenced to several months in prison for being a member of the Korean Communist Youth League. With his entry into youthful anti-Japanese poli-tics, Kim ended his formal schooling, having completed eight grades.

At the age of twenty-one, Kim graduated from politics to the military, joining a guerrilla band of Koreans that North Korean propagandists would later call the Korean People's Revolutionary Army, and it was at this point in his life that he began using the name Kim Il-sung. The Japanese were able to break up the group, but Kim eluded them and joined other resistance groups that were usually affiliated with contingents of the Chinese army. Most of the time the guerrillas fought the Japanese in Manchuria, but occa-sionally they conducted raids into Japanese-occupied Korea.

Thanks to his leadership qualities, Kim soon had command of his own small group of fighters, who rarely numbered more than a hundred men. His most famous "battle" was fought in and around Pochonbo, a small Korean town close to the Chinese border. Leading a band of two hundred men, grandly named the Sixth Division of the Chinese Second Army (of the First Route Army), Kim and his men staged a daring early-morning attack on June 4, 1937, destroying Japanese administrative offices, setting fire to a corner police office, the elementary school, and the post office, and quickly retreating back across the border. Although North Koreans are taught that Pochonbo marked a "decisive turning point" in the liberation of Korea, in fact skirmishes such as these had no effect whatsoever on the tide of war.[5] In 1940 or 1941, Kim and his soldiers took refuge in Russia, where Kim settled in a Soviet army camp outside the village of Viatsk (Viatskoe or Vyatskiye) near the city of Khabarovsk (Chabarovsk) and was commissioned a captain in the Eighty-eighth Independent Brigade. There he stayed for the remainder of the war, undergoing Soviet military training and marrying Kim Jong-suk, one of the Korean women who had joined his guerrilla group. Their first son, Yura, later to be known as Kim Jong-il, was born on February 16 in 1941 or 1942 (some sources say his birth date was moved back a year so he could be exactly thirty years younger than his father).[6]

On September 19, 1945, just over a month after the Japanese surrender, a Soviet naval vessel carried Capt. Kim Il-sung and sixty of his Korean comrades to Wonsan, Korea. Back in Pyongyang, Kim was installed in office and controlled by the Soviet military, who considered him to be a disciplined and reliable surrogate communist leader. After a few administrative false starts on the part of the Russians, who were not sure how best to govern North Korea, a provisional people's committee was formed in February 1946, and Kim was appointed to lead it.

To make a long and complicated story short, over the next several years Kim used his political talents, along with the advice of his Soviet advisors and the support of Soviet troops, to take control of the newly established Korean security and military forces, thereby enabling him to outmaneuver political rivals who lacked a military base. By 1950 he had consolidated his position and created a miniature version of the Soviet Union in the northern half of the Korean Peninsula.[7] His next goal was to extend his control over the southern half of the peninsula. What the North Koreans call the "Great Fatherland Liberation War," known to foreigners as the Korean War, began with a surprise attack on June 25, 1950, although the North Korean people are told that the Korean People's Army (KPA) was launching a counteroffensive against a South Korean attack.

In the years immediately following the war, Kim's generalship was questioned, and those who naively believed that he was the first among political equals made a political attempt to unseat him.[8] As is often the case when people are gradually deprived of their individual freedoms, Kim's political opponents did not realize that he was well on his way to becoming a totalitarian dictator. Kim used his political skills, as well as the backing of the army and secret police, to purge political opponents and secure his regime, and by the late 1950s he had firmer control over the country than before the war. Kim Il-sung incorporated the guerrilla lifestyle that had enabled him to survive in China into his governance of North Korea and wedded it to the regimented economic and political structures that had made the Soviet Union a world power and kept Stalin in office.[9]

A decade after the Korean War, Premier Kim (he would take the title of president under a new constitution in 1972) could be proud of himself. Despite having little formal education and no political connections, he had become the unrivalled leader of half a country. Communism continued to spread through Asia, and Kim surely believed that the tide of history was on his side. He rarely traveled outside his country, except for occasional trips to China and the Soviet Union, but in his own little corner of the world, he was a god-king.

Kim ruled by what seemed to him to be common sense, and technocrats had little impact on policy. He traveled around the country giving what the press called "on-the-spot guidance." In this sense he was like a king traveling among his subjects, dispensing advice on matters great and small. His people loved him, and most foreigners who met him thought him a charming man. It was hard to believe that behind the hearty handshake and jovial manner was a man who had ruthlessly started the Korean War and cold-bloodedly purged his political rivals and who oversaw a gulag system that imprisoned hundreds of thousands of Koreans for crimes no more serious than questioning his policies.

Kim's thoughts and actions were more like those of the mayor of a small city or the lord of a fiefdom than the leader of a twentieth-century state. Policy mistakes, of which there were many, were covered up by aid from China, the Soviet Union, and Eastern Europe. His people were kept so isolated that they could not compare their standard of living with that of the South Koreans or Chinese. The one sphere of life in which Kim had to stay on top of his game was domestic politics; he had a sixth sense about how to influence and control people, a sense that his son would develop as well. Motivated by adoration for their leader and by their own self-interest, party officials created for Kim a cult of personality that he gracefully accepted. He was not an evil or intentionally corrupt man. Better to say, he was a normal human being who gradually succumbed to adulation and privilege and who used whatever power his followers granted him.

The goal of Korean reunification continued to elude him. After the Korean War truce, he kept looking for an opening, but South Korea grew faster than the North and remained firmly under the protection of the

United States. The Korean War had turned most South Koreans into ardent anticommunists who accepted their own military dictatorships as a necessity for national survival. In the late 1960s, Kim increased North Korea's commando raids into the South, but they were repulsed and made the South Korean people even more hostile toward the North.

Judging by his lack of significant policy initiatives, Kim did not seem to notice that international communism was losing its legitimacy as a provider of people's welfare. The gap between rich and poor was smaller in communist than in capitalist economies, but communist economies were never healthy, and North Korea found itself locked into a trading system with other inferior economies. North Korean factories turned out third-rate products that were traded to other communist countries for their second-rate products. Meanwhile, South Korea was joining the other East Asian economic "dragons" on its way to prosperity.

In the 1970s, as the shortcomings of North Korea's economy were becoming more evident, Kim was in his sixties and beginning to sink into a comfortable semiretirement. It seems likely that in the 1980s and 1990s, Kim Jong-il was running the country with his father presiding over formal diplomatic tasks and public appearances. Kim Il-sung reportedly died of a heart attack at 2 a.m. on July 8, 1994, although the exact circumstances of his death are not likely to be known until after the secretive North Korean regime has been replaced. News of his death was announced thirty-four hours later on the Korean Central Broadcasting Station (KCBS), the country's only domestic radio station, and an hour after that to the international community by the Korean Central News Agency (KCNA). Millions of sobbing mourners appeared at the thousands of Kim Il-sung monuments scattered across the country to pay their respects (although one former North Korean we interviewed said that she only pretended to cry in order not to stand out from the crowd and attract the attention of the police). To this day, a visit to the Kumsusan Memorial Palace, where Kim's body lies in state, is a moving experience for the tens of thousands of North Koreans who go every year.

Two days before he died, Kim Il-sung reportedly gave a talk to a small group of officials in which he outlined several tasks to be accomplished, not knowing of course that this would be his last instruction.[10] After his death, his words were enshrined as a sacred "behest," and whenever it was convenient, his son invoked the behest as the mission his father wanted him and the North Korean people to accomplish, reminiscent of Stalin's pledge at Lenin's funeral to carry on his work. Kim's last instructions showed how out of touch he was with economic reality. He instructed his officials to construct

The Life of the Leader ⌒ 23

oil-powered power plants to help solve the chronic energy shortage, although North Korea had to import all its oil from abroad. He urged the repair of a large fertilizer plant and the "normalization" of the cement industry. He also ordered that the production of steel be increased. All these industries had been failing for years and would continue to fail because he could not tell the people where to get the resources to run them. He wanted to see an increase in trade with Southeast Asia, for which one hundred large cargo ships should be built—although North Korea only has the capacity to build small cargo ships. He also instructed his economic officials to go abroad to study modern business practices, although the country really needed a better economic system, not better businessmen. Kim's final instruction was significant: to "achieve the complete victory of socialism and the fatherland's reunification," that is, the reunification of the peninsula under communism.

The Rise of Kim Jong-il

North Korea is one of the rare cases of successful hereditary succession in national politics. As the oldest son of the founder, Kim Jong-il had an inside track on succession, even though hereditary rule has never been a notable feature of communist regimes.[11] But being a dictator's son was not enough to guarantee Kim Jong-il the succession. He had to prove himself, because his father was not foolish enough to put the country he had built into the hands of an incompetent. The approval process lasted from the time Jong-il graduated from college in 1964 to the time he was publicly presented as the future leader in 1980. Along the way there were purges and banishments and most likely a few dead bodies. Once in power, Kim Jong-il took the country as it had been shaped by his father and, with a view to staying in power, made no substantial changes.

According to an early edition of North Korea's *Dictionary of Political Terminology*, hereditary succession is "a reactionary custom of exploitative societies," but that inconvenient characterization was deleted in later editions of the work. From 1974 to 1977, and sometimes even in later years, the North Korean media referred to Kim Jong-il only as the "party center," leaving people to guess the exact identity of that individual.[12] Why he was not identified by name is not known, although the most popular guess is that he or his father was concerned about how the public would react to such an obvious case of nepotism. When he was mentioned by name, he was often referred to as "Dear Leader Comrade Kim Jong-il" (*kyongaehanun jidoja Kim Jong-il dongji*).

The official story of Kim Jong-il's birth has this auspicious event taking place in a log cabin on the forested slopes of North Korea's Mt. Paektu, where his father's guerrilla band was allegedly based. The mountain above the cabin, originally called Chang-su Peak, was later renamed Jong-il Peak. In fact, Kim was not even born in Korea but rather in a Russian military camp near Khabarovsk. In late November 1945, two months after Kim Il-sung was escorted back to Korea by Russian troops, the three-year-old Jong-il and his mother landed at the small eastern port of Unggi, later renamed Sonbong, meaning "leading torch." Kim's younger brother, Shura, who had been born in 1944, died in a drowning accident at the family home at the age of five. Kim also had a sister, Kyong-hui, born in 1946, who would become one of his closest associates.

His mother, Kim Jong-suk, died while giving birth to her fourth child in 1949, and in about 1953, Kim's father married the attractive Kim Song-ae and had a second son, Kim Pyong-il, a handsome and popular boy. Kim Jong-il disliked his stepmother and stepbrother, and when he gained political power, he saw to it that both of them were kept out of the circle of influence, his mother under house arrest and his brother permanently assigned to ambassadorships in Bulgaria, Hungary, Finland, and Poland, where he was kept under close surveillance.

Kim discarded his Russian name of Yura at about the time he graduated from high school, and he would later change the Chinese characters of his Korean name to make them fitting for a member of the ruling family, because in Asia names carry more meaning than they do in the West. Jong-il, originally written in Chinese characters meaning "righteousness the first," was changed to "righteousness the sun" when Kim made his political debut in 1980. The "sun" name is the same as the first character of his father's name, Il-sung. Kim's mother's name, Jong-suk, originally written with the Jong character meaning "virtue," was posthumously changed to the same Jong character for "righteousness" that is part of her son's name.[13] Thus, Jong-il ended up with one name from his father and one from his mother, signifying that he is firmly in the family "revolutionary bloodline."

Kim's childhood was typical—for the son of a dictator. He was treated with great deference by one and all and thoroughly spoiled. His father probably did not have much time to spend with his son, and having a father who was worshipped as a great hero and almost a god set a very high standard for the young Kim, who was always trying to gain his father's respect. After middle and high school in Pyongyang (except for a few years in China during the Korean War), Kim enrolled in the university named after his father, Kim

Il-sung University, and graduated with a degree in political economy in 1964. Kim's university dissertation, perhaps ghostwritten (he was a bright, but somewhat distracted, student who had special tutors to assist him), was titled "The County's Position and Role in the Construction of Socialism." In 1964, Kim joined the Korean Workers' Party's (KWP) Propaganda and Agitation Department, which was headed by his uncle, Kim Yong-ju. By 1967 the young Kim was chief of the Culture and Art Guidance Section of the department, rising to department vice director in 1970.

Testimony from North Korean defectors suggests that Kim played an active role in the management of party and government affairs from the time of his first party appointment in the mid-1960s, including (according to the North Korean press) bearing direct responsibility for the capture of the U.S. spy ship *Pueblo* in 1968 and the ax killings of American soldiers at the border post of Panmunjom in 1976.[14]

Kim moved steadily into his role as successor. In 1973 he became a Central Party secretary, and the next year he was appointed to the Politburo. His leadership succession was made official at the Sixth Party Congress in 1980, where at his father's direction he was appointed a member of the Politburo Standing Committee, secretary of the Central Party Committee, and member of the Central Military Committee. Only two other persons held such prestigious posts: his father and the top general, O Jin-u, who, not being a family member, could not be in the line of succession.

It appears that the junior Kim ran most of North Korea's domestic affairs from about 1980 onward. He issued commands in the name of his father and, by that token, had to be obeyed because his father's word was quite literally the law of the land. Because he served as his father's principal administrative assistant, reports sent to Kim Il-sung had to go through Kim Jong-il, who therefore decided what information his father would receive.

In the 1990s, Kim Jong-il was given (or took) several titles and top posts to consolidate his control over the military, the only institution that could conceivably block his succession. In 1990 he was elected first vice chairman of the National Defense Commission (NDC), an entity whose only significance at the time was that Kim Il-sung was its chairman. In 1991 Kim Jong-il was named supreme commander of the KPA, and the following year, on the KPA's sixtieth anniversary, he received the title of marshal (his father took the title of grand marshal). While reviewing the military parade commemorating the KPA's anniversary, Kim made the only publicly broadcast utterance of his career, calling out in a high-pitched voice, "Glory to the heroic KPA officers and men." According to one South Korean source, his words were only supposed to go out on the public address system, but due to a sound engineer's error, his brief speech was picked up by Korean Central Television (KCTV), a mistake for which several broadcasting officials were duly punished.[15] In 1993, Kim Jong-il succeeded his father as chairman of the NDC.

When Kim Il-sung died on July 8, 1994, no one other than Kim Jong-il was even remotely positioned to succeed him, but it is likely that Kim had to do some additional work to consolidate his political position now that his father was no longer around to back him up. To this end, Kim placed even more emphasis on the military as his main source of support and the "pillar" of North Korean society. He continued to reward and promote KPA generals, usually announcing the promotions on Kim Il-sung's birthday, thereby making the officers loyal to both him and his late father.

Many observers of North Korea, ourselves included, doubted that Kim Jong-il could hold on to power after his father's death. The reasons for such skepticism were numerous, but two stand out. First, the junior Kim was riding to power on his father's coattails. It seemed quite possible that the KPA generals might not rally around the great leader's son, who had no military experience, even though North Korean propagandists called him "a military genius who has boundless military insights, limitless boldness, extensive military knowledge, and political insights."[16] This line of skepticism failed to consider, however, that the top generals, most of whom were of Kim Il-sung's generation, recognized that they could not run the country themselves. They were, after all, uneducated warriors who owed their positions to having fought alongside the senior Kim fifty years before.

Another reason for discounting Kim Jong-il's staying power was his relative obscurity. Unlike his father, who loved to meet people and give speeches, the junior Kim avoided the public and never gave a public speech or made a media broadcast. He even failed to utter a word on the fiftieth anniversary of the country's founding in 1998, when the Supreme People's Assembly (SPA) convened for the first time since his father's death. Instead, the assembled delegates were treated to a recording of a speech made by his father in 1990. But, of course, the North Korean people have no voice in politics, so even though they were skeptical of Kim Jong-il's leadership ability, it hardly mattered.

By the mid-1990s the North Korean economy was in disastrous shape because Russia had ended its concessionary trade relations with North Korea, and China had curtailed them. Food rations began to run short even before floods hit the country in the summer of 1995. For three years after his father's death, while millions were going hungry and even starving, Kim Jong-il lived in seclusion. The press said he was such a loyal son that he was honoring a traditional three-year mourning period. Only in 1997 did he come out of his self-imposed seclusion to have himself appointed to his father's position as general secretary of the KWP. The appointment was made without convening a party congress, which had not met since 1980 (nor has it met since). In 1998, when Kim finally convened the Supreme People's Assembly, the delegates adopted a new constitution that retired the position of president, thereby making his father North Korea's "eternal president." Kim chose to be reelected as NDC chairman, a position declared to be the country's top leadership post. In the North Korean media, Kim is often referred to by the full complement of his ruling titles: Comrade Kim Jong-il, chairman of the Democratic People's Republic of Korea (DPRK) National Defense Commission, general secretary of the Korean Workers' Party, and supreme commander of the Korean People's Army.

First-Person Accounts of Kim Jong-il

Kim Jong-il is hidden person number one in North Korea. He has shrouded his life in secrecy as a first line of defense against domestic and foreign threats to his regime, and it would seem that secrecy is also an important characteristic of his lifestyle and mode of governance. He has said, "We must envelope our environment in a dense fog to prevent our enemies from learning anything about us."[17] Kim's penchant for secrecy makes it difficult to get behind the persona of the "respected and beloved general" and his international reputation as a crazy playboy. In reality he is not crazy, and although he likes to think of himself as a bold leader, his most important decisions are made with calculation and, more often than not, with caution.

Kim's international debut could be said to have occurred when he welcomed South Korean president Kim Dae-jung to Pyongyang for a summit meeting in June 2000. The meeting went well, and some Korea observers expected that Kim's public success would prompt him to adopt a more open leadership style. As it turned out, Kim was not about to become a public figure or international globe-trotter, and he never got around to making a promised reciprocal visit to Seoul. The leaders of China, Russia, Japan, and South Korea have come to Pyongyang, as has an American secretary of state, but Kim has continued to lead a secluded life and stayed close to home. Except for making a few trips to China and Russia, where he can feel at home among fellow autocrats, he has avoided going out into the world.

Clues about his personality, leadership style, and personal goals can be gleaned from the testimony of the relatively small number of North Korean defectors and foreigners who have come into contact with him. They describe him (to use what psychologists call the "big five" personality traits) as publicly retiring, impulsive, open to experience, alternately good-natured and irritable, and tense and insecure.

Kim Loses His Ideological Theorist

To date, the highest-level North Korean official publicly known to have defected is Hwang Jang-yop. When he defected in February 1997 while on an official visit to China, the seventy-three-year-old Hwang was chairman of the foreign policy committee of the Supreme People's Assembly and had previously been president of Kim Il-sung University and secretary of the KWP's international department. Hwang's interests lie mainly in the realm of ideology.[18] He appears to be a strong believer in socialism and a severe critic of Kim Jong-il, whom he accuses of betraying socialism and misguiding Kim Il-sung. Hwang claims that the senior Kim was "a perfect leader" until Kim Jong-il began to exert his influence around 1974, adding, "Kim Il-sung committed errors because of Kim Jong-il."[19] By the time he defected, Hwang was no longer in close touch with Kim, but he still knew much about the upper echelon of North Korean officialdom. When he defected, accompanied by his associate Kim Tuk-hong, Hwang left behind a wife believed to have committed suicide, one daughter who may also have committed suicide, another daughter, a son, and granddaughters, all presumably sent to prison camps. Hundreds, perhaps even thousands, of his friends and associates were fired from their jobs, imprisoned, or banished to the countryside. The thoroughness of this purge reveals the anger that Kim Jong-il can show when betrayed.

Hwang's greatest contribution to the body of knowledge about Kim Jong-il is his description of how the younger Kim ingratiated himself with his father and maneuvered to gain the succession. Hwang says the young Kim would stand beside his father and help him put on his shoes, even when his father was fully capable of taking care of himself. Kim Jong-il was an artist and manager, not a military man like his father, but his staging of patriotic films such as *Sea of Blood* and *Flower Girl* apparently impressed the old soldier. The young Kim successfully sidelined Kim Il-sung's younger brother, Kim Yong-ju, and wooed the politicians and military generals of his father's first generation of revolutionaries. In public at least, Kim showed respect to these older men, although once he had grasped power, he made it clear to them that he was the boss.

Hwang doesn't want to say much about Kim Jong-il's personality, but he does say that Kim is a suspicious person and very emotional in showing his likes and dislikes. Kim's moods and opinions change quickly, and he wants things done immediately. When making decisions, he does not consult advisors as readily as his father did. He likes to appear knowledgeable on a wide variety of subjects and presents himself (and probably thinks of himself) as a modern, liberal individual, more sophisticated than the officials who surround him. He is a micromanager, going so far as to choose apartments and cars for his top officials.

According to Hwang, Kim has an "animal's instinct for judging one's loyalty." He likes to get people drunk, the better to study them when they are off their guard, and the customary entrance fee for attending Kim's parties is to gulp down a glass of cognac. He does not trust nondrinkers, or at least he does not share his thoughts with them. He speaks boldly, always talking about war, but, according to Hwang, Kim takes care not to overplay his hand because he has no desire actually to fight a war and has never engaged in combat himself, although he is an excellent marksman with a pistol. He fancies himself a great general, but like certain other dictators—Hitler and Stalin come to mind—he thinks he knows more about military affairs than he actually does. Hwang says Kim does not read books but does review the hundreds of reports that reach his desk every week.

Hwang believes that Kim Jong-il has a clear view of his political interests. Unlike Kim Il-sung, who appeared to care for his people, the younger Kim seems not to be shocked by the hardship they face. Both Hwang and the abducted movie director Shin Sang-ok quote Kim as saying that having too many people in North Korea makes ruling difficult; Hwang even believes that Kim considered the famine of the mid-1990s a good way to weed out the untrustworthy people, who were the first to have their rations stopped.

Kim Abducts a South Korean Film Director and His Actress Wife

The South Korean film director Shin Sang-ok and his actress wife, Choe Un-hui, had the unwelcome opportunity to get to know Kim during their forced stay in North Korea. Choe was kidnapped from Hong Kong in January 1978 and brought to North Korea. According to her testimony, when she disembarked from the boat, she was met by Kim Jong-il himself, who said, "You have gone through a lot of trouble to come here. Honorable Miss Choe, I am Kim Jong-il." Choe was then taken in Kim's car to a Pyongyang guesthouse, which was to become her prison for a time.[20]

Six months later Choe's husband, director Shin, was also kidnapped from Hong Kong where he had gone when his films came under attack from the authoritarian government in South Korea. As Kim Jong-il later explained to the couple, who on several occasions secretly recorded their conversations with him in order to secure evidence that they had been abducted and had not willfully traveled to the North, he was aware that Shin was unhappy in South Korea and "wanted to show that South Koreans, people from the southern half, do come to us, to the bosom of the Republic, and make genuine movies while enjoying true freedom, not worrying about anything." Another time, he said, "It would be natural for you to say you came here to exercise your rights of creative freedom, instead of saying you were forced to come here."

When he arrived, Shin had no idea that his wife was in North Korea. He was confined to a guesthouse, but after an escape attempt in his first year of captivity, he was put in prison for several months. After trying to escape a second time the following year, he was imprisoned for four years, and he did not meet his wife or Kim Jong-il until 1983. Shin and Choe gradually gained Kim's trust and made ten films for him in North Korea. Kim wanted to make North Korean films known worldwide—"Make sure that the bastards envy us," he said—so he encouraged Shin and Choe to travel abroad, although they were always accompanied by a security detail. On a trip to Vienna in 1986, the two eluded their minders and asked for political asylum in the United States, where they lived for several years. Shin returned to South Korea in 1994 and died in 2006. Choe Un-hui reportedly divides her time between the United States and South Korea.

Most remarkable about Kim's comments as recorded by Shin and Choe is how realistically he describes conditions in North Korea. "As you may have seen, comrades, or rather Mr. Shin and Mrs. Choe, in short, we are people who only see things within the perimeters of our own fence, and believe we are the best (all three laugh)." After criticizing the "backwardness" of his film industry, Kim says, "If other people were to say this, these people would be criticized for not being satisfied with what they have (he laughs). That is, they would be branded flunkeyists [that is, subservient to capitalist enemies of North Korea]." Kim did not need to add that such critics would be sent straightaway to a prison camp.

Kim expressed awareness of socialism's shortcomings: "Socialism is fine, but there are many internal problems that need to be solved." Speaking of his screenwriters, he said, "The state gives one living expenses, even when one does not write. Therefore, one has no motivation." Twenty years later, in 2003, Kim voiced the same complaints about socialism, this time to the visiting chairman of South Korea's Hyundai conglomerate: "The evil of socialism is that there are too many people who want a free ride."[21] According to Kim, the solution to this problem of poor motivation and lack of responsibility is to change people, not the system: "The spirit of the socialist life of labor should be established so that people leading a dissolute life or getting a free ride do not exist."

In his talks with Shin and Choe, Kim even showed he was aware that the adulation he received from the people was not always genuine. According to Shin, one day when band members were cheering him, Kim said, "Mr. Shin, that is all fake. They are not cheering from the bottom of their hearts."[22]

Kim seemed to understand the bind he was in as the dictatorial ruler of a poor country. On the subject of permitting North Koreans to learn about the outside world, he admitted, "Say we constantly broadcast foreign films on television; then, the people will feel a sense of futility. Under the situation in which the country is divided, how can I let the people worship foreign things at a time when we need to arouse national pride, patriotic struggle, and other things? We have to develop our technology before opening up to foreign countries, but again, this is self contradictory."[23] This was still Kim's dilemma twenty-five years later: how to introduce foreign technology and attract foreign investment without exposing his people to foreign ideas that would weaken their loyalty to the regime or kindle thoughts about alternative forms of government.

Kim Adopts a Daughter

A fascinating close-up of Kim in the 1980s is provided by his "adopted daughter" Yi (Lee) Nam-ok, who was actually his niece. In the late 1960s Kim had taken as a mistress Song Hye-rim, a beautiful and popular actress who was already married. They began living together around 1969 and had a son, Kim Jong-nam, born in 1971. Song had a widowed sister, Song Hye-rang, who had a daughter named Yi Nam-ok and a son named Yi Han-yong. Because the illegitimate Kim-Song household had to be kept secret, not just from Kim Il-sung but from all of North Korean society, little Kim Jong-nam was not permitted to associate with children outside the family.

To keep him company, Song Hye-rang was brought to the house in 1979 so that her little daughter, Nam-ok, then age thirteen and five years older than Jong-nam, could become his live-in playmate. Nam-ok came to think of Kim Jong-il as her father, although there was always some distance between Kim and his family. Song Hye-rang defected with her sister in 1996 (her sister subsequently returned to Moscow) and published her memoirs in

Korean (the English title is *Wisteria House*).[24] So far as we know, she lives in Europe. Her daughter, Nam-ok, defected to France in 1992; since then, she has lived a secretive life as a French citizen.[25] With a French writer she wrote a manuscript titled *The Golden Cage* but later thought better of it and blocked its publication.

According to Nam-ok's testimony, Kim Jong-il was absent from home much of the time; he was, after all, running the country and had a wife and various other extramarital affairs to attend to. When he was home, his changeable moods put everyone on edge. Nevertheless, Nam-ok's impression of Kim was favorable—at least according to what she has said. The "golden cage" in which the family lived was distinctly Western, complete with imported furnishings. Nam-ok recalled many examples of Kim's interest in the latest foreign products. For example, he was always sending away for Japanese electronics (his favorite brand was Sony), he drove Western cars (Mercedes), and his son's playroom was filled with more toys than a toy store.

Nam-ok says Kim doted on Jong-nam, who physically resembled his father, and Jong-nam in turn was devoted to his father and bitterly missed him when he was later sent to school in Switzerland with Nam-ok. According to Nam-ok, Kim Jong-il hated protocol and flattery and had no interest in attending public gatherings. He always seemed to know what people were thinking and doing: "If a bud of a [political] 'faction' sprouted, he would not leave it to grow bigger."[26] He loved to laugh and have a good time, but she never saw him drunk and never saw him physically mistreat anyone, including family members, although he yelled and frightened them.

Kim Relaxes with His Japanese Chef

A treasure trove of information about Kim Jong-il's luxurious lifestyle and impetuous personality, some of it perhaps exaggerated, has come from the testimony of a Japanese chef, "Kenji Fujimoto" (a pseudonym he later adopted to protect himself), who was recruited in 1981 by a Japanese trading firm with connections in North Korea and ended up spending thirteen years working for Kim.[27] For Fujimoto, life in North Korea was one long adventure, although he had to endure constant surveillance and was always at the beck and call of his unpredictable boss.

Much of Fujimoto's testimony is about Kim Jong-il's food, parties, and hobbies. He speculates that Kim liked him as a companion because Fujimoto was a playful soul ready for almost anything. Fujimoto's first encounter with Kim, before he even knew who Kim was, reveals how the "Kim court" works. At the time, he was working as a sushi chef at a North Korean hotel, and one night the hotel manager told him to prepare sushi materials for twenty to thirty people. Three Mercedes picked Fujimoto and his assistants up and drove them two and a half hours to a villa at Wonsan beach. The kitchen crew finished preparing the sushi, and at 2 a.m. they were called into the banquet hall to serve Kim Jong-il and his guests.

After preparing sushi for Kim two or three times a month for several years, Fujimoto was invited to join in card games and other entertainments, and eventually he became a member of Kim's personal secretariat, traveling around the country with him and taking on added responsibilities such as house-sitting with Kim's children.

After Fujimoto became estranged from his wife and family back in Japan, Kim Jong-il observed that his chef was attracted to one of the young entertainment women attending Kim's parties and arranged a marriage. Fujimoto and his bride were married in a ceremony attended by Kim—but not by the girl's parents, who were not permitted to associate with the Kim court. The couple was given an eight-room apartment, complete with imported furniture and appliances. The girl's family, who lived in a one-room apartment (later upgraded to two rooms), was eventually permitted to make a visit to the Fujimoto household, where they were amazed to discover that running water was available twenty-four hours a day, not just for a couple of hours in the morning and evening as is the case in most Pyongyang apartments.

Fujimoto had a particular interest in Kim's cuisine and kept records of some of the dinners. Here, for example, is a menu for a family dinner: chilled flowering fern, radish dressed with vinegar, quail egg jelly, grilled pheasant, sautéed rice noodles, sautéed mushrooms, fried octopus with ginkgo nut, Chinese cabbage stew, and dog meat soup, not to mention the usual selection of side dishes that accompany every Korean meal.[28] According to Fujimoto, Kim's tastes in food are eclectic, but he particularly appreciates the delicate flavor of Japanese food, including sushi, noodles, and shark fin soup. Kim also likes Western food and even hired two Italian chefs to come to Pyongyang and teach his staff how to make pizza.[29]

The domestic ingredients for Kim's meals come from special farms. For example, Kim's beef comes from a cattle ranch staffed by former bodyguards who enjoy a princely standard of living but are prevented from leaving the ranch to mix with ordinary people.[30] A defector who had a relative working on one of Kim's farms told how the organic apples were cultivated by adding sugar to the soil (sugar is very hard to come by in North Korea) and severely pruning each tree to produce just a few sweet apples.[31] Foreign ingredients for Kim's table are procured by North Korean officials stationed in embassies around the world.

Of course, the North Korean media give an entirely different description of Kim's diet: "We all know what simple meals the great general takes on the road when giving on-the-spot guidance. Rice balls, some roasted potatoes, a bowl of porridge and kimchi. What hot tears all the people of this country shed every time that the anecdotes about his simple meals were reported in the newspapers!"[32] Or consider this "apology" to the dear leader (published in the party newspaper, *Nodong Sinmun*) by a writer who describes the pain Kim is said to have felt when he realized how hungry his people were: "It was heart-breaking to see the general in such agony. We were ashamed of ourselves for having brought anxiety to the general through our poor performance. At that moment, I came to see more clearly why the general was always on the move from front to front, having short and uncomfortable sleep in the car, instead of staying home and getting a comfortable sleep in his own bed, and why he ate rice balls and scorched rice gathered from the bottom of the pot on the road instead of eating proper meals prepared by the people."[33]

Fujimoto describes how Kim travels around the country, estimating that he is away from Pyongyang about three hundred days a year. His entourage is not informed about trips until the last minute—obviously for security reasons. Kim usually travels at night or early in the morning in an attempt to avoid surveillance from U.S. satellites. For trips lasting more than a few hours, Kim may take his personal train; shorter trips are made in a caravan of Mercedes, with Kim's car in the lead driving as quickly as the roads allow. Kim's travels take him to one of a dozen or so villas situated in the country's scenic mountain and seaside locations. On the larger estates guests can move around the extensive grounds in golf carts, and on one estate they are even given cars.

Fujimoto and other sources have provided detailed descriptions and photographs of some of Kim's country hideaways.[34] Each house has a resident staff, and Kim travels with a retinue of as many as one hundred security people, staff, and guests. All but one of the houses has a movie theater, a shooting range, and a basketball court. Three houses have indoor swimming pools. Most of the furnishings are imported from Japan and Europe. The Wonsan house, where Hyundai founder and chairman Chung Ju-yung stayed on one of his visits to North Korea, may be Kim's favorite. It faces the East Sea (Sea of Japan) and is convenient for water sports in the summer and duck hunting in the winter. The house also has a basketball court (the Kim boys loved basketball) and a nine-hundred-meter horse racetrack. Guesthouse No. 72, on the sea near Hamhung, has a beautiful beach, and Kim used to enjoy jet skiing there, although in recent years it is doubtful that his health allows him to engage in such strenuous activities. The Hamhung Guesthouse actually looks like a modern condominium, standing seven stories high with three of the floors underground. The Mt. Myohyang Guesthouse has two basketball courts. The Tanchon Guesthouse is located at a hot springs, as is the Sinchon Guesthouse. The Changsong Guesthouse, along the river border with China, is another place Kim enjoyed jet skiing. The Chindale Guesthouse, near Pyongyang, has a three-hole golf course. Guesthouse No. 22 has a three-thousand-meter horse track and a small amusement park. So far as we know, no other members of the elite class are permitted to own such villas, although top officials, like their Russian counterparts, are permitted to vacation in modest countryside dachas.

Fujimoto reports that Kim is an impulsive buyer. For example, one day Kim gave the chef a catalog and asked him to pick out two motorcycles. Two weeks later the motorcycles arrived, and the two went racing around the grounds of one of the guesthouses. Kim introduced Fujimoto to pistol target practice, at which Kim was an expert. The targets at one guesthouse were cutouts of American and Japanese soldiers (these are the standard targets at children's parks as well). At least in years past, Kim loved to stage sporting contests and watch people compete against each other. In shooting matches, he would offer prizes of chocolates, clothing, women's underwear, cash (in dollars or yen, not the local currency), liquor, and home appliances.

In the 1990s, Kim started inviting army generals to his parties, and guests enjoyed singing Japanese military songs and South Korean popular songs, which it was forbidden to sing in public. In addition to drinking a glass of brandy as an "admission fee" to his parties, guests were invited to engage in drinking contests for prizes. Kim himself rarely drank, but he loved to watch other people getting drunk. His brother-in-law, Chang Song-taek, often served as toastmaster. At parties a troupe of entertainment women, generally known to foreigners as the "joy team" or "pleasure team," often sang and danced in scanty outfits.

Fujimoto had more freedom to travel than do most North Korean officials, although he was always required to obtain Kim's permission. One time he was sent to Moscow, along with three cooks and three waiters, to prepare box lunches for a private Moscow-Pyongyang flight carrying members of Kim's family back to North Korea. Another time he joined a small group of officials sent to Macao to test a gambling system Kim had developed. He was sometimes sent to Japan to purchase fish and other ingredients for Kim's meals, and on one of those trips, in 2001, he decided to stay at home. Since returning to Japan, he has written books about his North Korean experiences—and lived in fear of assassination.

Kim Travels across Russia with a Diplomat

Few foreigners have had the opportunity to meet with Kim Jong-il on a daily basis over a period of several weeks. One who did was Konstantin Pulikovskiy (Pulikovsky), who accompanied Kim on a trans-Siberian rail journey to Moscow in the summer of 2001 as President Vladimir Putin's personal envoy.[35] Kim's train, consisting of five North Korean and seven Russian railcars, crossed into Russia on July 26 and returned on August 18. As Pulikovskiy said, "I had always wanted to cross our vast country by rail at least once in my life, of course, but I never would have chosen to make it a round trip." Kim Jong-il's railcars included his private car, a car for meetings, a dining car, and a car that carried two armored limousines. The North Korean staff lived in their own railcar. Among Kim's entourage was a "charming young woman" who acted as Kim's assistant, as well as four attractive young women entertainers who danced and sang in Korean and Russian. Koreans addressed Kim as "Great Military Leader" or "Beloved Leader," bowing deeply when they entered his presence and speaking to him in the third person.

Kim understood some Russian words and phrases and was always inquisitive, showing considerable interest in how private Russian businesses had developed since the end of state socialism, although he told Pulikovskiy that it would be impossible to run his own country as a market economy because providing for the welfare of so many people in a small country required an authoritarian government.

The train had a satellite hookup so Kim could keep up with the news, and he was well aware of what the Russian and world press said about him. "The Western media have made up so many stories about me. . . . I am the target of criticism throughout the world. This is what I think, however: As long as people are talking about me, I must be doing something right."

Dinners on the train consisted of fifteen to twenty dishes prepared by Kim's chefs, although, like Fujimoto, Pulikovskiy reported that Kim ate only a small portion of each dish. Kim revealed his keen interest in food by discussing the next day's menu with his Russian host. Four times during the journey, the North Koreans flew in a plane-load of fresh food and flew back the garbage. Kim also had French Bordeaux and Burgundy flown in from Paris, thus belying the claim made by the North Korean press that "the whole world knows that his state visits to foreign countries are not as luxurious and comfortable as those made by foreign presidents, and that they are partisan-style, field operation-style."[36]

The daily conversations between Kim and Pulikovskiy ranged over many topics, with Kim easily switching from one to another. On the subject of

Secretary of State Madeleine Albright's recent trip to Pyongyang, Kim said, "I believe that she found my character to her liking." On the subject of his 2000 summit meeting with South Korean president Kim Dae-jung, Kim Jong-il said that he only understood about 80 percent of what his counterpart said because of their different dialects. In a discussion of drug use in Russia (North Korea also has a serious drug problem), Kim said he had ordered drug dealers and users in North Korea to be shot, and he told Pulikovskiy that if he came across any Korean drug addicts, he had Kim's permission to shoot them as well.

Security for Kim was tight. The train was protected by a contingent of fifty Russian security guards and about two dozen North Koreans. One locomotive traveled seven minutes ahead of the train and another followed. In Omsk, where local officials remained unsure until the last minute as to whether the train would even stop, Kim's train pulled into the station with Korean riflemen running alongside, causing his Russian hosts to wonder what Kim feared. A Russian official explained, "We were obliged to take into account the different mentality of the representatives of North Korea. It is no secret to anyone that this mentality is totally different even from that of Soviet people not just 15 years ago but even perhaps about 40 years ago."[37]

Much of the Russian press coverage of Kim's trip was negative. Reporters complained that his travels disrupted the lives of thousands of Russians, and they criticized Kim for avoiding the press. More ominously, Kim's presence, and the respectful reception he received from Russian officials, reminded many reporters of Russia's own dark, totalitarian past. One article in the press asked, "Does Russia, which is dreaming of becoming part of the modern world, need to do business with this historical anachronism?"[38] Aleksandr Bovin, a Russian political scientist, offered the opinion that Kim Jong-il was "a guest from the past—but this is our past as well."[39] A writer for a government-owned newspaper said he had expected Russian officials to view Kim's visit ironically, considering that Kim embodied Russia's past, but instead, in order to play the game of "big politics," Russian officialdom gave Kim a "totalitarian framework" for his visit.[40] A weekly paper characterized Kim as "a representative of an odious political system which our nation rejected in 1991" and called Kim's visit a "humiliation" for Russians.[41] *Izvestiya*'s description of Kim's arrival in St. Petersburg spoke of the "frozen faces" of the gray-suited members of the Korean delegation, "reminiscent of the Soviet Union 50 years ago."[42]

The few Russian officials who met Kim seemed to have a generally favorable impression of their guest. Pulikovskiy described him as a "very sociable man" who cracked many jokes and was cheerful and gregarious.[43] The governor of St. Petersburg (which Kim insisted on calling Leningrad) described Kim as taking a lively interest in history, culture, and the economy, and he quoted Kim as saying repeatedly that North Korea is a "very open and friendly country."[44] Kim's talks with Putin, especially the second, when Kim received a surprise invitation for a "home-cooked" meal, apparently went well.

As usual, the North Korean media kept Kim's travels a secret as long as possible, presumably in order to foil possible coup plots on the part of his domestic and international enemies. On the day of his departure, the media announced that Kim would soon pay an official visit to Russia without mentioning any date.[45] Three days after Kim's departure, the Korean People's Army received an order over Kim's name to increase its combat readiness, and at about the same time, the media reported that Kim had sent letters of thanks to railway workers, bank officials, and coal miners, as if he were working at his office. Only after his official meeting with President Putin, nine days into the trip, did the North Korean media announce that Kim was in Russia.

Kim's return, however, received immediate and widespread coverage. The Party Central Committee, the Central Military Commission, and the National Defense Commission issued a joint communiqué announcing Kim's return, saying he had "carried out energetically external activities" for over twenty days.[46] KCBS, in a veiled reference to the earlier news blackout, said that Kim "set out on a journey to a faraway foreign country so silently. . . . People who regard themselves as politicians generally go to great pains to make the media circle's attention center on them. The respected and beloved general does not enjoy this."[47] Although the visit did not produce anything other than the usual formal document of friendship, the papers treated the visit as a historic occasion. "The world watched each step of the respected and beloved general while holding their breath. This was how things went. It was obviously a shock. It was a shock that instantly shook the world. . . . Every day, some 5 billion people of the world's five continents saw and heard news of the respected and beloved general's historic official visit."[48]

Kim Speaks Frankly to Loyal Korean Japanese

In April 1988, Kim met with a group of visiting delegates from Japan's North Korea association, Chongnyon (Japanese: Chosen Soren or Chosoren).[49] In the presence of this friendly crowd, Kim spoke frankly, dispensing opinions right and left and saying things he would not want the public to hear (a tape or transcript of the meeting was procured by a Japanese intelligence organization). In his talk, Kim adhered to the North Korean custom of referring to Americans, Japanese, and South Koreans as "bastards" (*nomduri*, "devils" in polite parlance).

On the subject of the United States, he said,

> Our People's Army regards the United States as its sworn enemy but our people [who are] engaged in trade address the Americans with much respect. This is called the principle of "hard inside, soft outside."

On the North Korean economy, he said,

> We continue to ask the World Red Cross for food assistance, because we are in fact short of food; but the main reason is that our seeds have degraded thanks to Suh Kwan-hee's treachery. . . . We are replacing them with better seeds but it will take about three years to fully recover. . . . Suh became a traitor in 1950. [Suh, the DPRK's agriculture minister, was made a scapegoat and publicly executed.]
>
> Earlier, when foreigners had come on visits, we used to take them only to the best-looking places and best-working places to make them think we are living happily without being envious of other countries. But more recently, we have come to think that now when enemies are scheming to isolate and annihilate this country, the better way of doing things for us is to use a buffer and conduct a "crybaby operation."

On socialism and capitalism, he said,

> Our socialist system is people-centered and we say that we serve the people, but the truth of the matter is that our economic system is not quite like that. In a capitalist society, customers are catered to and their pockets are picked clean in every possible way. The socialist system is ice-cold and indifferent to the customers. In our country, our store workers take the attitude that they don't care if the customers buy anything or not. Instead of servicing the customers and trying to sell something, they would rather that patrons did not show up so that they won't have to do anything.
>
> Today, Party cadres and security officers operate outside the law without exception. . . . In a capitalist nation, even the prime minister and president are prosecuted if they break the law. We must study how to strengthen our legal system.

On foreign policy, he said,

> Now, if you take a look at the United States, Japan, and South Korea, you will notice that they have become weak-kneed and friendly toward us since the point

of time when we made "military-first" our forefront policy. Because the American bastards have started approaching us, taking a low posture, the Japanese and South Korean bastards have started to say they are willing to provide us with anything we want. South Korea is the most anxious one of them all.

Kim Addresses an Audience at Kim Il-sung University

In April 1997, the South Korean news magazine *Wolgan Chosun* published the text of a lecture that Kim Jong-il had allegedly delivered the previous December on the fiftieth anniversary of the founding of Kim Il-sung University.[50] The lecture was not intended for publication in the North Korean press, so it was not filled with the usual propaganda. Exactly where the lecture was given and who was in the audience is not known, but it sounds very much like Kim. At the time, North Korea was in the depths of the 1995–1998 famine, most factories had stopped operating, and people were moving from town to town looking for food.

Kim shows an acute awareness of the country's hardships but offers no practical solutions. He complains that most party officials, including those in the Central Committee, are not working hard. He claims he began assisting Kim Il-sung in the 1960s but that today party officials can give him no assistance because of their incompetence. Kim overlooks the obvious fact that he has been the party leader for the last twenty or thirty years, and if anyone were able to instill spirit and vigor, it should be him.

Then he launches into a defense of his leadership: "At this time when the situation is complicated, I cannot solve all knotty problems, handling practical economic work. . . . When he was alive, the leader told me not to get involved in economic work. He repeatedly told me that if I got involved in economic work, I would not be able to handle party and army work properly. . . . Administrative and economic functionaries must take charge of economic work in a responsible manner."

Kim's solution to the food problem, for that matter, to all problems, is for the officials to get out of their offices and work with the people, somehow meeting the country's challenges simply by being on the front lines. He ignores the fact that his years of on-the-spot guidance have not revived the economy.

He demonstrates an amazing faith in the power of propaganda and agitation, recommending that party officials go to the employees and "ask them to produce and to ship more fertilizer, farming goods, and people's commodities." With people literally dying in the streets from starvation, he says, "If we tell our people they should eat only 450 grams a day [a starvation diet] and donate the remainder as rice for the army, all of them will willingly comply."

With excellent foresight, Kim warns that if people become responsible for finding their own food, black market activity will increase and erode support for the party. As it happened, five years later Kim put an end to the ration system and told people to earn their own livings, with exactly the consequences he had predicted.

Kim Jong-il's Governing Style

Decision Making

We only partially understand how decisions are made at the highest levels of the North Korean government because no close aide to Kim Jong-il is known to have defected. Throughout most of his career, it appears, Kim did not consult with advisors as often as his father did; however, since suffering a stroke in 2008, he has very likely begun relying heavily on other top officials to help him make decisions.[51] He intervenes in even the smallest affairs if they come to his attention and engage his interest. On important matters, Kim turns to his subordinates for policy suggestions, telephoning them at any hour of the day or night and encouraging them to discuss and argue among themselves. These subordinates forward their recommendations to Kim, who evaluates them in terms of what is good for national security and what is good for himself.

Kim works late into the night, a practice he says he picked up during the years when he was preparing reports to put on his father's desk first thing in the morning. Kim Jong-il's adopted niece, Nam-ok, says he often brought work home, and one of his associates says Kim would sometimes sneak out of late-night parties he was hosting in order to work in his office. It is not known whether Kim engages in a true exchange of ideas or simply solicits opinions and then makes unilateral decisions. Kim's imperious behavior in public suggests that he uses the latter decision-making process. There is little doubt that once Kim has made a decision, no one can question or contest it. The North Korean political system lacks checks and balances because the legislature and courts must answer to the party, and the party is, first and last, a tool of Kim's leadership. Even in the era of military-first politics, the top generals seem to have no political agenda and, in any case, live and work under close party surveillance.

Because Kim governs by personal power rather than organizational position, the best way to assess how much political power officials exercise is to look at their personal relationships to Kim. Those closest to him may never appear in public, but they are probably the most powerful people in the regime because they have Kim's ear and, more importantly, his trust. High-ranking officials who appear at meetings with foreigners are often only front men. A good example is the chairman (also called "president") of the presidium of the Supreme People's Assembly. Even though he is the highest official in the government, he probably has less political clout than some party officials. In any case, the SPA is nothing more than a part-time legislature that convenes for a few days each year to ratify the party's decisions. Likewise, Kim surrounds himself with high-ranking generals who follow him around on inspection tours, thereby demonstrating to the army and to the public that Kim is the man in charge.

Real power resides in what could be called Kim's inner cabinet. The makeup of this informal cabinet, whose members presumably never convene as a group but instead work with Kim at his office or socialize with him at his parties, has always been the subject of much speculation among foreign analysts. Most of the people who seem to belong to this inner circle are of Kim's generation or younger; all are presumably loyal to him and believe that their interests coincide with his. Some hold positions of power in the military, others in the party, and others in the government. Many hold multiple positions. Some in the inner circle are members of Kim's own family, such as his sister and his brother-in-law.

Kim's personal secretariat, which screens incoming reports and communicates Kim's instructions, has offices next to his. An Yong-chol, a former officer in the KPA, has written about the secretariat and described the physical layout of Kim's office, which is in the three-story headquarters of the KWP's Organization and Guidance Department, the most powerful of the party organizations.[52] Formerly housing Kim Il-sung's office, the building is in a special party compound in downtown Pyongyang, surrounded by tall trees and an eleven-meter-high wall. It is believed that Kim can commute to his office by way of an underground tunnel from one of his Pyongyang houses.

To keep Kim better informed than anyone else, information channels are vertical, not horizontal. Over the years, Kim has developed an extensive reporting system that keeps him apprised of what is happening in all sectors of society, while people in those sectors do not have accurate information about what is happening outside their domains. Officials are expected to transmit information to Kim in a timely fashion, and if he receives that information from another source first, heads may roll. The regime's principal security organizations—the Ministry of People's Security (MPS), State Security Department (SSD), and Security Command—have separate communication channels with Kim and often compete among themselves to provide him with information.[53] Kim's spies are everywhere, and people in critical lines of communication, and therefore with the most power, are the most carefully watched. The top elites, such as cabinet ministers, party secretaries, and KPA generals, must account for their comings and goings.

Defectors say that reports sent to Kim are often doctored to make conditions look favorable to the departmental bureaucrats, a phenomenon that characterizes most bureaucracies. Kim is nobody's fool, but he certainly does not know many things about his country, if only because officials keep bad news from him, just as he kept bad news from reaching his father. A possible case in point is the regime's decision to end World Food Program (WFP) aid in 2005, even though the WFP estimated that North Korea would continue to experience a serious food shortfall. Three months later, with food already running out, Kim relented and permitted a partial resumption of food aid. A plausible explanation for this fiasco is that Kim's agriculture officials misinformed him about the size of the 2005 harvest.

Although Kim has a wealth of information about the outside world available to him from foreign media sources and from intelligence provided by North Koreans stationed abroad, he has limited first-hand experience with foreign lands and people. As a teenager he accompanied his father on a trip to Moscow in 1957 and to Eastern Europe in 1959. In 1965 he and his father visited Indonesia, the only time either of the Kims is known to have traveled by air. Since the 1980s Kim Jong-il has made occasional trips to China, and in 2001 and 2002, he visited Russia. In short, he has much less exposure to foreign lands than do many of his officials. The prism through which he views the world may be distorted by the movies he loves to watch, and his officials' reluctance to be frank with him deprives him of a sounding board for his impressions and opinions. Interestingly, lack of experience has not inhibited his forming opinions about other countries or conducting international relations, as illustrated by the closed-door talk he gave to visiting Chongnyon officials.

For Kim's style of personal governance to be effective, he must have loyal and dependable followers. To garner this loyalty, he needs funds to reward followers because he is hardly the kind of leader who inspires others through his example or charisma, although some may follow him because they feel that their fate depends on keeping the regime in power or because they respected his late father. On the birthdays of Kim Jong-il and his father and on New Year's Day, the top twenty thousand or so cadres receive special gifts, such as liquor, clothing, foreign food, and wristwatches.[54] People who please him especially, like his former Japanese chef, receive more expensive gifts, including luxury cars. Ordinary party and government officials receive coupons on Kim's birthday for, say, a bottle of liquor and a carton of fruit. In 2008, local-level officials, depending on local economic conditions, received something like a domestic bottle of liquor, a toothbrush, and a bar of soap, while school children received several pieces of chewing gum, a few rice crackers, and a small pack or two of candy.[55]

Kim's On-the-Spot Guidance

In ancient Korea, the king would send out officials, sometimes in disguise, to report on conditions around the kingdom. Unlike the ancient kings, Kim Il-sung liked to conduct inspections personally; according to the North Korean press, Kim made eight thousand "on-the-spot guidance" tours in his lifetime, and Kim Jong-il has continued this tradition. In fact, these carefully arranged visits are practically the only time Kim appears in public. Since the late 1990s, he has made about one hundred public appearances a year, over half of them at military bases. These inspections keep people on their toes and serve a public relations function by suggesting that Kim cares about his people.

A special unit called the Support for Inspection Unit (*bojangjo*) goes around preparing for these "number one" visits by sprucing up the inspection sites so they will please Kim.[56] People who live in the vicinity undergo new background checks to confirm their political reliability. Those not deemed reliable are cleared from the area or told to stay in their homes on inspection day. People who will come in contact with Kim are given health checks to insure they will not pass on any germs. If an adoring crowd is needed to welcome Kim, actors and the most attractive children and adults in the area are selected, trained, and provided with appropriate clothing and flags to wave. Old equipment at the inspection site is swapped with new equipment from other organizations. Food supplies are provided. If the military base or factory to be inspected raises livestock on the side, a full complement of animals must be procured.

Shortly before Kim arrives at the inspection site, it is swept by his bodyguard personnel, and all entrances and exits are sealed. If Kim is inspecting a military base, small arms ammunition is locked up, and tanks and artillery pieces are secured with their gun barrels pointing away from where he will be standing. At a time of his choosing, Kim appears briefly, speaks to the top officials or commanding officers, walks around the site, has his photograph taken, and departs in his caravan of black Mercedes. A plaque will later be placed at the site commemorating Kim's visit, and if he sat in a chair or at a table, the furniture will be taken out of service and preserved as a historical relic. Anyone fortunate enough to meet him can expect to receive a measure of preferential treatment for years to come.

Kim's guidance tours are not always immediately reported by the North Korean media, and since 2003 no date is ever given for a visit—the better to keep Kim's schedule secret—although it seems that most of his appearances are reported within a day or two.[57] Press coverage of Kim's on-the-spot guidance dominates the entire first page of *Nodong Sinmun* (the first page is pretty much "Kim's page" anyway). Because there is no way to confirm that Kim actually made a visit, some of the reports may even be fabrications; this is especially likely since his stroke in 2008.

A typical news report of Kim's guidance to a military base goes something like this: "Comrade Kim Jong-il, great leader of our party and our people, who is general secretary of the Workers Party of Korea, chairman of the DPRK National Defense Commission, and supreme commander of the Korean People's Army, inspected KPA Unit Number 802, honored with the title of O Chung-hup-led Seventh Regiment."[58] Then follows a list of the generals who accompanied Kim on the visit.

The news report will claim that Kim acquainted himself carefully with the unit's operation, especially emphasizing his interest in the soldiers' living conditions: "Comrade Kim Jong-il looked into every detail of the soldiers' living, ranging from entertainment means and room conditions to every photograph they had taken and their personal belongings."[59] Kim also inspects any agricultural operations run by the unit to support itself, such as pig farms, catfish ponds, orchards, and cornfields. According to the press reports, Kim is usually satisfied with what he finds and declares that the unit is highly prepared to protect the people and defeat any aggressors. At the conclusion of his visit, he has his photograph taken standing in front of the assembled soldiers and gives the unit a few commemorative presents, typically an engraved rifle and pair of binoculars. These "number one articles" will be displayed in the special room set aside at every military post and civilian factory to study the works of the two Kims.

News reports of Kim's military visits usually conclude by painting a word picture of the soldiers enthusiastically cheering the departing Kim: "All the officers and soldiers . . . were full of burning determination to death-defyingly protect the nerve center of the revolution, becoming guns and bombs like the members of the anti-Japanese Seventh Regiment did, and to defend the outpost of the fatherland as an impregnable fortress."[60] Follow-up news reports often explain how Kim's guidance benefited the people he visited.

For example, in a television program titled "Legend of Love That Blossomed on the Path of On-the-Spot Guidance," Kim is credited with providing uniforms to soldiers, instructing that barracks be built with smaller windows to keep the cold winter air out, and instructing that soldiers be provided with heavy blankets (to be provided by a "magnificent blanket-producing factory" commissioned by Kim). Kim is said to have supplied soldiers with toothpaste and toothbrushes (rare commodities in North Korea) and even taught the soldiers the correct way to brush their teeth.[61]

On his guidance tours, as well as at all other times, Kim Jong-il's security precautions are probably more thorough than those of the president of the United States—and for good reason. American soldiers captured the leader of another "axis-of-evil" country, and President George W. Bush made no secret of his dislike for Kim Jong-il and his preference for "regime change." When U.S. forces attacked Baghdad in 2003, Kim disappeared from public view for two months, and for several weeks after the July 2006 North Korean missile launch, which the international community condemned, the domestic press made no mention of Kim's activities and whereabouts.

Although there is no firm evidence, rumor has it that over the years more than one coup or assassination attempt has targeted Kim and his father. In 1992, a group of officers who had received training in the Soviet Union allegedly plotted to turn their tank cannons on an assemblage of top government officials, and in the aftermath, officers throughout the army who had received training in Russia were purged. In 1995, officers of the army's Sixth Corps also may have been planning a coup against Kim Jong-il, leading to a purge of many of the corps's officers. In April 2004 a large explosion rocked the rail yard in the northern city of Yongchon, leveling an entire section of the city. The North Korean security services appear to have received information that the explosion was meant to assassinate Kim Jong-il, whose train was passing through the city around that time. Moreover, it was believed that a cell phone was used to trigger the detonation. Within weeks all cell phones were banned in North Korea, and only in late 2008 was the ban partially lifted.

The Bodyguard Command or General Guard Bureau (the names and organizations seem to shift over the years) is the organization tasked with guarding Kim. Separate from the Ministry of People's Armed Forces and under the control of the party, its soldiers are fiercely loyal to Kim. A number of other party offices close to Kim also provide security and keep him informed about possible threats.

Important testimony about Kim Jong-il's security arrangements has been provided by Yi Yong-kuk. In 1977 Yi was recruited at the age of seventeen to become a member of Kim Jong-il's bodyguard unit, which numbered only about three hundred at the time. Yi served for eleven years, until security officials discovered that one of his cousins had become a chauffeur for Kim Jong-il. Since only one family member is allowed to work for Kim, presumably to ensure that the bodyguards are more loyal to Kim than to anyone with whom they work, Yi had to retire. According to Yi, the bodyguard unit was so secretive that it took security organizations six years to discover that he and his cousin were related! During the entire time Yi worked as a bodyguard, he was not permitted to communicate even once with his family.[62]

Bodyguards are recruited from families with spotless working-class credentials. After rigorous training, they are housed in apartments isolated from the rest of Korean society, and if they marry, their wives come to live in the same quarantined housing. Upon retirement from the Bodyguard Command, soldiers are sworn to secrecy and given comfortable positions in the party or government. While in service, bodyguards live as well as top party and government officials, but Yi admits that there is a cost: the people working close to Kim are always on edge, never knowing how Kim will react from one moment to the next. Sometimes Kim praises the guards for stopping his car when the driver does not follow proper security procedures; at other times taking the same precautions is grounds for dismissal.

In public, Kim is surrounded by a half-dozen senior bodyguards, with another hundred bodyguards forming a second circle at a range of about a hundred yards. On the outer perimeter of the security field, guards from the SSD and MPS secure the neighborhood. Kim's travel plans are secret; even the bodyguards receive only an hour or two's notice before Kim departs. Security personnel at the destination of Kim's travels are given sufficient time to prepare for his arrival, but they will not know the exact hour of his arrival. When Kim is moving from place to place, people living along his travel route must stay indoors, and all other cars or trains along the route are halted.

Kim Jong-il's Personal Qualities

Because of the wide latitude of behavior granted to a dictator, his personality has particular relevance to his leadership and, consequently, to the welfare of his country. The North Korean press, somewhat incoherently, describes Kim's work style as "aiming high at all times and making a bold operation, the skillful organization and extraordinary sweep of achieving a target with the mobilization of all forces, the staunch propelling power of attaining one target after another for leaping progress without marking time."[63] Yet, on important matters, Kim is not as reckless as his reputation might suggest; instead, he always seems to leave himself room to maneuver. Time and again, North Korea (i.e., Kim) has issued a threat (such as to blow up South Korea's *Chosun Ilbo* newspaper) or a promise (such as to make a summit trip to Seoul), only to let the matter drop. Those experienced with North Korea are not unduly alarmed by even the shrillest North Korean threats.

Kim Jong-il is a very private person. Few North Koreans know anything about his life other than that he is the son of Kim Il-sung. They do not know who his wives and mistresses are, who his children are, or where he lives. In fact, he has gone through multiple wives and mistresses, even though a party lecture condemning divorce opens with the following Kim quote: "In our society the home is the foundational unit of life. Home life must be wholesome and happy for overall social life to be carried out cheerfully and energetically."[64] They do not know what he eats or how he amuses himself (other than listening to "meritorious military choir groups"). While his father was alive, Kim's secrecy was popularly explained as his playing the role of an obedient Confucian-style son. But since his father's death, Kim has continued to work behind the scenes, suggesting that some combination of his personality, concerns for his personal safety, and a particular pleasure derived from ruling in secrecy better explains his avoidance of the public.

Kim is often uneasy among strangers. In his on-the-spot guidance to farms, factories, and military bases, he rarely meets the people, instead making quick administrative visits and often watching an art troupe perform. A 1999 *Nodong Sinmun* article claimed, "The appearance of the respected and beloved general, touring farms across the country unceasingly with the lofty intent to bring glory to this year, precisely is a replica of the father leader's." The article painted a picture of farmers working in the fields and thinking, "Maybe our general is coming here along the footpath between the fields."[65] In reality, most North Koreans have pretty much given up on Kim Jong-il, no longer expecting him to be a people's president like his father was (or like they *thought* he was). A former North Korean reports that people parody the song "Where Are You, General, We Miss You," with the words "The general is not visible; where is he hiding?"[66] Yet when Kim meets world leaders, he has no trouble playing the role of chief of state. On meeting South Korean president Kim Dae-jung at the June 2000 summit, he was a gracious and expansive host, a performance he repeated when U.S. Secretary of State Madeleine Albright visited Pyongyang that October. Kim seemed stiff or ill at ease during a formal meeting with President Putin in Moscow in 2001, but when Putin invited him several days later for a private visit, Kim was delighted and revealed his pleasant side.

Kim likes to portray himself as a great general, although he has never actually served in the military. From his father, he has inherited what Adrian Buzo aptly calls the guerrilla style of leadership, and the younger Kim has even amplified his military leadership in the form of the "military-first" politics that has become North Korea's guiding policy and ideology. There are obvious political advantages to being a "wartime president" (as President George W. Bush proclaimed himself to be). The entire nation can legitimately be called upon to give the leader unquestioning support and to endure hardships for which the enemy can conveniently be blamed.

In public at least, Kim is supremely confident; indeed, arrogant would be a more accurate description. Even as a young man, he often treated senior officials like subordinates, speaking to them with his hands in his pockets or clasped behind his back (like his father), or smoking in front of them, or failing to greet them when he entered a room. His demeanor unnerved those around him. Koh Young-hwan, a former diplomat, said that when he was in Kim's presence, he became so nervous he could hardly breathe.[67]

Kim speaks rapidly in a rather high-pitched voice, usually in unfinished sentences, jumping from one topic to another. When he gets an idea, he wants it implemented immediately. For example, it is said that when his artistic eye rested on an empty Pyongyang vista, Kim would order that buildings be erected to fill the void. After his 2002 visit to eastern Russia, where he was impressed with the architecture of a Greek Orthodox church, he ordered that a similar church be built in Pyongyang within the year (it was finished in 2006), even though ordinary North Koreans who publicly worship anyone other than Kim and his father can expect to be sent to prison. Kim's ideas are often impractical, such as his decision to build a 105-story hotel that remains unfinished a quarter of a century later because of structural flaws or his order to build thousands of small hydroelectric plants throughout the country (in the manner of China's disastrous Great Leap Forward), few of which generate sufficient power to pay for themselves.

Kim has a hot temper, but he can quickly forget his anger. He sometimes sends close associates to reeducation labor camps for weeks or months at a time when they displease him, but after they have served their time, they are often allowed to resume their old positions. Then again, some are never released, perhaps because Kim has forgotten about them. When very angry, he can even go as far as to order that someone be put to death, as he has done on more than one occasion, the most famous case being the public execution of his agriculture minister in 1997.

It is Kim Jong-il's tragedy that in nearly all respects he cuts a less impressive figure than his father. Physically, he is short and stout (although, since his stroke, he has lost much weight). At about 5 feet, 5 inches tall (165 centimeters), he is several inches shorter than his father. To add a few inches to his height, he combs his thinning hair in a bouffant style and wears elevator shoes (since his stroke, he has occasionally appeared in public wearing sneakers). His weight, which has been a problem since childhood, was about 175 pounds (80 kg) when he was healthy. He has squinty eyes and frequently wears large-framed, heavily tinted glasses, which the North Korean press explains is to keep the people from seeing how red their leader's eyes are from hard work and lack of sleep.[68]

Kim has a distinctive taste in clothing. Before the 1980s, he sometimes wore a Western suit, which made him look like a portly young businessman, but for most of his life, he has worn light tan slacks with a matching working-man's zipper jacket, often referred to in the foreign press as a jumper, but in North Korea his attire is known as *inminbok*, or "people's clothes." Actually, with his stout build and unruly hair, he somewhat resembles the bus driver character Ralph Kramden, played by the comedian Jackie Gleason on the old television series *The Honeymooners*. On formal occasions, he may wear a longer Mao jacket, but even when meeting heads of state, he usually wears his work clothes. The North Korean press says that Kim's attire reflects his lifestyle as a workingman and that it shows his solidarity with soldiers, although they do not wear jumpers. "Our general is always dressed in the same outfit, a field uniform, regardless of the changing seasons. Our general's field uniform would always be wet from the sweltering heat and pouring rain that comes down irregularly in the midsummer season, and from sleet and heavy snow in the cold winter season. . . . Our respected and beloved general has no time to take off his field uniform."[69] In point of fact, Kim does wear short sleeves in the summer, and in the winter he wears a heavy parka and thick gloves. His clothes are tailor-made of the finest fabrics. It is difficult to believe that he is ever drenched in sweat or covered with snow.

Kim has an eye for attractive women, and his position as dictator gives him ample opportunity to meet them; however, as he has grown older, he seems to spend less time hosting parties and chasing women. He has had many affairs, but it is hard to tell how many serious relationships and how many wives. Marriage as a legal institution hardly applies in his case because he is above the law. Some believe that Kim's first wife or mistress was Hong Il-chon, a graduate of Kim Il-sung University and later a member of the Supreme People's Assembly, whom he may have married in 1966 and divorced or separated from in 1971. In the late 1960s, Kim began an affair with Song Hye-rim (mentioned above in connection with Kim's niece, Yi Nam-ok). Song was five years older than Kim and already married, but she divorced her husband, began living with Kim in 1969, and had a child, Kim Jong-nam. Neither Song, whose political origins were suspect because she had been born in South Korea, nor her son was ever presented to Kim Il-sung, and it is not known if the father even knew about their existence. Kim eventually lost interest in Song, her mental health began to deteriorate, and she spent the rest of her life in Moscow receiving psychological treatment. She died in 2002.

In 1973 or 1974, apparently to please his father, Kim took as his official wife Kim Yong-suk, a typist in his father's office. They had at least one daughter, Kim Sol-song, who reportedly works in Kim's private office, and perhaps one son. Kim Yong-suk may be living in an official residence in Pyongyang, but other reports say she has died. Just a few years later, in the mid-1970s, Kim fell in love with Ko Yong-hi, a beautiful Osaka-born dancer working in North Korea. He moved in with her in the late 1970s and fathered three children: two sons, Kim Jong-chol and Kim Jong-un, and a daughter, Kim Ye-jong. Ko Yong-hi died of cancer in 2004 after undergoing treatment in Paris. Kim Jong-il's name has been associated with other mistresses, and in 2006, foreign news reports identified one Kim Ok, a professional pianist who had been Kim's secretary since the 1980s, as his new "wife." The North Korean people know nothing about these women, although a vague propaganda campaign glorifying Ko Yong-hi (although not by name) began around 2002, possibly to prepare the way for leadership succession by one of her two sons.

Kim's health has been the subject of much speculation in the foreign press, although it is a taboo subject in North Korea. Over the years, he has been rumored to suffer from epilepsy, diabetes, liver trouble, brain damage (from a car accident or fall from a horse), and heart trouble. In May 2007 Kim was absent from public view for about a month, and during the same time a team of eight heart specialists from the Berlin Heart Institute traveled to Pyongyang. The head of the team said they performed surgery on three workers, a nurse, and a scientist, but not on Kim Jong-il.[70] A spokesperson for the institute likewise denied that the team saw Kim Jong-il, saying the rumor was "all nonsense"; yet, no one can explain why such a high-powered team of specialists would travel to Pyongyang to treat ordinary people.[71] The best guess is that either the doctors lied (people who become involved with North Korea often finding themselves doing things they would prefer not to do), or the team backed up North Korean surgeons who performed a heart procedure on Kim, most likely the expansion of a blood vessel (angioplasty) leading to the heart rather than the more serious bypass surgery.

In August 2008 Kim reportedly suffered a stroke and failed to appear in public for over two months, most notably at the sixtieth anniversary of the country's founding on September 9. A French neurosurgeon admitted to having gone to Pyongyang to consult on treatment for the stroke but said no surgery was involved. By the beginning of 2009, Kim was once again making on-the-spot inspections, but in the six months following the incident, he met only one foreign delegation—comprising Chinese officials who, being ideological friends of the North Koreans, could be counted on not to disclose anything about his health. During this period, photographs show Kim to have aged considerably and shed much weight, and he has trouble moving his left arm.

The Kim Family Cult

It is not unusual for people to project a positive image of themselves. Sometimes they conduct this impression management by themselves; sometimes they have public relations organizations perform this service. Political leaders find it necessary to create a good impression if they want to be reelected, and leaders like Kim, whose tenure is not subject to election, find it easier to govern if people respect them. And since dictators usually remain in power longer than elected leaders, they are able to do a more thorough job of impression management. Totalitarian dictators, who control most information sources in their countries, are even in a position to make themselves into cult figures. This is the case with Kim Jong-il, whose propaganda organs have created an image that elevates him far above the people and any political contenders. Of course, the hazard of a cult image is that it is based largely on lies that must be covered up with other lies, and each of these lies is a potential threat to the leader.

Kim not only has to protect himself from the lies that have been told about him, but he must also protect the lies that surround his late father. During Kim Il-sung's fifty-year reign, an elaborate image was fabricated for him, first by the Russians who put him in charge. Once the North Korean government was well established, by the 1950s, the propaganda and agitation people began to rewrite North Korean history to put Kim Il-sung at its center, downgrading and later expunging the roles played by other people and even by other countries. As an interesting example, on Kim Jong-il's 2002 trip to eastern Russia, the head of port operations at Vladivostok reminded him that it was from this port that Soviet soldiers had embarked in 1945 to accept the Japanese surrender in North Korea. Kim ignored the opportunity to thank the Russians and merely said, "Please tell me about the future of this port." Later, when a Russian reporter asked him if North Koreans celebrate the Soviet liberation of Korea, Kim responded, "I plan to talk about current issues with the president. I do not intend to talk about history."[72]

The elder Kim was—and still is—portrayed as a superior being. Most North Koreans believe that Kim Il-sung was a truly great leader who brought them independence and put them on the path to prosperity, although they have serious doubts about his son. On the third anniversary of Kim Il-sung's death, it was announced that from that point forward calendar years would be counted beginning with the year of the elder Kim's birth (1912), making 1997 "Juche 86" and thereby lending a dynastic tone to the Kim regime.

Millions of North Koreans have visited the Kumsusan Memorial Palace, where Kim Il-sung's body lies in state, and foreign delegations are frequently taken there to "pay their respects." The palace, formerly the Kumsusan Assembly Hall, was where he had his offices, and after his father's death, Kim Jong-il ordered the KPA to remodel the hall into his father's final resting place at a cost of at least $100 million, even while the government was appealing to the international community for food aid.[73] When Russian president Putin traveled to Pyongyang in July 2000, the North Korean press reported that he paid "sublime homage" to Kim at the palace.[74] On the occasion of U.S. Secretary of State Madeleine Albright's visit to the palace in October 2000, the press reported that she also "paid homage" to Kim, adding that she was "harboring admiration for the respected and beloved leader who is lauded by people for his immortal accomplishments for the era and history."[75]

Another way to pay respects to the departed great leader is to visit the Mansudae Grand Monument, a twenty-meter-high bronze statue of Kim Il-sung on Mansu Hill (Mansudae) erected for Kim's sixtieth birthday in 1972. The bronze Kim stands proudly, head held high, one arm outstretched as if to offer a welcome or a blessing, overcoat flapping in the breeze. Foreign visitors are usually brought here directly from the airport, and to honor Kim properly, they must offer a bouquet of flowers. Some Koreans returning from abroad purchase their flowers in Beijing and carry them back on the airplane.

Every year around the time of Kim Il-sung's April 15 birthday (the "sun's day") and the July 8 anniversary of his death, the media carry stories about the appearance of natural wonders. Some of the stories are downright curious, such as the KCNA report that on the seventh anniversary of Kim's death in 2001, "three beautiful birds" landed on the windowsill of an apartment in the port city of Nampo and perched there for one hour and forty minutes, blinking at the wall portrait of Kim Il-sung. The one hundred apartment house residents who witnessed the event unanimously agreed that the birds were paying "respectful homage to the president, not forgetting July."[76]

On the senior Kim's birthday, North Koreans are expected to bring flowers to one of the thousands of Kim monuments scattered throughout the country. On that day people also receive from the government a small "gift," such as a little meat or liquor, to remind them of the great leader's and his son's benevolence. Children receive a small bag of candy, and theaters show special movies. If possible, normal electricity service is restored for the benefit of those who have television sets. In the evening, people attend folk dances. On the following day, party meetings are convened at which people swear to uphold the Ten Principles of Kim Il-sung thought.

The annual Kimilsungia festival is also held around the time of Kim Il-sung's birthday. On his visit to Indonesia in 1965, Kim admired a purple Indonesian-bred orchid, which President Sukarno renamed in Kim's honor. Ten years later, when the Kimilsungia (also known in North Korea as the "flower of loyalty") was ready for general cultivation, a sample was sent to North Korea, where it has been grown in greenhouses throughout the country. Since 1999, a Kimilsungia festival has been held every year with a large display of the potted flowers in an exhibition hall. Organizations throughout the country (and even a few foreign ones) display their prize Kimilsungias, and crowds of visitors view the flowers arranged in front of giant paintings of Kim, with music playing in the background.

Kim Jong-il, too, has his own flower and flower show. A Japanese botanist introduced the Kimjongilia, a large, red South American begonia, as a gift in 1988, and it is displayed at its own festival around the time of Kim Jong-il's birthday in February. The flower is said to be grown in at least sixty countries "to be loved by hundreds of millions of people around the world."[77] The point of these cult displays honoring the two Kims is not to exhibit flowers but to show how much the people and the international community worship North Korea's leaders.

In the tradition of Chinese emperors, to whom delegations of foreigners brought gifts from afar, the gifts that Kim Il-sung and Kim Jong-il have received from foreign visitors are displayed in the two buildings (the smaller one is for Kim Jong-il's gifts) comprising the International Friendship Exhibition at Mt. Myohyang outside of Pyongyang. By 2006, the number of gifts was said to total 160,000, including many offered to Kim Il-sung posthumously. Visitors to the exhibits must cover their shoes with plastic socks to avoid scuffing the teakwood floors, and they are supposed to bow in front of a lifelike wax replica of Kim Il-sung. The featured gifts for the two Kims include automobiles from Stalin and Mao, an alligator-skin bag from Castro, a piece of pottery from Rev. Billy Graham, and from U.S. Secretary of State Madeleine Albright, a basketball autographed by Michael Jordan (Kim Jong-il's two younger sons are avid basketball players).

The number of references to Kim Il-sung in the North Korean press has declined over the years. On what would have been his ninety-first birthday in 2003, the long-running KCBS sign-on, "Long live the revolutionary thought of Great Leader Comrade Kim Il-sung; long live the glorious Workers' Party of Korea," was replaced with "Long live our glorious fatherland, the Democratic People's Republic of Korea; long live the Workers' Party of Korea, the organizer and guide of all the victories for the Korean people."[78] Mention of Kim Il-sung's name in the annual New Year's Day message has dropped from about two dozen instances in the last years of his life to fewer than a half dozen since 2000. In recent years, it has been Kim Jong-il's birthday on February 16 that nature supposedly celebrates. For example, in 2001, KCBS reported that thunder, lightning, and a rainbow appeared during a snowstorm on his birthday, causing residents to say, "Even nature seemed to congratulate Kim Jong-il, illustrious commander born of heaven, on his birthday."[79] However, the North Korean press is building up the importance of the year 2012, the centenary of Kim Il-sung's birth, by which date the country is supposed to have become an economic power.

Kim is even credited with some of the magical powers his father was said to have (some references to Kim Il-sung in the North Korean media claimed he could transcend time and space). In 2006 *Nodong Sinmun* published an article titled "Military-First Teleporting" claiming that Kim Jong-il, "the extraordinary master commander who has been chosen by the heavens," appears in one place and then suddenly appears in another "like a flash of lightning," so quickly that the American satellites overhead cannot track his movements.[80]

As the years passed and people's memories dimmed, propagandists became bolder in rewriting Kim Jong-il's biography. By 2002, North Korean radio could make the claim that "Great Comrade Kim Jong-il already earned the people's admiration as early as the 1940s and the 1950s of the last century [he was born in 1942]. He spearheaded our people's struggle to complete the *Juche* cause, undertaking all the heavy tasks of the revolution all by himself in the 1960s, 1970s, 1980s, and 1990s."[81] Kim Jong-il is now credited with all the attributes of his father, including his father's military abilities. To extend Kim's nonexistent military career into the past, he is now described as being at his father's side during the Korean War, helping him to plan battles, although at the time he would have been only eleven years old: "Sometimes he sat up all night together with Comrade Kim Il-sung at the table for mapping out a plan of operation, asking about the situation of the front, thinking of how to frustrate the intention of the enemy and learning Comrade Kim Il-sung's outstanding commanding art."[82] Kim Jong-il's distinctive military-first politics, first mentioned in the press in the late 1990s, is now said to have originated with a visit by the eighteen-year-old Kim to a military base on August 25, 1960.[83]

In point of fact, the closest Kim has ever come to fighting a war was his declaration of a "semiwartime state" in response to American pressure over the nuclear issue in 1993. However, his lack of combat experience has not prevented the North Korean propagandists from making Kim out to be a war hero. In North Korea's long-running cold war with the United States, Kim is said to have taken a very active part: "Not escorted by tanks or armored cars, he has passed the ridge [Chol Ridge, site of a Korean War battle] and crossed the rivers for forefronts without eating or sleeping. By doing so, he has devotedly tided over the crisis of the country and the revolution, winning one victory after another in the war without gunshot."[84]

And then there is Kim Jong-il's vaunted benevolence. Until recently, North Koreans were taught from childhood to think of his father as their father, like the Russians were taught to love "Papa Stalin." Children thanked Kim Il-sung for everything good that came their way. Now the thanks go to Kim's son. An article in a propaganda magazine targeting foreigners says that children and students in the DPRK "liken the embrace of the leader Kim Jong-il, who takes good care of them and has their dreams fully realized, to that of father."[85] The article quotes the first verse of a touching children's song titled "I Will Tell Him Everything":

> When I said I wanted to become a doctor or general
> My friends laughed at me and said I was greedy.
> I will tell the General about it when I meet him.
> Then they will not laugh at me any more.

Most of the propaganda boasting of Kim Jong-il's benevolence is made out of whole cloth. He is portrayed as a man who understands the suffering of the people and suffers for them: "Day and night, I always think about ways to have our people live more affluently."[86] *Nodong Sinmun* says that while he was being driven through the countryside during the 1990s' famine, "his thought, heartrending as it was, went to people said to be ranging hill and dale to pick wild spinach in an effort to stave off hunger. He had to bring his car to a halt to pull himself together before resuming the trip."[87]

The myth of Kim's benevolence is designed in part to make all North Koreans, even those stigmatized as members of the wavering and hostile political classes, feel that they are part of the same national family. Kim's image of benevolence is also intended to persuade the South Korean people that they could live happily in a unified Korea under his leadership. Even in North Korea few people have been convinced by this propaganda because since Kim came to power, economic conditions have gone from bad to worse, and instead of helping the people, Kim has elevated the army. In private, people say, "Kim Il-sung took the people's train, but Kim Jong-il takes the military train."

According to the cult propaganda, there is nothing that Kim does not know or is not good at. At the university, in contrast to recollections of former students who say he was not a serious student, the press now claims that Kim authored more than fourteen hundred works.[88] His memory supposedly enables him to remember "all the exploits performed by the famous men of all ages and countries, all the political events, big and small, and the significant creations of humankind and their detailed figures. He also remembers the names, ages, and birthdays of all the people he has met."[89]

Kyongje Yongu, which is as much a propaganda journal as the country's leading economics journal, claims that Kim's *Juche* ideology "includes all areas of economic theory, and is an economic ideology with perfect features as the most correct directional guide of economic activity for realizing independence in the relationship with nature."[90] According to another article, when the "genius of geniuses" visited a computer laboratory in the North Korean Academy of Sciences in 1998, he taught the academy's staff about computer memory capacity and processing speed and understood the computer programs "better than experts."[91] Scientific articles in North Korean scientific journals often begin with a nod to the wisdom of Kim Il-sung or Kim Jong-il. For example, an article titled "On the Vortex Method of Pulverized Coal Gasification (Part One)" leads off with a quotation from Kim Il-sung, after which the authors can safely say, "In respectful accordance with the instructions of the Great Leader we have advanced the study of fluid flow characteristics"—certainly a good way to get one's manuscript accepted by journal editors.

Not to put too fine a point on the matter, Kim (and the party) are never supposed to be wrong about anything, no matter how badly things turn out:

> Today [2004], our nerve center of the revolution [i.e., Kim Jong-il] is leading the new century with the most accurate ideas and lines. The correctness, scientific accuracy, truth, and invincible vitality of all the ideas and lines put forth by the respected and beloved Comrade Kim Jong-il, including the line of party- and state-building, the line of military development, and the line of economic and cultural development, have been clearly proved in the course of the arduous and prolonged struggle that we waged over the past decades [i.e., during a period when hundreds of thousands of people died of hunger].[92]

Kim Jong-il has been honored with many titles in North Korea. After he succeeded his father in the early 1970s, but before he was presented to the public, the press referred to him as the (anonymous) "party center."[93] In the late 1970s, he was variously referred to as "dear leader," "sagacious leader," and "esteemed leader." After he was introduced to the public as his father's successor at the 1980 party congress, the press began to refer to him as Secretary Kim Jong-il, including both his title and his name. He also became the *yongdoja* or *jidoja* ("leader"), whereas his father was and is the *suryong* ("top leader").[94] After he was appointed to head the military in the early 1990s, he gained the title of "supreme commander." Since the mid-1990s, the press has favored the phrase title "respected and beloved general," and he is the only person in North Korea who can simply be called "the general," although the KPA has some fourteen hundred officers of that rank. Kim Jong-il is also referred to in the press as the "nerve center," the "supreme brain," and the "heart" of the North Korean people, as well as their "mother," as in "The people follow the great general—the mother of the revolution—who takes charge of and looks after his children's destiny and future by devoting his whole life."[95]

The Kim cult embraces other Kim family members, except for those who are out of favor. The reputation of Kim's mother, Kim Jong-suk, who died in 1949, grows stronger by the year. Although historical records suggest that she merely performed housekeeping chores in the guerrilla group led by her husband, the North Korean press touts her as one of the "three generals of Mount Paektu" (the other two being Kim Jong-il and his father). An internal propaganda document from 2004 describes her as "a famous master shot, a seasoned intelligence agent, and a determined communist who would not give in to any cruel challenge or difficult obstacle."[96] According to words attributed to Kim Il-sung, his wife was "his most valuable and closest comrade," and "the greatest meritorious deed that she left behind in the revolution" was "having raised Comrade Kim Jong-il as the leader of the future and putting him up before the party and the fatherland." In short, she is described as the kind of person that Kim wishes all North Koreans would be—people who think first of protecting the leader.

Kim Jong-il's grandfather on his father's side—the schoolteacher, clerk, and herbal pharmacist—is portrayed as an "indomitable revolutionary fighter."[97] Kim Jong-il's paternal grandmother is described as a patriot who defied the Japanese when they were chasing her son, Kim Il-sung, and who told him that he would have to take the cause of independence over from his father; thus, the line of revolutionaries continues in the Kim family from one generation to the next.[98] Koreans who believe such accounts may become used to the idea of being ruled by a member of the Kim family, as if that is a defining characteristic of their country. This hereditary lineage not only confers legitimacy on Kim Jong-il but prepares the groundwork for one of his sons to succeed him.

The central theme of the Kim cult is that the highest duty of every North Korean is to protect the leader—although from what is not clearly specified. People are told that the country is nothing without the leader; therefore, protecting Kim comes before protecting the country. "If one fails to worship and uphold one's top leader [suryong, in this case Kim Il-sung] and leader [jidoja, i.e., Kim Jong-il] absolutely, one cannot defend national dignity, nor safeguard the socialist gains won with blood, nor avoid the fate of stateless slaves."[99] An internal document aimed at those cadres who might be more concerned about their own welfare than that of their country bluntly warns, "If they fail to defend the nerve center of the revolution, our commanding members will be the first to climb up the enemy's gallows."[100]

Protecting the leader also means protecting the "number one articles" associated with him. The most ubiquitous of these are portraits of the Kims found in virtually every room in the country. After a devastating explosion on the rail tracks at Yongchon, KCNA reported approvingly that a Mr. Choe and Mr. Jon, on their way home for lunch, rushed into a burning building that was collapsing "to die a heroic death" in an attempt to rescue portraits of the two Kims hanging on its walls.[101] According to another KCNA story, during the summer floods of 2006, one Kim Tok-chan awoke from a sound sleep to hear the roaring sound of a landslide. He took down the portraits of the two Kims from his living room wall, wrapped them with care, and prepared to flee the house, but he was too late. He did, however, manage to hand the pictures to his wife and push her to safety before he was buried in the landslide.

One of the more curious manifestations of Kim worship is the "slogan tree," whose bark bears what are said to be carvings made by Kim Il-sung's band of revolutionary fighters in the 1930s and 1940s. Thousands of trees have been "discovered" since the 1980s, leading most skeptics to assume that members of the party's propaganda department have been busy with their carving knives. Dozens of the trees located near historical sites are surrounded by special curtained glass enclosures to protect them from the elements. *Nodong Sinmun* says that when forest fires threatened these trees, seventeen soldiers "did not hesitate to throw themselves into the fire, in the flower of their youth, to protect a slogan tree that is the treasure of ages to come. After they were burned to death with their bodies covering every inch of the slogan tree, it came to light that they died clutching President Kim Il-sung's portrait [lapel] badges in their hands."[102]

In the Kim cult, the slogans carved on these trees play the same role that the three wise men play in the biblical story of the birth of Jesus; that is, they foretell the future greatness of the newborn Kim Jong-il: "Birth on Mount Paektu of the bright star, heir to General Kim Il-sung" and "Longevity and blessing to the bright star above Mount Paektu who will shine with the beam of the sun" (Kim Il-sung is the sun and Kim Jong-il is the moon).[103]

The Next Succession

Unless he departs from office in an untimely fashion, Kim will someday have to appoint a successor; perhaps he has already done so. In early 2009, his health seems so precarious that there may well be a sense of urgency to prepare for the succession. According to the logic of the Kim cult, which sets the Kim family apart from all others, Kim must choose one of his sons to succeed him. The tradition of Confucianism, on which the Kim cult is based, would favor his eldest son, Kim Jong-nam, born in 1971. Jong-nam, a taller and fatter version of Kim Jong-il, is the son of Kim's former mistress, the actress Song Hye-rim. He is said to be adept at using computers (a rare skill in North Korea) and has played various background roles in the party, primarily, it is believed, in the technology field. In 2001 he had the misfortune to be detained by immigration authorities while entering Japan on a forged Dominican Republic passport—not the first time, it seems, that he had traveled illegally to Japan. Press photos showed him to be a fat man with chin stubble, accompanied by two women and a small boy. The Japanese government decided to deport the group rather than press charges, but the immigration issue made him a laughing stock in Japan, caused his father to lose face, and might prove an inauspicious public debut for a future North Korean leader. Since then, Kim Jong-nam has lived in exile in Macau, only occasionally visiting his homeland.

In 2002, the North Korean propaganda organs began to elevate to cult status Ko Yong-hi, perhaps signaling that one of her two sons may be first in line for succession. In 2003, a classified document prepared for soldiers said, "The respected mother, assisting the respected and beloved Comrade Supreme Commander from a place closest to him and serving him with all her loyalty, is precisely in the same position as Comrade Kim Jong-suk [Kim Jong-il's mother], the anti-Japanese heroine, was in the days of the anti-Japanese war upholding the fatherly leader and laying the firm basis of succession for our revolution to be carried forward generation after generation."[104] Although the identity of the "respected mother" is not revealed, since Ko was known to be Kim's favorite consort, the reference is undoubtedly to her.

According to an internal party directive dated September 2005, the Party Central Committee "a while ago solemnly declared that it would highly uphold respected Comrade Kim Jong-chol, who inherited the spirit of Paektu intact, as our party's nerve center in response to our party and our people's unanimous cherished desire."[105] The "unanimous desire" is pure fiction, of course, because Jong-chol's name has never been mentioned in the press. The directive went on to indicate that Jong-chol should be addressed as "respected comrade chief deputy department director," that his portrait should be "cordially placed" in party conference rooms and offices but not in people's homes, and that his orders should be implemented without question. At the time, Kim Jong-chol was only twenty-five.

For top cadres, much is riding on the succession choice. Those close to the successor will rise in the party organization, and associates and supporters of other succession candidates may even end up in prison. It is not at all clear that Jong-chol will be his father's choice. In 2009, Ko's younger son, Kim Jong-un, seemed to have become the succession favorite. One would think that Kim Jong-un, only twenty-six years of age, would be too young and inexperienced to be named as the successor. After all, Kim Jong-il was in his early thirties when his father chose him, and his succession was not announced to the public until he was almost forty. But Kim Jong-il's deteriorating health may push the succession process forward more quickly than anyone had anticipated, and it would probably be better for him to name a young successor than none at all.

Little is known about either of Ko's two sons. Like Kim Jong-nam, they both spent a few years of their youth studying at schools in Switzerland (under false names). Neither has been mentioned by name in the North Korean press, and the general public does not even know of their existence. If in the near future Kim Jong-il becomes seriously incapacitated or dies, perhaps one of the sons will begin his reign at the head of a collective leadership group, with eventual leadership succession to be decided by domestic power struggles.

Summing up Kim Jong-il

Kim Jong-il, the "respected and beloved general," has never been particularly respected or loved by the North Korean people, but he has been accepted in North Korea's Confucian-based culture because he is the first son of the respected and beloved father. Perhaps more importantly, after a half century of life under the Kim dynasty, the North Korean people cannot imagine who else might lead them. It would be a gross exaggeration to say that the people support Kim Jong-il; rather, it does not occur to them to oppose him. In any case, what the people actually think of him is largely irrelevant because they have no political power. On the other hand, the military does have the power to contest Kim's rule, and the top generals, most of whom he has appointed, cannot be happy with the state of the economy, which has hurt morale and impaired military readiness. To keep the military in line, Kim spies on his generals and lavishes them with gifts. In any case, the generals would not know how to run the country without Kim.

The foreign press often calls Kim crazy, but there is little evidence to support such an assessment. Kim is a rational thinker, able to arrive at reasonable conclusions based on information he receives from loyal cadres. Given his desire to remain in power for a lifetime, his policy choices usually make sense. It would be a mistake to think Kim has made poor decisions just because North Korea's economy has collapsed and the people are suffering. His decisions are made for the benefit of himself and his supporters, not the people. Totalitarian socialism may have weakened his country and brought suffering to his people, but at the same time it has kept him in control and kept his people preoccupied with survival. Impulsive though he may be, Kim seems capable of weighing costs and benefits and employing North Korea's limited resources to protect his regime from the indifference and hostility of foreign powers.

The greatest flaw in his character is his attitude of exceptionalism. Although he has orchestrated a propaganda campaign to make the North Korean people selfless socialists, he himself is a confirmed capitalist. Even in a capitalist society, he would be called a "fat cat." The propaganda stories about Kim's frugal lifestyle ("I do not care if I only eat soup") might fool some of the masses some of the time, but they do not fool his top officials in Pyongyang, who, thanks to personal observation and rumor, are aware of his disdain for socialism.

It is doubtful that Kim has ever seriously considered loosening his grip on the people or adopting the kind of reform policies that have transformed other current and former socialist countries. The fate of former dictators teaches that reform is usually accompanied by political change. A day of reckoning came for each of the former communist European dictators: Hungary's János Kadar was deposed in 1988 and died the following year; East Germany's Erich Honecker was deposed in 1989 and subsequently arrested for corruption and manslaughter; Czechoslovakia's Gustav Husak, deposed in 1989, was expelled from the party the following year and died in 1991; Bulgaria's Todor Zhivkov was deposed in 1989, expelled from the party, and arrested for embezzlement; and Poland's Wojciech Jaruzelski was deposed in 1990 and later charged with crimes committed as defense minister. Yugoslavia's Josip Tito and Albania's Enver Hoxha were spared humiliation accompanying the collapse of communism only because they died in 1980 and 1985, respectively. Romania's Nicolae Ceausescu, whose cult of personality, nepotism, love of grand monuments, and reign of terror paralleled the ruling style of his good friend Kim Il-sung, was so hated by his people that after he fell from power, three hundred members of the military vied for a place on the three-man firing squad that executed him and his wife on Christmas day in 1989. With these examples before him, Kim Jong-il has not heeded Mikhail Gorbachev's famous advice to Honecker in 1989 that "life punishes those who delay." Gorbachev himself has disappeared from political life, as have most of the first generation of reformers who followed the dictators. Kim Jong-il has delayed and remains as firmly in power as he was in 1990. Life often rewards those who persevere as well.

To remain in control, Kim or his successor must reserve power for himself. He must accept corruption, which helps a dysfunctional society survive, although he must not allow top cadres to become too corrupt or they may amass sufficient power to threaten him. As for the masses, as long as they are preoccupied with making a living, and as long as they have reason to fear the police, they will be reluctant to engage in politics. Kim does worry about foreign influence and intervention, especially from the United States. In light of this threat, he desperately needs a guarantee from the United States of support for his regime and noninterference in its domestic affairs. Kim's conception of Korean unification follows the same line: economic support from South Korea coupled with acceptance of the North's dictatorial system. Only if Kim keeps his eyes focused on the supreme goal of staying in power can he and his successor and associates survive in a world where socialist dictatorships are an oddity and an anachronism.

As for the twenty-three million other North Koreans, it is their misfortune that Kim and his father have been free to pursue their own interests at the expense of the peoples'. As long as Kim or like-minded North Korean rulers remain in power, the best the people can do is look out for their individual interests and try to stay out of trouble with the authorities.

CHAPTER THREE

The Economic System

Nothing more immediately influences the lives of the North Korean people than their economy—an economy that did not evolve to suit their needs but was imposed on them by politicians. Even when it became apparent that the system was not working, the country's leaders kept it in place because it served their political purposes. Although the millions of North Koreans who suffer from this poor economy neither understand the economic principles that underlie their daily lives nor are aware of the economic statistics that describe the economy, these principles and statistics can help us understand why, from one year to the next, the economy continues to struggle. By the late 1990s the socialist command economy had eroded to such an extent that most people abandoned it and tried to create a new economy for themselves. Chapter 4 addresses how they are doing this in their day-to-day lives. This chapter looks at the underlying health of the economy.

Communism is an alluring social and economic vision: communities of farmers, workers, and intellectuals banding together as equals to selflessly produce and distribute the fruits of their enthusiastic labor according to their needs. No capitalists lord it over them and take a large slice of the proceeds for themselves. All for one, and one for all. This vision was still popular throughout much of the world when Kim Il-sung came to power in the late 1940s, although it was most often practiced in the form of a central-command socialist economy directed by the Communist Party. Whatever its shortcomings, this economic model was uniquely suited to the needs of a Stalinist government, a fact that the budding dictator Kim must certainly have appreciated. Kim knew nothing about economics and would have adopted any economic system his Soviet mentors told him to, but in the late 1940s, he could have had no misgivings about adopting the socialist economic model.

The central-planning aspect of socialism seemed preeminently logical: why let businesses produce whatever goods they wish? Overlooking the self-correcting nature of the market economy, socialist economic ideologues believe that market economies produce too much of some things and not enough of others. Yet, economic bureaucrats trying to run command economies find it next to impossible to direct them in such a way that all the parts work together. Even in a country as homogeneous as North Korea, it is not possible to control and coordinate the lives of twenty-three million people, much less coordinate the domestic and international economies. And yet, the Kim regime continues to place its faith in centralized economic control. A 2009 *Nodong Sinmun* article quotes Kim Jong-il as saying, "It is the intrinsic demand of the socialist economy to rapidly develop the economy in a planned manner under the unified guidance of the state."[1] If after sixty years the state has not managed to "rapidly develop" the economy in a unified direction, it is not likely to do so in the future. Later in the article, the author gets to the important point: "The observance of socialist principles in guiding and managing the economy is not a simple working-level economic matter, but it is a serious political issue that is related to the destiny of socialism." And, of course, to the destiny of the Kim regime.

For dictators, a great attraction of socialism's central control is that it enables them to withhold goods and services from people who refuse to obey. Until recently, North Koreans who left their workplaces or made unauthorized trips away from their hometowns were unable to obtain food rations. Today, people rarely receive rations even if they show up at work, so the regime cannot count on starving them into submission. Yet another advantage of central control is that those who control the economy essentially own the means of production. To gain resources, it is unnecessary to levy taxes or charge fees; the elites can simply help themselves to the output of factories, mines, fields, and forests. The Kim family has appropriated for themselves North Korea's most valuable commodities, including the output of its gold mines. Kim Jong-il is rumored to have stashed away billions of dollars, although this estimate is probably highly inflated.

In order for communism to work, workers must be motivated by a collective work ethic. Such workers embody the "new man" that both the Stalinists and Kimists vainly tried to create among the workers, although the creators themselves remained unchanged egotists. In North Korea, the Kims themselves were the most selfish and least socialistic of the lot. Although many North Koreans did buy into the communitarian ethic, so many people either went along for a free ride or tried to make the system work for their personal benefit that the system ultimately failed.

Under the most favorable circumstances, a centrally controlled socialist economy can provide a basic living for the people, but in North Korea's case, absence of trade with advanced economies, failure to receive continuing support from fellow socialist economies, natural disasters, and a degradation of the economic infrastructure have rendered socialism unsustainable. As North Korean authorities admitted in 2002 (to party cadres, not to the general population), the government is bankrupt. Only by receiving billions of dollars in foreign aid can it continue to function at all, and hundreds of billions of dollars will have to be invested to repair the economic infrastructure. Unfortunately, instead of trying to solve its financial problems by abandoning socialism in whole or in part, the regime's solution has been to push the financial responsibilities onto the people, who are still supposed to work within the socialist economy.

Although much is not understood about North Korea's economy, the outlines are clear. In the absence of meaningful economic statistics from the North Korean government, statistics from North Korea's trade partners and close analysis by foreign economists provide a fairly clear picture of North Korea's economy. For example, estimates of the factory-operating rate, around 25 percent, are based on aerial photographs of smoke spiraling from chimneys and counts of the number of people going to work in the morning. Aerial photography is likewise one method used to estimate crop yields. Trade statistics are notoriously unreliable because North Korea's most important trade partner, China, is secretive about its dealings with Pyongyang, and much of the trade along the Chinese border is not even recorded by the Beijing government.

North Korea's major economic indices, as compiled by South Korea's Bank of Korea, should be taken as only a rough indication of the state of the economy.[2] At least until the economic collapse of the 1990s, employment was fairly evenly divided between the three sectors of mining and manufacturing, agriculture, and services. Gross national income (GNI) for 2006 was estimated at $25.6 billion (the purchasing-power parity gross domestic product estimate by the CIA was $40 billion), with a per capita GNI of $1,108. South Korea's GNI was thirty-five times greater, and per capita GNI was seventeen times greater. Until 1990, North Korea's economy was growing at an annual rate of 2 to 3 percent, after which it fell by an average of almost 4 percent a year before returning to the black at the end of the 1990s, with annual growth averaging about 2 percent a year.

Although the North Korean economy cannot survive on its own, trade relations with other economies are weak. Estimated total trade volume, which had been in the $3 to $5 billion range in the 1980s, fell to $1 to $2 billion a year in the 1990s and rebounded to the $4 to $5 billion range after 2000. In 2006, total trade was about $3 billion (including foreign aid), whereas South Korea's total trade was approximately 240 times greater, at around $719 billion. For decades North Korea has run an annual trade deficit of $1 to $2 billion, which it makes up with foreign aid and by failing to repay its debts. In 2008, net debt, which is in default and has not been serviced for two decades, was estimated at $18 billion, which is almost as large as North Korea's GNI.

Before the collapse of communism in Eastern Europe, North Korea's major trading partners were the Soviet Union, China, and Japan, in that order. In the 1990s China became the largest trading partner, followed by Japan and South Korea, while trade with Russia almost ceased after Moscow demanded that trade be conducted on a cash basis rather than on concessionary terms. Since 2000, North Korea's trade with China and South Korea has increased, while trade with Japan has plummeted, especially after 2002 when the Japanese government began imposing trade sanctions to pressure Pyongyang to give up its nuclear program and reveal information about Japanese citizens who had been abducted years earlier. By 2006, China and South Korea accounted for an estimated 39 percent and 27 percent of North Korea's trade, followed by Thailand, Russia, and Japan. In late 2006, North Korea's nuclear weapons test worsened its relations with Japan, and a new South Korean administration that took office in early 2008 proved unwilling to continue the unreciprocated aid program of the previous two administrations, resulting in a precipitous decline in North Korea's trade with these two neighbors and an even greater reliance on trade with China.

Statistics for trade and investment between the two Koreas can in any case be deceiving. First, like statistics from other countries, they often include foreign aid transfers. In 2006, out of the $1.3 billion in inter-Korean trade, about 60 percent was foreign aid.[3] Second, few foreign companies actually make money in North Korea, so while their investments look like business decisions, they are based largely on the hope that things will improve in the future, or they are patriotic investments in the homeland.

A Brief Economic History

Why is North Korea economically on a par with some of the poorest states in South Asia and Africa, while South Korea has become one of the world's most successful economies? Both started in the same place, and for two decades North Korea was economically more successful than South Korea. When Soviet troops arrived in Korea in 1945 to take control from the departing Japanese, the northern half of the peninsula had 76 percent of Korea's mining production, 92 percent of its electrical-generating capacity, and 80 percent of its heavy industry.[4] The southern half of the peninsula was the country's rice bowl, a differentiation in economic potential attributable to climate and topography. Thanks to Japanese development and the natural endowment of the land, the northern half of Korea had the potential to respond to the Stalinist preference for heavy industry over agriculture and light industry.

Kim Il-sung's elementary school education had not prepared him to direct the country's economy, and his trusted colleagues, soldiers like him, had no more economic expertise than he did. He initially followed the advice of his Soviet sponsors, who were rather ignorant about Korea and, for that matter, not very knowledgeable about economics. Fortunately for Kim, the brute force of centralized organization and the high motivation shared by Koreans emerging from years of colonial oppression were sufficient to jumpstart the economy. As a soldier, Kim had developed a talent for organizing and motivating people, which fit in well with the needs of a socialist command economy. Consequently, the North Korean economy reestablished itself in the 1950s and continued to function adequately into the early 1960s, at which time Kim made the fateful decision to give priority to his military industry, and the rest is sad history, at least for the people. The shortages that people in a market economy face during wartime are a reminder of what North Koreans contend with all the time.

By the end of the 1960s, the North Korean government had stopped publishing economic statistics. In the 1970s, the country defaulted on its foreign loans, and the government increasingly relied on propaganda to motivate workers to do more with less. The Kim regime tried to induce foreign investors to pump capital and technology into the economy by drafting a foreign-investment law in 1984 and opening the country's first foreign trade zone at Najin-Sonbong in 1991, but laws drafted by a government that was above the law did not fool investors, and only a few small Japanese companies loyal to North Korea, along with a few Chinese entrepreneurs, took the bait. Foreign aid from the Soviet Union, Eastern Europe, and China barely kept the North Korean economy afloat, and by the late 1980s, some North Koreans were going hungry.

North Korea's economic lifeline was severed by the demise of European communism in the late 1980s and early 1990s, and in an unprecedented move, the government admitted that its 1987–1993 economic plan had failed to achieve its objectives. Fulfillment failures were nothing new for these economic plans, which in typical communist style ran for a period of six or seven years with a one- or two-year "catch-up" period, but this was the first time the "infallible" party admitted that it had made a forecasting mistake. After Kim Il-sung died in 1994, the government took no economic initiatives, leaving the people to fend for themselves. Severe floods in 1995 set the stage for three years of extreme hardship that the media called the "Arduous March" (*konan ui haenggun*), when a half million or more people died of starvation.

While his father was alive, Kim Jong-il had only limited scope to try out new economic ideas, not so much because his father might disapprove but because the entire top level of the leadership was of his father's generation, and as long as they continued to lead a comfortable life, they saw no need for change. But after the three-year mourning period, which largely overlapped with the three Arduous March years, Kim tried to revive the economy with two related campaigns, both announced around the time the Supreme People's Assembly was convened in 1998. The *kangsong taeguk* ("economically strong nation") campaign called for the people to return to the glory days of the 1950s, when great strides were made in heavy industry. By the 1990s, many of North Korea's industries, such as the steel industry, were hardly in better shape than they had been after the Americans bombed them during the Korean War.

The other campaign, launched by Kim to firm up his political position with the generals, was "military-first politics," whereby the military not only had first call on the country's resources, which had been the case since the 1960s, but would serve as a model for the rest of society. Neither of these campaigns promised a way out of North Korea's economic difficulty: expecting people to think and act as they did in the 1950s was not likely to work in the twenty-first century, and devoting the country's best resources to the military would only keep the economy unbalanced.

In 2001, Kim urged North Korea's bureaucrats to "make fundamental changes in their ideological view, their ways of thinking, their ways of acting, and their fighting spirit."[5] Henceforth, the guiding economic principle would be to achieve cost-efficient results, rather than results at any cost—as long as business was done within the bounds of the socialist command economy: "If the results of economic activities barely compensate or cannot compensate at all for materials consumed for production, compared to expenditure, and if products fail to have utility value or give negative influence to labor conditions, living conditions, and living environment, no matter how great the results of economic activities may be, we cannot say that such results actually contributed to the nation's development and prosperity and to promoting the people's living."[6] The key to getting results is supposed to be high technology: "Every sector and every factory and enterprise of the national economy are, without exception, left unable to make headway even a step without modernizing and renovating their obsolete processes, equipment, and production methods."[7]

Economic bureaucrats must take care when implementing this campaign because if any of their policies fall outside the scope of "Kim's intent," they might be out of a job and on their way to prison. For the North Korean worker and factory manager, the key question is where to get new technology, given North Korea's lack of foreign reserves and its status as a strategically embargoed state. Kim puts the burden squarely on the shoulders of the people: "To modernize local industry plants with up-to-date technology is a major requirement that each local organ of power has to meet to fulfill its duty as the householder responsible for local economic development and improvement in the residents' living conditions."[8]

The July 1 Economic Management Improvement Measures

On October 3, 2001, Kim met with high-level economic officials and gave shape and substance to his "new-thinking" idea, at the same time making clear that he and the party had made no mistakes in formulating previous economic policies; instead, Kim blamed economic bureaucrats for failing to carry out their duties properly, although he did concede that the party's earlier economic policies were not necessarily appropriate for North Korea's current economic situation.[9] He also insisted that the Chinese economic model, the results of which he had briefly observed on his trips to China, was not one that North Korea should imitate.

He said the State Planning Commission would continue to set broad economic goals (under the direction of the party), but it would be up to local officials and managers to set their own goals—up to a point. Managers would be free to set prices (within state guidelines), decide how to sell their products (after supplying their quota to the central government), and figure out how to procure raw materials. They could also set up foreign trading companies to sell surplus goods and purchase supplies abroad. Companies that could not secure raw materials must send their workers out to earn money in other endeavors. Prices for food, housing, fuel, and similar daily necessities would henceforth be set according to their cost to the state, which would continue to provide social welfare programs, such as health care, schooling, and retirement, free of charge (although in a much degraded state). The goal of the changes was not to replace the planned socialist economy with a market economy but rather to make the planned economy work better so that the people would stay in it.

The 2002 New Year's editorial, beginning as usual with the boast that an economic "breakthrough" had been made in the preceding year, announced, "Our socialist construction, which experienced hardships for several years, has now entered a new phase of radical change. We can dare to say with pride that we have taken an offensive position in the building of an economic power, fully ready to launch an overall offensive." The only reference to the specifics of a new economic plan was the vague statement, buried in the middle of the editorial, that the "main orientation" of economic management would be to "ensure the highest profitability while adhering to socialist principles."[10]

On June 1, 2002, an internal government document distributed to upper-level military and economic cadres outlined a new economic policy. "At present, commercial transactions are rampant because state prices are lower than those of farmers' markets. As a result, we see a phenomenon in which goods are lacking in the state but are piled up for individuals [i.e., a few fortunate individuals]. To be frank, the state does not have money at present, but individuals have money exceeding two year's of the state's budget. . . . From now on, regardless of who they are, all will live on living expenses accorded to them. Nothing will be free of charge, and there will be no egalitarianism."[11]

July 2002 would prove an otherwise typical month for North Korea. The Arirang mass gymnastics festival, scheduled to close at the end of June, was held over, although foreign attendance was sparse. Relations with South Korea were strained in the wake of a June 29 North Korean attack on South Korean patrol boats in the West Sea, although at the same time the North Koreans were requesting South Korean aid, which they were confident of receiving from the ever-optimistic South Korean government of Kim Dae-jung. Pyongyang's relations with Washington continued to be strained. After the West Sea clash, the U.S. government informed the North Koreans it was canceling a plan to send a delegation to Pyongyang in July to discuss bilateral issues.

At noon on July 1, local meetings were convened across the country to convey to the people the gist of the new economic measures that would take effect immediately. News of economic changes resulting from what came to be called the July 1 Economic Management Improvement Measures (*Kyungje Kwalli Kaeson Jochi*) slowly trickled out of North Korea over the next month. Foreigners, especially those who were optimistic about North Korea's future, often refer to the measures as "reforms," but the North Korean government avoided using that term because it implied there had been something wrong with the original economic system.

The most comprehensive reports on the measures came from *Choson Sinbo*, the pro–North Korean newspaper in Japan. A July 29 article reported that the North Korean government would no longer provide food and housing subsidies. "At their homes, people now have to do some mathematics to find out how much they can spend monthly and they have to save as much as possible."[12] According to the article, the price of a Pyongyang city bus or subway ride had increased twentyfold, from 0.1 to 2 won, to cover operating expenses. Prices of other consumer goods and services were likewise rationalized. The price of a kilogram of rice rose 550 fold, from .08 won (virtually free with a ration card) to 44 won. Prices of most domestically manufactured goods increased twenty-five-fold. The government began to charge rent on houses and apartments and to tax farmers for the use of their small "private" plots of land. Price tags were put on almost everything. According to one former North Korean, inspectors visited homes and assessed fees on electricity according to what lights and appliances were being used. While they were there, they might also search for unregistered items such as radios and videotape players, forcing homeowners to pay bribes to stay out of trouble. Before July 1, the cost of food (when rations were available), accounted for only a small percentage of the household budget; at the new prices, food purchases consumed half or sometimes much more of the budget.

To cover the costs now intruding on their lives from every direction, the average worker's monthly wage rose from 200 to 300 won to 4,000 to 6,000 won. As the *Choson Sinbo* article explained, "Factories and enterprises that increase their earnings will receive proportionally higher shares of distribution. Workers' pay will also rise proportionally. Only naturally, if these entities' revenues go down, the workers will also have to live on pay that is lower than that provided by the government so far. Good-for-nothings will not be able to live."

The flaw in the new economic measures was that in order for the payment-for-results model to succeed, work organizations had to be able to operate and make a profit so they could pay the workers. However, if workers, whom the state assigns to their jobs, are unable to produce anything at their workplaces, they have the choice of starving or finding employment in the black market economy.

Before the July 1 measures were enacted, cooperative and state farms were supposed to sell most of their crops to the government, which distributed food through the Public Distribution System (PDS) at a nominal cost to consumers. In the distribution, some people received more than their share not because they did more work but because they had political connections; by the 1990s those without connections received hardly any rations at all. Farmers preferred to sell their crops in the markets, where they could earn hard cash rather than the modest payment provided by their cooperatives, thereby creating a tremendous grain leakage that starved the government's ration system. This same process operated in other economic sectors. Coal miners could earn more money selling their coal directly to households rather than to the government.

To revive the socialist economy, the central government allowed factories to sell much of their output on the open market and, in turn, to take responsibility for procuring their own resources. The government would continue to set guidelines for production and pricing, but it was up to factory managers to find a way to keep their factories running. This was an entirely new responsibility for the managers, and it came at a time when the entire economy was short of resources. Many factories began to make alternative products for which local resources or markets were available. For example, an aluminum factory might switch from making aluminum sheeting to making cooking pots, which were more marketable and required less metal. The government recommended that factories that found it difficult to operate should send their workers out to alternative jobs such as growing crops or cutting trees, but this was hardly a suitable substitute for the regular operation of the factory, in terms of either the revenue that could be gained from these makeshift jobs or the efficient use of workers' skills. Workplaces were also given the responsibility of providing for the welfare of their workers, for example, by finding food for them.

Whether workers stayed in their workplaces or went out on their own, they had to cope with another problem triggered by the July 1 economic measures: inflation. Prices increased dramatically after July 2002. For example, by late 2005 a kilogram of rice was selling for between 600 and 1,000 won in the market, which was the only place most people could procure it. By early 2008, the price was about 2,500 won—a significant jump from the "official" price of 44 won in July 2002. The government's exchange rate jumped from 2.2 won to the U.S. dollar to about 140 won, where it stayed into 2008. However, since 2002, the market exchange rate has ranged from 2,500 won to 3,500 won to the dollar, meaning that a typical North Korean's monthly wage of 5,000 won would buy no more than $2.00 in hard currency.

The July 1 economic measures roughly paralleled the New Economic Policy (NEP) instituted by the Bolsheviks shortly after the Russian Revolution in that the NEP was not the direction the communists wanted to take, but they needed to get the economy moving before taking firm control of it. The NEP lasted only a few years in the early 1920s and differed in one important respect from the July 1 measures: the NEP was meant to be a springboard to communism, whereas the July 1 measures, coming fifty years after the communization of North Korea, were a desperate attempt to rescue the North Korean economy from communism.

The July 1 economic-improvement measures provided valuable, if difficult, lessons for the North Korean people. They lost the innocence of living in a low-grade socialist "paradise," and they came to realize there is no free lunch and that free riding imposes serious costs on the economy, even if those costs are not directly laid at each individual's doorstep. With the measures, the Kim regime hoped that people would become more responsible and productive socialists. Instead, people concluded that socialism is a sham and that the only real economy is the market economy. That economy is a harsh environment for many North Koreans, who have few economic resources (e.g., capital) to work with, virtually no laws to protect them as they trade in the market, and limited market education and experience to guide them. And finally, as a consequence of the breakdown of the socialist market, Kim Jong-il's image as a benevolent ruler and economic genius has been irreparably damaged.

Manufacturing and Marketing

A reasonable estimate is that by 2002, three-quarters of all factories had shut down. The transportation sector is a shambles: most intercity roads are unpaved, decrepit trains travel at twenty miles an hour, when the power is available, and some open-bed trucks, the main means of intercity transportation, have been converted to charcoal burners. The country's principal exports are minerals and fishery products, not manufactured goods. North Korea's heavy-industry plants are obsolete, a great irony considering that heavy industry is supposed to be the cornerstone of Stalinist economies. The one bright spot is North Korea's weapons plants, which manufacture everything from small arms to missiles, but these plants are operated by the military and provide no income to the civilian economy.

The marketplaces are filled with mostly inexpensive Chinese-made goods, along with homemade products, farm produce, and scavenged scraps from dormant factories. The Kim regime has never looked kindly on these marketplaces, which stand as an indictment of the socialist ration system and compete with it. But markets must be tolerated because now that the PDS has collapsed, they are the only source of daily necessities for most people. In the markets, prices for formerly rationed staples, such as rice and cooking oil, are supposed to be controlled, but officials overseeing the markets can be bribed to look the other way.

In a society where people are supposed to live, work, and play under the watchful eye of the party, the markets provide a means of economic and social escape. Not only can people buy and sell what they want, but they can exchange information. Markets are also a school for capitalism. People learn about marketing, a woefully underdeveloped practice in socialist economies, where traditional consumer skills include discovering what stores have something to sell on a given day, how to bribe the store clerks, and how to combat the boredom of standing in line for hours. For all of these reasons, the Kim regime has tried to marginalize the markets. A Party Central Committee instruction sent out in October 2007 quotes Kim Jong-il as warning, "The market has degenerated into a place which eats away at the socialism of our own style . . . and [is] a birthplace of all sorts of non-socialist practices."[13]

The July 1 economic measures officially recognized markets as necessary but tried to keep them within the controlled economy. More radical changes in the official view of markets took place in early 2003, when the government stopped referring to them as "farmers' markets" and started calling them simply "markets," an indication that items other than farm products could legally be sold. Shortly thereafter, the Democratic People's Republic of Korea (DPRK) cabinet approved new regulations for the operation of markets.[14] The regulations began with an assurance that Kim Jong-il himself had directed that markets be established in order to make the lives of citizens more "convenient." The ministry of commerce was put in charge of authorizing markets and overseeing their operation. According to the new regulations, all markets should have a paved floor, a roof, and necessary storage and sanitation facilities. Their hours of operation should be set so that people could visit them in the evening after work. "Farm products, foodstuffs, daily necessities, and other commodities produced domestically or imported" could be sold, with the exception of certain "state-controlled items." Ceiling prices would be set according to market conditions for such staples as rice, cooking oil, sugar, and seasonings. Sellers would pay fees for their stalls and be taxed on their earnings. "Illicit transactions" and "nonsocialist incidents" would be punished, although these terms were not defined, thus opening the way for market officials to levy fines and demand bribes at their own discretion.

With the government's open recognition of markets, it was necessary to define them in a manner consistent with socialism. For example, the director of the State Planning Commission was quoted as saying that markets were "part of the socialist circulation of goods."[15] A vice director of the DPRK ministry of commerce explained that the use of markets was an "interim feature of a socialist society," adding that the markets "do not at all mean that our socialist planned economy is being changed into a market economy or a free market economy."[16] *Choson Sinbo* referred to the new economic measures as "practical socialism" and insisted that even though other countries might view these measures as an adoption of capitalism, there was a "stark difference" between the North Korean measures and capitalism, presumably the fact that the markets were run by the state.[17] Readers were assured that "although they are taking an unknown path, they [the North Korean authorities] know what they are doing."

The North Korean authorities have been reluctant to reveal much to foreigners about the hundreds of markets now operating in the cities, small towns, and countryside. Foreign visitors are rarely allowed to enter or photograph them, as if they are something shameful. The attempt to hide their existence is another irony, considering that the outside world views them as one of the most promising aspects of the North Korean economy. In 1999, after the markets had already expanded to include nonfarm products, the Korean Central News Agency (KCNA) labeled a Japanese news story about them "a wholly unfounded fabrication" and insisted that the only thing happening at the farmers' markets was the sale of surplus agricultural products.[18]

Farming

Another economic adjustment made by the Kim regime around 2002 was a further move to abandon the socialist farming system. In 1946, even before the official founding of the North Korean state, the communists distributed much of the landowners' holdings to the peasants. After the Korean War, as Kim Il-sung embarked on the nationalization of the economy, the land was taken away from farmers and given to agricultural collectives of up to five hundred families. Today, most farms are still collectives. Each is assigned a quota of farm products to be remitted to the state, and any surplus is to be distributed among the members of the collective, although in practice the party cadres help themselves to a disproportionate share. People are assigned to work on farms usually because their parents are farmers. State planners tell farms what crops to grow, and the government is supposed to supply seeds, fertilizer, and machinery free of charge. The farm managers, who are party cadres, assign teams of workers to specialized tasks, such as cultivating rice, repairing farm equipment, tending mulberry trees, and raising poultry. All workers receive food and other basic necessities from the collective rather than from the PDS. Each family is also permitted to cultivate a small garden plot of about one hundred square meters where table vegetables such as peppers can be grown.

In 1964, Kim Il-sung's "Theses on the Rural Question" advocated converting collectives to state farms, where workers would be paid a basic wage, just as if they worked in a state-run factory. Interestingly, the opposite has happened, and for economic reasons the collectives have become more like large collections of private farms than like agricultural factories. The obvious problem with both collective and state farms is that farmers do not directly benefit from their labor. Hard-working farmers receive the same rations and pay as lazy farmers. Political connections, bribery, and party affiliation are the main determinants of reward. Under these circumstances, many farmers do as little work as possible in the fields, pilfer as much as they can, and devote their attention to their private plots or to working outside the farm.

To combat the problem of what psychologists call "social loafing," managers have organized workers on collectives into ever smaller work teams. By this means performance can be more accurately measured and payments more equitably calibrated. These work teams originally comprised fifty to one hundred people, but in the 1990s, collectives introduced the concept of "sub–work teams," which had a dozen members or fewer, often all members of one family. Each work team or sub–work team is given an output quota and may dispose of any surplus as its members wish. This devolution of responsibility is as far as the regime is willing to go toward decollectivizing the farms. However, as part of the July 1, 2002, economic measures, private farming was introduced on an experimental basis in a few places.[19] Individuals and families are granted a plot of land and allowed to farm as they wish. Former North Koreans report that individual farms range in size from six hundred to thirteen hundred square meters (a sixth to a third of an acre), depending on the fertility of the land. The government takes a portion of the harvested crops to pay for seed, fertilizer, and fuel. In a complicated system of many gradations, land-use fees are assessed, but they are never referred to as taxes because the government has always boasted that North Korea is the only country in the world without taxation.

The life of the North Korean farmer has always been hard. Despite fifty years of government campaigns to improve the standard of living in rural areas, most people would prefer to live in the city if they had a choice. City dwellers may complain about shortages in housing, electricity, and clean water, but these are worse in the countryside, where North Koreans are living as South Koreans and Chinese did in the 1960s.

During planting and harvesting seasons, Koreans from all walks of life— office workers, soldiers, students—are sent to the countryside to assist the farmers for two months in the spring and two weeks in the fall. The party sends agitators to erect red flags in the fields to motivate the people engaged in this "rice-planting combat." Even people who happen to be traveling in the countryside may be abducted by officials to help with the farmwork. The seasonal farmworkers live in farmers' houses and village halls and are issued special ration cards for food, although more often than not they rely on the local farms for food. The North Korean media boast that representatives from foreign embassies and organizations volunteer to help in the countryside in a show of solidarity. But for all this effort, North Korea comes up short in food production almost every year.

Money and Banking

North Korea's primitive banking system is one of the factors preventing the economy from making the kind of giant leap forward that the Kim regime dreams about. Before markets became popular, people had little to spend their money on, creating an "overhang" of savings that most people preferred to keep under their mattresses rather than deposit in a government bank under the scrutiny of party officials. Even state organizations have avoided using banks. A 2006 article in the party's economic journal virtually implored government organizations to use banks, even quoting Kim Jong-il on the subject. Those who deposit their money in banks find that they are sometimes unable to withdraw their savings because the bank is short of cash, and in this case, since the government owns the bank, the depositors can do little to retrieve their savings. Now that people are forced to shop in the markets, where prices are far higher than in the PDS, some personal savings may have been soaked up, but people are understandably reluctant to disclose the amount of their savings for fear that government officials will confiscate some of it under one pretense or another. Instead of depositing money in banks and going there for loans, North Koreans who want to invest do so as part of small cooperative groups of friends and acquaintances (usually groups of housewives), which are also popular in South Korea.

One approach the government used in the past to get people to put their money in banks was to replace the currency periodically. People with the old currency had to bring it to a bank and exchange it for the new, often with a limit on how much could be exchanged. The limit was imposed based on the assumption that citizens of a socialist economy, where wages are low, have no legitimate means of amassing large amounts of cash.

The government can also soak up hidden cash by selling bonds. This method had previously only been employed during the Korean War, but in March 2003 it was announced that a new series of bonds would go on sale, despite the fact that communists have always denounced bond issues as an evil of capitalism that robs working people of their money. In an attempt to counter this argument, the vice president of the DPRK's central bank gave the following nonsensical explanation of the new People's Life Bonds on national television:

> Generally speaking, capitalist countries issue bonds to take away what is in people's pockets and use it to maintain and strengthen their oppressor institutions and wage wars of aggression. These capitalist countries pay back the bonds with taxes that they squeeze from people. Therefore, bonds in capitalist countries definitely are a further exploitation of the working popular masses. Contrary to this, bonds in socialist countries, in essence, are issued to temporarily mobilize and use people's unused cash funds to develop the people's economy and improve people's lives. They are people-oriented because all the mobilized funds are returned to the people.[20]

The part about returning the funds to the people is difficult to verify in a society as secretive as North Korea's. Bond purchasers are eligible to win lotteries. In the first two years (2003 and 2004), a lottery was held twice a year, with winners receiving prizes corresponding to the size of their bond investment. After that, drawings have presumably been held once a year. For example, among those holding 1,000-won bonds, one lucky winner is supposed to receive 50,000 won with other prizes of 25,000 won, 10,000 won, and 5,000, including the returned principal. Those who do not win the lottery began receiving their principal (but no interest) beginning in 2008 "on a phased basis," with all money finally to be repaid by 2013.[21]

Purchase of the bonds was supposed to be entirely voluntary, but officials let it be known that purchasing bonds was the patriotic thing to do. For example, purchasers of 1-million-won bonds received a Letter of Commendation for Patriotic Deed and a state decoration. Local people's committees in the neighborhood and workplace put considerable pressure on people to purchase these bonds because these committees had been given bond quotas to meet. Even so, bond sales, which apparently ended in December 2003, were sluggish. A Korean Central Television news report at the end of 2007 announced the winning numbers for the latest prizes but did not indicate who held the numbers or how large the prizes were.[22] By then, most people had presumably forgotten about the bond scheme, considering it to be just another form of taxation rather than a legitimate financial investment.

Foreign Trade and Investment

Given the dire straits into which the North Korean economy has fallen, it very much needs foreign trade and investment, neither of which directly affects the lives of most North Koreans, who rarely come into contact with foreigners and are unable to purchase foreign goods other than inexpensive Chinese products that are trucked across the border. Because the North Korean media have imposed an almost total blackout on foreign news, only party members who work for trade organizations know anything about the international market.

In 1984, as it became clear that the North Korean economy was faltering, the government promulgated the Foreign Joint Venture Law. Kim Il-sung had visited China in 1982 and made another visit the following year to observe the success the Chinese were having with their own Joint Venture Management Enterprise Law. However, North Korea's law was not particularly successful in attracting investment for several reasons: its provisions were not detailed enough to satisfy skeptical foreign investors, the government had long since reneged on its foreign debt, and North Korea's transportation, communication, and power infrastructures were grossly inadequate to support modern business ventures. Most of the foreign investors who took advantage of the joint venture opportunity were Chinese and pro-DPRK Koreans living in Japan, with the total amount of investment estimated to be only $150 million, not the billions being invested in China.

From the beginning, the Kim regime was wary about foreign investment because it would inevitably be accompanied by foreign influence, which would poison the artificial political culture of *Juche* ideology and Kim cult worship. In China, foreign investment was initially concentrated in a few trade zones where the government could limit the impact of foreign culture and keep an eye on the foreigners, and following this conservative model, the North Korean government decided to funnel foreign investments into its own trade zone. To maximize the economic impact of investment, a trade zone would ideally be located near a big city or port, which would offer the best infrastructure and the most skilled workers. But because political considerations took priority in the North Korean case, the first trade zone was located as far from Pyongyang and other business centers as possible, over three hundred miles away as the crow flies, in the remote and undeveloped northeast corner of the country.

In December 1991, a 621-square-kilometer Najin-Sonbong foreign economic trade zone was created, encompassing the towns of Najin (Rajin) and Sonbong. After the two towns were merged in August 2000, the name of the trade zone was changed to Nason (Rason). The zone was within a larger area designated by the United Nations Development Program (UNDP) as an international development area, and the UNDP provided seed money for planning and research. The North Koreans initially had high hopes for the zone because their lack of economic sophistication caused them to think in terms of geography rather than economics. They saw the site as a slice of land advantageously situated at the junction of a navigable river (the Tumen River) along the border with China and Russia, affording the opportunity to become an international hub of economic activity. Add cheap labor and tax incentives, and the zone looked like a fair imitation of China's successful trade zones set up in Zhuhai, Shenzhen, Shantou, and Xiamen in the late 1970s—with the important difference that China's zones were located close to the thriving capitalist centers of Taiwan and Hong Kong. One of the first preparations for the Nason zone was to enclose it with barbed wire and replace those of its residents considered to be "politically unreliable" with former soldiers.

The zone was connected to Russia by a dirt road. On the dirt road to China, the bridge over the Tumen River had been built by the Japanese during the colonial period. A rail line ran into the Russian city of Khasan, but the Russians (like the Chinese) complained that the North Koreans tended not to return their railcars. Roads from Nason to Pyongyang and the more developed western region of North Korea were likewise unpaved, and a train ride to Pyongyang could take anywhere from twenty hours to several days. Nason lacked both an airport and a container cargo port.

The zone has had a rocky history, and almost twenty years later, little progress has been made in its development. The original plans were to develop—or, rather, to have foreign investors develop—the zone in three stages, with an investment of $1.3 billion by 1995, another $1 billion by 2000, and yet another $1 billion by 2010. In September 1996, the North Koreans convened a grand business forum to attract foreign interest. A few curious businesspeople came from the United States and Western Europe, but most of the prospective investors were Chinese and Korean Japanese. The South Korean government, angered by the North Koreans' refusal to extend invitations to over half of the fifty-three South Korean applicants, kept its entire delegation at home.

In a case of extremely bad timing, just three days after the investment conference ended, a South Korean taxicab driver spotted what turned out to be a North Korean spy submarine that had run aground on a South Korean beach. Searchers discovered eleven members of the submarine crew nearby, shot dead in an apparent murder-suicide pact. Another crew member was found alive, and in the days to follow, thirteen commandos who had disembarked from the submarine were hunted down and killed by thousands of South Korean forces, with one commando escaping back to North Korea. In the course of the manhunt, the commandos killed four South Korean civilians, eight soldiers, and two policemen. The incident reminded prospective investors of how unstable the political situation was on the Korean Peninsula and decisively turned South Korean president Kim Young Sam against reconciliation with the North. Investor confidence was further shaken when Kim Chong-u, the North Korean economic official who presided over the conference, abruptly and permanently disappeared from view along with several of his associates the following year. The best guess is that they were purged for taking financial advantage of their economic positions, something that virtually all North Koreans who travel overseas do.

Although contracts amounting to $286 million were signed at the conference, since then almost the only discernible development in the zone has been the 1999 construction of a Chinese-owned hotel and gambling casino, but even that investment ran into trouble when a Chinese government official who embezzled several million yuan was found to have gambled much of it away at the casino. The Chinese government thereupon pressured the hotel's owners to close the casino down in 2005, virtually shutting down the hotel as well, although the hotel reopened two years later. In 2007, Nason still reportedly had no traffic lights, no billboards, and only one small market. A Chinese tourist describes his visit to Najin as "travel back in time."[23] On the other hand, as a remote tourist attraction, the zone has much to recommend it: the air is clean, the scenery beautiful, and the seafood delicious.

A more successful zone was established in the beautiful mountain region of Kumgang (Diamond Mountain), in the far southeast corner of the country along the border with South Korea. The North Koreans fenced the area off and opened it to foreign (mostly South Korean) tourists, who began arriving in November 1998. The North Koreans chose Hyundai Asan, the branch of the Hyundai conglomerate that undertook the project, because Hyundai's chairman, Chung Ju-yung, had originally come from North Korea. Yet Hyundai encountered numerous problems along the way, and it is not clear that the investment will ever become profitable, although as a symbol of inter-Korean reconciliation, it has continued to receive a measure of support from the South Korean government.[24] In 2004, tourists began traveling to Kumgang by bus across the Demilitarized Zone rather than by ferry, and in 2008, visitors were permitted to make the four-hour drive in their own cars for a fee of $330. A new hotel and reunion center was built and paid for by the South Koreans. By the end of 2007, over 1.7 million tourists, mostly South Koreans, had visited the mountain resort, and the Kim regime had received over $1 billion from tourist fees and business rights for the project.

Unfortunately, the Kumgang project encountered the same sort of political problems that plagued the Nason project after the submarine incursion. In the early morning hours of July 11, 2008, a North Korean soldier shot and killed a female South Korean tourist who had wandered onto an off-limits beach adjoining the hotel. The South Korean government demanded a joint investigation, and when the North Korean government refused, the South Koreans shut down the tour pending an investigation, whereupon the North Korean military expelled most of the South Korean resort staff. When the tours might resume is hard to guess.

With the Nason industrial investment zone going nowhere, the Kim regime looked for another doorway through which to attract foreign capital. In this case, a bizarre twist of fate prevented the zone from even getting off the drawing board. Plans were announced in 2002 to make the border city of Sinuiju in the northwest corner of the country into a special trade zone. Sinuiju, with a population of six hundred thousand, lies across the Yalu River from the thriving Chinese city of Dandong, the gateway to most of China's trade with North Korea. The two cities are connected by a single-track railway and a one-lane road that cross the Friendship Bridge, built by the Japanese colonial administration.

To make Sinuiju attractive to foreign investors, the DPRK adopted the Basic Law of the Sinuiju Special Administrative Region, which provided the city with the same kind of autonomy that Hong Kong enjoyed when it was under British jurisdiction.[25] For the next fifty years, Sinuiju would have its own executive, legislative, and judicial systems, staffed by foreigners and North Koreans. The city's top executive, holding the rank of governor, would be a foreigner

Pyongyang's selection for Sinuiju's first governor ultimately doomed the new trade zone. The North Koreans' choice for this responsible position, Yang Bin, one of China's wealthiest businessmen, had become known to Kim Jong-il during a visit to China in 2001, during which Kim observed greenhouses producing fruits and vegetables in the middle of winter. Yang Bin's company had built these greenhouses as part of Yang's extensive tulip-growing business, and Yang was invited to Pyongyang to discuss building greenhouses in North Korea. He signed a $20 million contract, making a very good impression on the North Koreans, and it was as a result of this investment, in addition to his great wealth, that he was invited to become the governor of Sinuiju.

Yang estimated it would cost between $50 and $100 billion over ten years to build the necessary infrastructure in Sinuiju. Once the zone was up and running, foreigners would be permitted to enter without a North Korean visa, but North Korean citizens would only be allowed in with special permission. Yang planned to relocate two-thirds of Sinuiju's residents out of the zone (offering each of them $100 above anything their own government might provide them), then to sell the vacated land to investors. Sinuiju's basic law stipulated that the zone would be turned into "an international financial, trade, commercial, industrial, up-to-date science, amusement, and tourist center," but Yang reportedly decided to push tourism and entertainment, that is, gambling, in order to get a quick infusion of capital from China.[26]

Apparently, government officials in Beijing were not consulted about the plans to make Sinuiju into a gambling destination, and when they heard that a Chinese citizen would be heading up what could become a major gambling city just across from the Chinese border, they were miffed.[27] On the day Yang was to travel to Sinuiju, he was arrested by Chinese police and subsequently charged with a variety of crimes related to his business activities in China, including illegal use of agricultural land, fraud, and bribery; that is, he was accused of the types of crimes that any Chinese citizen would have to commit in order to become fabulously wealthy. In 2003, he was sentenced to eighteen years in prison, and Kim Jong-il needed to find another governor for Sinuiju.

Chapter two of the Sinuiju saga opened in September 2004 with news reports that the front-runner to replace Yang Bin was a Chinese Korean American woman by the name of Sha Rixiang, with the American name of Julie Sa.[28] Born of Chinese parents in South Korea (her father came from Dandong), Sa emigrated to the United States and made money in real estate and a chain of Chinese restaurants in California. In 1992, she was elected to the city council of Fullerton, one of the cities in the metropolitan Los Angeles area, and in 1994 she served briefly as the city's mayor.[29] As a successful Korean American businesswoman, she was introduced to Kim Il-sung and Kim Jong-il in 1993. Although the DPRK government never officially announced that Sa had been picked as the new governor of Sinuiju, in a South Korean television interview in September 2004, Sa said she had been offered the job right after Yang Bin's arrest.[30] What happened after that is not clear because little more was ever heard about the proposed Sinuiju zone. As China–North Korean trade has increased, business in Dandong is booming. Why the Chinese, who hate the rapacious North Korean customs inspectors, would want to promote Sinuiju as a competing business center is not clear.

What might be called North Korea's four-corners investment-zone strategy was completed by another business zone, this one in the southwest corner of the country. Years ago, Hyundai's chairman Chung Ju-yung discussed with Kim Il-sung the possibility of establishing a manufacturing zone in the North, with the preferred location being near Pyongyang. However, the closest the Kim regime would allow foreign businesses to get to Pyongyang was Kaesong, 160 kilometers south of Pyongyang and 70 kilometers north of Seoul. Before the division of the peninsula, Kaesong was famous as a city of businessmen. In the initial partition of the Korean Peninsula, it fell within South Korea's borders, but it was lost to North Korea during the Korean War.

Shortly after the inter-Korean summit of 2000, Hyundai received permission from the North Korean government to lease a sixty-six-square-kilometer zone outside the city of Kaesong. The zone would remain under North Korean jurisdiction, but foreign companies would be permitted to rent land in the zone for a period of fifty years. South Korea would provide the infrastructure, including the electricity. By early 2009, over one hundred South Korean companies were operating in the Kaesong Industrial Complex, employing almost forty thousand North Korean workers. Because the South Korean government hopes that investment will stimulate North Korea to engage in broader economic reforms, various investment guarantees and insurance coverage are available to the mostly small and medium-sized companies going into Kaesong.

Even so, the odds against profitability are great. In addition to the usual logistical problems that bedevil any project involving North Koreans, such as getting permission to visit one's own factory or communicate with the home office, the zone faces problems because of North Korea's problematic trade status in the international community. Numerous trade embargoes, especially of "strategic" items, make it necessary for South Korean companies to screen production equipment destined for Kaesong carefully. Another problem companies in the zone face is that North Korea does not have preferential trade agreements with many of the Organization for Economic Cooperation and Development countries, so Kaesong-made products exported beyond South Korea are subject to stiff tariffs. South Korea's Roh Moo-hyun administration, which left office in early 2008, considered Kaesong the economic cornerstone of inter-Korean reconciliation but viewed the project more as a political confidence-building measure than a hardheaded business investment. President Roh, a former human rights lawyer, not a businessman, pushed companies to invest, saying that "businessmen had better move a step forward to enhance inter-Korean economic exchanges and explore the North Korean market."[31]

For its part, the Kim regime has undoubtedly always planned to keep tight control over the Kaesong zone. Only authorized North Korean workers are allowed into the zone, and South Korean workers are not permitted to leave the zone to go into Kaesong city; they must commute directly between South Korea and the zone, and they may do so only with the permission of the North Koreans, who can revoke that permission at any time. Only a few non-Korean foreigners have been permitted to visit the zone, even though it is supposed to be an international trade zone. Commercial advertising, which is practically banned throughout North Korea, is permitted in the zone, but regulations ban "any advertisement hamstringing the process of improving the north-south relations, decadent and fraudulent ads, ads for commodities whose production, sale and supply are prohibited, banned services and those ads unreasonably comparing or slandering other enterprises or commodities or services."[32]

And then there are the political problems inherent in doing business in North Korea. From the very first, at the December 2004 inaugural ceremony for the zone, North Korea's government representative, presumably in protest against what he considered slow progress in building the zone, walked out on the speech of his South Korean government counterpart. In February 2008, Lee Myung-bak, a hardheaded businessman (known as "the Bulldozer") and former mayor of Seoul, was elected president of South Korea, and the Kim regime flew into a rage. In an apparent bid to turn the South Korean people against their new president, the regime instituted what could be called a full-court press against South Korea, cutting off government-to-government dialogue, imposing travel restrictions, and issuing threats to take military measures. As one of the few cases of ongoing inter-Korean contact, Kaesong became an obvious target of the Kim regime's ire.

One month after President Lee's inauguration, the eleven South Korean officials assigned to Kaesong were expelled. In June, the North Koreans began to restrict the border crossings of South Korean businessmen going to and from Kaesong. In November, a group of North Korean army officers paid an unexpected visit to the zone and pointedly asked factory managers how long it would take for them to shut down their operations. In December, half of the sixteen hundred South Koreans working in the zone were expelled, seriously crippling operations. During the annual U.S.–Republic of Korea (ROK) military exercises in March 2009, the North Koreans cut all communication links between South Korea and Kaesong, forcing even more South Koreans to return home. In May 2009, the North Koreans shredded all contracts relating to Kaesong, claiming that because the South Korean government had become hostile to the North, the previous "favorable" contract terms were no longer appropriate. Faced with a demand for dramatically higher land-use fees and wages, most South Korean companies began looking for a way out. As this book goes to press in 2009, it is uncertain if the Kaesong zone will survive; in any case, it offers yet another lesson about how difficult it is for foreigners to do business in North Korea.

Many foreign observers have suggested that North Korea must inevitably follow the Chinese model in its foreign trade and investment policies, but business conditions in North Korea differ in several important respects from conditions in China, where, along with private farming, the first foreign trade zones were the major drivers of the economic boom that began in the 1980s. Unlike North Korea, China had a vast domestic market to which goods could be sold, and wealthy Chinese living abroad became early investors. More importantly, China never insisted on the high degree of control over the zones that North Korea does. For example, the factories can freely hire Chinese laborers, whereas in North Korea the state provides the workers and rotates them to prevent their being unduly influenced by their market experience. Finally, the North Koreans at least pretend to believe that foreign investors, especially those from South Korea, should invest for patriotic rather than business reasons. Responding to the criticism that many South Korean companies find it difficult to make a profit in North Korea, a North

Korean official said, "Why is money a priority? Inter-Korean business must be about something more than just monetary calculations."[33]

Realizing that it lacks the financial and technical resources to develop a modern economy solely by its own efforts, the Kim regime has become more accepting of foreign investment outside the trade zones. A few South Korean entrepreneurs have established joint ventures in Pyongyang and other cities, generally to their regret. North Korea's only automobile plant, which assembles cars from imported parts, is a joint venture with Pyonghwa Motors, a South Korean company affiliated with the Unification Church. It produces only a few hundred cars a year, most notably, the "Whistle" (*Hwiparam*). In recent years, the North Koreans have been making a strong investment pitch to the Chinese, who already have a variety of joint ventures throughout the country, including a contract to run the Pyongyang Department Store No. 1 and joint ventures in a number of large mines.

North Korea is an exceptionally difficult country to conduct business with, and doing so is a hardship tour for the few foreign businesspeople who live there. The government provides land, natural resources, and labor, while foreign investors are expected to provide everything else, including infrastructure. Bribes must be paid at every turn, and signed contracts are considered merely the first step in continuing negotiations. When a foreign business begins to turn a profit, rather than rejoicing, the North Koreans try to squeeze out more of those profits for themselves.

The business viability of North Korea's trade zones remains very much in doubt. According to two separate surveys of businesses reported by South Korea's *JoongAng Ilbo* newspaper in 2005, 45 out of 150 South Korean companies that had signed contracts to do business with North Korea had ended their business ventures within six years, and only 22 out of 241 companies that had opened factories there continued to do business after five years.[34] In a 2008 poll conducted by the Korea Chamber of Commerce and Industry, 80 percent of South Korean businesses in North Korea said they were experiencing difficulties, and over half said they believe China or Vietnam would be more attractive foreign business sites than North Korea.[35] The businesspeople's most common complaints relate to problems traveling between the two Koreas, customs procedures, limited access to telecommunications, and the ban on importing strategically important goods into the North for manufacturing purposes.

A South Korean newspaper article sums up the results of a survey with this "first commandment of investment in North Korea": "Don't."[36] A Korean American industrialist who had business dealings in North Korea for fifteen years before finally pulling out recounts some of his experiences.[37] Looking back, he admits that his investments were motivated more by compassion for the North Koreans than by good business sense. He first planned to start a ship-repair facility, but two years of delays changed his mind. Instead, he built a farm to harvest scallops, but once it was built, the North Koreans wanted to run it themselves and would not permit his technicians even to visit the farm. Since the North Koreans knew nothing about running the business, it failed. A shoe factory he set up likewise failed because worker morale was so low that production could not keep up with his shoe factory in China. Other business ventures likewise failed.

The Court Economy

While North Korea's socialist economy struggles to survive, a parallel economy seems to have done quite well for itself. Operations directed by Offices 38 and 39 of the Korean Workers' Party supply funds to support Kim Jong-il's lavish lifestyle and to reward his followers. Legitimate funds come from party-owned trading companies that sell the country's most marketable commodities, including minerals such as gold, agricultural products such as pine mushrooms, and seafood such as sea urchins. Trade statistics from other countries suggest that the regime may also earn as much as several hundred million dollars a year from the sale of illicit drugs and counterfeit pharmaceuticals (most notably, Viagra), currency (dollars and yen), and cigarettes. North Korea's arms exports contribute tens or hundreds of millions of dollars a year as well, but the military controls the trading companies selling arms, and presumably most of the profits stay in the separate military economy.

The party further raises funds by requiring the people to contribute local products such as sesame, salt, scrap metal, and rabbit skins. It also collects money from people in the form of "contributions" to a variety of national causes, including Kim Jong-il's birthday celebration. People have always grumbled about these donations, and in recent years the grumbling has been growing louder and more public.

The party also withholds a significant portion of the wages of North Koreans working overseas as "contributions." Furthermore, diplomats engage in smuggling to support embassy operations and to remit donations to the party offices back home; in fact, smuggling could be considered an integral part of a North Korean diplomat's job. Diplomatic pouches are used to smuggle goods such as gems, ivory, gold, counterfeit or foreign cigarettes, alcohol, and compact discs from one country to another, and diplomatic status protects the smugglers from conviction when they are caught. According to a U.S. government source, since 1976 North Koreans have been arrested for smuggling at least fifty times in more than twenty countries, including Sweden, Finland, Estonia, Russia, China, Nepal, Thailand, Cambodia, and Egypt, as well as various other African countries.[38]

One of the largest cases of North Korean smuggling was revealed on a stormy night in April 2003—on April 15 (Kim Il-sung's birthday) to be exact—when two crewmen from the small North Korean freighter *Pong Su*, which was standing just off the Australian coast, unloaded 125 kilograms of pure heroin. One of the crew members transporting the drugs to the beach drowned, and another was captured, along with a three-man shore party waiting to receive the drugs. When the Australians ordered the *Pong Su* into port for investigation, the ship fled and was only apprehended after a four-day chase. At the trial, the surviving courier and the three shore-party members were convicted on drug charges, whereas the *Pong Su*'s captain, party secretary, first mate, and chief engineer were acquitted by a jury who chose to believe the improbable defense argument that the men had no knowledge of the smuggling operation. Because the ship had been involved in drug smuggling, the Royal Australian Air Force confiscated and sank it. After the acquittal was announced, the North Korean press issued its own version of events, somehow managing to make the United States the guilty party:

> The United States, a past master at lies and deception, is now suffering bitter shame before the international community for a series of conspiratorial plots hatched by it recently. This is proved by the recently announced results of the final investigation into the case of the ship "Pongsu," a trading cargo ship of the DPRK. . . . The High Court of Australia declared the crewmen of the ship not guilty and set all of them free. . . . The above-said case inflicted no small damage upon the DPRK's ship and its crewmen. The U.S. should make a formal apology and compensation for its piratical act and political swindle.[39]

Why Doesn't the Regime Reform the Economy?

It is a notable characteristic of socialist command economies such as existed in the former Soviet Union and Eastern Europe and still exist in Cuba and North Korea, that they are plagued by chronic shortages, especially of consumer goods.[40] To improve the situation, the party promises to "perfect" the system under the assumption that the basic characteristics of socialism are "scientifically correct." Even a leader as enlightened as Mikhail Gorbachev could not escape the commitment to communism, saying in 1988, "Trying to restore private ownership means to move backward, and is a deeply mistaken decision."[41] The people who get blamed for the system's defects are not the leaders who impose it but the mid-level bureaucrats who administer it and the working people who use it. Socialist organizations are constantly reorganized, officials replaced, and new economic plans announced with great fanfare, but nothing changes.

It is a great irony that socialists criticize the market economies for being chaotic and claim that socialism is superior because it follows a plan, but it is the plan that defeats socialism. There is nothing wrong with planning, if it can be done well, but poor plans are worse than no plans at all because they lead people in the wrong direction. And once a plan has been put in place and people have become committed to it, it is difficult to change just one part of the economic system because doing so tends to destabilize the whole. This is one important reason why the Kim regime has tried to stick with the economic system already in place.

Fortunately for the leadership, most people in failing communist economies do not demand a change. The economist Janos Kornai lumps economic actors into three groups.[42] The elites generally profit from the system and thus support it. The masses are generally ignorant of how much better conditions are in other economies; in any case they have few ideas about how to make fundamental changes in their own economic system because that system is linked to the political system over which they have no control. And then there are a few intellectuals who have some understanding of the system and a desire to change it, but they are easily silenced. The result is that the masses are stuck in an unworkable system in which they participate as little as possible, instead of putting their efforts into an alternative economy.

Foreign analysts have identified a long list of problems plaguing the North Korean economy, and we can be sure that some North Korean economists are aware of these problems as well but know that it is unwise to criticize the Kim regime's economic system. In the United States, Marcus Noland and Nicholas Eberstadt have separately discussed most of the problems the North Korean economy faces.[43] Eberstadt's list includes the following: breakdown of central planning, too many resources devoted to the military, too few resources devoted to the consumer sector (to improve quality of life and give people something to work for), overreliance on barter, lack of a banking and loan system, refusal to service external debt, restrictions on trade with developed economies, and a generally inhospitable domestic economic environment.[44]

For Kim and his elite supporters, the economy is secondary in importance to the politics of control that keeps them in power. As a rule of thumb, it could even be argued that the more reforms Kim introduces to the command economy, the weaker his political position becomes. One might think that a strong economy would please the people and confer legitimacy on the regime, but Kim can look at what has happened in other countries that adopted reforms. All those formerly communist economies that have "reformed" are under new management. Even China, where the Communist Party is still firmly in power, has had several leaders. Only North Korea and Cuba, the two unreformed economies, are still ruled by the same family.

One thing that hasn't changed over the years is the regime's eternal and unwarranted optimism. Every year the North Korean media promise that an economic takeoff is at hand, and every year is the same as the previous year, with new campaigns to achieve the same old economic goals. As far as outsiders can see, the socialist economy has not made any progress at all. It is the emerging people's economy, which forsakes socialism and embraces small-scale capitalism, that is keeping the people alive and giving them a measure of hope. This is the economy that we turn to in the next chapter.

CHAPTER FOUR

The Economy of Everyday Life

The North Korean people must struggle to make a living, but at least they are not as sick and hungry as they were during the famine of the mid-1990s, now that many of them have learned to go into business for themselves. Yet their lives are marked by uncertainty as the economy and society change within the confines of an unchanged political system, and like millions of Americans who lived through the Great Depression, they have an underlying fear that another famine may be just around the corner.

Before the economic changes that were ratified—but not initiated—by the July 1, 2002, Economic Management Improvement Measures, the task of describing the life and work of the average North Korean was comparatively simple, thanks to the party's efforts to impose uniformity on society. After graduating from secondary school at the age of sixteen, most males went into the military for ten years or more. Women were assigned to clerical or blue-collar work. After marriage in their twenties, women worked part-time until their children were older. Upon completion of military service, men could marry and were assigned lifetime jobs according to the needs of the local economy. Since daily necessities were obtained from the Public Distribution System (PDS) with ration coupons distributed at work sites, people of the same political class ate the same foods in approximately the same amounts, wore the same clothes, and had the same household articles. The government assigned housing, and physicians assigned to each workplace or locality provided a minimum standard of health care.

This stable, low-grade life began to change in the 1980s. The tens of thousands of visitors to the World Festival of Youth and Students in Pyongyang in 1989 introduced new styles and ideas to the city's residents, who communicated them to people around the country. Word of the collapse of European communist regimes in the late 1980s and early 1990s seeped into the country, leading people to wonder how long their own socialist system would survive. That collapse also resulted in a drastic reduction in foreign aid, quickly triggering shortages of oil, electricity, and manufacturing materials. By the early 1990s, the PDS was beginning to run short of goods, and by 1995 it had ceased to function, except in Pyongyang. The nominal wages paid to workers became almost worthless because there was nothing to buy. Factories stopped operating. The most immediate impact of this economic collapse was the shortage of food. Those who showed up at their assigned workplaces and waited for public rations starved. Those who looked for work on their own survived.

More than ten years later, the socialist employment and distribution systems still have not recovered, but most people no longer starve because they have found a thousand ways to eke out a meager existence. There are few rules to guide them and few laws that absolutely must be obeyed. Describing this rapidly changing, chaotic environment is challenging. It is easier to say what it is not than what it is or where it is going. The recent history of former socialist economies in Eastern Europe or the current socialist economies in transition in such places as Vietnam and China may provide some clue about what is happening today in North Korea, but it is not certain that North Korea will follow the same economic path as these other countries, and for that matter the Kim regime has vigorously insisted that it will not.

Working for the State

Until the 1990s, private enterprise was forbidden and hardly existed. Instead, North Koreans worked for state or collective enterprises. The North Korean urban workplace paid low wages, but more importantly, it issued ration coupons for food and other daily necessities, which could then be purchased for just pennies. Farmers were provided for by the management of their agricultural collectives. The workplace was also the center of social and political life. Political education sessions were a part of every workday, and workers were occasionally mobilized for special work assignments such as construction and harvesting. To reinforce the workplace connection, urban workers in the same unit were often assigned to the same housing complex.

Since the early 1990s, it appears, only about a quarter of North Korea's factories have been operating at near normal capacity. The operating rate of mines may be even lower due to extensive flooding during the mid-1990s and in 2007. Party officials have called on factory managers to "grasp the labor forces of all individual plants and enterprises which have temporarily become idle due to the material and resources problems" and to send them out to find substitute jobs that can contribute to the cash flow of the crippled workplaces.[1]

The labor market is supposedly run in a rational and egalitarian manner. In principle, workers' education, skills, interests, and physical condition are used to match employees to the needs of local employers. People are rarely given permission to move far from their hometown—the better to keep track of them. As they go through the motions of job hunting, job candidates submit to the labor department of the local party committee a resume, career statement, list of desired occupations, and certificate of graduation. The applicant's secondary school or military unit also submits relevant documents. In practice, if there is a large factory, farm, or mine in the area, workers will be sent there regardless of their job preferences. And if there is a shortage of workers at a major construction site somewhere in the country, the party committee may dispatch a contingent of workers to the site to fill the local labor levy. Job preferences are only honored when a person has good political connections or can afford to pay hefty bribes.

There are two exceptions to this peremptory method of assigning workers to jobs. First, much care is taken when recruiting someone for a sensitive political or security position such as in the Bodyguard Bureau or special forces. In these cases, extensive interviews are conducted, along with an investigation of the political history of the candidate's extended family, including nephews and nieces. The slightest hint of political unreliability, such as having relatives in South Korea, will disqualify the candidate. The other exception involves highly talented students, especially in the sciences, who are identified at an early age and sent to "number one" schools in each locality—the North Korean equivalent of magnet schools.

Women with young children are not automatically assigned to the workforce, although at an early age the children are sent to state nursery schools, thereby allowing the mothers to enter the state labor force. A woman's life is doubly difficult because North Korea remains a male-dominated society in which women are expected to take primary responsibility for raising the children and taking care of the home, in addition to holding down a state-assigned job. On the other hand, women today have one great economic advantage in that because they are under less pressure than men to hold a full-time job, they have more freedom to work in the private sector, where there is money to be made. As a consequence, the wife is often the main breadwinner in the family, a situation that threatens the self-esteem of North Korean husbands and leads to dissension in the family.

Workers are required to join one of the national party-controlled labor unions, such as the umbrella General Federation of Trade Unions or the Union of Agricultural Workers, which function as indoctrinating and controlling organizations rather than as representatives of the workers. According to the 1996 version of the [North] Korea Encyclopedia, a labor organization is "an auxiliary organization of the party that advocates, protects, and supports the party and is an important link between the party and the public."[2] It is the role of such an organization "to educate the working public from all walks of life, keep them closely under the control of the party and the great leader, and mobilize them in implementing party policies."[3] Women who do not work outside the home are expected to join the Korea Democratic Women's Union, and men between the ages of fourteen and twenty-six join the Kim Il-sung Socialist Youth League. Children from the ages of nine to thirteen join the Korea Children's Union. Identified by the red neckties they proudly wear, these organized youngsters patrol neighborhoods and report suspicious activities to the police. Their slogan, "Always ready," is reminiscent of the American Boy Scouts' "Be prepared." Under Kim Jong-il's military-first politics, these youths have adopted the slogan "Let's become three million bombs [to protect our great leader]."

The government has designed an elaborate schedule of wages that takes into account type of work, training and education, and seniority. Until the early 2000s, the socialist work model stipulated that all workers doing the same job should receive the same pay, regardless of how productive they were. On collective farms, when the workers brought in a bumper crop, they collectively shared a larger food distribution, with the diligent workers getting as much as the lazy ones, although the collective's managers, who were party hacks, benefited disproportionately.

As part of the July 2002 economic measures, wages were raised across the board, but since prices were also raised by about the same amount, the pay raise did nothing to motivate workers. Within a few months, many work organizations stopped paying wages altogether, and in the years since, inflation has destroyed the value of the North Korean won. In 2008, the average worker was receiving only enough money to buy about a week's supply of food for one person at market prices, and prices for household goods and appliances put them out of reach of those who relied on government wages.

In those workplaces still operating more or less normally, a typical workday starts at 7 a.m., with a half hour of warm-up exercises followed by another half hour of instructions for the day and political study. Workers take an hour for lunch and quit work at 5 p.m.; they are then required to attend political study and self-criticism sessions for one to three hours. Workers must also show up on Saturday for more political study or special labor duties, but they have Saturday afternoons and Sundays off. Workers on collective farms take off every tenth day, which was the traditional Korean market day.

Work hours are extended during "speed battles," when the authorities try to whip an organization or an entire economic sector into a frenzy in order to complete whatever project the officials in Pyongyang desire. These battle periods, usually lasting several weeks or months, are modeled on the Stakhanovite movement of the Soviet Union. In rhetoric, although not in practice, the speed battles can be extended for years, as in the phrase "speed of the nineties." In 2009, a countrywide "150-day" battle was waged from May to October. To take an example at the local level, the workers of the Sinuiju Shoes Plant, said to be "permeated with the great general's immortal leadership achievements," went all-out to achieve goals set in the 2003 New Year's Joint Editorial.[4] The local party committee organized a "siren-sounding unit" and employed "visual-aid propaganda, oral propaganda, and situation propaganda (chonghwang sondong)" to create a work site "seething like a battlefield." The Sinuiju workers were reminded that the United States was trying to crush their country and that "the bosom of their mother is the very bosom of the great general." In short, standard practice is for young party members to show up at a work site with red flags (no work site is complete without its red flags), bang drums, shout slogans, and sing songs. To judge by first-hand accounts and economic statistics, the effect of this agitation is fleeting at best.

Work on major construction projects is generally conducted in speed-battle style by unskilled workers, including students and soldiers drafted for the projects. The workers are organized into "shock brigades" that toil up to twelve hours a day with very little food. Work conditions are difficult, and deaths from construction accidents and malnutrition are common. According to an article quoting the "battalion political instructor" of one of these shock brigades, during the three years of construction on facilities at Mt. Paektu, shock brigade members "gathered stones from the beds of rivers where ice was floating," "dragged huge tree trunks down the mountainsides," and "transported and supplied almost all the granite and marble needed for the overall construction work."[5] This sounds like a modern-day version of building the pyramids. According to one defector, twenty thousand workers carrying dirt and rocks in sacks on their backs built the Samsu power plant.[6] Each day a worker received 580 grams of corn (equivalent to two or three cups, the exact amount depending on whether the distributed corn was cooked or raw), with side dishes of salted bean-paste soup and pickled radishes. On Kim Il-sung's birthday, each worker received new underwear, a pair of socks, and two bags of cookies.

One of the most famous "youth" construction projects in recent years was the Youth Hero Motorway, a forty-three-kilometer, twelve-lane expressway linking Pyongyang and the port city of Nampo, completed in 1998. To please Kim Jong-il, who is a great fan of the theater, this accomplishment was immortalized in a "light comedy" titled *Youths Shine*, depicting "the lives of the bright and merry youths mixed with tears of laughter and deep emotion."[7] North Korea has hundreds of other such projects, including the Anbyon Youth Power Station, the Jangsongang Youth Power Station, the Unsong Youth Reservoir, and the Hamhung City Youth Goat Farm—all accomplishments of what the North Korean press lauds as "the wisdom and stamina of the youth."[8]

A detailed account of worker motivation is provided by a former labor battalion commander of a workers' shock brigade assigned to construct the high-rise apartments that Kim Jong-il commissioned for Pyongyang in advance of the 1989 World Festival of Youth and Students.[9] In addition to reporting on the unsafe work conditions (he claimed to have seen statistics showing that an average of one worker died per day during a three-year period of construction), he described how difficult it was to motivate his men. To get to their work sites, the workers first had to climb twenty to thirty flights of stairs. "Upon reaching the top, I would find my men loafing, enjoying the panoramic view of Pyongyang like sparrows perched side by side on a telephone line. . . . I had no strength to scold them, so I would quietly sit down near them. . . . Only after I prompted them several times, would they slowly get up and get ready for work. Half an hour passed this way. Some mean fellows still remained sitting, protesting in silence." Throughout the day they worked only sporadically. "Wherever the regimental commander and the political director went, the mobile propaganda team appeared beforehand with bugles blowing, and the battalion and company commanders barked at their men blowing whistles and pointing their fingers at them. Each tried to show that they were the masters in creating a 'combat atmosphere.'" All that the typical worker could bring home after two years of labor was some saved food-ration coupons, a few biscuits, and such necessities as toothpaste and facial soap obtained from friends or relatives in Pyongyang, where such items are available.

Anecdotal evidence from defectors suggests that job satisfaction in North

Korea is low, which is hardly surprising given how little control people have over job selection and how low their wages are. With few material incentives for superior performance, working for the state is drudgery; but then again, until recently that drudgery was all that people knew. Consequently, most of the people, most of the time, do not work hard—not because they are lazy but because they do not have the opportunity to work for themselves in a productive environment. The government launches one campaign after another in a vain attempt to persuade workers to honor the "480-minute" workday as a "sacred duty" and to think of their time "like combat hours at a decisive battlefield."[10]

Kim Jong-il seems to hope that eventually the North Korean people can be made to love labor for its own sake, motivated only by political and moral incentives, thereby making it possible to dispense with the need to provide them with any material incentives. The press is filled with calls for officials to "properly conduct labor education so that the working people will love to work, participate in social labor voluntarily and faithfully, and thoroughly abide by socialist labor life norms and the labor discipline."[11] But Kim, and presumably everyone else in North Korea, realizes that socialist motivation alone will not run the country. The official explanation of the continued need for material incentives is that socialist society is in transition, still burdened by the bad habits and outmoded thoughts of the old capitalist society—not that many North Koreans ever had the opportunity to be capitalists.

The North Korean press claims that in a theoretical work dating from the 1960s, Kim Jong-il "completely elucidates the directions and methods necessary to realize the political and moral incentive and the material incentive," thereby providing "a theoretical weapon which we should persistently maintain throughout the entire course of socialist construction."[12] But Kim has only offered the notion that political and moral incentives should always take precedence over material incentives, and this remains the official doctrine.[13] That said, on Kim's recommendation labor administrators have tried to boost the role of material incentives since the advent of the July 2002 economic measures, even while articles in the press continue to stress the primacy of political and moral incentives. Workers are told they are the "masters of the society and the economy," and thus "the material and cultural wealth created in the socialist society is absolutely the property of the masses of people, and used for their independent and creative lives."[14] In the 1950s and 1960s, most North Koreans truly believed they were building a prosperous state and would soon be living in a socialist paradise, and every year their lives improved. But today, after several decades of economic decline, and seeing before them the corruption of party officials, the people largely discount political and moral incentives.

Another aspect of work motivation that has received much attention in the North Korean press since July 2002 is the matter of "socialist distribution." Those who know communism from the textbooks will be familiar with the precept "From each according to his ability, to each according to his need." Instead, in today's North Korea people are told, "Those who have contributed more to the society and the group receive more material incentives and proper political assessments suitable for their achievements."[15] Now the problem for the bankrupt state is to find resources with which to reward top performers.

As one can imagine, when people are assigned to jobs they have not chosen for themselves, and when their efforts are not materially rewarded, they use whatever extra energy they have to pursue sideline occupations such as tending a vegetable garden, raising chickens, or trading in the local market. Since the mid-1990s, sideline employment has become an economic necessity as the availability of goods in the PDS declines and state wages can hardly buy anything at the markets. Time spent at the office or the factory is time wasted.

Working for Oneself

North Korean propaganda organs teach that if people are boundlessly loyal to the party and the leader, they can even "grow flowers on rocks if the party wishes them to."[16] It turns out that people who ignore the party line and go to work for themselves are the ones who can perform economic miracles. Yet, even though most factories are not operating and the distribution system is bankrupt, people are still supposed to show up for work.

A partial exception to this work regime is the case of women, who, as mentioned earlier, are less likely than men to be assigned full-time jobs. Thus, they have more opportunity to work outside the socialist economy as small traders and merchants, selling household goods and homemade articles. Women also take jobs as waitresses or maids (because householders in a communist economy are not supposed to have servants, employers may introduce their maids as "distant relatives"). Some women become mistresses of the newly rich, and others engage in prostitution.

In the absence of a functioning domestic manufacturing sector, most of the goods in the market are imported from China by big traders, who then export North Korean antiques, narcotics, counterfeit pharmaceuticals, and natural resources such as ginseng, mushrooms, and herbal medicine. Traders who work for themselves must have access to hard currency, usually through family connections in China or Japan. Other traders work for state, party, and military organizations, who enlist their own employees or hire outsiders to purchase manufacturing resources and food for the organization. If an organization hires a trader or manager who provides his own operating capital, he is registered as an "honorary" employee and pays the organization a portion of the profits. Traders, whether they work for themselves or for an organization, also end up paying a sizeable portion of their profits as bribes to border guards and security personnel who intercept deliveries along the way. Whatever the trading or business endeavor, the important principle for earning money is to keep one step ahead of the competition—and the police—by discovering new businesses or new ways to do business.

To get out of their useless job assignments, men often buy out their work contracts, so to speak, by paying the workplace management a nominal fee to keep their absence from being recorded. Some organizations that have no work for their employees simply permit workers to sign in for work in the morning and then go out and produce something of value for the organization, such as homemade consumer goods. Workers are even permitted by their workplace managers (but not by the central government) to sell the organization's assets, such as machinery salvaged from a factory that is no longer operating. The most notorious case of factory-stripping occurred at the Hwanghae Steel Mill, where, according to what Kim Jong-il told members of a visiting delegation from Japan's North Korea organization, "Some bad elements of our society in cahoots with the mill management began to dismantle the mill and sell its machines as scrap metal to Chinese merchants. . . . [The bad elements] bought out party leaders and security officers, and consequently, no one had informed us about their thievery. Everybody was on the take at the mill and we had to send in the army to retake it."[17]

Even those who do not engage in marketing or trading as a full-time business have become part-time small-scale merchants and traders, producing handmade goods at home, growing vegetables, collecting firewood to sell on the street or at the market, or buying goods in one place and selling them in another. For example, cheap consumer goods purchased in China or along the border are transported in bundles to the southern part of the country, rice grown in the south is sold in the north, and fish from the seashore is sold inland. There is no evidence that the economy is actually producing more goods (other than homemade goods); rather, more people are trying their hand at trading.

Selling goods in a local market is a popular way to make money. Almost anything can be purchased there, although most vendors sell inexpensive articles such as soap and homemade food. The markets also attract criminals, including the *kotchebi*, or "swallows"—orphaned children who work alone or in small gangs picking pockets and swiping bags and merchandise.

The authorities have relaxed the ban on street vending. In Pyongyang and other cities, food stalls sponsored by party, government, and military organizations sell snacks. On the back streets, women squat on the sidewalks with a few articles for sale: a couple of chickens, a half-dozen fish, some knitted socks, a few bottles of homemade liquor, herbal medicines, and so forth. The scene is reminiscent of South Korea in the 1950s and 1960s, and the variety of goods is so vast that it is said, "You can buy everything except cat's horns." Merchants also conduct business in houses and apartments located near the markets, especially when they have been chased off the street by the police.

Workers also sell their labor. Referred to variously as *ppolppori* ("people who sweat for a living"), *sakbari* ("people who receive small wages"), and *ilkkun* ("ordinary workers"), these individuals assemble at informal day-labor sites and hire themselves out for 1,000 to 2,000 won a day, far more than the official government wages of 4,000 to 6,000 won a month.[18]

Because private enterprise is antithetical to socialism, people who engage in business activities are walking on thin ice, politically and legally, and thus are easy prey for those in a position to demand bribes. Small businesspeople bribe local officials; big businesspeople bribe higher-level cadres. Whether sitting on the sidewalk, standing in a street stall, or selling in a market, people must bribe police officers and market officials for permission to sell, and (at least in the markets) it is also necessary to share a portion of the profits. Raids conducted by inspectors sent down from Pyongyang temporarily disrupt business. While the visiting inspectors are in town, merchants lie low, hence the term "locust markets," referring to markets whose vendors flee like locusts at the sight of inspectors. If the visiting inspectors stay for long, the merchants become acquainted with them and buy them off just as they do the local officials.[19]

Working Abroad

An estimated fifteen to thirty thousand North Koreans work abroad legally, not counting diplomatic and military personnel.[20] One large group of workers includes the five to ten thousand laborers employed in the Russian Far East to work in North Korean–run logging camps, at construction sites, and on fishing boats. Approximately seven thousand North Koreans are engaged in construction work in the Middle East, primarily in Kuwait, Qatar, and the United Arab Emirates. Several hundred workers are also employed in Eastern Europe, mostly in the garment industry, and North Korean waitresses staff hundreds of North Korean–owned restaurants in China and Southeast Asia. And then there are the thousands of North Koreans employed by South Korean companies in the Kaesong Industrial Complex.

Foreign and South Korean companies hire North Korean workers from a labor pool supplied by the North Korean government, and workers' wages are paid to the government, which then pays the workers only a portion of them. Even in the Kaesong zone, the South Korean government does not know how much money the workers actually receive, and the workers themselves do not report their earnings for fear of being excluded from the labor pool.[21] It has been estimated that their take-home pay is a quarter to a fifth of their wages. Still, because North Koreans working for South Korean and foreign companies are able to escape the stifling conditions of the North Korean economy, they are extremely grateful for the opportunity. Even difficult jobs such as logging in Siberia are much sought after, and only politically reliable people are sent abroad. For example, the attractive singing and dancing waitresses working in North Korean restaurants in China and several other countries are likely to be the daughters of high-level party officials in Pyongyang and certainly not working-class women from the provinces. Applications for jobs with foreign companies in Kaesong or abroad far outnumber the available positions, and in order to be accepted into the job pool, workers must bribe North Korean officials.

Foreign employers are enthusiastic about North Korean workers because they do whatever their government handlers tell them to do, typically working ten hours a day or longer, seven days a week, with no absences. A Polish foreman supervising several North Korean welders working in Gdansk told news reporters, "They are perfect welders. They do not cause any problems and never come to work with a hangover. Do not write anything bad about them because my department will come to a standstill if those Kim Ir Sen [Kim Il-sung?] guys take them away. One North Korean is worth five Poles."[22]

North Korean guest workers live in crowded dormitories, are not permitted to associate with foreigners, and go to work in company vans or on foot, accompanied by North Korean security agents. Foreign human rights organizations and labor departments have tried, usually unsuccessfully, to investigate their wage payments and working conditions, but neither the employers nor the North Korean government is willing to release information. Nevertheless, the situation where North Korean "prisoners" are working in the midst of a democracy is anomalous and, to many, morally wrong. In 2007, the Czech government decided not to renew work visas for North Korean laborers because of negative reports about their working conditions.

Even though they are thousands of miles away from their country, North Korean workers are expected to behave as if they were back home. They are required to write letters of loyalty to Kim Jong-il on his birthday and to donate money to the various campaigns glorifying their leader. North Korean workers rarely defect not only because they come from the loyal political class but because their families are held hostage in Pyongyang. After a few years abroad, they are called back home, bringing with them some hard currency and foreign-made goods. For them, the overseas work experience is just a taste of what the outside world is like, but that is better than nothing. As one North Korean welder in Gdansk said, "We are well fed now and enjoy a glass of beer every day. Every day seems to me like my birthday."[23]

A Soldier's Life

In the late 1990s, Kim Jong-il designated the military as the leading political force of the revolution, replacing the working class. "No other people in this land today are bigger, more precious, and more sacred than soldiers."[24] A 2004 *Nodong Sinmun* essay titled "Love Gun-Barrel Families" states that "the gun-barrel family is a new type of family for mankind, where all the family members regard wearing a military uniform and holding a gun as the greatest happiness and the best family tradition and where they all become soldiers." The article goes on to claim that the "three generals of Mt. Paektu" (i.e., Kim Jong-il and his parents) were the first gun-barrel family.[25]

Kim's heavy reliance on the army does not, however, translate into a better life for soldiers. Conditions in the Korean People's Army (KPA) have materially worsened since the 1980s. Formerly, soldiers were fed, clothed, and housed about as well as the general population, but in recent years, despite Kim's "military-first" policy, soldiers in the enlisted ranks must scramble to find food to eat and suitable clothing to wear, with the consequence that military morale has plummeted. Foreign analysts estimate the size of the KPA, which includes the country's navy and air force, at 1.2 million out of a population of 23 million. If the various police and security agencies are included, the number is closer to 1.8 million. Adding reserve units, including 1.7 million in reserve training units, 4 million in the Worker-Peasant Guards, and 1 million in the teenage Young Red Guards, the total number of North Koreans ready to bear arms is over 8 million. This large military force is consistent with Kim Il-sung's Four Military Lines of 1962, which called for the entire country to be fortified, the entire population to be armed, the military to be modernized, and soldiers to become absolutely loyal to the regime.

Until the 1990s, soldiers could at least look forward to the opportunity to join the Korean Workers' Party on completing their military service, and in order to attain this goal, they were more concerned about pleasing the political officers than the units' commanding officers (every unit has a parallel political-military command). Today, however, party membership has only limited economic value, so the decade of military service is increasingly seen as a waste.

According to the law, all able-bodied men are required to serve in the military. Men serve for ten years (formerly thirteen years), and women who choose to enlist (comprising 5 to 10 percent of the army) serve for six or seven years. It is possible to get a deferment if one has good political connections or has been accepted by a top university (which in itself requires good political connections), and defectors say that by paying a few hundred dollars in bribes, it is possible to obtain an early release from military service.

Local security officials begin tracking males when they reach the age of fourteen, and when they graduate from middle school at age seventeen, they receive a draft notice. In addition to those with educational exemptions, men who come from families with unfavorable political backgrounds (one member has a criminal record or the family is registered in a low rank of the "hostile" class) or who fail to meet the minimum height requirements (148 centimeters or 4 feet, 10 inches) and weight requirements (43 kilograms or 95 pounds) are passed over. Since the famine of the 1990s, the North Korean soldier has been "downsized." The robust soldiers that tourists see at the Panmunjom truce line are the best of the best. In photographs surreptitiously taken by tourists traveling in other parts of the country, soldiers look like scraggly Boy Scouts in baggy clothes and cheap sneakers. Those North Korean youth who do not meet the minimum physical, mental, or political requirements for enlistment are sent directly into the workforce, and their failure to serve in the KPA will be a black mark against them.

During their long years of service, soldiers are granted only one or two home leaves, for example, to attend family funerals. Training can be brutal, and afterward life in the barracks is tedious, with the added burdens of having to undergo political indoctrination and struggling constantly to find enough to eat. Ironically, this struggle takes place in peacetime—for, to its credit, the North Korean army has not engaged in large-scale combat since the Korean War.

The daily life of a soldier is not much different from the regimented life of the civilian population. After morning exercises, soldiers sit through a newspaper-reading session and a talk delivered by their political officer. Then there follows breakfast, morning duties, lunch, afternoon duties, and dinner. After dinner, soldiers attend political-criticism sessions, followed by "cultural" activities, often with a political purpose. Saturday mornings are filled with military duties, and the afternoons with camp-cleaning chores. Sundays are free, but soldiers are rarely permitted to leave camp.

The KPA takes the lead in many of North Korea's major construction projects, building dams, tunnels, roads, bridges, buildings, and the thousands of monuments honoring the Kim family. Most of this work is manual labor done without the aid of heavy machinery. Like civilians, soldiers are drafted to help out on farms during planting and harvesting seasons.

For soldiers, the greatest sources of stress are lack of food and lack of female companionship. Beginning in the 1990s, the government shifted much of the burden of feeding the troops onto the individual military units, so an important part of a soldier's duties includes provisioning the camp by working on farms attached to it. Even so, enlisted men rarely get enough to eat. Except on special occasions, meals consist of rice or some other grain, with side dishes of vegetables, peppers, and radishes. Bean paste is sometimes available, and occasionally there is fish. A small piece of low-quality pork is served once or twice a year. Soldiers constantly seek means to supplement their diet. A sample of food-related article titles in military magazines includes "Raising Rabbits in Summertime," "Smoke-Drying of Catfish," "Growing Bean Sprouts in Caves," "Pickling Mountain Garlic," "Ways of Cooking Cabbage," and "Beans Are Multiple Vitamins." Soldiers who become too malnourished to perform their duties are housed in a special barracks where they can rest, although they still do not receive sufficient food. Those who become seriously ill are returned to their homes for a few months of recovery. Officers get more food than enlisted men because they are able to siphon off the best of the rations and accept bribes from soldiers in return for special assignments, promotions, and leaves.

Under the "military-first" slogan, soldiers sometimes go into the markets and demand food. Acting alone or with the connivance of their officers, they also erect checkpoints to rob traders and travelers and raid farms for food—

sometimes the very farms they are supposed to be guarding. In an internal document smuggled out of the country in 2003, Kim Jong-il issues the following instructions to his soldiers: "Never lay hands on the people's belongings; do not commit acts of violence against the people; do not engage in inappropriate relationships with women."[26] Another internal document from 2003 warns, "Officers must not commit such un-party-member-like crimes as organizing soldiers to steal farm produce under various pretexts."[27]

Soldiers posted along the border with China are subject to particularly severe temptations, with a land of relative plenty just across the river. Notes for lectures to be delivered by officers to border guards complain that "[soldiers] peek over at the splendid facade of the neighboring country [China] and thoughtlessly belittle the things of their own country."[28] The lecture document accuses guards of holding border crossers for ransom, overlooking smuggling and human trafficking, and engaging in illegal activities by selling government property. Reference is made to the raids that North Korean soldiers occasionally stage across the border into China: "Because of the improper behavior of some soldiers, citizens of the neighboring country have scorn for the People's Army and even swear at them with abandon."

The second major stress on soldiers is their limited social life. During their initial ten years of service, they are not permitted to marry, which means that they are supposed to postpone all sexual activity until their late twenties. According to a military lecture, "Once soldiers become infatuated with women and start to have inappropriate relations with them, the soldiers lose interest in their military duties and in their army lives. They do not hesitate to go absent without leave or even desert from the army. In order to win the hearts of women, they steal property of the army and government and even of civilians."[29] Predictably, the celibacy policy promotes clandestine sexual relationships and hidden marriages. Female soldiers, local women, and even the wives of officers are potential girlfriends for the lonely soldiers.

Low morale and lax discipline are combated by motivational lectures that caution soldiers never to relax their vigilance, no matter what news they hear about the outside world. Soldiers are told that their government is conducting a two-track foreign policy: "The KPA troops must never let themselves get distracted by dialogues the party holds or by whatever the party does. They must use their heads only in completing preparations for a war."[30] "When the gun barrel is strong, the enemies will be forced to come to the dialogue venue holding a white flag."[31] Other military study materials use similarly harsh rhetoric: "Just because the enemies kneel before us and visit us with smiles on their faces, it does not mean at all that their true nature has changed." "Illusions about the enemy amount to death." "Let us further accelerate fighting preparations without regard to North-South dialogue, cooperation, and exchanges." "For the fatherland's reunification, there exists only one method: the force of arms."[32]

Finding Food

A Rice Culture

Putting food on the table is the first concern of most North Koreans, who vividly remember the dark days of the Arduous March. By Western standards, North Korean cuisine is limited. Polished sticky white rice, the center of every meal when people can get it, is eaten with fresh vegetables or with pickled vegetables in the form of kimchi, the national dish. On special occasions, fish or small pieces of chicken or pork may be added to the meal, although many North Koreans get the chance to eat meat and eggs only once or twice a year. Corn, barley, wheat, and potatoes are considered second-class foods but have largely replaced rice in the diets of poor people.

Kim Jong-il has tried to shift the people's diet away from rice, which is difficult to grow in North Korea's relatively cool climate, to other grains and to potatoes. Indeed, Kim has been a champion of the potato, just as his father put faith in growing corn. Kim himself, it should be noted, is such a connoisseur that, according to his former chef, every grain of rice destined for his dinner table is inspected for quality and shape. The party has called on the people to obtain good-quality potato seeds that "require low amounts of fertilizer, have high productivity, [are not] infected by viruses, and [are] resistant to pests."[33] Potatoes can be difficult to cultivate, especially in North Korea's overfarmed acidic soil. They require large amounts of scarce fertilizer and are vulnerable to numerous diseases and insects, which North Korean farmers are unable to combat in the absence of chemical controls, and with their high moisture content, potatoes are difficult to store. One North Korean farmer complained that the number of potatoes he harvested was less than the number of seed potatoes he started with, so instead of planting seed potatoes the following year, he planned to preserve them carefully and submit them in the fall as his required contribution to the harvest![34]

Meat is a luxury in North Korea. Beef cattle and oxen are state property, and a person can receive the death sentence for slaughtering a cow.[35] Given the severe shortage of farm tractors, cows are used as farm animals until they are too old to work. Pigs can legally be raised as private property, and even people living in the city may raise a pig in their apartment or on a veranda.

Fresh pork is supposed to be sold to the state in return for payment in grain, but people often try to sell their pigs in the market, where they will fetch a much higher price. Dog meat, a popular health food in North Korea, South Korea, and China, is especially valued for making a person healthy and virile, but North Korean dogs are understandably in short supply.

The party has frequently sponsored campaigns to raise rabbits and goats as another source of meat. A front-page article in *Nodong Sinmun* in early 1999 says,

> Rabbit raising is something that is worth a try for anyone, and is a work to be carried out by the entire masses. Each person has had experience in raising rabbits. Therefore, rabbit raising can be carried out in schools, homes, work sites or any other places. People often think that rabbit raising is a work for children. However, this is not true. It is an important policy-level issue for implementing the party's policy. . . . Thus, we should bring about a new turning point in the work of upgrading people's living standards by raising more rabbits in response to the party's intention.[36]

A few months later, the vice minister of agriculture weighed in with some advice on raising rabbits, noting that rabbit raising was "vigorously under way according to the firm determination of the respected and beloved general."[37] On closer inspection, it seems that raising rabbits is not entirely trouble free. The vice minister advises that superior rabbit breeds be secured (a batch was flown in from Switzerland), special breeding stations set up, grass fields created, and rabbit diseases prevented. Presumably the Kim regime finds rabbit farming so attractive because people can do it without government assistance.

One indication that North Korea is not about to be overrun with rabbits is that seven years after the above articles appeared, *Nodong Sinmun* published another front-page article titled "Let Us Raise Many Rabbits As a Mass Campaign."[38] The article covers the same ground as earlier articles, emphasizing that organizations and individuals should "push forward the work of raising rabbits through to the end without abandoning it halfway." For breeding stock, the North Koreans this time went to Germany. A retired chauffeur was mentioned in a German paper in connection with the "German giant grays" he raised, each almost the size of a beagle. In late 2006, the North Korean embassy in Berlin contacted him, and he agreed to sell six of his rabbits (or twelve, depending on the source of the story).[39] The rabbits were shipped to North Korea in dog carriers, and a couple of months later the German rabbit breeder was again in the news, this time complaining that the North Koreans had not invited him to their country so he could show them how to raise the rabbits. Suspecting that his rabbits were already dead, he said, "I will never sell to North Korea again."[40] He may well have been correct about the fate of the rabbits. According to the chairman of Germany's State Association of Rabbit Breeders, the giant grays are not particularly profitable to raise for food because they require "wheelbarrow-loads of hay, vegetables, and rabbit chow to bring them to maturity."[41] In late 2007, a report out of China said that the North Koreans had recently purchased one hundred "AAA-level fine-breed otter rabbits" along with various rabbit-farming materials and medicines and that four hundred bunnies had subsequently been bred from the original batch.[42]

Army posts, collective farms, and schools are often assigned quotas of rabbits, goats, and chickens to raise, and in the run-up to an inspection, members of the organization must buy or steal animals to fill their animal pens. Duck and ostrich farms "equipped with modern facilities and based on the latest technology" have also been mentioned in the press, as have turtle farms and catfish breeding ponds.[43]

Most of the pork, beef, and chicken produced by farms goes to feed the cadres and their foreign guests. Ironically, despite the increasing prevalence of obesity in South Korea—in 2005 the government prepared to set up a National Obesity Control Committee—a South Korean company called Porky Trading Korea said it had obtained Republic of Korea (ROK) government approval to import forty tons of North Korean chicken and hoped to import a total of two thousand tons by the end of 2005.[44] If the hard currency North Korea obtained from the sale of chicken were used to purchase less expensive, but equally nutritious, food to feed the people, such a deal would make sense, but in recent years the Kim regime has spent very little on food imports, preferring to spend hard currency on monuments, military equipment, and luxuries for the elite class. Today, South Koreans throw away more food (an estimated four million tons annually) than North Koreans are able to produce, and 30 percent of the wasted food is fish and meat—foods that North Koreans rarely get to eat.[45]

The diet of the Pyongyang elites, who receive special rations or can afford to pay high prices for food at the markets, is far more varied than is the diet of the twenty million ordinary North Koreans. One of the strange food stories in the North Korean press is about that Western favorite, hamburgers. In a long December 2003 article, *Nodong Sinmun* called readers' attention to "the silvery white vehicles running busily through the intersections of the socialist capital every morning."[46] The destination of these vehicles was said to be the country's premier universities, and the purpose was to deliver hamburgers (whether just the beef or already prepared burgers the article does not say). "Loaded to capacity on these vehicles are hamburgers to be supplied to university students. The hamburgers [are] filled with the ardent benevolence of the great general!" According to the article, in September 2000, Kim had ordered that hamburgers and fried potatoes "in our own way" (french fries?) be provided "even though the country was still in a difficult situation."[47]

The End of the Ration System

The effective end of public food distribution in the mid-1990s dramatically changed the lives of the North Korean people, who had depended on the system since Kim Il-sung abolished private enterprise in the late 1950s. Every two weeks, at their workplace, workers were issued ration coupons (*yanggwon*, also known as "food tickets," or *yangpyo*), which they took to their designated PDS center where they were entitled to purchase food and staples for a nominal fee—as long as the items were in stock. Ration coupons could also be used to purchase food at restaurants, except those that accepted only foreign currency. Travelers needed a special kind of ration coupon to purchase food. The amount of food that could be purchased with the ration coupons depended on occupation, age, and political status, and the coupons were issued in denominations of grams, where 200 grams of rice equal about a cup of uncooked rice (3 cups when cooked), and the daily requirement for a working adult is between 500 and 600 grams (2,000 to 2,500 calories, the equivalent of 9 cups of cooked rice). Workers in nationally strategic and difficult occupations such as mining and heavy industries received the most generous rations—as much as 900 grams a day. High-ranking military officers received 850 grams, officers with special qualifications, such as pilots, 800 grams, and party members 700 grams. At the other end of the scale, women over 55 and men over 61 received 400 grams worth of coupons and children 200 to 300 grams, which is how much food many prisoners received. To complicate matters, party members and military officers would receive most of their grain ration in white rice, whereas ordinary workers would receive only 30 percent rice and the least fortunate 10 to 20 percent rice, with the remainder usually being corn. Beginning in the early 1970s, two days of rations were deducted from every fifteen-day ration period as a contribution to "wartime reserves," and other deductions were often made for one campaign or another.

Party and government officials could supplement their rations with money or food obtained by bribery, so they were never as reliant on the PDS as the workers were, and farmworkers were paid in grain produced on the farms. In the 1980s, PDS distribution centers began running out of rations, rendering the coupons of dubious value. By the mid-1990s, distribution centers could provide only a few days' rations every month.

On special occasions, such as the birthdays of Kim Il-sung and Kim Jong-il, people received special rations, and those "gifts of the leader" have continued. For example, in 2006, households received ration coupons authorizing the purchase of one kilogram each of rice, corn, soy sauce, and bean paste, a bottle of domestically made liquor, and one hundred grams of seasoning. An extra six hours of electricity was supplied for three nights so people could watch television. Children received two hundred grams (about one cup) of snacks, two hundred grams of candy, one hundred grams of popped rice, and five pieces of chewing gum. The latter delicacy was long denounced as a capitalist product but is now manufactured by the Pyongyang Chewing Gum Factory under the brand name of *Unbangul* ("silver bell").

After the PDS collapsed, most North Koreans had to work to eat and eat to live. Kim Il-sung famously said, "Rice means socialism," and when rice was no longer forthcoming, people turned their backs on socialism. The betrayal was very real. North Koreans vividly remember the 1990s famine, when even some members of the elite political class died of starvation. In those days it was common outside of Pyongyang to come across dead and dying people in the streets. A video smuggled out of North Korea shows dirty, shoeless children scrounging in the marketplace for scraps of food, even picking single grains of rice out of the mud. Ten years later, millions of North Koreans still suffer from malnutrition, and some continue to die of starvation. No one can be sure how good the next harvest will be or how much of the annual food shortage will be covered by foreign food donations.

Rations were discontinued during the famine because of temporary economic conditions, but the Economic Management Improvement Measures of July 2002 formally ended the ration system except as it continued to provide for the top one or two million cadres. So much farm production was being illegally diverted to the markets, rather than dispatched to the PDS, that the system was near collapse. For example, the state paid farms 0.8 won for a kilogram of rice and sold it to those with ration coupons for .08 won. The same rice was available for purchase in the markets at around 45 won per kilogram. Farms could thus earn far more by illegally selling their crops in the markets than by selling to the government. After July 2002, the government paid 40 won for a kilogram of rice and sold it in the PDS for 44 won, which was approximately the going rate in the markets, but inflation soon raised the market price.

In March 2003 the prohibition against selling rice and other rationed items in the markets was lifted, and the government began referring to the markets simply as "markets" rather than "farmers' markets." Farms were no longer required to sell most of their crops to the state. After reimbursing the state for its costs (amounting to about 50 percent of the harvest), farming collectives were permitted to dispose of the remainder of their crops in the markets. Prices of food in the markets were supposed to be capped at approximately the PDS rate, but this did not happen. Over the next few years, prices continued to climb, even though wages, when they were paid, remained the same. In 2007, at the average monthly salary of 5,000 won, a person could buy six kilograms of rice, equivalent to ninety cups of cooked rice—if all the household income was devoted to food. Without an income source outside of the assigned workplace, starvation was almost inevitable. According to defectors, after July 2002, people spent as much as 80 to 90 percent of their income on food, compared to next to nothing when the rationing system was in place.[48] Clothing was the second largest expense, followed by housing, heating, electricity, and then miscellaneous government fees, including education expenses.

Food prices fluctuate according to how much food is in the market, rising in early spring after most of the fall harvest has been consumed and peaking in early summer before the barley harvest. Prices also reflect how much food aid North Korea is receiving because, even if most of the aid doesn't go to ordinary people, the aid going to the upper political class and the military takes pressure off the food system and lowers prices in the market for everyone else. Because of transportation difficulties, prices also differ among provinces, with the lowest prices in farming areas and along the Chinese border. A class of entrepreneurial traders has sprung up to take advantage of these price differences by trucking rice and other products from one locale to another. Some of these traders operate on their own, and some work for party, state, and military organizations. "First runners" bring large quantities of goods from China to North Korean border cities. "Second runners" buy smaller quantities of these goods for a few hundred dollars and sell them to small-time entrepreneurs operating stalls in local markets.

In addition to food imported from abroad, North Koreans have increasingly depended on food grown on small patches of private and semiprivate land. In 2004, the Democratic People's Republic of Korea (DPRK) cabinet issued instructions on land use that included this key provision: "Measures shall be worked out to allocate arable land to organizations and enterprises and have them resolve food shortages for their workers and office employees on their own."⁴⁹ This directive ignored the fact that few workplaces have any experience in farming; moreover, allocated farmland is often some distance from the workplace. After paying all expenses, many organizations hardly break even in the farming business.

In small towns and in the countryside, people grow food in garden plots and public land that they appropriate secretly or by bribing the officials in charge of land usage. The legal size of kitchen gardens has been expanded from one hundred to one thousand square meters, although most gardens are smaller than that. In these gardens, which serve the same purpose as the "victory gardens" tended by Americans during the two world wars, farmers conscientiously grow vegetables such as beans, cabbage, radishes, peppers, garlic, potatoes, corn, and pumpkins. Houses in the countryside are covered with vegetable vines and surrounded by edible plants, while in the fields of collective and state farms, the crops are thin. Individuals and organizations seek out "patch fields"—small abandoned plots of land—and farm these as well, although they have no legal right to do so. When they are called to account by a party or government official, a small bribe usually settles the matter. To prevent thieves from raiding garden plots, farmers sleep outdoors next to their crops as harvest season approaches, and collective farms post guards.

Chronic Food Shortages

Reliable statistics are hard to come by, but the high point of domestic grain harvests apparently occurred in the 1980s, with production in the range of five to six million tons.⁵⁰ Since the early 1990s, grain production has slipped to three to four million tons, which is one to two million tons short of the minimum domestic demand.⁵¹ When foreign aid donations do not make up for the shortfall, people simply starve. Food was not plentiful in the 1960s, 1970s, and into the 1980s, but most people had enough to live on and even enjoyed the occasional extra dish. By the late 1980s the food supply was dwindling, and in the early 1990s, the government launched a "Let's Eat Two Meals a Day" campaign. The worst period of hunger, at least since the end of the Korean War, was from 1995 to 1999, when anywhere from twenty-five thousand people (an overly conservative estimate) to three million people died of hunger and illnesses caused or worsened by malnutrition. The most credible estimates fall in the range of six hundred thousand to one million, constituting 3 to 5 percent of the population.⁵² To put these figures in perspective, a comparable death rate in the United States would translate into nine to fifteen million people dying of hunger over a three-year period. If the higher estimates of two to three million North Korean deaths are closer to the truth, the comparable death tolls for the United States would be thirty to forty-five million dead.

The reasons for North Korea's chronic food shortages are not hard to find. Agricultural productivity is sapped by lack of incentives for farmers and the severe limitation that centralized socialist economic management imposes on agriculture (and the rest of the economy, for that matter). Localities have gained more responsibility for making agricultural decisions, but they are still supposed to implement the central government's plans, usually without adequate resources. Kim Jong-il and his economic officials are unable to resolve food-shortage problems without abandoning the centralized socialist model that enables them to exert a large measure of control over the people.

The land and climate also limit how much food North Koreans can grow. The northern half of the Korean Peninsula is mostly hilly and mountainous. In 2001, for example, North Korea had cleared 1.57 million hectares of farmland, 15 percent more than South Korea, but probably produced only 3.9 million tons of grain compared to South Korea's 6.2 million.[53] In order to expand agricultural land, hillsides have been extensively terraced, a practice that leads to soil erosion during the heavy summer rains. Authorized logging for export and unauthorized logging to provide fuel for heating homes worsen the erosion problem. The temperatures in the north are lower than is ideal for growing rice, and the North gets less rainfall than the south. In short, looking at topography and climate alone, trying to be self-sufficient in food production may be a losing battle in North Korea.

North Korean fields are overused. For years, fertilizer helped keep them productive, but with little money to import fertilizer and with domestic fertilizer factories idled, productivity has plummeted. Until recently, the South Korean government donated several hundred thousand tons of fertilizer to the North annually, or the situation would be even worse. Electricity is often unavailable in rural districts, limiting the use of pumps to irrigate fields. Farm machinery has not been replaced for years, and in any case there is little fuel to run it. According to a United Nations report published in South Korea in early 2005, only 60 percent of North Korean farm tractors are operational, and over half the land is being tilled by hand or plowed by oxen.[54] Shortages of trucks and fuel make it difficult to get crops to market before they spoil. In addition to fertilizer, farmers need more insecticides and plastic sheeting to cover seedbeds in the springtime.

In the 1990s, when the PDS ran low on food, the government simply cut off food deliveries to large groups of people living in the remote countryside. Foreign food-aid monitors are prevented from traveling to some of the remoter areas, especially in the northeast part of the country, so conditions there must be gauged by testimony from North Koreans who defect or travel to China. The people of Pyongyang receive the best food rations, but even during the famine some of them died of hunger.

During the famine, those who had money went to the markets and paid high prices for what was available. City residents asked relatives who lived on farms to send them food, for which they traded household possessions. They also went on the street to beg, and some turned to burglary, robbery, swindling, and prostitution. People living in the countryside cultivated whatever small plots of land they could find around their homes and in the mountains. They also cut down trees and sold them as firewood. One defector tells how people would spend a day in the hills cutting trees (an illegal activity) and then walk ten hours carrying the wood on their backs to sell in the nearest city for enough money to buy a bowl of noodles and a half dozen cups of corn. In the last stages of hunger, people went into the woods and fields to pull up grass and peel bark off trees, then ground this material up and mixed it with a little grain. These alternative foods wreak havoc on the digestive system while supplying little nourishment.

The short-term consequences of the food shortages are easy to see, but one can only guess the extent to which the chronic food shortages will physically and mentally weaken the North Korean people in the long term. As one visitor observed, "Nobody is apple-shaped or pear-shaped. Everyone is banana-shaped."[55] Those who are most immediately affected are the young and the old. In late 1998, at the end of the three-year famine period, a survey of children from age six months to seven years, sponsored by the World Food Program (WFP), found 16 percent wasting, 62 percent stunted, and 60 percent moderately underweight.[56] A WFP survey in early 2005 found 7 percent of sampled children under the age of six to be wasting, 37 percent stunted, and 23 percent underweight.[57] After the age of six, stunting is largely irreversible, which accounts for the difference in height and weight between North and South Koreans. By their size, North Korean children look several years younger than their South Korean counterparts, and throughout their lives these undernourished children are likely to suffer from a mental and physical "disease burden."[58]

The reality of the suffering of millions of North Koreans is better delivered by photographs of severely malnourished children and their gaunt parents than by looking at tables of statistics, and to truly appreciate what the chronic food shortage means to millions of North Koreans, one must skip a few meals and then imagine what it must be like to live with that feeling of hunger for years on end. One defector told a pathetic story about how the regime prepared a small delegation of students to meet a famous South Korean radical student, Im Su-kyung, who traveled illegally to North Korea in 1989. The members of the North Korean welcoming delegation were housed in a Pyongyang hotel for a week before the visit and fed meat, bread, fresh fruit, and milk to fatten them up for the meeting with the South Korean.[59]

Although North Korea had been receiving an undetermined amount of food assistance from its socialist allies for much of its history, in the mid-1990s, and especially after the floods of 1995, the Kim regime began to appeal to the international community for food aid. Since that time, the major sources of food aid have been the WFP, which channels aid donations from member countries, and the ROK and Chinese governments. WFP aid started in 1996 and continued annually with about one million tons a year. In addition to providing annual food shipments, the WFP, with a resident staff of about one hundred at its highest point, set up nineteen factories to manufacture high-nutrition food such as biscuits and noodles. A rough estimate is that during this period the WFP was feeding about 6.5 million North Koreans (i.e., almost a third of the population), with the target population being children, pregnant mothers, and the elderly.

The first South Korean delivery of aid, 150,000 tons of rice, was made in 1995, after which about 100,000 tons of grain and 300,000 tons of fertilizer were sent to the North every year until 2008, when the North Korean government froze all relations with the South Korean government to protest the election of its new president. American food aid, mostly delivered through the WFP, began in 1996 and peaked in 1999 with 695,000 tons, before declining. By 2007, the total American contribution was just over two million tons, at a cost of about $700 million.[60] In 2008, the United States pledged another five hundred thousand tons of food aid, but not all of it was delivered.

The WFP has frequently argued with the North Korean government about how to keep track of donated food in order to ensure that it goes to the deserving poor. WFP monitors are required to put in a travel request a week or more in advance before making a trip outside of Pyongyang, thus giving local officials plenty of time to prepare for the visit and set the stage for whatever play they want to perform—whether to make things look bad in the hope of getting more aid or good to indicate that progress is being made. Monitors are accompanied by North Korean security cadres, and the WFP is generally not permitted to bring Korean-speaking aid workers into the country, presumably for fear they will learn too much about North Korean society. Aid workers must therefore rely on North Korean government translators to speak with the people, and needless to say, no North Korean is going to speak candidly in the presence of a government official. To someone unfamiliar with North Korea, these government restrictions might seem extraordinary, but the WFP dares not object too strongly for fear of being prevented from delivering any food aid at all.

Much of the donated food is transported by the military, the only organization with sufficient fuel and operating trucks to move large amounts of goods around the country. At every step of the way, beginning at dockside, military and party organizations have the opportunity to siphon off some of the aid for their own consumption or to sell in the markets, but it is not known how much of the aid is diverted. Stephan Haggard and Marcus Noland, who have provided a balanced and well-researched view of North Korea's food situation, cite estimates that 10 to 30 percent of the aid is not making it to its intended destination.[61] On numerous occasions the WFP has vigorously denied that significant amounts of food are being diverted, but in the absence of a more rigorous monitoring system, this defense lacks credibility. Staff from other aid organizations, which find it impossible to insist on stricter monitoring while the bigger WFP accepts the Kim regime's restrictions, have been anonymously quoted as taking a more pessimistic view of the diversion situation. One says, "Everything is a lure and a facade here!" Another says, "We still don't have a minimal degree of transparency."[62]

One policy that the WFP has firmly adhered to is to distribute aid only to areas where it is possible to send monitors. This means that large swaths of North Korea, primarily in the East and Northeast, have never received WFP aid because the North Korean authorities refuse to let monitors visit those areas, ostensibly for security reasons. In an attempt to discourage diversion of food aid to the wealthier classes, the WFP has substituted corn and other less desirable grains for rice, on the principle that only poor people would be willing to eat those grains, although unscrupulous people could still sell the grains in the markets.

In late 2004, the North Korean government placed further restrictions on food monitoring, explaining, implausibly, that local residents found the monitoring trips too "intrusive," whereupon the WFP reduced its food distributions by 20 to 30 percent. In October 2005, the North Korean government requested that the WFP close its local food factories, suspend its food distribution, and send its workers home by the end of November, claiming that there was now enough food coming in from domestic and other foreign sources (presumably directly from South Korea and China). At the same time, the government said it would welcome "development-oriented" assistance.[63] Most other aid organizations received the same expulsion notice.

In November 2005, Kim Young-hoon of the (North) Korea Rural Economic Institute told the ROK minister of unification that if South Korea continued to deliver food aid for one or two more years, the North would then be able to "resolve the food issue."[64] Worse than wishful thinking, this was a lie. The WFP and other NGOs pleaded with the North Korean government to let them stay, and foreign human rights activists criticized the Kim regime for its wanton disregard of people's needs, prompting the regime to assert that choosing *not* to receive humanitarian aid was its "sovereign right" and insisting that the government "has a way to overcome its difficulties, as they are temporary."[65] However, as the 2005 harvest (which was indeed somewhat larger than in previous years) was consumed, reports of hunger surfaced, and the regime was forced to relent. After lengthy negotiations, the WFP was permitted to return to North Korea in May 2006 with a dramatically scaled-down program.[66]

We can only guess at the calculations that went into the decision to expel NGOs from North Korea. A decision of this magnitude could only be made by Kim Jong-il, and it is quite possible that his agriculture officials mislead him about the food situation. The year 2005 was officially designated as the year of agriculture, and even if the officials knew better, they might have been reluctant to admit to Kim that their campaign had come up short. After all, only a few years earlier Kim had ordered that his agriculture minister be publicly executed for failing to deliver sufficient crops. Another possibility is that the North Korean military, which draws most of its food from domestic stocks, might have objected to the foreign aid monitors and pressured Kim to throw them out. Or perhaps the expulsion and readmission were simply ploys to force the WFP and other aid organizations to be more responsive to North Korean demands for reduced monitoring.

The Kims, father and son, have addressed the perennial food shortages in their own ways, relying on their intuition and on the advice of homegrown agricultural experts who recommend solutions consistent with the principles of the command socialist economy. Under Kim Jong-il's rule, a four-prong attack on food shortages has been mounted. In a continuation of his father's enthusiasm for creating more usable farmland, the younger Kim has emphasized "large-scale land rezoning" designed to combine smaller fields into larger ones suitable for mechanized agriculture, despite the lack of such machinery. Kim also pushed the "potato revolution," the "seed revolution" (developing or importing seeds suitable for North Korea's growing conditions), and the "two-crops-a-year farming policy" (typically corn and wheat in cooler weather and rice in the summer).[67] None of these initiatives has materially increased the annual harvests, suggesting that the agricultural problem lies elsewhere.

Kim Jong-il must suspect that the key to improving harvests will be found in agricultural management, a perennial concern of socialist economists. One issue is how to "correctly combine the unified guidance of the state with the creative initiative at each unit" (to borrow North Korea's words).[68] Favorite prescriptions include injunctions to "rationally deploy" farming resources and pursue "farming-at-the-right-place" and "farming-at-the-right-time." A second management problem concerns how to employ incentives, a perennial issue (discussed earlier) that the North Korean media discuss in the context of determining the "scientifically correct" combination of political, moral, and material incentives to use. Arguably the greatest boon to North Korean agriculture is right under Kim Jong-il's nose, but he either refuses to see it or realizes that it is too dangerous to adopt. The productivity of farmers' private gardens far surpasses the productivity of the collective and state farm fields. Farmers do not have to be told what seeds to plant in their gardens or when to plant them. That is to say, farmers are using the type of creativity that Kim wants them to use, but they are being creative outside the bounds of socialism, and this is not acceptable to Kim. In short, the most obvious way to increase agricultural production would simply be to give the land back to the farmers, like the Chinese government did beginning in the late 1970s.

The Kim regime holds its people hostage to hunger, and dealing with hostage takers involves making distasteful compromises. Kim obviously cares less about his people's welfare than do international aid organizations, not just because he is hard-hearted but because he is concerned first and foremost about his own security, which he believes foreigners threaten—thus the strange and unfortunate situation in which food-aid donors must plead to be allowed to continue to feed the North Korean people.

When all is said and done, North Korea remains as dependent as ever on foreign food aid and has manipulated the international community in order to continue receiving it on the best possible terms. Direct aid from South Korea and China is preferred over aid from the WFP, which is accompanied by more monitoring. The South Korean government under Presidents Kim

Dae-jung and Roh Moo-hyun bristled at the charge that it was not doing enough to track where its donated rice was going, but the numbers speak for themselves. According to a South Korean newspaper, in 2004 only ten South Korean inspections were made of the distribution of over three hundred thousand tons of rice, whereas the WFP made over four thousand spot inspections.[69] The same article reported the ROK unification ministry's explanation: "Because it [rice aid] was given as a loan, we are limited in terms of our participation in the distribution process."[70] This refers to the pretense that some aid is in the form of a loan, despite the fact that nobody expects the loan will ever be repaid. As for China's aid to North Korea, it is a matter between two secretive communist governments.

Haggard and Noland, in their study of the North Korean economy, have noted that as food aid began to arrive in the mid-1990s, the North Korean government cut back on its purchases of foreign food to the point where over 90 percent of food imports were in the form of aid.[71] This action was taken even though the food aid was insufficient to save all North Koreans or bring them back to full health. So, not only does unmonitored bilateral aid seem to be crowding out WFP aid, but aid in general has crowded out commercial imports of food.

What is the Kim regime doing with its money and with its domestic food harvests? Much of the domestic harvest goes to the military, in line with Kim's "military-first politics," and a considerable portion of the government's income goes to the construction of monuments to the Kims. In an internal communication from August 2004, Kim supposedly boasted about how construction proceeded in the DPRK even during the famine period. The projects listed were the Kumsusan Memorial Palace (believed to have cost at least a hundred million dollars), statues, and other commemorative monuments built "for the indoctrination of revolutionary tradition."[72] Reports in 2006 indicate that Kim Jong-il museums are being built throughout the country to supplement the Kim Il-sung museums found in every city, province, and county.[73]

Health Care

International concern about North Korea's chronic food shortages obscures another serious threat to the people's health: their broken health-care system. The system is broken not because of any shortage of qualified medical personnel, although North Korea's doctors have limited access to cutting-edge medical knowledge, but because the collapse of the economy has deprived medical personnel of equipment and medicines to work with, and malnutrition makes people vulnerable to a host of ailments. After the introduction of the July 2002 economic-management measures, which shifted the burden of living costs to the people, the government promised to continue providing free health care, but descriptions of the health-care system in the North Korean press bear little resemblance to actual conditions.

Workplace accidents are common. Construction work performed with machinery in developed societies is done by hand. Mines are death traps. "Speed battles" force workers to work too quickly under exhausting conditions. A German technical advisor who worked for several foreign aid organizations in North Korea reported that North Korean managers considered adequate safety measures an extravagance, and he noted that in the provinces doctors were forced to amputate the limbs of injured workers because they did not have instruments and medicines for surgical treatment.[74]

According to a United Nations Children's Fund (UNICEF) report, as the economy deteriorated during the 1990s, the availability of potable water declined: in 1994, 83 percent of North Koreans had access to piped water, but by 1998 only 53 percent did.[75] Without electricity to run pumps, high-rise apartment buildings are without water except during a few hours in the morning and evening. According to a survey conducted by the DPRK government and jointly sponsored by UNICEF and the WFP, only about half of North Korean households have flush toilets.[76] Outside of Pyongyang, chlorine to purify drinking water is in short supply, and pumping stations often cannot operate for lack of fuel and spare parts, forcing people to get their water from the nearest stream or river, which is often polluted because waste-treatment plants are not operating.

Since the 1960s, public health care (there is, of course, no legal private care) has taken the form of a "doctor-in-charge" system whereby a general practitioner, an obstetrician, and a pediatrician are assigned to a geographical area or designated workplace comprising about fifteen hundred persons. Patients are first seen in local clinics. More serious cases are supposed to be referred to a local hospital, then up to a county hospital, then to a hospital in the provincial capital, and finally to a hospital in Pyongyang. In fact, none of these medical facilities has adequate medicine or equipment to treat serious cases, except for a few of the Pyongyang hospitals that treat the elite cadres. The most famous of these elite hospitals is the Pyongyang Maternity Hospital, a favorite spot for North Korean officials to take foreign visitors in order to demonstrate the alleged superiority of their health-care system. In 2004, a Korean Central News Agency article reported that Kim Jong-il had sent "scores of tons of wild honey to the hospital on at least 30 occasions," along with "rare tonics including bear hoof, deer's placenta paste, black hens and pine-nuts." This list suggests that even at this hospital, modern (or at least modern Western) medicine is lacking, forcing doctors to resort to more traditional Asian herbal remedies, which in North Korea have come to be called "*Koryo* medicine."[77] Because indigenous (or Chinese-origin) medicine does not rely on foreign research and technology, the Kim regime is especially proud of it, in line with the official ideology of *Juche*, but North Korean doctors are sometimes skeptical of its effectiveness.[78]

Getting admitted to well-equipped hospitals like the Pyongyang Maternity Hospital, the Pyongyang Medical University Hospital, or the Kim Manyu Hospital is only a dream for most people. Even if those hospitals admitted ordinary people, which they rarely do, getting timely transportation to them would be extremely difficult. Travel from one city to another often takes days and requires the payment of bribes to get on trains, buses, or, most commonly, open-bed trucks, nicknamed *ssobicha*, or "service cars." Most patients are treated locally with herbal medicines gathered and mixed by a physician or pharmacist. An article in the North Korean press praises local hospitals and clinics that procure their own medical supplies for their efforts to "lighten even a bit of the burden shouldered by the great general who takes great pains to promote the people's health."[79] Patients in need of complicated operations or modern medicines such as antibiotics must pull through by themselves.

North Korea's doctors perform as well as they can under the circumstances. As employees of the state, they receive only subsistence wages, although they benefit from gifts of food and homemade consumer goods donated to them by grateful patients. Doctors dedicated to treating their patients perform heroically, for example by using old X-ray machines that expose their own bodies to dangerous levels of radiation. What must be most difficult for medical professionals is the frustration of watching patients suffer and die from diseases that could easily be cured if the proper medicines and equipment were available. The World Health Organization has estimated that North Korea depends on foreign donors for 70 percent of its most basic drugs.[80]

Norbert Vollertsen, a German physician who worked as an advisor in North Korea from 1999 to 2000 and later became an outspoken critic of the Kim regime, documented some of these frustrating conditions: "There were no bandages, scalpels, antibiotics or operating facilities, only broken beds on which children lay waiting to die."[81] A German technical advisor to a foreign aid group reported, "The hospitals, nurseries, kindergartens, and schools I witnessed personally were, in a word, 'hellish.' . . . Bacterial infection and diarrhea are epidemic in the regions outside of Pyongyang, and because pharmaceuticals such as antibiotics are depleted, most of the residents live with one or two kinds of chronic disease."[82]

The North Korean government has been so unhelpful to visiting health-care workers that some of the foreign medical organizations, including Doctors without Borders, Oxfam, and CARE, have withdrawn from the country.[83] Beginning in 2006, the International Red Cross scaled down its assistance programs, diplomatically noting that the year was "marked by increased complexities in the implementation of the programs."[84]

In 2006 the (South) Korea Center for Disease Control and Prevention examined the health history of over one thousand North Korean defectors.[85] The average North Korean defector was three inches (eight centimeters) shorter than his or her South Korean counterpart and weighed seventeen pounds (eight kilograms) less. Of the North Korean sample, 77 percent had contracted diphtheria and rubella, 64 percent mumps, and 53 percent measles; 44 percent had a history of carrying parasites (a figure twelve times higher than in South Korea). Syphilis was eight times more frequently found in defectors than in a comparable South Korean sample. The United Nations' 2006 World Population Status Report estimated the life expectancy of North Korean men to be sixty-one years, compared to seventy-four years for South Korean men (the ROK Ministry of Health says seventy-eight years); the comparable figures for women were sixty-seven and eighty-two years. North Korea's estimated infant mortality was forty-three, compared to South Korea's three, per one thousand.[86]

On the other hand, an entire mini-industry is devoted to the health care of Kim Jong-il, who, along with his top cadres, has access to the Ponghwa (Bonghwa) Clinic, which appears to provide medical care comparable to that found in hospitals in developed countries. A handful of top cadres have also been permitted to travel abroad to receive medical treatment in Beijing, Moscow, and Paris, and top medical specialists are sometimes flown into Pyongyang to advise North Korean doctors on special procedures to treat Kim.

Housing

It is difficult to determine what housing conditions are for the average North Korean because foreigners are not permitted to visit their homes, although foreigners are occasionally invited to see the apartment of a model citizen in Pyongyang. The capital city was almost completely destroyed during the Korean War and rebuilt in a modern design. Under the direction of Kim Jong-il, the city got a major facelift to prepare for the Thirteenth World Festival of Youth and Students in 1989 with the construction of rows of thirty- and forty-story apartment buildings on Kwangbok ("liberation") and Tongil ("unification") streets.

Compared to most large cities, Pyongyang is serene and orderly. High-rise buildings set among parks and monuments line broad but empty streets. Except when sand blows in from China, the air is clear because there are few vehicles on the streets and few factories operating. Visitors often find the city not so much quiet as disquieting, like an enormous Potemkin village, although hidden behind the tall buildings one can glimpse neighborhoods with winding streets and old-style tile-roofed houses.

The top cadres in Pyongyang live in large apartments or detached homes with small gardens located in neighborhoods surrounded by guarded walls to keep ordinary Koreans well away. They may also enjoy the use of a modest dacha in the countryside. Officials of somewhat lower rank live in high-rise apartments of three or four rooms, while mid-level officials get a one- or two-room apartment. Many people in Pyongyang and other cities live in single-story multiplex buildings of simple design or in traditional Korean dwellings. In the countryside, old tile-roofed and some thatched-roof houses from the early twentieth century can still be found.

The most prominent building in Pyongyang is the 105-story pyramid-shaped Ryugyong (Ryukyong, Yukyong) Hotel, designed to be Asia's tallest hotel. Construction began in 1987 and was supposed to be completed in time for Kim Il-sung's eightieth birthday in 1992. However, work stopped in 1989, and the French consultants withdrew the following year, complaining they were not being paid. Because of structural flaws and lack of materials, only the superstructure and façade were completed, and the building remains an empty eyesore overlooking Pyongyang, with a construction crane still perched at the top. There has never been an official explanation of what happened, and the North Korean media never mention the structure, even though it dominates the Pyongyang skyline. In 2009 Orascom, an Egyptian construction company, installed glass panels on the building to make it look less abandoned.

Visitors to Pyongyang stay at one of a handful of hotels catering to foreigners, the most popular being the twin-towered Koryo Hotel and the newer Yanggakdo Hotel, which is located on a small island in the Taedong River.

Power outages in these hotels are less frequent than in other buildings, but to conserve electricity hallways are kept unlighted most of the time. High-ranking foreign officials visiting Pyongyang are usually put up in government-owned guesthouses.

The state or a collective owns most dwellings in North Korea, although it is said that in the countryside there are some old homes that the communists never nationalized because their owners were from solid working-class stock. Until July 2002, housing was almost free, but under the new economic-management measures, the government now charges rent on homes and fees for utilities. As in other socialist countries, housing in North Korea has always been in short supply. Extended families often live in two-room apartments, and newlyweds typically wait several years before they can move into their own apartment.

Power outages are a daily occurrence, and residents of smaller cities and towns may be without electricity for days or even weeks at a time. At night, people use kerosene lanterns and candles for lighting, even in Pyongyang's high-rise apartment buildings. Streets are not lit, but monuments to the Kim family are brightly illuminated. Without power, there is no running water or elevator service. Only the homes and apartments of the elites enjoy central heating. Other residents warm themselves with small stoves, insulate their windows with vinyl sheeting, and huddle under blankets.

The head of the *inminban* (neighborhood or people's group consisting of twenty to forty households), who is usually a housewife or retired worker, recruits residents for all manner of local activities, including neighborhood security, cleaning, maintenance, recycling, and road repair. The group leader also checks to see that the households participate in required communal activities, including composting and farming assistance. In apartment buildings, residents take turns acting as security guards, recording the comings and goings of nonresidents.

Changes in the economy and a weakening of government control are beginning to transform the housing market. Although houses and apartments cannot be privately owned, people find ways to buy and sell their homes anyway. The usual procedure is for two individuals to agree to trade homes and then to bribe housing authorities to change their residency registrations. In some cases people trade away their homes for needed cash and end up homeless. It even seems to be possible to construct private housing. According to one report, a business enterprise, usually an arm of a government, party, or military organization, uses money from investors to buy out owners of existing dwellings, tear down their homes, put up a new building, and sell the condominiums for a tidy profit. Considerable bribery is necessary to complete such a project, and relevant housing officials may even receive ownership of one of the new units.[87]

Because apartments and condominiums in desirable downtown locations can fetch thousands of dollars, and condominiums in Pyongyang sell for as much as $30,000 to $40,000, real estate purchases must be made with illegally gotten money.[88] After all, the annual wage for most North Koreans is less than $100 in hard currency. Houses near marketplaces are in particularly high demand because when the authorities crack down on a market, vendors can take their customers to a nearby house and continue their business. A political lecture for domestic consumption mentions the existence of private inns in North Korea. Titled "Let Us Thoroughly Eliminate Private Accommodation Facilities and Give No Room for Enemies to Maneuver" and dated May 2004, this lecture alleges that private rooming houses springing up near railway stations and highways throughout the country can be used as hiding places for foreign spies.[89] The lecture also notes that "ill-behaved women" entertain men in these houses.

The Uncertain Future of the New Economy

The Kim regime's willingness to loosen economic restraints on the people and devolve economic responsibility to lower levels has fundamentally changed the character of the civilian economy, which has gone from being a struggling socialist command economy to an emerging protomarket economy. How far this change will go is hard to say. Those foreign analysts who see great promise in North Korea's economy since the introduction of the July 2002 economic measures are really only seeing the emergence of a nation of very small shopkeepers. At the present stage, the reformed part of the economy is largely engaged in buying and selling cheap cottage-industry and Chinese-made goods, an activity that livens up the streets but does little to build a strong economy. It might not be an exaggeration to say that this is the sort of economic activity conducted in market towns in the Middle Ages. The sidewalk vending that is becoming popular in North Korea today was common in South Korea in the 1960s and 1970s, but in South Korea, by the 1970s, factories were beginning to turn out manufactured goods for the domestic and international markets, and by the 1980s South Korean heavy industry was taking its place in the front rank of the major economies. It is hard to imagine that North Korea's dilapidated industries can make such progress in the coming years.

The economic changes that have come from the people, not the regime, are creating a new economic class of people with hard currency, usually earned illegally, while the rest of the population depends for its livelihood on barter and the worthless North Korean won. Formerly, the privileged economic class consisted of top party and government officials, who receive better rations than the common people and whose positions of authority make it possible for them to exact bribes. Today, the rich people, who are sometimes the same party and government officials, are those who know how to earn foreign currency. This phenomenon is similar to what happened in Russia in the 1990s. In North Korea, many of the newly wealthy class get their start with money from relatives in China or Japan. Most of their businesses involve trading: they have not progressed to the stage of buying up North Korea's decrepit industries, which have not yet been put on the market, although entrepreneurs may "rent" some of them by taking a management position in return for infusions of cash or resources.

These nouveaux riche, who have foreign connections and whose families are often not native Korean, were formerly discriminated against as members of the unreliable political class, but now their foreign currency connections eclipse their political liabilities. They can rehabilitate themselves by providing generous donations to public projects, such as school improvements, and by being generous to members of the party and government bureaucracy. In fact, like flies to honey, cash-poor party members, bureaucrats, and police officers are drawn to these wealthy new entrepreneurs, forcing them to pay out money right and left in order to get things done and stay out of trouble. A former North Korean truck driver reports that he would lose 50 to 60 percent of his cargo on the drive from China to Pyongyang because each time he was stopped by security forces, he had to offer them some of his cargo as a bribe to let him proceed.[90]

The state continues to intervene in the economic lives of the people by promulgating and sporadically enforcing strict rules for market activity. In the absence of resources to feed the people or any enthusiasm for the market economy, the government and the party exercise a constraining, rather than a facilitating, influence on economic life. Now that the socialist economy has collapsed, the state is trying to raise funds by taxing private economic activities. This taxation is bitterly resented by the people, who feel that they have been abandoned by state socialism and now are being taxed for finding an alternative livelihood.

Rich people are beginning to flaunt their wealth by driving private cars, wearing expensive clothes, and living in apartments and houses they have illegally purchased, although they risk exposing their riches and falling afoul of crusading authorities. The Kim regime intermittently launches campaigns against nonsocialist activities and wealth and sometimes makes an example of these people, but they seem willing to take their chances. Entrepreneurs in China and Russia expose themselves to similar risks.

There is a limit, however, to how much the North Korean economy can change. Deep and enduring economic changes must await political change, and once politics begin to change, people will ask why they had to suffer for so many years and why North Korea has fallen so far behind. People will no longer believe the propaganda claims that "imperialists," primarily the Americans, are responsible for North Korea's economic failures. They will begin to ask questions about how Kim and his associates have been running the country, and at that point it will be all over for the Kim family regime.

In food, housing, and health care, the stealthy transition from a command socialist economy to a protocapitalist economy is teaching North Koreans to become entrepreneurs and consumers.[91] The transition is also creating a gap between the very rich and everyone else. Koreans with good political connections, business talent or experience, access to foreign currency, or good luck are beginning to make thousands and tens of thousands of dollars in business. The majority of Koreans only earn enough to buy food and other basic necessities, and some people still die of starvation.

It is difficult to predict North Korea's economic future. The tension between the growing market economy and the regime's continuing hostility toward capitalism has resulted in an awkward economic transition. The regime periodically rolls back market initiatives, as it did in May 2004 when it banned the use of cell phones, and then relaxes enforcement of the bans. In 2007, the government tried to prohibit women under the age of fifty (in some places, forty) from selling goods in the markets. According to an October 2007 Korean Workers' Party document, which quotes Kim Jong-il's instructions, the major problems with markets are that "women in their prime and workable age" are at the markets rather than at state factories and offices, that merchants are making "exorbitant" profits, and that the sale of South Korean goods is "spreading illusions about the enemy."[92] The instructions portray markets as instruments of North Korea's enemies who seek to "employ all vicious means to disintegrate us from within."

In late 2008, rumors circulated widely that the government had decided to transform the markets into the old-style farmers' markets that met only three times a month. The order was supposed to go into effect at the beginning of the new year, but nothing happened.[93] If the markets were limited to selling food, it would be a severe blow to North Korean commerce and a hardship on the people. It would also deprive the local officials of the money they earn legally and illegally from running the markets, and for this reason alone, such a move would meet with resistance.

Groups of inspectors are dispatched from Pyongyang to try to stamp out such "antisocialist" activities as viewing smuggled videotapes and using Chinese cell phones along the border. These "secret *gruppa*" ("groups," from the Russian, which may also be the same as "724 Gruppa" and "No. 5 Anti-Socialist Inspection Groups" mentioned by various defectors) include officials from several security organizations, the party, and the state prosecution, perhaps in order to have personnel from the different organizations keep an eye on each other. The inspection teams are supposed to be on the lookout for activities occurring outside the socialist economy, but since everyone is at least partially engaged in these activities, the inspectors' efforts are doomed to failure.

The transition from socialism to capitalism seems to have gone too far to stop. The more people turn to the markets, the fewer resources are available to the state—unless it creates a more systematic form of taxing private incomes. People are unable to plan for their future because they cannot know what the economic situation will be from one year to the next, but they can be sure that they must continue to struggle in the new marketplace because the old socialist economy is unlikely to return.

The two architects of North Korea. Kim Jong-il escorts his father at the dedication of the Juche Tower on the occasion of the senior Kim's seventieth birthday in April 1982. *Choson ui Yanggwang*, Pyongyang, 1984.

This photo of Kim Il-sung accompanied an article in a pro-North Korean-Japanese newspaper announcing his death in 1994. *The People's Korea*, No. 1,657, July 16, 1994, 1.

This photo of Kim Jong-il accompanied an article titled "Let Us Exalt Brilliance of Comrade Kim Il-sung's Idea on Youth Movement and Achievements Made under His Leadership." *The People's Korea*, No. 1,757, September 7, 1996, 2.

Kim Jong-il, nine months after his stroke (his left arm is hanging at his side), casts his ballot in the military constituency in which he is registered. As a candidate in the March 2009 election of delegates to the Supreme People's Assembly, Kim received a 100 percent approval vote, as did all of the party's 687 candidates. Behind him is General Hyon Chol-hae, in full military dress, while Kim wears his trademark "people's clothes." Permission of Yonhap News.

Downtown Pyongyang, 2008. Courtesy of a friend.

A 2008 photo of the shell of the 105-story Ryugyong Hotel in Pyongyang, begun in 1987 but never completed. Since the photo was taken, an Egyptian construction company has covered the crumbling concrete shell in a sheath of glass to make it more attractive. Courtesy of a friend.

A performance at the 2008 Arirang Festival celebrating the country's sixtieth anniversary. The card section spells out "A Ri Rang," which is the title of Korea's most popular folk song. Courtesy of a friend.

Woman bowing at a monument to Kim Il-sung, one of thousands in North Korea. This one is near Mt. Kumgang, and the date is July 8, 2004, the tenth anniversary of Kim's death. Photo by Bill Brown.

Women transport goods in the countryside by "dubal-cha" (two-legged car). Permission of Good Friends USA.

Goods are transported in the countryside by man-powered cart. Permission of Good Friends USA.

Children help to push a family cart. Permission of Good Friends USA.

A busy informal roadside market. Permission of Good Friends USA.

A woman sells food at a roadside market; her face is blurred to protect her identity. Permission of Good Friends USA.

Women peddle goods at an official local market. Permission of Good Friends USA.

Peddlers at a roadside market.
Permission of Good Friends USA.

A few peddlers gathered along the road. Permission of Good Friends USA.

Children use wooden boxes to hunt for clams or other aquatic food. Permission of Good Friends USA.

CHAPTER FIVE

The Information Environment

Although the Kim regime has gone to great lengths to restrict the information available to its people, information control is breaking down. North Koreans today live in two information environments. The regime has fashioned the public environment of party speeches, propaganda banners, and communist-inspired culture for its own purposes, and it is filled with falsehoods. People treat this environment the way most Westerners treat their commercial environment—by ignoring it as much as possible. And then there is the hidden information environment of news and entertainment that seeps in from outside North Korea's borders. Because this information is hard to come by, it is much sought after. Even Western-style television commercials and print advertisements are eagerly viewed by those few North Koreans with access to them. The question of how much impact this information has on people will be taken up in chapter 6, leaving this chapter to survey the official and unofficial sources of information available to the North Korean people.

People need information to navigate their social and physical environments and make optimal choices; information is also sought for its entertainment value. Systems theorists have observed that closed systems, which do not communicate well with the environment, eventually falter and die because they cannot adapt to the larger systems of which they are a part.[1] These systems may be countries or companies or social groups. Open systems have a better chance of surviving, but they are vulnerable to change imposed upon them by their environment. The Kim regime has struggled with the trade-off between the benefits of open and closed systems. North Korea cannot survive by relying solely on its own knowledge and inventions. Yet, information from the outside world inevitably provides a standard against which North Koreans can compare their difficult lives. How can Kim Jong-il let in the information necessary to make his economy competitive without introducing ideas that challenge the official ideology? The attempted solution is to drape what Kim Il-sung described as a "mosquito net" around the country, letting in some things and keeping out others.[2]

One reason that Kim and his associates have been able to stay in power for over half a century is that they have been able to control information channels. A former North Korean has characterized the people as twenty-three million frogs living at the bottom of a deep well. The people not only lack knowledge about what is going on outside their country but are even ignorant about what is happening within North Korea. Without information about alternatives, including alternative political systems and standards of living, their options for change are limited. Since it began publishing its annual world index of press freedom in 2002, Reporters without Borders has placed North Korea dead last on the list every year except in 2007 and 2008, when it was next to last (after Eritrea and just ahead of Turkmenistan, Burma, Cuba, Vietnam, and China). By monopolizing information, the political elites have erected a protective wall around themselves. At the center of things, Kim, who has more knowledge than anyone else, including about what the other elites are doing, has built an inner wall around himself to guard against coups, much like the keep or inner tower within a walled castle.

North Koreans live in a propaganda-rich, information-poor environment. During the Cold War, citizens of the Soviet Union and Eastern Europe had much more information available to them about life outside their country than do North Koreans today. In the heyday of communism, perhaps only the Chinese and Russian peasants were as ignorant of the outside world as today's North Korean villagers. To be sure, not all North Koreans are uninformed about what is going on in their country and the world. Those in the upper political class have more knowledge about international events than do the peasants, and Kim Jong-il has full access to the international media. Below them, most party cadres get their news from the government-controlled media, supplemented by whatever they pick up from rumor and clandestine listening to foreign radio broadcasts. Ordinary North Koreans must rely on radios with dials fixed to the government station and televisions that can only receive the nearby government stations to get the news, and electricity shortages prevent even those who have radios and televisions from using them much of the time.

Because the government owns and operates the radio and television stations and the newspapers, they provide a single source of information, with one media channel reinforcing another. Consequently, North Koreans cannot judge the reliability of one news medium by comparing it with another. And not only are most North Koreans deprived of reliable information, but they are saddled with large amounts of misinformation. For example, North Koreans are told that in 1945 Kim Il-sung won the war against Japan and that several years later he successfully defended North Korea against a joint American–South Korean invasion that started the Korean War. They are also told that in his day Kim Il-sung was recognized throughout the world as one of the great leaders of the twentieth century and that Kim Jong-il holds that position today.

Authorized Sources of Information

The Role of the News

The role of the media in a communist state is to make people loyal supporters of the regime. As Lenin said, "Newspapers are free not for the sake of the circulation of news but for the purpose of educating and organizing the working masses toward the attainment of goals clearly defined by the thoroughgoing leadership of the party."[3] Article 67 of the constitution of the Democratic People's Republic of Korea (DPRK) provides for freedom of the press, publication, assembly, demonstration, and association, but "freedom" in North Korea is defined as what "corresponds to the interests of the popular masses"—and party officials decide what is in their best interest.[4] The DPRK has never been shy about admitting that the primary role of its media is to indoctrinate. *Nodong Sinmun*, the party newspaper, calls the press a "sharp ideological weapon dedicated to staunchly defending and safeguarding the leader" and urges the press to "dye the whole society one color, the color of the revolutionary ideology of the great leader."[5]

The Kim regime places great faith in its media's ability to transform people from what it calls "egotists" into socialists loyal to the Kim family. Countless articles have emphasized the important role the media play in molding people's socialist outlook, with several themes predominating: obey the leader and the party without question, protect the leader with your life, adhere to the military-first policy by supporting the army, be optimistic about the country's future, work hard for the good of the community and country, do not be tempted by capitalism and its products, be proud of Korean culture and hold to the traditional ways, hate the Americans and Japanese, and if you are a bureaucrat or manager, get out of your office and go among the people to lead them by setting a good example. Yet, despite this flood of propaganda, the North Korean people have actually become less socialistic and more capitalistic with each passing year. It is probably not wrong to infer from the media's repetition of propaganda themes that their opposite is closer to reality: people do not obey the leader and the party when they can get away with it, they harbor ill will toward the military, they work for themselves rather than the community, and they are mightily attracted to the products and pleasures of capitalism. The only propaganda themes that seem to strike a chord are nationalism and hatred of the Americans and Japanese.

The North Korean press publishes little news about the outside world except items that reflect badly on other countries—the better to foster the belief that North Korea is the finest place in the world to live. Any foreign news story that does make it into the media is likely to be brutally short. For example, following a visit to Pyongyang by a former official of the Clinton administration, North Korean domestic radio broadcast this item: "Bill Richardson, governor of the state of New Mexico of the United States, and his party left Pyongyang on 20 October. They were seen off at the airport by functionaries of the relevant sector."[6] Why Richardson was in Pyongyang, how long he had been there, and whom he was talking to—none of that is supposed to be the business of the North Korean public.

Nor are the people given any substantive information about their own leaders and government. Promotions, demotions, and dismissals of officials are rarely mentioned, and when a top official dies, the news report is usually limited to a few lines noting that Kim Jong-il sent a wreath to the funeral. It is unusual to run across a story about accidents or crimes inside North Korea. Even during the period from 1995 to 1998, when hundreds of thousands or even millions of people were dying of starvation, no casualty statistics were published in the press, which simply observed that the country was experiencing a "food problem." Occasionally, the media will mention a domestic tragedy if it has produced a hero worthy of emulation. For example, *Nodong Sinmun* published an article titled "Phoenixes Who Overcame Difficulties with Faith" about how, in a mine disaster in October 2006 (the report coming two months after the fact), two miners survived and "overcame the crisis of death with ideology and faith" by singing "Where Are You General, for Whom We Yearn?" and reciting the poem "Please Forgive."[7] It should be added, however, that the media seem to be opening up in recent years. For example, the press covered the 2007 summer floods quite extensively—although, of course, the damage was attributed to an act of nature rather than to mistakes the party has made in managing the environment.

Like all organizations in North Korea, the print and electronic media operate under the dual control of the party and the government. Party officials vet items for broadcast or publication carefully because if a published item reflects badly on the leader or the party, those responsible for its publication may lose their jobs and possibly even be thrown into prison. According to a former scriptwriter at the Korean Central Broadcasting Station (KCBS), news writers and editors receive monthly topic lists from the Korean Workers' Party's (KWP) Propaganda and Agitation Department. Before being published, news items are submitted to an in-house review panel and then sent to the director of the news organization. From there, stories work their way through layers of officials until they reach the General Bureau of Publications Guidance and the appropriate news department of the Propaganda and Agitation Department. Editorials and important commentaries are in all likelihood submitted to Kim Jong-il for his personal review and approval. Owing to this extensive review process, news articles may not be timely, but they do provide a reliable glimpse into what the authorities are thinking. Foreign news items are sometimes published days or even weeks after the events they report, giving the North Korean propagandists time to evaluate the events and decide how best to present them. According to a former North Korean journalist, most newspaper copy is submitted a month ahead of time, and over half of the typesetting is completed several days before publication.[8]

For the domestic audience, North Korea has four major newspapers, one AM radio station, and three television stations. Each province also publishes a daily newspaper comparable to the capital city's *Pyongyang Daily*. The only news agency is the Korean Central News Agency (KCNA), whose employees gather international and domestic news, process it for publication in the domestic press, and publish some of it internationally in English and other languages, for example on the KCNA website.[9] At least until the mid-1990s, about a thousand top cadres received *Chamgo Tongsin* ("reference news"), a briefing publication that provided its readers with foreign news and current issues to think about.

Newspapers

The DPRK's premier news outlet is *Nodong Sinmun* ("daily worker"), the six-page organ of the KWP's Central Committee published five days a week. Its editor in chief, who holds the rank of a cabinet minister, oversees a staff of six hundred reporters and editors.[10] *Nodong Sinmun* articles, especially the editorials and commentaries, signal the direction of the Kim regime's thinking. The paper usually takes the lead in breaking stories and presenting viewpoints; on the same day or soon thereafter, radio and television stations and KCNA quote articles from the party newspaper. The newspaper has twelve departments, with names like Propaganda for Juche Theory, Party History Cultivation, Revolution Cultivation, Party Life, Industry, Agriculture, International, South Korea, and, of course, Editorials.

Page 1 of the paper is largely devoted to articles and photographs about the Kims (these days, mostly Kim Jong-il), including reports of Kim's on-the-spot guidance. Editorials and commentaries also appear on the first page. At the very top, to the left and right of the newspaper banner, one-sentence teachings of Kim Il-sung and Kim Jong-il are displayed. Page 2 is similar in content to page 1, with more articles and photographs about the Kims. Page 3 is the domestic news page, with stories about organizations that have reached or exceeded their production goals, examples of heroic workers, and descriptions of how the party's correct policies are being realized throughout the country. Page 4 features more domestic news, along with articles on arts and culture. In terms of news content, the last two pages of *Nodong Sinmun* are of the greatest interest to readers, although even here the articles are chosen for their propaganda value. Page 5 is the pan-Korean or Korean-unification page, and page 6, the international page, features articles praising North Korea and criticizing other countries. *Nodong Sinmun* has no sports, business, or comics pages.

To provide a flavor of what passes for news in North Korea, here are article topics for *Nodong Sinmun* for a random date, December 18, 2003:

Page 1:
- Kim Jong-il thanks managers and workers for supporting the army.
- People in various countries study the classic works of Kim Jong-il.
- The DPRK's achievements in various fields are celebrated.

Page 2:
- Kim Jong-suk's development of national handicrafts is celebrated (she is the mother of Kim Jong-il).
- Representatives from various countries lay wreaths at the statue of Kim Jong-suk on the occasion of her eighty-sixth birthday.
- Supreme People's Assembly president Kim Yong-nam sends greetings to the president of Niger on its founding anniversary day and to the king of Bahrain on its founding day.

Page 3:
- Achievements of various organizations are presented under the heading "Let Us Endlessly Create Production Upsurges with the High Spirit of Victors."

Page 4:
- Articles and photographs highlight the achievements of Samjiyon County under the heading "People's Paradise That Sings of the Creation of a New World."
- A film about Kim is shown to foreign diplomats in Pyongyang on the occasion of the twelfth anniversary of Kim's appointment as the Korean People's Army (KPA) supreme commander and the eighty-sixth anniversary of the birth of Kim Jong-suk.
- The Russian ambassador hosts a New Year's friendship party.
- A friendly gathering of North Korean and Chinese youth league representatives is held.
- The DPRK's ambassador to Iran pays its president a farewell visit.

Page 5:
- A special article celebrates the theme of *Uriminjokkiri* ("our race only").
- Republic of Korea (ROK) news is reviewed, including ROK criticism of President George W. Bush's diplomatic policies.
- Japan's Chongnyon (the North Korean association in Japan) is praised for its efforts in nationalist education.

Page 6:
- A special article warns against the dangers of war presented by the relocation of U.S. forces in the ROK.
- A commentary explains why a DPRK nuclear deterrent is the only way to prevent war.
- A spokesperson for the foreign ministry sees evil designs behind the passage of the U.S. sanctions law against Syria.
- The Cuban army minister vows to crush U.S. provocations.
- Developing countries are making progress in science and technology.
- An article headline warns, "We Should Be Cautious of Japan Emerging as a Country of Aggression."[11]

Articles in *Nodong Sinmun* are written in the communist authoritarian style, with little effort to engage the reader's interest, although in recent years all the media are trying to become a bit more consumer friendly. Even though the paper is meant to be a vehicle for instruction and agitation, it fails on both counts because it is extremely boring. Those Koreans who have direct access to the paper (in contrast to those who are read a few of its articles during the daily newspaper-reading session at school and at work) ignore the first four pages. *Nodong Sinmun*'s circulation is nominally rated at a million copies, but newsprint shortages probably prevent the paper from reaching this circulation goal.

Nodong Sinmun prints the names, titles, and quotations of Kim Jong-il and his father in boldface, much like some Bibles print the words of Jesus of Nazareth in red ink. Newsprint with photographs of the Kims must never be torn or crumpled. In October 1997, North Koreans discovered a copy of *Nodong Sinmun* with a photograph of Kim Il-sung in the wastebasket of a dormitory where South Korean workers were staying while building the KEDO light-water nuclear reactor; as a consequence, they were confined to their quarters for several days.[12]

The government publishes several other newspapers of no more interest to the general reader than *Nodong Sinmun*. *Minju Choson* ("democratic Korea"), the paper of the government cabinet, informs readers about government policies and urges their implementation. *Pyongyang Sinmun* ("Pyongyang daily"), the Pyongyang city paper, carries more entertainment and cultural articles than *Nodong Sinmun*. The daily paper of the KPA is *Choson Inmingun Sinmun* ("Korean People's Army daily"), which prints information tailored to the needs of military personnel. And the daily paper of the Kim Il-sung Socialist Youth League is *Chongnyon Chonwi* ("youth vanguard"). Between them, the party, government, military, and youth papers cover just about all of the population.

Kulloja ("worker"), the party's theoretical journal, publishes explanations and justifications for party policies. *Kyongje Yongu* ("economic studies"), a quarterly journal explaining and justifying North Korean economic policies, also tries to teach its readers the rudiments of market economics and international trade on the theory that North Korea must be prepared to deal with nonsocialist economies until capitalism destroys itself and the world embraces socialism.

Difficult economic times have placed operating constraints on the news media. The quality of newsprint is poor, except in *Nodong Sinmun* and *Minju Choson*. Articles in the press allude to problems with getting newspapers to readers: "The post and telecommunications sector must make sure that the publications, including the official party newspaper, should be immediately distributed without delay."[13] In government offices, about ten people share one copy, and in factories and other workplaces, one copy is shared by thirty or forty people. Copies are also posted on the street and distributed to neighborhood leaders to serve as a basis for political discussion sessions. In 2003 the newspaper became available on the North Korean intranet, where cadres are urged to read it first thing in the morning in order to "learn about the party's intention and demands in a timely manner."[14]

The New Year's Joint Editorial

When Kim Il-sung was alive, he recorded a New Year's message that was broadcast on the radio and published in *Nodong Sinmun*. Since his death, the message has been replaced by a joint editorial that is not attributed to any individual. No item published in North Korea receives more attention from North Koreans or is read more carefully by foreign analysts than the annual New Year's editorial, which is comparable to the American president's State of the Union address. For weeks after its publication, the editorial is discussed in political sessions, and school children are required to memorize parts of it. Its composition involves some of the best writers in the country, and Kim Jong-il certainly provides guidance and criticism. Perhaps to show that Kim is above any single organization, even the party, the joint editorial is published simultaneously in the newspapers of the party, the military, and the youth organization. It is also read on the radio, although not by Kim Jong-il, who has never made a public speech.

For all the attention it receives, the editorial is pretty much the same from one year to the next. The title is meant to be shouted: in 2005, "Let the Whole Party and Army and All the People Unite as One in Mind and More Strikingly Demonstrate the Might of *Songun* [military-first politics]"; in 2006, "Make a Higher Leap Full of Great Ambition and Confidence"; in 2007, "Usher in a Great Heyday of *Songun* Korea Full of Confidence in Victory"; in 2008, "Let Us Glorify This Year of the 60th Anniversary of the Founding of the DPRK As a Year of Historical Turn That Will Go Down in the History of the Fatherland"; and in 2009, "Glorify This Year As a Year of a New Revolutionary Upsurge Sounding the General Advance."

The editorial begins by boasting of the progress made in the preceding year: In 2005: "Last year, *Juche* 93 [2004], was a year of worthwhile struggle in which a revolutionary offensive was conducted on three fronts: politics and ideology, anti-imperialism and military affairs, and economy and science—to make a breakthrough toward fresh success in the efforts to build a great prosperous powerful nation." In 2006: "Last year was a year of fruitful efforts and a year of great creation and changes." In 2007: "Last year was embroidered as a great year of victory and a year of upheaval when the dawn of a powerful socialist state broke." In 2008: "Last year was a year of proud victories in which the great vitality of our party's military-first revolutionary line was powerfully proven and great advances were made in the building of a prosperous and powerful fatherland." In 2009: "Last year was a year of historic turn which had written a chapter of brilliant victory in the proud 60-year annals of the DPRK." Of course, Kim Jong-il is given credit for all victories and accomplishments, as in, "These shining victories and successes made by our army and people last year are a shining fruition of leader Kim Jong-il's unquestioned leadership prestige and invincible political caliber."

The editorial then turns to the coming year, with predictions of even greater successes, building on the alleged firm foundations of the preceding year: In 2005: "*Juche* 94 [2005] is a worthwhile year which will witness a great turn in the Korean revolution and in the efforts to accomplish the cause of building a great prosperous powerful nation." In 2006: "New year *Juche* 95 [2006] is a year of general offensive that will make a great leap forward in the building of a great prosperous powerful socialist nation." In 2007: "The new year of 2007, *Juche* 96, is a year of great changes, a year which will usher in a new era of prosperity of military-first Korea." In 2008: "The new year, *Juche* 97, is a year of a magnificent struggle and an auspicious year in the history of the nation, in which a great turn will be brought about in the history of our fatherland and revolution." In 2009: "The new year, *Juche* 98 [2009], is a year of a new revolutionary surge in which all the people should launch a general offensive in response to the party's call to make a historic leap on all fronts in the building of a prosperous nation."

After the review and pep talk, the editorial presents the main theme for the new year. In 2005 and 2006 the theme was agriculture. In 2007, it was improving the people's standard of living and stepping up technological innovation. In 2008, it was, once again, boosting the people's standard of living, with a somewhat ominous emphasis on the need to "keep to socialism in its original form." In 2009, it was the need to recapture the spirit of the great socialist upswing in the economy of the 1950s. After discussing the main issue, the editorial turns to ideology and politics, urging the people to follow the dictates of the party and support the military. The next major topic is unification, followed by a brief discussion of the international situation, usually criticizing American attempts to intimidate North Korea.

The editorial's tone is upbeat and militant. Every year the claim is made that a foundation for success has been laid and now is the time to build on that foundation. The country is said to have reached a "turning point," after which things will get better. People are told that they have everything they need to achieve a brighter future, if only they will give "fuller play" to the correct policies laid down by Kim and the party. Unfortunately, every year turns out to be pretty much like the year before, with little or no economic progress. Consequently, people pay no more attention to the New Year's editorial than is absolutely necessary.

Radio, Television, and the Third Broadcasting System

For most North Koreans, televisions, especially color sets, are still luxury items. There may be only four million radios and a few million television sets in the entire country of twenty-three million people, although no statistics are available. In Pyongyang and other major cities, most households have a television; in the countryside, perhaps only one in ten or twenty do. Radios manufactured in North Korea have analog dials soldered to receive only the broadcast frequency of KCBS, which has transmitters throughout the country.

KCBS and Korean Central Television (KCTV), its companion television station, carry more domestic news and less international news than KCNA provides to the international audience. In addition to KCTV, which offers news and other programming on weekday evenings and during the weekend, Mansudae Television provides entertainment programs on weekends and holidays, and Korean Educational and Cultural Television broadcasts programs for three hours on weekdays and longer on weekends. The PAL television signal broadcast by North Korea (also used in Europe and China) is incompatible with the NTSC South Korean television signal (also used in the United States and Japan). For comparison purposes, here are the major news stories carried by KCBS and KCTV on December 18, 2003, the date for the preceding list of articles from *Nodong Sinmun*:

KCBS (eighteen-minute news cast)
- Kim thanks officials for planting trees and protecting historical relics.
- The twenty-fourth anniversary of Kim's work on "living in our own style" is celebrated.
- The works of Kim and his father are displayed at the *Juche* exhibition hall.
- New Kimilsungia and Kimjongilia greenhouses are built.
- People visit the Kim Jong-suk relic room at a museum on the occasion of her birthday.
- ROK authorities are denounced for their antireunification act of suppressing students.
- Japan's budget for a missile-defense program is denounced.

KCTV (twenty-nine-minute news cast)
- One of Kim Jong-il's books is published in Angola.

- Various countries, including Egypt, celebrate the eighty-sixth birthday of Kim Jong-suk and the twelfth anniversary of Kim Jong-il's appointment as KPA supreme commander.
- Kim thanks a boat crew for their accident-free work at Kumgang.
- People are shown listening to a lecture at the Historic Place of Revolution on the occasion of Kim Jong-suk's eighty-sixth birthday and Kim Jong-il's appointment as supreme commander.
- Archive footage shows on-the-spot guidance at a food institute given by Kim and his father.
- The winner of the Kim Il-sung poetry prize and his family are shown enjoying a "birthday table" of food sent by Kim Jong-il.
- A video shows progress in land rezoning work in North Hamgyong Province.
- A video shows progress in the construction of the Orangchon Power Plant.
- A video celebrates the year-end acceleration of production at the Nanam Coal Mine Machinery Complex.
- The operation of the Tokchon Chicken Plant is shown.
- Medical researchers at the Academy of Koryo Medicine talk about their recent achievements.
- A "meritorious" technician is shown working in a laboratory at the 5 October Automation Apparatus Plant.
- A visiting delegation of Vietnamese is shown paying their respects to the late Kim Il-sung and reviewing exhibits on display at the Kumsusan Memorial Palace.
- Representatives from various countries are shown laying wreaths at the statue of Kim Jong-suk on the occasion of her eighty-sixth birthday.
- The announcer claims that in 2003 the world's progressive people supported the DPRK's anti-U.S. policy.
- A DPRK foreign ministry spokesperson reports on the interest of various countries, including the Czech Republic, Russia, and China, in the resumption of the Six-Party Talks on the nuclear issue.[15]

Radio and television programming is not devoted exclusively to news, but it *is* mostly about politics in one way or another. Documentaries tend to be about the Kims. Interview and discussion shows highlight the virtues of Kim Jong-il's military-first politics. Children's stories and songs likewise provide political teachings. One can imagine who "The Boy General" is about. "Chodong and His Father" discusses "the need to assist the army," and "A

Boy Defeats Robbers" teaches that "one can find a way to beat any formidable enemy [for instance, the United States] and emerge victorious." Cartoon shows, including *Three Ant Brothers* and *The Clever Raccoon Dog*, try to impart the values of hard work. Since 2001, a few children's stories and cartoons from the West, such as episodes of *Tom & Jerry* and programs based on "Cinderella" and *Alice in Wonderland*, have appeared on North Korean TV, apparently in line with Kim Jong-il's instruction that people be cautiously exposed to information about the outside world.

Songs (or "paeans," as the press has been known to call them) extolling the virtues of Kim Il-sung include "Long Live Generalissimo Kim Il-sung," "Our Leader Is Always with Us," and "Song of the Sun Will Be Everlasting." And plenty of songs praise Kim Jong-il, including "We Will Death-Defyingly Defend the Nerve Center of the Revolution," "The General Is the Banner of Victory," "The General Leads the New Century," "Peerless Patriot General Kim Jong-il," and "We Will Display Victory While Flying the Supreme Commander's Flag." In addition to dominating the airwaves, these songs are sung at concerts and in schools, and children sing them (under the direction of the class leader) as they march to school in the morning.

North Korea's "third broadcasting system" is a wired network of speakers in homes, public buildings, and outdoor spaces. Third-broadcasting messages differ from those on radio and television largely in that they are tailored to specific locales and less concerned about promoting a positive image of the country. People are instructed about how to behave when a visiting foreigner is expected in the neighborhood, or they might be warned to be on the lookout for those responsible for a rash of local burglaries. The messages are sent out for about two hours a day, and the volume on home speakers can be turned down but not off, although electricity shortages and the general deterioration of North Korea's communication infrastructure have hampered the operation of the speaker system. In a tape of a town meeting smuggled out of the country in 2006, the mayor warns people that an official will be coming around to homes checking that the speakers are properly installed, and if residents do not admit the official, they will be suspected of hiding illegal radios, operating an illegal gambling den, or even of being spies.[16]

Intranet and Internet

Kim Jong-il is eager to have his people adopt the latest technology as a means of reviving the economy, although how people might actually get their hands on it remains a mystery. Perhaps only 5 percent of the population has access to a computer, and probably no more than a few thousand have access to the Internet. Thousands more use computers at schools and workplaces to log on to the *Kwangmyong* ("brightness") intranet, where they can retrieve information and communicate by e-mail. A 2001 article in *Nodong Sinmun* is purportedly written by an intranet user who does not forget to thank Kim Jong-il for this electronic miracle: "Filling the computer screen with this endless joy, I just want to write my first letter to the great mentor, our close parent, who has brought us all to the summit of modern civilization, carrying us in his bosom."[17]

North Korea is unable to manufacture its own computers because it lacks the technology to make critical components. Apart from manufacturing constraints, the international Wassenaar Arrangement forbids countries from exporting technology that could have military uses to North Korea, although some countries, most notably China, are lax in their export controls, and the North Korean residents of Japan seem to have been particularly helpful in transferring technology and equipment to North Korea over the years. Only about 10 percent of offices in North Korea have computers. Most elementary schools lack computers, but middle schools are likely to have a handful. Local colleges also have only a few, and a university may have a few dozen. Individuals who wish to purchase a home computer must apply for various permits, and the cost is far beyond what the average Korean can afford.

By 2002, fiber-optic cable connected North Korea's major cities, and the intranet operates on this network, overseen by officials of the State Security Department (SSD). So far as we know, the network is not connected to the Internet, which makes use of different telephone links, although a few portals allow intranet e-mails to be forwarded to the Internet. Kim Jong-il is probably the only person in the country who can surf the Web free of SSD monitoring. When U.S. Secretary of State Madeleine Albright visited Pyongyang in 2000, Kim gave her his e-mail address, although whether they communicated is not known. Some government administrative and economic organizations, as well as North Korean trading companies, maintain Web pages on the intranet, and the electronic version of *Nodong Sinmun* may be found there as well.

The ".kp" domain has been set aside for North Korea, but there are no servers in the country, so there are no ".kp" addresses. North Korea's "official" websites are located on servers in China, Japan, and Germany. Several dozen websites showcasing the Kim regime's ideology are sponsored by North Korea or by sympathetic groups and hosted on foreign servers.

North Korean scientific articles occasionally cite Internet addresses, which scientists may have accessed directly or by way of the intranet, and

North Korea is believed to have a robust computer-hacking program, which must function through the Internet. A former North Korean professor of computer studies claims that skilled North Korean hackers, trained at North Korea's top technical schools such as Mirim University and Kim Chaek University of Technology, are sent abroad by the military to work undercover in other countries, especially China.[18]

Because information and technology can be used against the regime as well as for the good of the country, Kim Jong-il can hardly afford to let the general public get their hands on such politically powerful tools. Moving information around on the North Korean intranet is safer for the regime than letting people go on the Internet. Even the communist leaders of China, who continue to try to censor what their people can access on the Internet, have resigned themselves to a large measure of exposure to the international community. The North Korean press complains about the alleged oppressiveness of the South Korean "puppet" regime, while inadvertently revealing just how much freedom South Koreans enjoy. For example, KCBS has reported that South Koreans are using Internet sites to protest the American military presence in South Korea. What must North Koreans think about their own level of technology and degree of freedom when they cannot even gain access to a computer, much less use it to protest against anything?

Books

For a country of its size and with its high literacy rate, North Korea publishes relatively few books, which is hardly surprising given the chronic paper shortage and the authorities' reluctance to put nontechnical written material into the hands of the people. Apart from technical works, most books, like newspapers, are unabashed instruments of propaganda. The most popular book topics are the life and teachings of Kim Il-sung and Kim Jong-il. In 2008, fourteen years after the Great Leader's death, the number of volumes of his collected works had reached seventy-four, and more were being released all the time.

Most foreign-language books are kept in special reserve sections in libraries and are available only to party cadres on a need-to-know basis. The Kim regime is particularly proud of the library at the Grand People's Study Hall in Pyongyang, but few ordinary Koreans spend any time there. When a French visitor asked how many volumes the study hall had, he was told thirty million. When he asked how many of the books were in the catalog, he was told twenty-five hundred.[19] So the number of volumes is presumably somewhere in that range. A German visitor to the study hall was told that the two Kims had written over 10,800 works, a figure that his Korean hosts stuck too under further questioning.[20] According to KCNA, Kim Jong-il performed "great ideological and theoretical exploits which ordinary people could hardly accomplish in all their life" by authoring more than fourteen hundred works ("treatises, talks, speeches, conclusions, and letters") during his four years as a student at Kim Il-sung University.[21]

Among the hundreds or thousands of books written about the Kims, *Collection of Legends of the Great Man* recounts "77 legends about the gifted intelligence, lofty outlook on the people, and noble traits displayed by leader Kim Jong-il."[22] Books in the socialist realism tradition include such titles as *Song of Humankind*, "based on the fact that President Kim Il-sung visited the Kangson Steelworks and called on its workers to bring about a great revolutionary upsurge in socialist construction," and *Arms*, which "shows the validity and vitality of the *songun* [military-first] politics pursued by leader Kim Jong-il."[23] Novels such as *Breath of Land* and *Swaying Abele* "depict farm and railway workers' efforts to implement the policies of the Korean Workers' Party."

An ongoing series of novels, including *Song of Desire for Reunification*, *Wealth*, and *40 Years in My Memory*, are based on the reminiscences of each of the sixty-three North Korean spies repatriated by the ROK government in 2000. These works purportedly show how these men "maintained their faith for scores of years in South Korea, undaunted by brutal torture, appeasement and deception, trusting only in Kim Il-sung and Kim Jong-il."[24] On their return to the North, the spies were given a hero's welcome and have been featured ever since in propaganda campaigns illustrating the loyalty of North Koreans. Unfortunately, the ROK government did not insist that the DPRK release any of the South Korean prisoners of war or abducted civilians that it has been holding for decades.

Films

North Koreans may not have access to many books, but they do like to go to the movies, whose primary function is to propagandize for the regime. Films are particularly well suited to a collectivist society because people watch them as a group, and for that matter, the films are produced not by individuals but by production companies, so both the production and consumption can be kept under the watchful eyes of the authorities.[25] Popular film themes include the adulation of the Kim family, the perennial conflict between socialism and capitalism, and the dangers posed by foreign culture.[26] Many films have historical anti-Japanese themes, with perhaps the most famous being the Kim Jong-il production from the late 1960s titled *Sea of Blood*, about a woman farmer who became a revolutionary and fought the Japanese colonialists in the 1930s. Another famous Kim film from that period is *Flower Girl*, about a peasant girl who receives a beating from a greedy landlord.

Korean propagandists say that Kim first showed an interest in films at the age of seven, when he supposedly commented that the snow in one movie looked too much like cotton.[27] A wall chart at the Korean Feature Film Studio outside of Pyongyang tallies 1,724 visits and 10,487 instructions made by Kim up to the year 1993.[28] Throughout the studio, large photos show Kim in the act of supervising, while much smaller photos show actors and directors at their work.[29] In his 450-page treatise on film titled *On the Art of the Cinema*, Kim covers all facets of filmmaking and emphasizes the importance of the director's role (presumably in life as well as in film).[30] Two of the book's chapters are titled "The Director Is the Commander of the Creative Group" and "The Quality of Acting Depends on the Director." As he took on more responsibilities for running the country beginning in the 1980s, Kim had less time to devote to the film industry, but his interest in film remained strong.

The North Korean film industry fell on hard times as the economy shrank, with film output declining to only about a half dozen major films per year in the 1990s, down from a full dozen in the 1980s. Multimillion-dollar film productions are now out of the question, and technology is so limited that films are routinely dubbed with sound after they have been shot. The poor production values and didactic quality of North Korean films goes a long way toward explaining why South Korean films smuggled into the country are so popular. The one bright spot in the film industry is animation: North Korean studios have established a good reputation for producing animated films on contract for the export market.

For want of anything more entertaining in the domestic market, the public likes melodramas-with-a-message in which individuals struggle against social and physical obstacles in order to follow the socialist path and in the process achieve their personal goals, including sometimes love. A modern example is the 1997 film *Myself in the Distant Future*, in which a lazy young man falls in love with a girl working on a construction brigade. The girl is not interested in the selfish suitor, and after her brigade has been disbanded, she returns to her village to serve the party as a farmworker. The young man follows her and, after failing to win her back on his own lazy merits, sees the light and invents a method to run farm tractors on wood instead of scarce gasoline. He performs a heroic deed with his wood-burning tractor, is awarded a medal, and finally gets the girl.[31]

Out-of-Home Media

North Korean buildings are plastered with hand-painted propaganda posters and banners that urge people to commit themselves to the *Juche* ideology and military-first politics and to be loyal to Kim Jong-il: "Let's Become Young Heroes in the Worthwhile Struggle to Glorify the *Songun* [Military-First] Era!"; "Let's Consolidate Our Political and Ideological Position Like Steel"; "All Working Class! Let's Vigorously Display the Example and Spirit of the DPRK Working Class of the Military-First Era!"; "Let the Functionaries Lead the Ranks Like the People's Army Commanders!" Other slogans address civic responsibilities: "Let's Plant Trees through the Entire Country"; "More of Our-Style Stockbreeding!"; "Let's Achieve Heroic Feats in the Construction of Hydroelectric Power Plants!"; "Let's Turn Our Villages into a Socialist Fairyland Where Crops Are Abundant!"

About 80 percent of the northern part of the Korean Peninsula is mountainous. This is bad for farming but good for rock carving. It has been estimated that over forty thousand characters (words and syllables) have been carved on rocks, especially in the scenic mountain regions around Mt. Kumgang and Mt. Paektu.[32] Although Koreans have a long tradition of rock carving, the propaganda cult carvings of the Kim regime did not begin to appear until around 1972 to celebrate Kim Il-sung's sixtieth birthday, and the initial carving project can probably be attributed to Kim Jong-il. Most slogans either praise or quote one of the three Kims. Carvings of Kim Il-sung's sayings are painted in red. In the Mt. Kumgang tourist area, some forty-five hundred characters are said to be carved on the jagged cliffs for which the mountains are famous. One of the most prominent of the carvings quotes Kim Il-sung: "'Kumgang is the celebrated mountain of Choson,' [signed] Kim Il-sung, September 27, 1947." The characters forming the words are twenty meters high and sixteen meters wide.[33] The phrase "Heaven-Sent Brilliant General Kim Jong Il" was carved in characters of similar size to honor Kim Jong-il's sixtieth birthday.[34]

Internal Documents

There exists a hidden universe of North Korean documents sent down from the party to provide lecture material at political study sessions. The internal documents, labeled "for internal use only" or "secret," are supposed to be collected after use, but thanks to the widespread corruption of cadres and the wide dissemination of the documents, it is hardly surprising that some of them end up in the hands of defector groups and foreign news media.

The value of these documents for foreign analysts lies in what they say about reality in North Korea. In a country supposedly without corruption, how is it that the fight against corruption is a perennial theme? Instructions on how to stamp out crime reveal much about its nature in North Korea, and lectures on preventing defections provide valuable information about how people defect. The lectures repeat what is presented in the mass media but cite social problems more concretely, whereas the newspapers tend to avoid any specific mention of problems in order to preserve the illusion that North Korea is a model society. The internal documents are also blunter in their language; for example, Americans and Japanese are routinely referred to as "bastards."

The documents follow a standard format. The first section introduces the issue to be discussed, the second explains why the issue is important, and the third discusses how to deal with the issue. Political instructors are urged to include local examples in order to relate the lecture to the audience's imme-diate concerns and experiences. Defectors report that people do not take these lectures seriously but are forced to attend and answer questions about them. It is highly likely that the instructors do not take the lectures seriously either, for it must be demoralizing to give the same lecture year after year, only to see the problems it addresses, such as the spread of capitalism, worsen rather than improve.

In lecture material distributed in 2002 titled "On Intensively Waging the Struggle to Smash the Capitalists' Ideological and Cultural Infiltration," marked "For Party's Internal Use Only," examples of capitalist infiltration include "reactionary and erotic" videotapes, American films, photo albums, picture books, novels, and Bibles. The videotapes in question are said to be circulated among friends and relatives, reproduced, sold, and rented in shops and in the markets, and viewed not just by individuals but by entire groups. The lecture also warns against possessing radio and television sets whose dials are not fixed to the authorized channels; singing South Korean songs; composing "bad songs and even replacing those elegant words of our great songs with vulgar and bad words" (presumably parodies); wearing "disheveled hair styles" and Western clothing styles, such as short skirts and "ugly pants that cling to the body"; using makeup in an "extremely grotesque manner"; getting divorced; engaging in superstitious behavior, including astrology and fortune-telling; believing in religion; and spreading false rumors.[35] This pretty much covers the gamut of the antisocialist "sins" prevalent in North Korean society.

In the introductory section to this same lecture, the "U.S. imperialists" are said to be intensifying their "slanders" of the DPRK with the help of the "Japanese reactionaries" and "South Korean puppet bastards." The lecture warns that "people will ideologically degenerate and weaken, cracks will develop in our socialist ideological position, and in the end, our socialism will helplessly collapse," as happened in the former Soviet Union and Eastern Europe. It is claimed that people and the party bureaucrats are "going ideologically slack and becoming habituated to the bourgeois ideological and cultural infiltration." Even bureaucrats in the Central Party organizations are said to be "infected with capitalist germs."

The lecture outlines four measures to "smash" this capitalist infiltration. First, North Koreans must "firmly equip [them]selves with the respected and beloved general's revolutionary ideology." The great irony here is that Kim Jong-il's behavior exemplifies almost all the cultural vices mentioned in the lecture, including viewing foreign films and divorcing one's wife. The lecture also advises people to follow the model of the Korean People's Army, where "bourgeois ideology and culture can never set foot." However, it is clear from other internal documents that exactly these same practices have taken root in the military—and the people surely know this.

The second means suggested to combat infiltration is to block the channels of communication by having radio dials fixed and asking people to surrender forbidden materials such as videotapes voluntarily. People are also told not even to look at such materials or to inquire about them because they may be seduced even by a glance. Instead, people should live "in a revolutionary manner." "Undisciplined life is a space where bourgeois ideology and culture can set foot and can spawn"—the North Korean version of the old Western saying "Idleness is the devil's playground."

A third anti-infiltration measure calls upon the assistance of party and government bureaucrats and police officers to be vigilant in finding and eliminating foreign materials: "Many of the functionaries have never seriously taken issue with it [the infiltration of foreign materials], even when capitalist elements [i.e., materials] were appearing around them; they pretended not to know about it." It is in fact widely recognized that many of these officials are avid consumers of forbidden materials and can best afford them.

Finally, the lecture warns that those caught with bourgeois cultural materials should be "punished in the name of the party and the law" (notice that the party comes before the law). According to Article 193 of the 2004 North

Korean criminal code, "Whoever, without authorization, brings in from other countries or makes or spreads music, dances, paintings, photographs, books, videos, or memory media such as CD-ROMs reflecting decadence, sexuality, and obscenity in content shall be sentenced to two years or less of labor discipline. In case the degree of culpability is serious, the offender shall be sentenced to four years or less of labor correction." Article 194 specifies two to five years of imprisonment for anyone listening to or viewing such materials. Article 195 provides for two to five years of imprisonment for listening to foreign broadcasts.

Three years after this lecture was written, the same themes were still being lectured on. A 2005 document titled "On Completely Destroying the Schemes of Our Enemies Who Are Spreading Exotic Lifestyles" condemns those who lead a "slovenly, corrupt, and rotten lifestyle," watch "unhealthy and decadent movies and recorded cassettes," and get divorced or live together outside of marriage. Koreans are urged to wear Korean-style clothing and traditional hairstyles, "make and eat lots of [Korean] food," and address each other with traditional greetings.[36] As a KCBS broadcast says, "When we sing, we have to sing with our own tunes, and when we dance, we have to dance with our own rhythm, and we have to positively preserve our national traditions and customs, including attire, food, and etiquette."[37]

Civilian and military lectures urge audiences to block illegal imports along the border with China. "Let Us Vigorously Wage the Struggle to Uproot Acts of Smuggling," dated 2003, blames smuggling on "South Korean puppet 'intelligence agent' bastards" who operate along the borders of "neighboring countries" (i.e., China) and instigate people to get involved.[38] The specific items to be on the lookout for are transistor radios, religious tracts, CDs, DVDs, and videotapes. Equally important is banning trade in the other direction that is used to pay for these items, including the selling of metals, agricultural products, and historical artifacts. Ironically, the lecture also warns against earning foreign currency by selling classified documents, such as "documents on our internal life, educational lecture plans, and state price tables." And so it came to be that the very lecture warning of smuggling out internal lectures was itself smuggled out.

The Stalin regime was famous for blaming the Soviet Union's troubles on "wreckers," said to be disloyal and traitorous individuals bent on ruining the socialist system (in most cases, they were simply people the regime did not like or trust). The Kim regime has its own designated wreckers, most notably, lazy bureaucrats who stay in their offices and give orders rather than go out among the people to lead them in Kim's teachings. Alleged spies also come in for some of the blame, although the mass media rarely refer to them because to do so would acknowledge that the North Korean police are not in complete control of society. A June 2004 SSD document titled "Mass Education Material for the Anti-Spy Struggle" provides a number of examples of people who have wrecked the system.[39] A certain "rascal" Ri Song-chun, formerly a trade bureaucrat, is blamed for being lured through sex while traveling overseas into the grasp of a CIA front organization and subsequently importing defective equipment and providing the CIA with economic intelligence. According to the lecture, Ri was "sternly judged by the people" for his crimes. Another "rascal," Kim Sun-chol, also a former trade bureaucrat, is accused of falling into a trap set by South Korean agents while on an overseas business trip and then embezzling his organization's funds. For his crimes he was "drastically punished."

In a country that has never publicly acknowledged a mine disaster, this internal lecture refers to two of them. In one case, a "spy who sneaked in [to the country] under the guise of a 'traveler on personal business'" is said to have bribed an electrician at a coal mine to sabotage a hoist, resulting in six coal cars crashing down into the mine. In another case, a spy "instigated impure elements" to steal an electric motor from a crane, and when the motor was replaced with manpower, an unspecified "commotion" occurred at the mine.

School Lessons

The North Korean regime has two goals for its education system: to make young people good communists and loyal supporters of the regime and to teach them the academic skills necessary to make North Korea a *kangsong taeguk* ("powerful country"). Article 43 of the DPRK constitution says that the goal of "socialist pedagogy" is to "raise the younger generation as resolute revolutionaries who wage struggles for the society and people and as new communist people equipped with knowledge, virtue, and physical health." The DPRK Education Law describes socialist education as "human remolding work" whose dual goals are to develop "independent consciousness" and "creative ability"—although these goals should not be taken literally.[40] "Independent consciousness" is better interpreted as subscribing to the Kim regime's *Juche* ideology, whose sole living interpreter is Kim Jong-il, and "creative ability" is limited to tackling economic problems without worrying the government about them.

Korea's Confucian society has always valued education deeply, and under the egalitarian communist system, eleven years of compulsory and free primary and secondary schooling boosted the literacy rate to almost 100 percent. North Korea's educational system was a great success in the 1950s and 1960s, but the quality of education has declined for at least three reasons. First, as the Kim cult developed over the years, studies of the Kim family began to crowd out standard academic subjects. Second, North Korea's self-imposed isolation has cut it off from foreign advances in knowledge. And third, economic problems have degraded the educational infrastructure. By the 1990s, the economy was in such bad shape that many students and even some teachers were skipping school in order to search for food. Meanwhile, school buildings fell into disrepair, and fuel was so scarce that classrooms were often unheated in the middle of winter.

After the collapse of European communism in the early 1990s, Kim Jong-il put greater weight on the importance of ideological training to prevent the younger generation of Koreans from imitating their European counterparts. Then, in 2001, it occurred to Kim that the only way to pull the country out of its economic slump was to remake the economy with modern technology, and to that end schools were urged to teach students the latest technology, which was unfortunately not available in North Korea. These two curricular areas, ideological indoctrination and technical training, remain the cornerstones of North Korean education. The priority given to ideological education makes sense from Kim's point of view because an economically successful North Korea without the Kim regime is of absolutely no interest to him. Better that people be poor and under his thumb than well-off and self-sufficient. Defectors have estimated that between 40 and 80 percent of school time is spent on ideological lessons, although since the 1990s more emphasis has been placed on science and technology and less on ideology. In elementary school, students learn about the lives and alleged virtues and accomplishments of Kim Il-sung, Kim Jong-il, and his mother, Kim Jong-suk. As children get older, they study the principles of communism and *Juche*; in college, they study *Juche* economics, *Juche* literature, and such. As an example of what teachers are taught, here are the titles of the first ten articles in the journal *Kodung Kyoyuk* ("higher education") for August 2006:

- "In the Days of the Military-First Revolutionary Leadership: While Leading to Be Always Faithful to the Cause of the Leader's Immortality"
- "The Great Leader Comrade Kim Il-sung Is Always with Us"
- "The Immortal Achievement Engraved in the Development of Educational Work at Technical Schools"

- "Introduction to a Military-First Animal: The Korean Bear"
- "In Order to Realize Kim Il-sung's Greatness with One's Heart"
- "Explaining in Depth Even a Single Piece of Educational Data"
- "On the Basis of Highly Practical Educational Data"
- "With the Faith of Sure Victory and Optimism Possessed by the Anti-Japanese Revolutionary Fighters"
- "Legend of a Great Man: Amazing Prophecy"
- "Introduction to a Military-First Animal: The Squid"[41]

Despite the regime's insistence that capitalism is evil and doomed to be replaced by communism, a few students are exposed to capitalist ideas to prepare them to do business with foreigners. As early as 1996, Kim Il-sung University offered a few lectures on capitalism—originally taught by professors visiting from North Korean–affiliated universities in Japan.[42] In recent years, North Korean students have also been sent abroad in small groups to study capitalism, for example, at Chinese universities. Students have also been sent to universities in Western countries, including several hundred to the United States. Syracuse University, for example, has had an ongoing exchange program in computer sciences with North Korea's Kim Chaek University of Technology.

It is difficult to say exactly how much ideological education students receive because academic subjects are suffused with ideology and the worship of the Kim family. The first songs students learn are songs of praise for the Kims. In history class, they study the military victories of the Kims. In math class, they work on problems about how many American soldiers North Korean soldiers can kill. In art classes, they draw pictures of the Kim family home. A reading lesson from a first-year book goes like this:

> I want . . .
> I want to be a KPA soldier
> To defend our motherland.
> I want to be a KPA soldier.
> I want . . .
> I want to be a hero soldier
> For our great general.
> I want to be a hero soldier.[43]

Another lesson shows little children gleefully playing with a remote-controlled toy tank:

Mini-tank advances,
Our tank advances,
Crushing American bastards,
Mini-tank advances.

Children have one year of preschool, four years of elementary school, and six years of senior middle school. The school year starts in April, and a typical school day begins as students assemble on street corners at 7 a.m. and march off to school behind their homeroom leader. The first half hour of school is devoted to listening to the teacher read the news or present political messages—the same activity their parents are participating in at work. Classes begin at 8 a.m., with a lunch break at noon. Elementary school children do not attend classes in the afternoon, but middle school students have classes until 3 or 4 p.m. In better times, children brought lunch boxes containing rice and vegetables, but today some students are lucky if they can bring a cupful of corn kernels.

Like adults, children are kept busy with group activities. After school, they perform school and community service, and once or twice a week, they participate in the children's version of political-criticism sessions, where they write down "mistakes" they have made and indicate how they will make their lives better. Children also participate in group sports activities, as do adults. Gymnastics is highly developed and showcased in mass displays in Pyongyang. Soccer, basketball, and table tennis are played outdoors at schools and in parks when the weather is warm; in the winter, ice skating is popular. Adults also enjoy traditional Korean folk dancing. All of these activities can be pursued with a minimum of equipment and facilities. Sports like tennis, bowling, and skiing are reserved for the wealthy, who have access to special facilities and equipment.

In line with the regime's 2002 economic self-sufficiency policy, it has become the responsibility of students, their families, and teachers to provide school supplies, repair school buildings, and bring wood or coal, if any is available, to heat the classrooms. In addition, the government requires that schools contribute quotas of recycled goods, such as metal and rubber, and locally sourced goods, such as mushrooms and seafood. Raising rabbits for their fur and meat is also a required task for many students; those who cannot provide, say, their quota of rabbit skins are supposed to bring money instead, and students who do not fill their quotas are publicly criticized. Older students are sent to rural areas to help with rice transplanting and harvesting. Students in Pyongyang are called upon to participate in gymnastic displays, parades, and mass rallies.

Due to a chronic paper shortage, most students share textbooks, which are often printed on *osari* paper made out of cornhusks. The print is difficult to read, and *osari* notebooks are difficult to write in. The school must purchase other educational supplies, such as computers, after conducting a money-earning drive. Students who want special attention or recommendations to college are expected to provide gifts to teachers and administrators in the form of money, food, cigarettes, and clothing.

In each district, students who show promise in science and mathematics are selected to attend special senior middle schools, known as the "number one" or "first" schools, where they will be prepared for advanced study. Knowing the reputation of universities as breeding grounds of dissent, the Kim regime keeps careful watch over its students, requiring them to engage in the usual extracurricular activities, including military training and political self-criticism sessions. Mandatory labor assistance (for example, on farms) may take them away from their studies for three to four months a year. North Korean university education is highly regimented; after all, the goal is for students to become productive members of Kim's socialist society, and in this sense college students are already employees or warriors of the regime, although most do not see themselves in this way. North Korean university students probably make up the most liberal segment of society, but they are also among the most privileged and must protect this status by behaving appropriately. Like soldiers, students are prohibited from marrying, and also like soldiers, they resort to secret love affairs.

University faculty members work under the watchful eye of the government and the party. A German professor who taught for a year at the prestigious Kim Il-sung University said she found little evidence of independent thinking among her students, who spent about half of their class time on ideological studies. Professors were required to obtain official approval for every lecture they delivered, and the German professor was not able to strike up a social relationship with any of her North Korean colleagues or visit any of their apartments.[44]

Unauthorized Sources of Information

If Kim Jong-il had his way, North Koreans would have absolutely no access to foreign sources of information, which compete with and contradict the official propaganda. It is a criminal offense to listen to foreign radio broadcasts, view foreign videotapes, or read foreign newspapers, magazines, or books. Even engaging in conversation with a foreign visitor can get a North

Korean into trouble. But the Kim regime does not have complete control over the information environment. When foreign radios are brought into the DPRK, they must be registered at the local police station and then taken to the local communications office, where the dial is soldered to the frequency of KCBS. Inspectors make surprise visits to households to check that the dials on their radios remain fixed, because for just a few dollars, a freelance electrician can unfix them. North Koreans returning from overseas sometimes discard their imported radios rather than live under a cloud of suspicion, or they bring home two radios, hiding one and letting the authorities fix the dial of the other. The government also tries to jam foreign radio broadcasts, but jamming is never entirely successful and in any case requires large amounts of electricity. During the Cold War, the Soviet Union reportedly employed ten thousand technicians to drown out foreign broadcast frequencies, an effort that required twice as much electricity as all the foreign stations were using to target the Soviet Union.[45] Television signals travel shorter distances than radio signals, but residents of Pyongyang can sometimes receive South Korean television broadcasts as long as they use (illegal) foreign-made television sets.

Voice of America (VOA) and Radio Free Asia (RFA) broadcast to North Korea on several frequencies. According to its charter, VOA "will present the policies of the United States clearly and effectively, and will also present responsible discussions and opinion on these policies." VOA, known in North Korea as Sori Bangsong ("radio voice"), broadcasts in English and fifty-two languages, including Korean, with programs originating in Washington, D.C. As of early 2009, VOA programs were being transmitted to North Korea for five hours a day on AM and shortwave frequencies (from 4 a.m. to 6 a.m. and 9 p.m. to midnight, local time), and VOA also hosts a website in Korean. VOA programming includes world news, U.S. headline news, correspondents' reports, editorials, news about Koreans in the United States, health news, economic news, an English lesson, and stories from North Korean defectors.

Radio Free Asia, like Radio Free Europe/Radio Liberty (beamed at Europe, central Asia, and Russia), is intended to function as a surrogate radio station that broadcasts information domestic Asian stations neglect to air.[46] The International Broadcasting Act of 1994, under which RFA was created, charges its radio broadcasting stations with the mission to "provide accurate and timely information, news and commentary about events in the respective countries of Asia and elsewhere, and to be a forum for a variety of opinions and voices within Asian nations whose people do not fully enjoy freedom of expression." Programming originates from Washington, D.C., with transmitters in about a dozen locations in Asia and Europe. As of early 2009, RFA was broadcasting to North Korea for five hours a day in AM and shortwave, from 6 a.m. to 7 a.m. and midnight to 4 a.m. A typical hour's programming includes world news, commentary, features, book reading, interviews, and an English lesson; like VOA, RFA has a Korean-language website.

The ROK public broadcasting system, Korean Broadcasting System (KBS), runs Social Education Broadcasting (Sahoe Kyoyuk Pangsong), which formerly beamed antiregime programs into North Korea. However, since the advent of the Kim Dae-jung administration in 1998, broadcasts hostile to the Kim regime have been banned. In 2004 KBS adopted new policies for its stations, making Social Education Broadcasting a "national network channel" whose purpose is to foster national reconciliation rather than broadcast news reports critical of North Korea.[47] At least up to 2007, it appears that the ROK government operated two "gray" (disguised source) radio stations broadcasting to the North, Echo of Hope (Huimangui Meari Pangsong) and Voice of the People (Inminui Sori Pangsong), but the government does not comment on them.[48]

Several other radio stations specifically target the North Korean people. The Korean station of Far East Broadcasting (known to Koreans as Kukdong Pangsong) is operated by a nondenominational Christian organization that broadcasts in 150 languages, including Korean, from thirty-two transmitters around the world.[49] Radio Free North Korea (Free NK or Chayu Pukhan Pangsong) began regular shortwave broadcasting in early 2006 and by early 2009 was on the air five hours a day. Operated by defectors, the website's offices have come under pressure from a minority of South Koreans for "obstructing" Korean reconciliation. The North Korean government strongly objects to the broadcasts, claiming that they violate the June 15, 2000, agreement signed at the inter-Korean summit talks that calls for Korean reconciliation. Radio Free Chosun also began broadcasting in 2006, with ninety minutes of shortwave broadcasts daily as of early 2009. Open Radio for North Korea, which also began regular shortwave broadcasts in 2006, lets members of the public, including a consortium of university radio stations under the name Broadcasting without Borders, air messages to North Korea.[50] It has been reported that all three stations are financially supported in part by U.S. government money channeled through Washington's private, nonprofit National Endowment for Democracy.[51]

In a February 2003 survey of 103 defectors conducted by the KBS Broadcasting Institute, 87 percent of respondents said they had listened to or knew about KBS's Social Education Broadcasting; 6 percent listened to Far East Broadcasting and 2 percent to Radio Free Asia. Some 40 percent reported listening to the KBS station once or twice a week, and the same proportion said they listened every day. Asked how they learned about KBS broadcasts, 50 percent said they discovered the station by accident, whereas 15 percent said the station was recommended by others. North Korean listeners liked "information about the ROK" most about the station.[52] Somewhat surprisingly, a similar survey conducted in 2005 found lower exposure to South Korean media: 24 percent of this sample reported being exposed to foreign media, with the most popular medium being radio and the most popular radio stations being Social Education Broadcasting (9 percent) and Radio Free Asia (3 percent).[53]

On July 31, 2003, the DPRK government closed down its "black" radio station, Voice of National Salvation, which had been broadcasting programs in the South Korean dialect since 1970 (a black station is disguised to appear as if it is broadcasting from the country of its target audience, in this case, South Korea). The stationed signed off with the following words:

> Our nation is now welcoming the 15 June era of reunification [referring to the June 2000 Korean summit meeting] in which the fellow countrymen will become one under Great General Kim Jong-il's military-first politics based on love for the country and people. . . . The North side, on the occasion of the 15 August Independence Day, proposed to stop all broadcasts that slander the other party. . . . The Editorial Bureau of the Voice of National Salvation, while extending full support to, as well as fully sympathizing with, the North's proposal, in response to such a proposal, inform all of you that we will actively and totally end our broadcast starting 1 August. From the bottom of our hearts, we extend our thanks to all of you who gave unsparing support to our broadcast and earnestly enjoyed listening to it and wish that greater results are seen in the future struggle. Good-bye, everyone.[54]

The DPRK asked the ROK government to make a corresponding gesture by ending broadcasts aimed at the North, although North Korea's Voice of Korea, formerly known as the Pyongyang Broadcasting Station or Radio Pyongyang, continues to broadcast propaganda targeted at the South Korean audience. The North Korean request was widely interpreted as a sign that the Kim regime was increasingly concerned about outside information reaching the North Korean people, especially in the wake of U.S. propaganda attacks on Iraq and calls in the United States to increase RFA broadcasts to North Korea. The Kim regime also realized that Internet sites provide a better medium for propaganda aimed at South Korea's computer-savvy younger generation.[55] Pursuant to its National Security Law, the ROK government has occasionally attempted to prevent its citizens from visiting these pro–North Korean websites, but the attempts are largely futile.

A good indication of the threat posed by international radio to the Kim regime can be found in North Korean press comments. Although the press occasionally complains about VOA, Pyongyang's reaction to RFA is altogether harsher. The North Korean people are told that in the former Soviet Union and Eastern Europe, thanks to Radio Free Europe, "large numbers of people, such as the youth . . . were imbued with illusions about capitalism," resulting in the collapse of communism and a worse life for everyone.[56] The United States stands accused of attempting to "disintegrate and transform us internally through shoving in numerous pocket size radios on the one hand and on the other hand through airing Radio 'Free Asia' programs in the Korean language day and night," thereby "falsely trumpeting the temporary difficulty we are experiencing due to natural disasters as if our system itself has 'huge shortcomings' or 'problems.'"[57]

Regardless of the warnings issued to them by their government, North Koreans continue to listen secretly to foreign radio broadcasts. Foreign-made videos on tape and disk smuggled in from China are now widely available on the black market. Pornographic videos make up some of this trade, but videos of South Korean television dramas are even more popular, and few people see anything wrong with watching them. The dramas are enjoyed for the stories they tell and for the scenes of South Korean life they offer. People pass them around and watch them at home behind closed doors. Those caught viewing or possessing foreign videos have their video equipment confiscated and are typically sentenced to a few days or weeks of labor "reeducation," although the punishment can be more severe for repeat offenders. Payment of a bribe to the police is usually sufficient to avoid any punishment at all, and the police keep the videos for their own viewing pleasure. Members of the North Korean elite class, supposedly the core supporters of the Kim regime, are the most likely to listen to foreign broadcasts and watch foreign media because they have the money to buy radios and televisions, and equally importantly, they can afford to bribe the police if they are caught.

Foreign communications reach North Korea in unconventional ways. Through the 1990s, some eight hundred loudspeakers along the ROK's side of the Demilitarized Zone broadcast music and political commentary across the border, targeted primarily at North Korean soldiers. Messages were also shown on a hundred giant electric signboards, the largest of which could be seen for a distance of fifteen kilometers. The North had its own speakers and signboards, but they were less effective, especially as the electricity shortage became severe in the 1990s. In 2004, the ROK government responded positively to the DPRK's proposal that both sides discontinue border broadcasts and signboard communication, although many South Koreans considered this a bad deal because the South was arguably winning the propaganda battle.

Another unconventional communication channel formerly used by the ROK government to target the North is the balloon drop. During the Cold War, the government would send up flights of small balloons to drift over the North carrying leaflets and small consumer goods such as candy and nylon stockings. In recent years, private human rights and missionary groups in South Korea have taken to flying these balloons, dropping hundreds of thousands of anti–Kim Jong-il leaflets along with small radios, small Bibles, food packets, nonprescription medicine, items of clothing, and cash. One group claimed to have sent two hundred large balloons with over a half million leaflets in 2007 alone.[58] The South Korean police often try to prevent balloon flights, although it does not appear that they have a legal right to do so. The ROK's unification ministry explains, "Domestic law does not ban such activities, but we urge them [South Korean activists] to stop immediately because they may strain the inter-Korean relationship."[59] In the past, North Korea sent its own balloons into the sky to drop pamphlets on South Korea, and some of these balloons have drifted to Japan. In the mid-1990s, balloons with timer devices and vials of harmless liquid drifted over Japan, presumably from North Korea.[60]

North Koreans can also learn about the outside world from the thousands of Korean and Chinese Korean traders who regularly cross the northern border. Information also comes from conversations with tourists, whose numbers have increased in recent years, although for the most part the tourists are kept well away from ordinary North Koreans. As inter-Korean relations have warmed, the number of South Koreans allowed into the North has increased dramatically. According to the unification ministry, between 1989 and 2005 a total of 168,498 South Koreans visited the North, not counting those on group tours to the Mt. Kumgang reservation.[61] During the same period, 5,243 North Koreans visited the South, all on official business.

At Mt. Kumgang, tourists can converse only with tour guides, who are trusted party members or Koreans from China, and these conversations must be conducted with great care to avoid violating DPRK government rules that prohibit remarks critical of North Korea. In June 2000 a South Korean housewife conversing with a North Korean forest ranger said that just as she was enjoying her tour at Mt. Kumgang, the ranger might enjoy life in South Korea after reunification. Apparently, the suggestion that a North Korean might one day want to visit or live in South Korea is considered a serious offense, and she was arrested for spying and detained for several days while her six-year-old son had to return to South Korea without her. After undergoing stressful interrogation and threats of a long prison term and receiving the death penalty, she was released.[62]

How Information Travels

A brief summary of communication flows in North Korea might look like this: most communications from the outside world are blocked, communications from the leaders to the people are ignored as much as possible, communications from the people to their leaders are not to be trusted, and communications among the people are restricted.

It is difficult to get a sense of the nature of personal communication in North Korea's relatively closed society. Because of security restrictions and infrastructure problems, most communication is face-to-face. Mail is easily examined by the authorities, and ownership of private telephones is limited to upper-level cadres and wealthy traders. There are no reports of anything like the samizdat that existed in the Soviet Union and Eastern Europe during the communist era.

The Kim regime has always viewed telephones with suspicion. It is not known how many telephones there are in the North; a 1997 estimate put the number at five per one hundred people. In the entire country there is only one telephone book, which is a classified document marked "secret," the better to keep people from learning about the structure of their government and society. A copy of the phone book's 2002 edition, acquired by a South Korean human rights organization, listed forty thousand numbers of organizations and government-owned businesses but no private numbers. Home phones cost the equivalent of about twenty years of wages for the average North Korean, so when people need to make a call, they line up at public phone booths. In the countryside, they can go to a local government communications office and make a call after presenting personal identification and a small deposit. In Pyongyang and a few other big cities, the telephone exchanges are automated, but in many places in the countryside, people have to go through switchboard operators. In 2005 it was reported that the government had blocked 90 percent of North Korea's 970 international land lines, leaving only a few for use by foreigners and government offices.

The mobile phone revolution, which swept South Korea in the 1990s, got off to a slow start in North Korea—and then faltered. The Ministry of Posts and Telecommunications, in a joint venture with a division of Thailand's Loxley Pacific Company, began cellular phone service in August 2002, employing the GSM standard used in China and the European Union, not the CDMA standard used in South Korea and North America. A year later, news reports out of South Korea said that Loxley was curtailing its expansion due to lack of demand. Cell phone service was extremely expensive by North Korean standards. The handset and initial subscription reportedly cost over $1,000, whereas the average North Korean worker brings home just a few dollars a month.

The government banned all cell phones in May 2004, although its reason for doing so is not entirely clear. There is much speculation that the ban was a response to the Yongchon railway explosion that just missed Kim Jong-il's private train as it returned from China. If it was an assassination attempt, perhaps the explosion was detonated by a cell phone. The government confiscated all the phones it could find, and the ban continued into 2008.[63] In May 2008, Orascom Telecommunications, a subsidiary of a large Egyptian conglomerate that has signed several investment contracts with North Korea, launched another GSM cell phone service, and cell phones began appearing once again in 2009.[64]

The first people in North Korea to use cell phones, as far back as 1997, were Chinese traders working in North Korea near the border, where they could receive signals from Chinese cell towers. The use of these Chinese cell phones has increased over the years, despite the North Korean cell phone ban. Chinese lend or rent the phones to North Koreans with whom they are doing business, and illegal businesses provide cell phones to North Koreans who want to talk with relatives in China or South Korea. The North Korean security services try to track down these phones by using spies and electronic equipment, and they sometimes succeed, although payment of small bribes usually keeps cell phone users out of jail.

With severe economic and legal restrictions on travel and poor telephone service, North Koreans have few ways to communicate with each other except by word of mouth. Train passengers are said to be an excellent source of information and rumor because their anonymity provides them a measure of safety. Where only two people are gathered, some freedom of communication is possible, because if one person reports to authorities that his interlocutor said something that could be construed as "counterrevolutionary," the other can always deny it—unless the reporter is an undercover agent. Among three or more people, a measure of paranoia sometimes motivates listeners to report disloyalty to the authorities before they in turn are reported upon by the other parties to the conversation. The security services employ hundreds of thousands of informants (mostly recruited on a temporary basis) to report on their comrades. North Koreans believe that as many as one out of ten or twenty citizens is reporting to the police at any given time. Parents must even be careful about what they say in front of their children, who are sometimes induced by overzealous teachers to report on their home life. Despite these constraints, news, rumors, and even indirect criticism of the Kim regime make the rounds, with a few people paying the price for their loose lips but most escaping any serious consequences.

Media Impact

Gaining access to information is one thing; interpreting it is something else. People screen incoming information to keep from being overwhelmed, especially when the information challenges their current beliefs. The screening process involves selective exposure, selective attention, selective understanding, and selective remembering. The more committed an individual is to current beliefs, the more rigorous the screening process. Consider how this might work for a typical North Korean who encounters information coming from outside the country.

Because the Kim regime is highly selective about what information it allows its people to receive from outside, the information that *does* get in easily makes it through the personal information filter of selective exposure. Nor is selective attention likely to be a significant second-stage barrier in North Korea's communication-deprived society because outside information is so scarce that people actively seek it out and pay attention to it. Selective interpretation, on the other hand, may prevent information from being correctly understood. North Korean propaganda has consistently taken the line that the United States is doing all it can to subjugate the North Korean people. Even American foreign aid is depicted as a kind of psychological operation. North Koreans who accept this viewpoint will be inclined to interpret any information coming from the United States and other capitalist countries as "imperialistic" propaganda delivered with an ulterior motive.

Such skepticism about U.S. intentions brings into relief two important and related issues in communication and persuasion: latitude of acceptance and communicator credibility. A communication is most readily believed when it is neither too different from nor too similar to the audience's current attitudes and experience.[65] If it is too similar, the new information is received with little thought and has little impact, falling well within the latitude of acceptance. If it is too different, the new information is rejected as implausible or incomprehensible, falling within the latitude of rejection. The width of these latitudes varies for each audience segment and even for each individual at different times and on different issues. A plausible hypothesis is that, having been for so long isolated and subjected to hostile anti-American propaganda, the North Korean people have developed a wide latitude of rejection for foreign (especially American) communications. Consider the case of a North Korean who escaped to China, where he came across an article in a Russian journal telling about how Kim Il-sung had actually started the Korean War. "If the journal had not been from Russia, I would have believed the article was fabricated by South Korea. So I decided to go to South Korea to learn more."[66]

The Kim regime has taken extreme measures to prevent its people from receiving and believing foreign communications, especially those coming from the United States. As the country opens itself slightly to foreigners, it has erected a mosquito net of censorship to let some information in while preventing unwanted influences from turning people's heads. Another measure to combat outside communications is the use of "inoculation," whereby North Korean propagandists contrast the ideal American life with its somewhat harsher realities in order to prevent the North Korean people from believing everything they hear and see about the United States. In a particularly graphic, and sometimes comical, example of inoculation, *Nodong Sinmun* published an article describing the experiences of an unnamed Russian tourist who visited the United States. According to the paper, the Russian's experiences were reported "some time ago" in a *Pravda* article titled "A Russian Citizen's Account of the Disgusting United States." The Russian reports on housing:

> Only a very small minority of people live in skyscrapers. These skyscrapers are few in number. They converge in the "commercial center," a small district that comprises a few streets in the heart of the city. The entire remainder of the city is a world of asbestos-board houses. . . . Most people live in pressboard or asbestos board houses that are singularly disorderly and swarming with roaches. The walls of these houses are such that just pressing on them with a finger leaves a mark, and one can push a nail into them with the bare hand. . . .[67]

One time I went into a house where eight households lived, with one kitchen and one bathroom. There were old people living in that house. Their lives were all but done. They sat and wept. The lighting was barely enough to see in front of one's nose. I sat down and considered how I might console them.[68]

Eventually, I returned to my home in the fatherland. When I set my trunk on the floor, U.S. cockroaches came crawling out of it. We threw the trunk out on the veranda. In the cold of the Russian February, the cockroaches crawled barely half a meter and froze to death.[69]

On the U.S. health-care system, the Russian says,

If one is not insured, then he cannot get an operation. Yet the cost of insurance is 300 to 400 dollars each month, and no one can pay that much. They go on living somehow, without dying. There is a "free treatment system" for pensioners called the "old-age health system." In fact, they call the old folks in every month to confirm whether they have died or not, then they insult them by asking why they live so long when they live poorly, and threatening to get rid of the "old-age health system."[70]

In North Korea, as in all countries with heavy censorship, inquiring minds learn to read between the lines of the official media. Even though the media are designed to be a propaganda tool of the Kim regime, they are not without some informational value because the propagandist needs the raw material of news content in order to tell a story. For example, in a *Nodong Sinmun* article arguing that U.S. forces fell into a "trap" set by resistance forces after invading Iraq in 2003, readers were informed that "it took only some 40 days for the U.S.-led coalition forces to occupy Iraq."[71] The astute reader could therefore infer that U.S. military power must be formidable if it vanquished the large Iraqi army in a matter of weeks. To take another example, a *Nodong Sinmun* article in 2003 reported that due to recent events, South Koreans no longer liked the United States. It is true that anti-American sentiment had increased at that time; however, the information in the article conflicts with the usual propaganda line that the South Koreans have *always* disliked the Americans.[72]

Sometimes so many facts are left out of a foreign news story that the audience can probably make neither head nor tail of it. For example, presumably referring to speculation in the international media that a nuclear transparency policy recently adopted by Libya might prove to be a model for North Korea, KCTV quoted a foreign ministry official as cryptically saying, "Recently, the United States has been extensively advertising the incidents they orchestrated in some Middle East countries and is having a hallucination that the effects from these incidents will be reproduced on the Korean peninsula. . . . To expect a change in our position is the same as expecting a shower from a clear sky."[73]

Although it is easy to characterize North Korea's information environment as impoverished and dysfunctional, the fact to keep in mind is that this environment has served its purpose as one of the most important means of keeping the Kim family in power for over half a century. On the other hand, the regime's restrictive information policy has prevented North Korea from modernizing and becoming internationally competitive. Information needed to make optimal choices, especially economic choices, is in short supply. More importantly (from our point of view), the lack of information about alternative political systems keeps the people, dissatisfied though they may be, from finding a way out of their political prison.

It is difficult to predict what would happen if North Koreans gained unfettered access to information about their regime and the outside world. Such information might empower them to restructure their society to their own benefit, but they would need more than information to free them from the grip of thousands of years of autocratic rule.

CHAPTER SIX

Hidden Thoughts

What is in the minds of North Koreans as they go about their daily lives? What motivates them? What do they love and hate, hope and fear? Have years of indoctrination brainwashed them? Do they believe the propaganda that proclaims, "Our leader is the best, our ideology is the best, our army is the best, and our system is the best"?[1] Or are their minds filled with contradictions, frustration, and resentment? The short answer to such questions is that the minds of North Koreans are in conflict, but they do not dwell on it. Their minds are filled with the teachings of the Kim regime, but they are guided in everyday life by beliefs of an opposite and far more practical nature. They heavily discount the official propaganda claiming that the North Korean economy is merely going through a bad patch on the road to socialist paradise, and they are beginning to doubt that the rest of the international community holds Kim Jong-il and the North Korean state in high esteem. With each passing year, they put less faith in the regime's teachings, but they have no coherent set of alternative values to guide them to a better future.

Values—that is, a culture's ideas about what is good and bad—provide very basic guidelines for behavior, although people do not always follow them, and they are usually open to interpretation and modification according to circumstances. For example, Americans value efficiency, hard work, freedom of choice, individualism, a judicious degree of conformity to social norms, and the rights of minorities. All cultures share these American values, largely inherited from European culture, with varying degrees of emphasis on each. Even traditionally collective societies, like those of the Japanese and Koreans, are today quite individualistic. North Koreans subscribe to most of these values as well, although they place more weight on social conformity and less on individualism than do most modern societies.

Attitudes—positive and negative feelings about objects as diverse as guns, carrots, and democracy, along with knowledge and beliefs about those objects—are a more precise guide to behavior than are values. Knowing something about a person's attitudes makes it easier to predict behavior. As it happens, attitudes may sometimes be formed as a *consequence* of behavior, as in the case of rationalizations, but once formed, attitudes guide people as they navigate a world of choices, suggesting what to approach and what to avoid. People also use attitudes to define themselves, as in "I am a proud North Korean."

Attitudes are transmitted by teachers, by the media, and by the people we respect. For over half a century, the Kim regime has devoted prodigious efforts to teaching a set of socialist, loyalist, and nationalist values and attitudes. Attitudes, and to a lesser extent values, are also formed by experience; in fact, the strongest attitudes are learned in the school of hard knocks. Every day, North Koreans face a harsh contradiction between attitudes they have been taught and attitudes they learn from direct experience with life. For example, the Arduous March of the late 1990s taught the lesson that the state would no longer look out for its citizens, even while the propaganda press told people to keep their faith in state socialism. Those who remained faithful to socialist principles became society's losers, while those who went into business for themselves survived.

It is difficult to describe the beliefs of people living in a totalitarian society, where many thoughts must be hidden from all but family members and a few close friends, and no public opinion surveys are conducted. Instead, we must rely on material gathered from individual interviews and surveys of North Koreans who have already left the country, realizing that these people are not a representative sample of North Koreans and that their postdefection thoughts may color and even crowd out the thoughts they had while living in their homeland. Much of the material for this chapter comes from two surveys of defectors conducted by South Korean organizations and from two hundred defector interviews conducted since the late 1990s by the book's second author, Kongdan Oh.

An Ideology "in Our Own Style"

The Kim regime is inordinately proud of its ideology. "Some countries are known for their economic prosperity and others for military strength and still others for rich cultural assets. But our country is the only country known for its ideological power."[2] From cradle to grave, North Koreans are exposed to this ideology, and a good place to begin studying what they think is to look at what they have been taught.

An ideology is a collection of mutually consistent values and attitudes on which a political system is based. The Kimist ideology, borrowing heavily from Confucianism, Stalinism, and Maoism, stresses the value of the family as a model for society, with the leader as the father figure and each citizen-family member having his or her own role to play. According to Confucianism, the leader in turn has obligations to his national family, and when those obligations are not met, the leader loses his ruling mandate and should expect to be replaced. Of course, in practice it is as difficult to remove the leader of a state as it is for a family to replace its father. Chinese dynasties were passed on from parent to child for generations. In North Korea's dynasty, through good years and bad, Kim Il-sung ruled for almost fifty years as the "father-leader" (*oboi suryongnim*).

The point in common between Confucianism and the various forms of communism is the autocratic nature of governance. Kim Il-sung borrowed many ideas from Marxism-Leninism as it was practiced in the 1930s and 1940s, including an emphasis on collectivism and on the perpetual revolution. Even in the 1940s it was difficult for many people living under communism to take this ideology seriously because it was obvious that their leaders were determined that the dictatorship of the *nomenklatura* should never give way to the dictatorship of the proletariat. By the twenty-first century, communist totalitarianism had become an anachronism found only in North Korea and Cuba, although communist parties in China and Vietnam continued to monopolize politics and guide their respective economies.

A truly socialist or communist society can succeed only if its people are remolded into citizens who place community above personal interests. In Stalinist Russia, the utopian citizen was called the "new man," and this new man is the ideal in North Korea as well. Party lectures, newspaper articles, radio and television programs, and movies and plays teach people that egotism has no place in their society. Unfortunately, this teaching goes against universal norms and may well violate biological survival instincts. Only when faced with a community emergency are people willing to put aside individual goals; the rest of the time, they revert to their own self-interest, none more enthusiastically than the communist elites.

Communism is acknowledged to be a work in progress. Because some people cling to the old individualistic values, the transition from socialism to communism is painfully slow. In fact, North Korea is all about transitions: year after year the propaganda press proclaims that a foundation has been laid or a turning point reached in achieving economic goals, but as with a mirage, those goals are never reached. Nothing gets built on the foundation, and one turning point simply leads to another, until the economy comes full circle in failure for the simple reason that the problem is not the economy but the political system that controls it. Given the transitional nature of communist society, it is especially difficult to get people to adopt a communitarian outlook when some are working for the community while others are working for themselves. The existence of so many free riders gives people the feeling that they are not being adequately compensated for their selflessness.

The Kim regime's ideology rests on a few key themes, some developed early on by Kim Il-sung and his ideological advisors, and others added by Kim Jong-il and his advisors. The senior Kim began with Marxism-Leninism; however, in the mid-1950s, facing the task of recovering from the Korean War and consolidating his hold on power, Kim needed a new ideology. Rather than rule as North Korea's representative of international communism, Kim wanted to be the originator and interpreter of his own ideology. In a speech he gave to Korean Workers' Party (KWP) propaganda and agitation workers in December 1955, Kim introduced the concept of *Juche* in its modern context, saying, "We are not engaged in any other country's revolution, but solely in the Korean revolution."[3]

Juche symbolized independence from the Soviet Union and China and conveyed a determination not to let Korea fall under the influence of foreigners, as it had done so often in the past. Subscribing to Marxism-Leninism would have put North Korea's ideology under the authority of foreign theorists, and although Kim appreciated the value of domestic unity, he was not so keen on international communist brotherhood except when he was asking for foreign aid. As North Korea's national ideology, *Juche* eventually supplanted Marxism-Leninism, mention of which was dropped from the 1980 charter of the KWP and the 1992 revision of the state constitution. But Kim could not afford to separate North Korea completely from his communist benefactors in Russia, Eastern Europe, and China, although it helped that in China, Chairman Mao was also distancing himself from Moscow's authority. The political ideologies of North Korea, China, and the Soviet Union may have diverged, but they shared the principle that the few should control the many under the guise of the dictatorship of the proletariat.

Juche can be roughly translated as national pride and self-reliance. It prescribes doing things in a manner suited to North Korean conditions (as interpreted by the Kims) and not mindlessly imitating others, even if others (e.g., South Koreans) are more successful. A half century after Kim introduced the idea, *Juche* remained the guiding ideology: "Achieving the strengthening and prosperity of the country and people is an arduous task. It can never be accomplished if we abandon our style and shift to another people's style to escape from ordeals and difficulties, or if we turn to another people for help without trusting our own strength."[4]

Consistent with *Juche* principles, the North Korean press routinely warns of the evil intentions behind U.S. foreign aid, which is often characterized as a type of psychological military operation: "The purpose of the United States' 'aid operation' lies in the paralysis of anti-U.S., independent consciousness by creating a fantasy about the United States in people and encouraging pro-U.S. flunkeyism that depends on the United States."[5] *Juche* has not, however, prevented the Kim regime from soliciting billions of dollars in foreign aid over the years, including over $1 billion (mostly in World Food Program donations and compensatory oil shipments) from the American government.[6] Of course, the *Juche* economy was a lie from the very beginning. To maintain the myth of self-reliance, considerate foreign governments sometimes pretend that aid to North Korea is a loan. North-South Korea talks about aid are called "economic cooperation talks," and aid from the United States, when it is acknowledged by the North Koreans, is sometimes described in lectures to the people as tribute forced from the United States by the great general, Kim Jong-il. The regime also uses *Juche* as a propaganda weapon against South Korea by emphasizing the fact that although Chinese and Soviet troops had left the North by the late 1950s, American and UN troops remained in the South.

In the 1950s and 1960s, conveniently overlooking his own years of service in the Chinese and Soviet armies, Kim Il-sung skillfully employed *Juche* to purge his political rivals by suggesting that those who had connections with South Korea, China, Japan, and Russia could not have the best interests of North Korea at heart. Hundreds of top officials, thousands of their followers, and hundreds of thousands of ordinary citizens were banished to the countryside, imprisoned, or executed for words or deeds that could even remotely be interpreted as praising or imitating another country or denigrating North Korea, although the real reason for their downfall was that they were viewed as being insufficiently loyal to Kim. Following the example of Stalin, who eventually eliminated almost everyone in the upper echelons of the Soviet Union's party, government, and military, Kim began his purges with attacks on leaders of rival political factions and then moved to purge rivals within his own faction.

Any exposure to the outside world puts a North Korean under a cloud of suspicion. People on the street are cautious about engaging in conversation with foreign visitors. Immigrants from the North Korean community in

Japan are relegated to the hostile political class. Among the top cadres, one famous example of a tainted official was Kim Dal-hyon, North Korea's competent minister of external economic affairs in the early 1990s and a frequent traveler to foreign lands, who, after returning from an official visit to South Korea, lost his government position and spent the rest of his days out of sight as a local official. Several years later the top official in charge of external economic affairs, Kim Chong-u, failed to show up for a meeting with a foreign delegation and was never heard from again. On a broader scale, in the aftermath of what some foreigners believe was a coup attempt around 1992, hundreds of North Korean army officers who had studied at Moscow's Frunze Military Academy were purged simply because a few of their number had participated in the coup attempt.

Juche was revised under the stewardship of Kim Jong-il, who from the early days of his political career had shown a marked interest in ideology. One of Kim's first jobs was in the KWP's Propaganda and Agitation Department, where he proceeded to make *Juche* the ideological bulwark of the regime by enshrining loyalty to his father as the ideology's cornerstone. In 1974 the Ten-Point Principle (Ten Principles) for Solidifying the Party's Monolithic Ideological System became the supreme political (in contrast to legal) set of commandments. The first principle stated, "All society must be dyed with Kim Il-sung's revolutionary ideology," and the other nine principles merely repeated or elaborated on this.

The collapse of European communist regimes in the late 1980s and early 1990s forced Kim to address the hard reality that socialism was not necessarily destined to defeat capitalism. North Korean propagandists had to acknowledge, "The socialist movement has not always been victorious. In the early 1990s, socialism was frustrated and capitalism restored in not a few countries."[7] Foreigners talked about the "winds of change" blowing toward North Korea, and although the North Korean people were kept largely ignorant of events in the outside world, some news of socialism's demise trickled into the country. Kim could not completely block this news, but he could offer his own interpretation of it. In two talks he gave to party cadres in the early 1990s, he introduced the idea that the retreat of socialism in some countries was only a "local and passing phenomenon," caused by the fact that the European socialist parties had become lax.[8] "These countries neglected the work of strengthening the working-class party, weakened its leading role and the function of the unified leadership of the socialist state, adopted the capitalist relations of ownership and capitalist methods of economic management, and compromised with imperialism in an unprincipled manner, instead of fighting against it."

As Kim saw it, in Eastern Europe and the Soviet Union, there had not been *enough* socialism, and he vowed that there would be no shortage of socialism in North Korea. Consequently, any talk of economic reform or political opening was absolutely forbidden, and the regime redoubled its efforts at political indoctrination. "If people in socialist society do not lead political life properly in the working class party and other political organizations led by the party, they cannot preserve their socio-political integrity and even play into the hands of the reactionaries."[9] Editorials and political lectures warned that if foreign ideas were allowed to circulate, they could prove more attractive than socialist ideas. Capitalism was portrayed as a drug that paralyzes consciousness: "Imperialists are seeking to get the normally sound mind of people in revolutionary and progressive countries to degenerate."[10] As a mental-health measure, foreign influences must be kept out, and *Juche* socialism must have no competitors. These teachings have continued unabated since the early 1990s.

Yet, it was not the decline of socialism in Eastern Europe that directly influenced North Koreans, cut off as they were from outside news, but rather the everyday trials of the Arduous March that snuffed out their socialist beliefs. People didn't care whether they lived under a socialist or capitalist system as long as they had enough to eat. When people turned to their own self-made market economy in the early years of the twenty-first century, North Korean propagandists issued a new warning: "People who like money and goods get caught in the enemies' evil hands without exception, and once they take the bait thrown out by the enemies, they start acting as the rascals suggest and ultimately end up as traitors and rebels to the revolution."[11] This is the socialist version of the Biblical injunction that the love of money is the root of all evil, but the message falls on deaf ears in North Korea, as it does almost everywhere else.

Military-First Politics

After mourning the death of their founder in 1994 and struggling to survive during the Arduous March, the North Korean people needed something to restore their faith in socialism and their new leader. During the Arduous March and then the Forced March to Final Victory, the party's pronouncements had sounded a note of pessimism. People were assured that "the more our generations undergo sufferings and shed sweat, the happier our future generations will be."[12] They were urged to "live today for tomorrow" and even to "resolve to voluntarily choose death for the sake of the party and the leader."[13] In 1998 Kim sought to counter this defeatism by injecting some of the spirit that motivated his father's generation when they were fighting the Japanese in the 1930s and 1940s. He also sought to recapture the economic motivation that enabled North Koreans in the 1950s and 1960s to make a rapid recovery from the war through a military-style mobilization of the workforce. Kim's new ideology placed an emphasis on militarism and the "fighting spirit of the 1950s," this time packaged as the "military-first" (*songun*) policy or politics.

In 1995, one year after Kim Il-sung's death, the press hailed the Korean People's Army (KPA) as the "pillar and main force of the revolution."[14] The term *songun* received its first prominent use in the 1999 New Year's Joint Editorial. Thereafter, *songun sasang*, meaning "military-first thought," appeared regularly in the North Korean press. An August 2003 domestic broadcast titled "Our Republic Is a Socialist Military Power" provided a good indication of what military-first politics represents: "A country can be called a military power if it has an ever-victorious and legendary brilliant commander at the highest position of national defense; if all of its people strongly arm themselves politically and ideologically and highly modernize militarily and technologically; if its unity between the army and people is firmly achieved; if the idea of giving importance to gun barrels and military affairs becomes a social trait; and if all of its people arm themselves and it is entirely turned into a fortress."[15]

Like *Juche*, the military-first ideology can take on multiple meanings. At its core it means that everyone should think and act like a soldier, not expecting an easy life but instead working to make the country strong enough to resist foreign aggression. The roots of military-first thought go back to Kim Il-sung's Four Military Lines policy, first presented in the early 1960s and subsequently enshrined in the North Korean constitution. The policy called for arming the population, fortifying the entire country, modernizing the military, and making soldiers into politically reliable communists. Kim's total militarization policy came at a time when North Korea's international environment was becoming "complex"—to use a favorite North Korean expression. The Soviet Union had adopted a softer domestic and international line after the death of Stalin, relations between China and the Soviet Union were becoming strained, and the United States had begun to take notice of the threat of communism in Southeast Asia. Kim Il-sung decided that North Korea needed to put greater reliance on its own military strength in this changing environment and not to count as much on its alliances with China and the Soviet Union.

The early 1990s were likewise a time of complexity for North Korea. The Soviet Union had virtually ended its economic relations with North Korea and, along with China, had effectively terminated its military alliance; the United States, as the world's only superpower, was flexing its military muscle against various smaller states, including Iraq. Also, as in the 1960s, North Korea was falling farther behind South Korea in terms of modern weapons, although Pyongyang's development of a nuclear weapons capability was one way to try to compensate for the growing conventional weapons gap.

The military-first ideology addresses both international and domestic issues. Enhanced military power helps deter North Korea's enemies, especially the United States. Among the North Korean people, military-first politics produces a wartime mentality—a perception that they are about to be attacked and can survive only if they stick together and follow their leader's orders. The North Korean press goes so far as to claim that military-first politics is the best policy choice for all "progressive" (i.e., noncapitalist) countries, serving as "a militant banner which humankind should uphold in the 21st century." According to this line of thought, world peace will come "only when military capabilities are mighty."[16] This is hardly new thinking. In the United States, the Strategic Air Command and its successor, the Strategic Command, promoted the slogan "Peace is our profession," even going so far as to print it on the fuselage of its nuclear bombers.[17] The North Koreans have assured their South Korean brethren that military-first politics benefits them as well: "When all is said, the [Democratic People's Republic of Korea's (DPRK)] military-first politics is a great politics of loving the nation that protects the well-being of not just the North but the entire Korean nation, as it is actually holding the United States' war of aggression in check."[18]

To keep the tension level high and to distract the people from their troubles, the North Korean press warns that a great battle against the United States is at hand. On numerous occasions, especially in articles discussing alleged Pentagon war plans, the North Korean domestic press has warned that the United States has essentially declared war already. *Nodong Sinmun* claims that cases of American "military provocation" average five *per hour*.[19] And on the first day of every month, *Nodong Sinmun* catalogs alleged instances of U.S. "aerial espionage" during the previous month, typically numbering between one hundred and two hundred. When North Korean writers let their imaginations run wild, they can paint a graphic picture of war during peacetime, as in this 2003 description: "There, on the front where a volley of battles between peace and war was being waged every minute of the day and where a hand-to-hand fight between life and death was ongoing, the nation's survival and the destiny for all of us were smack in the middle of a merciless decisive battle."[20]

Military thought permeates North Korea's media and culture. In the past, everything was supposed to be done in the *Juche* style—*Juche* poetry, *Juche* farming, *Juche* architecture, and so on. Now everything is to be done in the military way. Under military-first politics, the army serves as "a college of revolution," as "a blast furnace of ideological training and a school of self-perfection of human beings."[21] Party and government officials are instructed to conduct their work in a "frontline style just like the People's Army."[22] The propagandists have come up with catchy military-first phrases, including "gun-barrel family" and the "guns and bombs family."[23] A story broadcast on North Korean radio asserts that the "Mangyongdae family" (i.e., Kim Il-sung's family, who lived at Mangyongdae) "was industrious and diligent, but did not pass down any material assets to the next generation. . . . However, the Mangyongdae family possessed the most precious and valuable inheritance, which could not be measured by or compared to anything, and that was the two guns left by Mr. Kim Hyong-jik [Kim Il-sung's father, who was a pharmacist]."[24]

Foreign economists and presumably many North Korean economists as well realize that military funding impedes North Korea's economic recovery. To counter this idea, people are told, "If the respected and beloved general should have elected a line giving priority to light industry and agriculture by citing the reason that the food for survival comes first . . . our people would have degenerated into slaves of the aggressors, not just once but a hundred times by now."[25]

In a dramatic departure from Marxist-Leninist thought, which argues that the working class is the core of the revolution, the military-first policy casts the army in this leadership role. The reason given for the substitution illuminates the fragile nature of North Korean society:

Many countries in the world victoriously carried out the socialist revolution and socialist construction with the working class as the main force. Today . . . the working class's living situation is changing, and labor becomes more and more technological and intellectual. . . . Reactionary bourgeois ideology and culture is rampant. This strongly deters the working class's class awareness, consciousness, and revolutionization. . . . The People's Army has a firmer collectivist spirit, a higher sense of organization and discipline, and stronger power of unity than any other group in society. The whole army is perfectly harmonized with the supreme commander as its center; all act as one to the supreme commander's order and instruction; and the soldiers' military lives and activities are all organized and conducted according to military rules and regulations.[26]

It seems then that despite his prodigious efforts to indoctrinate them, Kim Jong-il has lost faith in the working class. As it happens, the average North Korean soldier is no better socialized to communism than is the average civilian, and Kim Jong-il is probably aware of this fact, but at least soldiers are more regimented than civilians and thus easier to control as long as their officers remain loyal to Kim.

The first duty of every North Korean is to protect the leader: "The course of building a powerful state is a course of making all the people turn into human bullets and bombs to death-defyingly defend the great general, [and] implement his orders in the heroic spirit of self-sacrifice by risking their lives."[27] More poetically:

> You fought off the raging storm
> And gave us faith, Comrade Kim Jong-il
> But for you, we wouldn't be here;
> But for you, the fatherland wouldn't be here either.[28]

Although military-first politics may be good for Kim, it is bad for the North Korean people. It focuses their attention on a bogus enemy, distorts their view of reality, and gradually exhausts them. It deprives the economy of badly needed resources and gives too much power to the military, which tends to abuse this power by lording it over civilians. The ultimate danger is that militarizing North Korean society may ultimately provoke the very international conflict that the regime claims it wants to prevent.

New Thinking

The "new-thinking" campaign, launched in early 2001, three years after the introduction of military-first politics, has already been discussed in connection with North Korea's economic policies. The first thing to notice is that this new economic campaign does not follow from, nor is it consistent with, the foregoing military-first propaganda campaign, once again highlighting the Kim regime's desperate, almost random search for ways to revive its economy while keeping its politics stable. In addition to changing the structure of the economy by shifting economic responsibility to local administrations and ultimately to individuals (in the 2002 Economic Management Improvement Measures), the campaign encourages people to find creative ways to solve their economic problems. They are instructed to free themselves of "outdated ideas" so as to give "full play to the superiority of our way of socialism."[29] The glory days of the 1950s and 1960s, which are often presented as a model for economic reconstruction, are relegated to history because "there have been major changes in the conditions and environment of our struggle." A key idea of the new-thinking campaign is that people should employ modern technology to improve their productivity (although they are not told where they can find such technology).

The new thinking is consistent with *Juche* self-reliance—not at the national level but at the local level and on the part of individuals. Ironically, in adopting capitalism, people are unwittingly following the example of Kim Jong-il, who has all along been a fat-cat capitalist, a man whom *Forbes* magazine in 2002 listed (presumably on the basis of little hard evidence) as a billionaire.[30]

New thinking, as interpreted by the people, turns North Korea's world of values upside down. Whatever people have previously been told is right turns out to be wrong. Selfless devotion and blind obedience to the party are not to be rewarded—at least not materially. Individual endeavors, egotism, and selfishness are what turns a profit. Materialism and the pursuit of money, which the party has always condemned, become the guiding values. Even the relative value placed on husbands and wives in marriage changes as women become the main breadwinners in many families, thanks to the relative freedom they enjoy to do business in the new marketplaces while their husbands are stuck in useless jobs.

What People Believe

The era of public opinion polling has not come to North Korea (although according to one defector, party officials are requested to make reports about public sentiments and send them up to party officials in Pyongyang). Consequently, in order for outsiders to assess North Korean beliefs, it is necessary to talk to North Koreans after they have defected. South Korean social scientists have conducted many opinion surveys of defectors. For example, in 2002, 163 North Koreans residing at Hanawon, the government's halfway house for defectors, were asked about life in North Korea.[31] In 2006, 314 defectors at Hanawon were asked to evaluate the durability of the Kim regime.[32] Using these sources and testimony from defectors we have interviewed, it is possible to estimate the strength and stability of those beliefs that supposedly serve as the cornerstone of North Korean society under the Kim regime, namely, socialism, *Juche*, nationalism, and the legitimacy of the Kim family's rule.

Many North Koreans no longer believe that socialism is a workable economic system. In the 2002 survey, 38 percent of defectors thought North Korea's choice of socialism as an economic system had been a mistake, and of those, 60 percent believed that the problem lay in how it had been implemented. Some 48 percent believed that the North Korean economy's troubles could be attributed to government and party mismanagement, whereas 47 percent blamed the Americans for trying to "crush" the North Korean economy.[33] Indeed, the 2006 defector survey suggests a steady decline in beliefs in the collective lifestyle since 1996.[34]

Years of poverty that prove North Korea cannot take care of itself have damaged belief in *Juche* as national self-reliance, and by now, most North Koreans are aware that their country receives foreign food aid. In the 2002 survey, 60 percent of defectors said they were very or a little bit familiar with foreign aid coming from South Korea, compared to 39 percent who were not too well or not at all familiar with it.[35] In the 2006 survey, belief in the value of national independence showed a steady decline since 1996, when food aid began to arrive in the country.[36] In the markets, foreign-made goods superior in quality to anything that North Korea can produce are flooding in from China and other countries.

North Koreans seem to have an inflated opinion of their importance in the international community, thanks to their isolation from international opinion and the fact that the media praise their country to the skies. For example, *Nodong Sinmun* boasts that "Korea continues to walk on its own road, standing right in the center of the world as strongly as a mountain."[37] And, "Our Pyongyang today maintains a firm grip on the justice and conscience of the world and brightly illuminates the path of independence, as something like the ideological center and source of light of our planet."[38] Undoubtedly, some of this feeling of importance can be attributed to the impact of North Korea's nuclear weapons on the international community. In recent years, the leaders of China, Russia, Japan, and South Korea, as well as a U.S. secretary of state, have visited Pyongyang. North Koreans can take the major powers' devoting so much attention to their country as proof that although they may be small and undergoing hard times, they are an important country nonetheless.

The image and memory of Kim Il-sung are still very much alive among North Koreans, although references to him in the North Korean media are diminishing. Few North Koreans are aware of the universe of lies that makes up the Kim Il-sung cult, and most still believe he was a great man. All North Korean defectors have some opinion about Kim Il-sung, even those who are too young to have a clear memory of what their country was like during Kim

Il-sung's time. After they arrive in the South, most defectors still express a positive opinion of the senior Kim; to do otherwise would be to admit that they have been fooled their entire lives. Yet, comments about Kim are often defensive: "Kim Il-sung was not a bad person"; "Not a bad human being"; "Can't hate him"; "Everyone cried when he died." All defectors agree that material life in North Korea was better while the senior Kim was alive. Remote as he was, by selectively appearing among ordinary people, Kim successfully fostered the impression that he cared for them. He was "a politician for the people," as one defector said. One of the few negative comments about him called him the "original sinner" because he was responsible for appointing Kim Jong-il as his successor. In the 2002 defector survey, 67 percent of the respondents said their former countrymen still considered Kim Il-sung to be the "greatest mind of humanity."[39] The reasons given for Kim's high standing were that he liberated North Korea from the Japanese (41 percent), built a socialist state (8 percent), won the Korean War (8 percent), improved the economic lives of the people (7 percent), and created the *Juche* ideology (2 percent).[40]

On the other hand, defectors almost uniformly voice negative opinions of Kim Jong-il, although they concede that he is smart. The most common complaint is that he doesn't care about the people the way (they thought) his father did. As a North Korean saying goes, "Kim Il-sung took the 'people's train,' but Kim Jong-il took the 'military train.'" Another complaint is that since Kim Jong-il took over from his father, the economy has suffered, although whether Kim can be held responsible for the downturn in the economy is something that few North Koreans are in a position to know. The consensus among foreign economists is that the economy was on the way to collapse long before Kim Il-sung died. In the 2002 defector survey, 55 percent said Kim Jong-il was not liked because of the bad economy, 12 percent thought it was because he did not earn his leadership position but was appointed to it, and 9 percent thought he was disliked because he lacked the capacity to be a good ruler.[41] In the same survey, 70 percent of the respondents said Kim Jong-il was respected only because he was Kim Il-sung's son.[42] Defectors show varying susceptibilities to the Kim Jong-il cult propaganda. Some actually believe he works all the time and lives on rice balls and short naps. Others never believed this. A few defectors (from the elite class) had heard rumors of Kim's luxurious life style and his multiple lovers and wives, but this information didn't seem to bother them.

Attitudes toward the United States are decidedly negative. The notorious Sinchon Museum, which graphically portrays American soldiers killing

Koreans during the Korean War, has strongly influenced generations of North Koreans. News coverage of the United States is uniformly negative. To support the image of Americans as imperialist aggressors preparing to invade their country, the media remind their audience of past American invasions of small countries, including Somalia, Haiti, Bosnia, Afghanistan, and Iraq. In addition to the destruction and cruelty of the Korean War, the media blame the Americans and their economic embargo for North Korea's current economic problems. When the lights go out due to power failures, people curse the American "bastards." One defector said he even found credible the rumor that the Americans had caused North Korea's perennial rice shortage by buying up the world's rice harvest and spitefully dumping it in the ocean. Few North Koreans seem aware that the United States has been one of North Korea's principal food donors. In the 2002 defector survey, 31 percent said North Korean perceptions of Americans were improving, 12 percent said they were more negative, and 53 percent said they were the same as in the past, which is pretty bad.[43]

North Koreans do not have a very high opinion of any country, for that matter. Whereas Americans are the number one enemy, the Japanese rank number two. As the North Koreans see it, the Japanese are always preparing to reassert their military dominance in the region (many South Koreans would agree). It does not help Japan's image that thousands of American troops are based there. Attitudes toward China are also negative, although North Koreans have a grudging respect for the great strides that the Chinese economy has made. Several decades ago, North Koreans pitied the Chinese as poor; now almost all North Koreans believe that the Chinese are wealthier than they are.[44]

Attitudes toward South Korea have changed over the years. North Koreans formerly believed that South Koreans were virtual slaves of the Americans, living a life of abject poverty. In the 2002 survey, fully 80 percent of North Korean defectors said that when they lived in North Korea, they would have agreed with the statement "South Korea is a colony of the United States."[45] The North Korean media continue to project this image, but thanks to South Korean goods and humanitarian aid that began to reach the North in the 1990s, most North Koreans have come to realize that South Koreans are quite wealthy.[46] However, South Koreans are criticized for being materialistic (a common criticism against people of wealth) and too much influenced by foreign cultures. It is true that the dialect of Korean spoken in the North is largely devoid of foreign words, whereas Korean as spoken in the South is peppered with them. Yet, many younger North Koreans are picking up the South Korean dialect from smuggled audio and videotapes and discs. Young women, in particular, like the Southern dialect, which is considered softer in tone than the Northern dialect.

The people almost universally hated inside North Korea are security agents. One defector's husband, who worked for the State Security Department (SSD), told his wife that if people knew he worked for the SSD, "they would kill [him]." Despite years of being exposed to Kim Jong-il's military-first politics, which upholds soldiers as models for the rest of society, many civilians consider them bandits and thieves. Government and party officials are viewed as corrupt slackers, a reputation that even the press occasionally promotes in order to shift the blame for the bad economy away from Kim and onto party and government officials.

To learn what North Koreans like and dislike and hope and fear in their daily lives, the second author of this book, Kongdan Oh, interviewed a sample of defectors who came to South Korea between 2002 and 2005 and who held white-collar positions in the North, which is to say, they were from a relatively privileged class. When asked what they liked most about their former lives, several mentioned the lack of competition in socialist society. Until the 1990s, doing one's job according to the relatively low standards of government service was sufficient to earn a decent living. Defectors who were party and government bureaucrats also said they were proud of their jobs and enjoyed the deference shown to them by less successful people. Some defectors also remarked that North Korea is a simpler and purer place than South Korea. The language is not filled with foreign words, and there are few electronic gadgets to master. Defectors also missed the simplicity of the market in North Korea; after coming to the South, they were overwhelmed by the wide variety of products in the marketplace.

Some defectors said that people in the North were more likely to help each other, when they could afford to, than people in the South. Once they arrive in South Korea, most North Koreans find they are on their own, shunned by South Korean society as outsiders and avoided by their distant relatives.

What defectors disliked most about life in North Korea was the state's control over their lives, including the ubiquitous party and police surveillance. Even outside of work, their time had to be accounted for. Local party watchdogs and security officials might pay unannounced visits to their homes. Because of the constant surveillance, people had to hide their true feelings and pretend to be satisfied with their lives, although some defectors said they did not realize how little freedom they had until they came to

South Korea. They were not happy living a life controlled by the party, but they were used to it.

When defectors were asked what they had wanted most when they lived in North Korea, they frequently mentioned personal desires. A woman recalled that she had always wanted to learn to dance. Another wanted to own a car. A third wanted to travel to some of the natural wonders in North Korea. A fourth simply wanted access to the latest knowledge in his occupation, which was computer science. Beyond these personal desires, most North Koreans wanted reunification with the South. Reunification was also the ultimate political goal of the Kim Il-sung regime, but after East Germany absorbed West Germany, many North Korean elites came to believe they would be better off if the two Koreas remained separate, whereas those lower on the social and political scale believed that reunification would bring an end to the economic shortages they had endured all their lives. In April 2000, a delegation of French visitors in Pyongyang heard a loud gong signaling that a special announcement was about to be made over the third broadcasting system's speakers. Their North Korean guides were worried because the last time they had heard the gong, it had heralded the announcement of Kim Il-sung's death. This time the announcement was that the two Koreas would hold their first summit meeting in Pyongyang in June. One Korean said, "Finally, finally, finally. You know, we could not take it any longer. . . . You cannot know all the sacrifices we endure, all the wealth and all the resources we sink into strengthening our army, to the detriment of everything else."[47] As it turned out, the summit talks led to only the first small steps toward Korean reconciliation and did little to improve the material lives of North Koreans, who continued to suffer as Kim Jong-il strengthened his military-first policy.

Defectors said their greatest fear in North Korea was for their personal safety. They most feared arrest by the security services, which is understandable considering that most North Koreans are forced to engage in illegal market activities in order to survive. If the police decide to crack down on a particular activity at a particular time, some people are inevitably caught in the net. Likewise, as social controls have broken down and economic hardships have multiplied, the incidence of crime has increased. Women are afraid to go out at night because street crimes such as robbery, rape, and even murder, all of which were formerly rare, are becoming more frequent.

What North Koreans spend their time thinking about depends in part on how old they are. Young people are interested in earning money to buy products that give them pleasure, emulating what they see in South Korean videos. They gather to sing South Korean songs, dance at discotheques, and wear Western clothing such as jeans and printed T-shirts. South Korean movies are having an especially strong impact on the youth, who imitate the clothing and behaviors they see. The Kim regime recognizes that the younger generation is most vulnerable to bourgeois culture and most lacking in "revolutionary discipline," and the media frequently warn that youth need to be subjected to stronger socialist indoctrination, but boring, heavy-handed communist propaganda is notably ineffective, and foreign culture has continued to spread among the youth.[48]

Religious Beliefs

Before the communists came to power, Confucianism was the most popular belief system in Korea, although unlike Western religions, Confucianism is an elaboration of principles about the conduct of human affairs rather than the worship of a supreme being. Buddhism was introduced into Korea in the fourth century and Christianity in the nineteenth century, around the same time that Chondoism (*Chondokyo*) emerged as an indigenous religion. Shamanistic practices and beliefs were, and to some extent still are, popular in the countryside.[49]

When Korea was liberated from the Japanese, a survey conducted in the northern half of the peninsula found 1.5 million practicing Chondoists, 375,000 Buddhists, 200,000 Protestants, and 57,000 Roman Catholics.[50] The first North Korean constitution, dating to 1948, declared, "Citizens have the freedom to engage in religious activities," but it was Kim Il-sung's typically communist opinion that "religion is a counter-revolutionary and unscientific view of the world. Once they indulge in religion, people come to have their class-consciousness paralyzed and will be deprived of the desire to carry out revolution. Religion can be compared to opium."[51]

Following the 1959 publication of a booklet titled "Why Should We Oppose Religion?" the Kim regime began to actively discourage the practice of religion by imprisoning religious leaders and forcing their followers to recant. In the late 1960s, with the completion of the nationwide political classification of the people, Protestants, Buddhists, Catholics, and Confucians were assigned their own subclassifications in the "hostile" class. The South Korean government estimates that virtually all North Koreans who openly practiced religion were killed or imprisoned between the end of the Korean War (when an estimated one hundred thousand Christians fled to South Korea) and 1970, effectively wiping out the public practice of religion.[52]

The 1972 DPRK constitution guaranteed freedom of religion, along with the freedom "to engage in anti-religious propaganda activities." The 1992 constitution took a more favorable position on religion, stipulating, "Citizens have freedom of religious belief. This right also guarantees the right to construct buildings for religious use, as well as religious ceremonies." But the constitution warned, "No one may use religion as a means by which to drag in foreign powers or to destroy the state or social order," a provision that effectively prevents the practice of religion. In his landmark 1995 text on ideological indoctrination, Kim Jong-il pronounced religion to be antithetical to North Korea's official ideology of *Juche*: "The religious and idealist views have been defined as if the people's activity is restricted or their destiny is determined by a mysterious supernatural being. Science has already proven the unreality of the religious and idealist view."[53]

In 1972, at a time when the two Koreas enjoyed a brief period of rapprochement, the Kim regime revived several defunct religious organizations so they could participate in the united front campaign against South Korea, whose religious organizations were largely opposed to the dictatorial military governments then ruling the South. The Korean Buddhist League reappeared in 1972, the Korean Christian Federation in 1974, and the Central Guidance Committee for Korean Chondoists in 1974. The Korean Catholics Association was established as a separate organization in 1988. The KWP Central Committee's United Front Department controls all these associations. Representatives of North Korean religious groups travel to international meetings, where they promote their government's political positions, especially calling for Korean reunification according to the DPRK's political formula.

After a half century of repression, most North Koreans seem no more interested in religion than in politics, and it is difficult to know what place religion would play in their lives if the authorities permitted it. In the late 1980s and early 1990s the Bongsu (Pongsu) Methodist Church, the Changchun Catholic Church, and the Chilgol Church were built in Pyongyang. Their congregations consist of a few party and security agents and a small number of religious believers who have somehow been permitted to practice their faith. Interestingly, the Chilgol Church is said to be built on the same spot as the church that the young Kim Il-sung and his parents attended in the days when Pyongyang was a center of Western religion in Korea. On his 2003 trip to Russia, Kim Jong-il got the idea of building a Greek Orthodox church in Pyongyang, which opened in August 2006 with a delegation of Russians attending, including the Russian ambassador and the metropolitan of Smolensk and Kaliningrad, who consecrated the church, known as the Jongbaek Church.

In addition to serving a political motive, controlled religion in North Korea has brought in hard currency. Most of the Pyongyang churches seem to have been built with foreign donations, and foreign (mostly South Korean) religious organizations have been generous humanitarian donors to North Korea. For example, between 1995 and 2006, the South Korean Catholic community sent $38 million in aid—certainly enough money to warrant the regime's toleration of one small Catholic church in Pyongyang.[54] Pyongyang's handful of churches also serve as a place of worship for the small community of foreign residents. The sponsorship of religious organizations and toleration of churches are also means to parry international criticism of the Kim regime's antireligious policies.

An unknown number of "house churches"—perhaps as many as several hundred throughout the country—hold services, sometimes with the knowledge of local officials. Worshippers meet in groups of a half dozen or fewer (more than that attracts notice and increases the chance that one of the worshippers is a spy), usually in someone's home. Children, who might be induced to report on their parents, are excluded from worship. People caught worshipping or found to possess religious literature can receive prison sentences of ten years or more for antisocialist activities, which often amounts to a death sentence. Koreans caught in China and returned to North Korea are vigorously interrogated, and if they confess to having been in contact with South Korean or other foreign religious organizations, they are sent to prison. A survey of 755 North Korean defectors published in 2008 found only ten who said they had participated (secretly) in church services while in the North, forty-three who said they had known of others who participated in church services, and thirty-three who said they had seen a Bible.[55]

Communism as Cult

In a number of respects, North Korea presents the appearance of a large cult, and to the extent that the parallel holds, the study of cults (the politically correct term is *new religious movements*) can provide some understanding of North Koreans and their belief system.[56] In cults, the selfishness of the individual ego is seen as separating members from the group and from their "true" nature, just as egotism and individualism are supposed to be enemies of the North Korean community. In a cult, the most menial tasks are valued as necessary and significant parts of a divine plan, providing members with motivation and giving them a sense of self-worth. In North Korea, the press praises the work of "hidden heroes," and citizens are urged to "silently defend their outposts, regardless of whether they are recognized or not."[57]

After cult members are indoctrinated with the group's beliefs, they have trouble assessing the extent to which their values are realistic or moral. One reason they hold on to their new beliefs is that they have already committed themselves to the cult with their effort, time, and possessions. The North Korean people have likewise sacrificed much in their journey toward a socialist paradise, and it will be difficult for them to admit they have been traveling the wrong road and following the wrong leaders for over half a century. When cult followers find something about their new belief system hard to accept or at variance with reality, they often blame their lack of understanding on limited knowledge and doubt their own judgment. In North Korea, only Kim Jong-il is said to have a clear vision of the future; it is the role of the people not to think but to obey Kim and have faith in his superior wisdom. Cult members are taught to be suspicious of the outside world, just as the North Korean media routinely disparage foreign countries. When a cult falls under the control of a dominating leader, as is usually the case, that leader tends to exploit members for his or her advantage. The obscene wealth enjoyed by Kim Jong-il is made possible by the work of millions of ordinary Koreans who will never enjoy the fruits of their labor and cannot begin to imagine the luxurious lifestyle their leader enjoys.

After they have left the cult, former members often recognize that they have failed to accomplish what they set out to do by joining and are often confused about what their next step in life should be.[58] They may discard some aspects of the cult's belief system but retain others. Likewise, North Koreans who arrive in the South are usually confused about what to do next. The transition to life outside the DPRK is much more difficult than the transition former cult members face because, except for those who have spent some time in northern China, defectors have no previous experience of the outside world. Moreover, defectors have usually left behind family and loved ones and lack close family members to support them in South Korea.

Once free of the cult, former members often reminisce about the more positive aspects of their cult experience, such as the community support they received, and they sometimes question the wisdom of having left the group. Likewise, North Korean defectors often ask themselves whether defecting was a good idea. In a 2004 survey of one hundred defectors, 69 percent said they would prefer to leave their difficult life in South Korea for another country such as the United States or Canada, and 33 percent said they would return to North Korea if they could (although to do so would almost certainly mean lifetime imprisonment).[59] By leaving their homeland, defectors exchange one set of problems for another, although most of them believe that by defecting they made the correct choice under very difficult circumstances.

Belief and Consequences

People are generally reluctant to abandon the values, beliefs, and attitudes that have guided their lives—even if their lives have not been very satisfying or successful. It is interesting to note that defectors often hold on to their positive attitudes toward Kim Il-sung even after learning how much he lied to them and how much damage he did to North Korea. A growing number of Koreans in the North can see that they have been given the wrong roadmap for life, but they do not know where to get a more accurate one. In contrast, a (dramatically shrinking) number of North Koreans maintain implicit faith in the mapmaker (by whom they usually mean Kim Il-sung, not Kim Jong-il) and believe that by following his teachings they will eventually make it to a socialist paradise.

The mental life of North Koreans is as bankrupt as their material life (we refer here to their beliefs about the economy, politics, and the world outside their country, not to their beliefs and emotions about self and family, which they hold in common with people of all cultures and countries). The Kim regime has failed in its effort to create a "new man" who is a Kim loyalist and a committed communist. Although most North Koreans no longer believe in socialism, that doesn't mean they like or understand capitalism. One of the great attractions of communism—but also an important reason why it does not succeed in the long run—is that people do not have to take personal responsibility for their life choices; they only have to follow the commands of the party. After defectors arrive in South Korea, most of the responsibility for their success or failure rests on their shoulders, and they find this experience troubling.

Surely one can find no other post–Cold War society where such a wide gap exists between propaganda and reality, between what one is supposed to do and what actually works. In particular, the North Korean elites, who know more about their country and about the outside world than ordinary North Koreans, confront a serious contradiction. On the one hand, their leader and his media say that North Korea is the best country in the world to live in; on the other hand, they know that domestic conditions are bad and that conditions outside North Korea are much better. Do the elites tolerate this contradiction in their minds, or do they somehow resolve it? Citizens of the former communist regimes in Eastern Europe faced a similar dilemma.

As one of Mikhail Gorbachev's aides recounted, "Gorbachev, me, all of us, we were double-thinkers, we had to balance truth and propaganda in our minds all the time."[60]

In our first North Korea book, written in the late 1990s, we concluded that the North Korean elites were indeed double-thinkers, although most of the time they did not dwell on contradictions. It appears that over the last several years, double-thinking has spread to the majority of North Koreans. As the saying goes, they are "daytime socialists and nighttime capitalists." People are still forced to attend political indoctrination sessions and hang portraits of the Kim family on their walls, but their thoughts are about the market economy. North Koreans lead a double mental life in another respect. In the narrow world of their personal experience, they have developed rudimentary knowledge about how to survive within the constraints of a ruined economy, but they are ignorant of the larger sphere of economics and politics. As a consequence, their newfound beliefs can guide their day-to-day affairs but cannot help them address the underlying macroeconomic and political problems that restrict them to the pursuit of a kind of precarious cottage capitalism. They do not know how things could be better; nor do they have the opportunity to protest against the way things are now.

How does a North Korean respond if socially prescribed means of success—such as going to work at a factory and joining the party—do not lead to a better life or to any life that is tolerable? Sociologist Robert K. Merton studied what people do when society's norms conflict with social reality.[61] In Merton's terminology, those who do what society dictates, even when aware that they are failing to achieve the goals that society promises, are *conformists*. *Ritualists* are those who follow the rules without even thinking about what goals they are trying to achieve. *Innovators* employ socially unacceptable (e.g., illegal) means to reach socially approved goals, while *retreatists* reject both the means and goals that society prescribes in favor of alternative lifestyles. *Rebels* also reject both means and goals, but like the early communists, they actively try to change society. In North Korea, many of the conformists and ritualists didn't survive the hard times of the 1990s. A relatively small number of retreatists fled to China. No one has rebelled. The majority, after years of conforming, have become innovators who are stealthily building a new economy and culture.

The anthropological work of James C. Scott, who studied how Indonesian peasants responded to the oppression of their employers and their employer-friendly government, suggests a somewhat similar way to describe how North Koreans have responded to the widening gap between what they are taught and what they must do to survive.[62] Scott observed that the Indonesian elites (like the North Korean elites) shaped the official ideology, and the Indonesian peasants (like North Korean workers) made no attempt to dispute that ideology or to rebel, even though their experience told them that the official ideology was false, and its promised goals were unobtainable for them.

Like the powerless in many places and at many times in history, the Indonesian peasants used the "weapons of the weak" to protect their interests and protest against conditions. These weapons included malingering at work, lying to superiors, and pretending to be ignorant of their duties. Peasants also resorted to pilfering and absenteeism, and in extreme cases, they committed sabotage and arson. None of these responses openly challenged their superiors or the government authorities; all of these responses are found today in North Korea. North Koreans occasionally grumble or, in recent years, even raise their voices at local meetings, but for the most part each person takes care of his or her own business, with the collective result being a kind of silent rebellion that holds back the socialist economy and makes a mockery of the regime's politics.

Like the Indonesian ruling class in Scott's study, the North Korean cadres pretend that everything is working. They hesitate to report crimes or failure to achieve economic goals because to do so would show them in a bad light to their superiors in Pyongyang. Instead, they send up rosy reports, and the people at the top do not ask questions because they do not want to be held accountable for failure either. At the very top, Kim Jong-il may be partly aware of how rotten North Korean society is, but there is little he can do about it, short of instituting the kind of reforms that would threaten to disrupt a half century of Kim family rule. And while the propagandists continue to grind out editorials and political lectures that fall on deaf ears, the people go about constructing their own reality—not a coherent ideology or worldview but a rough-and-ready guide to everyday survival.

CHAPTER SEVEN

~

The Law, Political Class, and Human Rights

The Kim regime's poor treatment of its people is a key element of its governing style. It is not a symptom of "system malfunction" or the "collapse of discipline and lack of control by the central government," as one South Korean professor has suggested.[1] Just as a democracy cannot exist without free elections, a dictatorship cannot exist without political oppression. The individual liberties fundamental to the Western concept of human rights confer power on the people that directly competes with the power of a leader. Simply put, the Kim regime is built on the violation of human rights—and not only the right to individual liberties but also the right to food, work, and safety. Only Kim enjoys the freedom to eat what he wants, live and travel where he wants, and read what he wants. North Koreans are granted these rights by the constitution, but in practice anyone who tries to exercise them will end up in prison.

North Korea is a society with many laws, but it is not a society *of* law as liberal democracies define it: "Rule by law basically refers to the use of law as a tool to communicate and enforce the will of a powerful subset of a society on the remainder of the society. Rule of law, on the other hand, refers to the concept that not only individual citizens but also the government itself is subject to and is limited by the law, and that certain human rights are protected by the law against infringement by other individuals or the government itself."[2] In an apparent attempt to convince the international community that it is a lawful society that protects human rights and the rights of foreign business enterprises, the government of the Democratic People's Republic of Korea (DPRK) now publishes many of its criminal and commercial laws.[3] In August 2004 the government published a collection of 112 laws, including the Law on the National Flag, the State Funeral Law, the Fruit Culture Law, the Library Law, and the Law on Fish Breeding.[4] As the titles indicate, most of these laws are state and party guidelines for how things are supposed to be done, with the added bonus for the regime that more laws are available to punish people for political mistakes.

The North Korean legal system is under the control of the party, as is stated plainly in Chapter 1, Article 11 of the 1998 constitution: "The DPRK shall carry out all of its activities under the leadership of the KWP [Korean Workers' Party]." Common to all dictatorships, the law is a tool to consolidate the ruling party and the authority of the ruling class, while at the same time providing a patina of legitimacy for the government. In a collective society like North Korea's, one should not expect the law to protect the rights of the individual; rather, it is the society as represented by the party and the leader that warrants protection. As Kim Il-sung said, "Our judicial organs are a weapon for carrying out the functions of the dictatorship of the proletariat."[5]

North Korea's controlling legal code is not even a state law but rather a list of party principles in the form of the Ten-Point Principle (Ten Principles) for Solidifying the Party's Monolithic Ideological System, mentioned in chapter 6. The principles appeared in 1974 and were attributed to Kim Jong-il during the days when he was making a reputation as the interpreter and enforcer of his father's *Juche* theory.[6] The first principle reads, "All society must be dyed with Kim Il-sung's revolutionary ideology," and the entire list can be paraphrased in the following manner:

> Accept the ideology of Kim Il-sung.
> Respect, revere, and be loyal to Kim.
> Make Kim's authority absolute.
> Believe in Kim's ideology.
> Carry out Kim's instructions with unconditional loyalty.
> Strengthen the party's unity and solidarity around Kim.
> Imitate Kim's personality and work methods.
> Repay Kim in loyalty for the political life he has given you.
> Establish strong discipline such that everyone uniformly follows Kim's lead.
> See to it that future generations inherit Kim's revolutionary task.

To promote the illusion that the DPRK is a democratic country, periodic elections are held that are wholly typical of totalitarian communist systems;

that is, they are forced votes of confidence in the party. On the advice and consent of higher levels, the members of the local party election committee choose one candidate for each office. In the run-up to election day, which is a national holiday, the media try to generate excitement. Banners with slogans like "Let us consolidate revolutionary sovereignty as firm as a rock by participating in the elections" are hung on buildings, and on election day agitprop teams beat drums and sing and shout outside the polling places to create a festive atmosphere.

The voting is anticlimactic. First thing in the morning, people of voting age (seventeen and older) proceed to their local polling places, where their registration cards are checked. After bowing to portraits of Kim Il-sung and Kim Jong-il, they receive a ballot with the name of the party's candidate. For a yes vote, the ballot is dropped into the ballot box. If anyone were foolish enough to vote *against* the candidate, it would be necessary to pick up a pencil and cross out the candidate's name before dropping the ballot into the box. Since a police officer, security agent, or party official is present at every polling place, a no voter would be immediately investigated. Everyone who is healthy enough to get to a polling place is required to vote, and those unable to make it to the polls can cast a ballot in a mobile ballot box or by proxy. A special problem concerns the thousands of North Koreans who have illegally left their homes for other towns or to cross over into China. If the entire family has departed, the local authorities can list them as deceased, but if some family members remain, they are held accountable for their missing members and will have to pay a hefty bribe to local party and police investigators to register the missing persons as dead. Otherwise, the missing family members would be classified as traitors to the state, and the entire family would be in trouble.[7] After voting, people are supposed to spend the rest of the day singing and dancing to show support for the regime and the election process. Election results are announced the same day and are always the same: a voter turnout above 99 percent (99.98 percent in the 2009 election for the Supreme People's Assembly) and 100 percent approval of the party's candidates. The media celebrate the election as a great victory for Kim Jong-il and the nation: "The election of deputies to the local power bodies [in the July 2007 nationwide local elections] marked an important occasion in reinforcing as firm as a rock the revolutionary government of the DPRK led by Kim Jong-il and further increasing the function and role of the people's power by electing persons of ability, who have devotedly worked for the party and the leader, the country and the people, in the local power bodies."[8]

The Political Class System

All societies have classes of one sort or another, and because communists come to power in a revolution of the working class against the bourgeoisie, communist societies will have at least two classes. The North Korean media frequently speak of the "uncompromising and merciless struggle" that the working class must wage against class enemies that include "remnants of the overthrown exploiting class and reactionaries."[9] Until the 1990s, North Korea's political class lines were so rigid that they resembled those of a caste system.

The Ten Principles are the basis for social, political, and economic stratification. North Koreans are classified according to their loyalty, or presumed loyalty, to the Kim regime. Kim Il-sung based his political purges, which commenced as soon as he took power in the late 1940s, on his assessment of loyalty rather than professional competence. In 1958, the entire population was subjected to political classification, with successive classifications culminating in a system of three classes and fifty-one subclasses announced at the 1970 party congress.[10] It seems the three-class structure has been maintained since then, although the subclass structure may have undergone some modification.

The three classes are the core class (*haeksim kyechung*), the wavering class (*tongyo kyechung*), and the hostile class (*joktae kyechung*), estimated (somehow) by Republic of Korea (ROK) authorities to consist of 30 percent, 50 percent, and 20 percent of the North Korean population, respectively. Some defectors (and South Korea's unification ministry) refer to a somewhat different class-labeling system, consisting of core, basic, and complex classes, with the complex class subdivided into wavering and hostile subclasses.[11] The Kim regime considers members of the core class, most of whom are party cadres, to be its loyal supporters. The DPRK has never made public the membership size of the KWP, but based on the proportional representation at the last party congress in 1980, membership in 2009 may number about three million out of a population of twenty-three million. The regime counts on the wavering class, consisting of workers, farmers, technicians, teachers, and enlisted soldiers, for nominal support but fears that enemies of socialism or their own human frailties could lead some of its members astray. Members of the hostile class are suspected of silently opposing socialism and the Kim regime. The classes are further divided into fifty-one subclasses. For example, the hostile class is broken down into subclasses including those who worked for the Japanese colonial administration before 1945, former members of the different religious organizations, and property owners. As one would expect, those who held the highest positions in precommunist Korea became members of the lowest political class, whereas at least some members of the low class moved up to the new privileged class. This was the case for Kim Il-sung and his military comrades, who became the leading figures in North Korea despite coming from working- and petty-merchant-class backgrounds.[12]

Forming a particularly unfortunate subclass are the thousands or tens of thousands of South Korean intellectuals and professionals who were systematically abducted by North Korean soldiers during the Korean War in order to build up the socialist state.[13] Foretelling this campaign, Kim Il-sung in 1946 said, "To solve the problem of lacking intellectuals, we have to bring them from the South, rescuing them from the American imperialists and their collaborators."[14] These abductees were put to work for the North Korean state, sometimes in their former capacities and sometimes as common laborers, but their record as former South Koreans remains a black mark for them and their descendants.

The first generation of North Korean leaders, including Kim Il-sung, received only a basic education. Kim never trusted intellectuals, who, throughout his fifty-year reign, suffered discrimination, even though the national symbol of the DPRK depicts a hammer, sickle, and pen, symbolizing the contributions of the workers, farmers, and intellectuals.

One feature of North Korea's class system that resembles a caste system is that people are primarily classified by family history. For example, children of soldiers killed in the Korean War are core class, children of craftsmen are wavering class, and children of officials who worked for the Japanese administration are hostile class. The same goes for the children's children. Members of the core and wavering classes who commit crimes, speak out against the regime, or are associated with those who commit political crimes are demoted to the hostile class. On the other hand, members of the hostile class who are law-abiding citizens remain in the hostile class.

The Core Class

No strict line separates the privileged core class from the masses, although there is a clear line separating the quasidivine Kim family from the rest of the core class, which explains why it is difficult to imagine that anyone from the privileged class other than a member of the Kim family could replace Kim Jong-il when he finally steps down or dies. The elites are best distinguished from the masses by their being part of the government and party bureaucracy. Because the state owns all means of production, it is important to be a part of, rather than to work for, the state—at least this was true until recently. Bureaucrats in the government and party can supplement their incomes by selling their services to the people in the form of bribes for such things as travel and housing permits, release from jail, and educational recommendations. Because the party is above the law, the only danger involved in accepting bribes is that it might come to the attention of Kim Jong-il, who despite being the biggest bribe taker in the country, has been known to punish those who follow his example.

The economy of corruption is hardly unique to North Korea: it is found wherever dictatorships exist. By all accounts, Victor Kuznetsov's harsh characterization of the typical member of the Soviet *nomenklatura* applies to the North Korean cadres as well: "A confirmed member of the *nomenklatura* had no respect for the law; he knew that Soviet laws were formal and not meant to be enforced or were to be observed only by ordinary citizens. As long as he followed the unwritten rules common to all members of the 'ruling upper class,' his status in the hierarchy was assured. Breaking a formal law was dangerous for him only because it could be used by other members of the *nomenklatura* in their own interests in the course of the unrelenting inner struggle to obtaining a more prominent post."[15]

The most privileged members of the core class live in Pyongyang, but being a Pyongyang resident and party member is no guarantee of a comfortable life. In hard times, even party members must live on reduced rations if they do not have the kind of job that enables them to solicit substantial bribes. Party members have no more individual freedom than do the masses; in fact, they are held to a higher standard than the rest of the population and are probably watched more closely, although they also have more resources to bribe their way out of trouble.

Members of the core class, especially at its upper reaches, live and die by politics, monitoring the most recent political lines embraced by Kim Jong-il. If for some reason Kim is currently sensitive to the spread of popular music, or long hair, or a particular type of clothing, one does well to avoid these things until Kim's attention is diverted elsewhere. Jealous colleagues or too much alcohol still sometimes trip up even those who try to stay within the bounds of current political trends. For example, a former North Korean medical professional tells how, while drinking at a party with friends, he complained that people in his profession could not procure adequate equipment for their work but that in China the equipment was available. "North Korea is now worse than those smelly Chinese, and China has become a new country with a reformed economy." One of the people at the party, who was the son of a high-ranking party cadre, reported the comments to security officials, who two days later raided the professional's home at dawn, arrested him, and interrogated his family members, associates, and even fellow students from his university days.[16]

To combat the ever-present danger of falling from grace, it is necessary to have a means to ward off, or bail oneself out of, trouble. Traditionally, the best means has been personal connections with powerful people, although as North Korea has transformed into a money-driven society, personal wealth has started to take the place of personal connections as a political insurance policy. In the case of the unfortunate medical professional, one of his patients with political connections arranged for his escape. Another defector tells how, with a bribe of $5,000, he was able not only to get his brother out of prison but to get him admitted to a North Korean medical college.[17]

Members of the privileged class pass on their privileges to their children. Those among the highest-ranking elites, numbering one to two hundred thousand, can send their children to the eleven-year Mangyongdae Revolutionary School, and after graduation, their family connections enable them to avoid military service and proceed directly to a university—if not Kim Il-sung University, then one of the other top schools in Pyongyang such as Kim Chaek University of Technology or the Pyongyang Foreign Language School. After college they are given jobs in the government or party bureaucracy. The most important requirement for success is to fit in socially and politically. Showing initiative can be dangerous because Kim Jong-il sets party policies, so the best course of action is simply to implement whatever policy the party is promoting at the moment; if this can be done in a way that reflects well on one's superiors, so much the better. Some university graduates succeed by dint of their professional skills in science and technology rather than through political connections, but these people are not likely to rise to the highest levels of the bureaucracy.

And so it has been for the last fifty years. But times are changing and a new economic elite class is emerging, comprising people who care little for party membership but know how to make money. They are not replacing the political elites, but their numbers are growing, and they often live better than many of the political elites.

Members of this new economic class, introduced at the end of chapter 3, must be sensitive to political trends and depend on well-placed officials to further their interests and protect them when they get into trouble. Because their economic endeavors are technically illegal, their lives are even less secure than those of the political elites. Few of these capitalists work for themselves. They develop affiliations with party, government, and military organizations that take a cut of their profits in return for offering them legitimacy and protection. Army regiments, police units, and factories all have trading arms that send people out to sell whatever is at hand. The more organized and powerful of these organizations send traders abroad; the less organized and poorer simply send their traders across the border into China.

The Hostile Class

No scarlet letter identifies members of the hostile class. Security services maintain their political records, but they themselves often do not have certain knowledge of their political class designation, although they usually have a pretty good idea of where their family stands in the class system. A former Korean People's Army (KPA) officer tells of how he surreptitiously gained access to his security file and discovered that he had been denied higher promotion because one of his father's cousins, a former police chief of Haeju City (then part of South Korea), had been arrested and killed by the communists during the Korean War.[18] This incident had happened forty years earlier and had nothing to do with the KPA officer, but the record remained in his file and limited his life chances. Other former North Koreans tell how their parents shielded them from knowledge of politically tainted relatives in the often vain hope that the family's class designation would not spoil their children's lives.

As in the case of the KPA officer, members of the hostile class are sometimes permitted to join the army officers' corps but will not be promoted much above the rank of captain. Nor will they be recruited for any of the security services. Hostile-class members who are arrested for ordinary crimes are likely to receive severer sentences than members of the other two classes. When people are publicly identified as hostile-class members—for example, they have been banished from Pyongyang to a small village—some of their new neighbors may avoid them for fear of political contamination. A defector tells of how, after her father was sent to prison, the family was banished from Pyongyang to a small town, where they were assigned to live in an abandoned shack. She had a three-month-old baby who suffered from flea and bug bites in the shack, but none of her new neighbors would have anything to do with the Pyongyang family. They were eventually able to move to another town where they were not known as banished people.[19]

Most North Koreans whose names appear in the police registers as members of the hostile class pursue their lives in much the same way as members of the wavering class. Until 2002, in good times they received state rations of food and clothing. In bad times they were the first to have their rations cut, but, then again, during the famine period almost no one outside of the core class received rations. Since 2002, when food rationing ended and government jobs became useless, hostile-class members' prospects have not been much worse than those of the wavering class. Still, hostile-class members are unlikely to be accepted at a university; nor can they receive permission to reside in Pyongyang. To foreigners, living in Pyongyang may not seem like a great privilege, but among North Koreans the capital city is considered such a special place that people boast about knowing someone who lives there.

Disabled people cannot reside in the central districts of Pyongyang, presumably because their presence would sully the country's image. One former North Korean says her father was informed by the local party secretary that his daughter, who walked with a limp, would have to leave the city. When the father objected to sending his daughter to live with relatives, he was told that the only alternative was to move the entire family.[20] The daughter was sent to live in a small town where she was teased so badly by the other children that she withdrew from school. After three years, the family bribed a local official to let the girl live with her grandmother on the outskirts of Pyongyang, but she was required to stay off the streets.

Members of the hostile class work on agricultural communes and in the factories and mines. The less fortunate have no jobs and no houses. The least fortunate are interned in prison camps. In lean times between harvests, members of the hostile class are the first to take to the road and wander around the countryside or cross over to China to look for food. A pitiable segment of the hostile class includes the children whose parents have died or abandoned them. These *kotchebi* ("swallows") travel from town to town and haunt the marketplaces and train stations looking for food. On September 27, 1998, Kim Jong-il ordered that they be rounded up and placed in "9/27" camps, typically unused factories and warehouses. There they receive little care, and most soon escape, only to be caught again. *Kotchebi* frequently turn to petty crime, sometimes forming small gangs of thieves and pickpockets.

In the former Soviet Union, numerous political, ethnic, occupational, and religious groups—in addition to the unfortunate kulaks, whose only crime was to have a bit more money or property than their neighbors—were assumed to be hostile to the regime. Likewise, in North Korea anyone with family ties to Japan, South Korea, or China automatically falls under suspicion because they can get resources (and information) from outside the country and are consequently not as dependent on the regime as ordinary North Koreans.

Although most members of the hostile class pose no threat to the regime, if disloyal cadres were allowed to rise to positions of authority, they might then pose a danger to Kim. Thus, to be on the safe side, the regime banishes or imprisons anyone suspected of being different or disloyal. The treatment of the hostile class follows the medical model in that its members are assumed to have the capacity to infect others and must therefore be quarantined or eliminated.

Because the Kim regime has always considered itself to be engaged in a warlike confrontation with the United States, it is concerned not only with regime security but with national security as well. Parallels can be seen in other countries that feel threatened. After the terrorist attacks of September 11, 2001, the George W. Bush administration took extensive homeland security precautions, including drawing up lists of possible terrorists and their supporters, classifying airline passengers according to the level of threat they were presumed to pose, and broadening surveillance of the general public. In North Korea, classification and surveillance systems are more comprehensive and efficient than in the United States, and their use is motivated more by fear of an attack directed at the regime than at the population or national infrastructure.

The Law

The North Korean criminal code, together with the entire justice system from judges to juries to attorneys, is a tool of the party. People detained by the police cannot consult with an independent lawyer—because all lawyers work for the state. Sometimes those accused of political crimes are not even told what crime they allegedly committed.

North Koreans from all three political classes know and fear the words "to the mines" or "to the Aoji coal mines." People are sent to prison for many reasons. Police officers from the Ministry of People's Security (MPS) investigate ordinary crimes, which are as common in North Korea as in other societies, although rarely reported in the press. Criminal suspects are entitled to a trial, but like the trial presided over by the King and Queen of Hearts in *Alice in Wonderland* ("Sentence first—verdict afterwards," says the queen, who by the end of the day has sentenced two *witnesses* to death), the legal proceedings are perfunctory because the accused are presumed guilty. This is to be expected when the prosecution is an arm of the party, which claims to be infallible.

Public executions are occasionally staged as a warning to lawbreakers, although they seem to be less common in the 2000s than in the late 1990s. Defectors have described many such executions, which are usually carried out by firing squad in a stadium or field on the outskirts of the city and often involve several convicts. According to announcements made at the executions, the capital crimes include espionage, smuggling, selling narcotics, stealing metal wire, stealing or butchering cattle, human trafficking, murder, Christian worship, distributing South Korean videos, listening to foreign radio, and using Chinese cell phones.[21]

A more perverse form of legal folderol is applied in cases of political crimes, that is, when someone is accused of transgressing one of the Ten Principles. If there is any trial at all, the accused is charged with one of the loosely defined articles of the criminal code. For example, Article 67, one of the ambiguous "Crimes against the State and the People," stipulates that anyone who commits a crime of "suppressing our people's movement for national liberation under the rule of imperialism or struggle for national reunification or a crime of selling Korean national interests out to imperialists, shall be sentenced to more than 10 years of hard labor correction. In case the circumstances are grave, he shall be sentenced to an indefinite term of labor correction, death, and confiscation of property." Often the procedural steps leading up to imprisonment (i.e., arrest, trial, conviction, and sentencing) are dispensed with entirely. The victim (one can hardly refer to the person as a defendant) and in many cases the immediate family are abducted by State Security Department (SSD) agents and taken to a concentration camp, where they can expect to spend the remainder of their days. SSD officers have even been reported to summarily execute individuals in public.[22]

One North Korean woman who was tried and convicted of a political crime but later escaped to South Korea has recounted the following experience: She was a county-level party bureaucrat in charge of distributing cloth to make jackets for party officials. The cloth was in short supply, so she provided each official with only enough material for one jacket, although the head of the local security agency asked for twice as much. She believes that due to her failure to comply with his request, she was arrested and charged with embezzlement. She thinks her arrest was also part of a power struggle between the local party office and security agency. In any case, she was imprisoned and tortured for seven months before agreeing to plead guilty—to save her husband and son, or so she thought. The trial, which was held in public so as to make an example of her, lasted only a few minutes—just long enough for her to confess to the charges and receive a sentence of thirteen years in prison. The attorney appointed to defend her never said a word; nor were her husband and son allowed to attend the trial (unbeknownst to her, they had already been banished).[23]

These days, most North Koreans are guilty of at least a few "crimes of undermining the economic management order," including engaging in "individual commercial activities" (Article 110) and "pocketing money or objects by doing illegal work or transport" (Article 120). One former railway inspector, who obtained his position by bribing railway officials, says he served ten years in a prison camp for extorting money from train passengers, an everyday occurrence.[24] Because many people lack the necessary documents to travel within the country, they simply bribe railway inspectors to let them stay on the train. The bribes thus collected amount to many times the inspector's annual salary. According to the former railway inspector (who told his story to a fellow prisoner, who later escaped to South Korea), he and a fellow inspector confiscated three kilograms of gold bullion being illegally transported by a gold dealer. In this case, however, the dealer was working for a high-ranking party cadre and a senior security officer. When the dealer informed his sponsors about what had happened on the train, the train inspectors were themselves arrested for embezzlement. Only by bribing the court officials were they able to negotiate "lenient" sentences of ten to fifteen years, which for most people is equivalent to a death sentence.

Some people are sent to the camps simply because they have said something directly or indirectly derogatory about the system or the regime. This is why people only voice complaints to family members and close friends. But occasionally people lose their temper or say something after drinking too much alcohol and find themselves charged with being "verbal reactionaries."[25]

The Prison System

If North Korea's political prisons were as secure as one would expect them to be, outsiders would know very little about them because, before they are released, North Korean prisoners are required to sign a statement promising never to discuss their prison experience.[26] The North Korean government's official position is, "There can be no 'concentration camp' in the DPRK as it is a man-centered society where man is valued most."[27] Occasionally, however, political prisoners are released—usually to their own surprise—and a few, such as the former party official mentioned above, manage to defect and tell their stories to the outside world. Several former prison-camp guards have also defected and identified some of the camps they served in from satellite photographs.[28] Sensitive to the bad publicity, the North Korean government has closed some of the camps and presumably relocated their inmates.

In recent years the most widely cited estimate of the number of political prisoners in North Korean camps is two hundred thousand, almost 1 percent of the North Korean population.[29] This may not seem like a large number considering that almost the same percentage of the American population is in prison, but this estimate does not include the ordinary prison population; in any case North Korean prison conditions are exceptionally harsh. Even people imprisoned for only one or two years are treated so badly that some of them die before completing their sentences.

North Korea has several kinds of detention centers. The Ministry of People's Security (the police) in every town and city has a local jail, or *gamok*, where prisoners are held for initial interrogation, often accompanied by beatings and torture. Defectors also speak of local interrogation or collection centers called *guryujang*, which are sometimes a separate part of the local jail. Prisoners whose cases warrant further investigation or punishment are transferred out of these jails within a few weeks. Those convicted of minor offenses are sent to local labor-training camps, or *jipkyulso*, to perform up to six months of very hard labor. At both the local jails and the labor-training camps, prisoners are beaten, work for long hours, and receive so little food that they rapidly lose weight.

North Korea operates two kinds of long-term prisons. Criminals who have committed felonies, which may be as minor as stealing food, are sent to the MPS's "reeducation centers," or *gyohwaso*, some of which are prison buildings surrounded by high walls, barbed wire, and guard towers. Larger prisons consist of one or more villages surrounded by barbed wire and located in remote mountain valleys. Prisoners who attempt to escape from the village must walk through miles of mountainous country, which is impossible for many inmates because by the time they arrive at the prison, they are already weak from starvation and beatings. Prisoners captured trying to escape are beaten so badly that they cannot stand and then dragged into camp to be executed by hanging or firing squad in front of other inmates, who may be forced to kick or throw stones at the corpses.

Former prisoners comment that upon arriving at the prison camp they were first impressed by the walking skeletons, many hunched over and limping, wearing dirty rags; very soon new prisoners come to look the same way. The daily prison diet consists of at most five hundred grams (two cups) of corn, potatoes, or cabbage. Resourceful prisoners supplement their diet with rats, snakes, insects, grass, and tree bark. Prisoners work in coal, gold, stone, copper, iron, or gypsum mines and logging camps for ten hours or more a day, seven days a week, with a half dozen holidays a year, including the birthdays of the two Kims. Prison factories make cement, bricks, glass, textiles, shoes, bicycles, and furniture. Because safety measures are lacking, workers are frequently maimed or killed on the job, especially in the mines. One former political prisoner reported that some are even forced to live down in the mines.[30] Prisons also operate farms to feed inmates and produce crops for the Public Distribution System.

Prisoners have little access to medical facilities. Those who are severely ill or injured may be sent to the prison sanatorium to die or back to their homes in order to save the prison the burden of having to bury them. If they should recover at home, local officials will return them to prison. The "reeducation" that prisoners receive is the same education that all North Koreans receive: evening study of the works of the two Kims. Prisoners are told they are guilty of failing to repay Kim for his benevolence and are not worthy to live, but through hard work they may redeem themselves.

Bad as conditions are in the *gyohwaso* prison camps, they are better than in the political detention camps, or *gwalliso* ("control and management centers"). No dictatorship can do without its political prisons to isolate critics of the regime. When the communists took control of the northern half of Korea, landowners, those who worked with the Japanese occupation authorities, and religious leaders were classified as antistate elements and sent to the first political camps. After the Korean War, captured soldiers were added to the camps. Throughout the 1950s and 1960s, Kim Il-sung conducted purges to eliminate potential political rivals, and these people also ended up in the camps. After the 1966–1970 countrywide political classification, an estimated fifteen thousand "antirevolutionaries," along with seventy thousand of their family members, were sent to the camps. By the 1970s Kim Jong-il was sending people to the camps on his own initiative as he consolidated his position in the leadership succession. In the 1990s, some of the North Koreans who had lived in or visited other socialist countries before their communist governments collapsed were sent to the camps to prevent them from "contaminating" their fellow citizens with knowledge about the outside world.

Immigrants and foreigners are two other groups who are sometimes sent to political prisons. Some of the ninety-three thousand Koreans (and their Japanese wives) who emigrated from Japan to North Korea in the 1950s and 1960s were imprisoned; certainly, almost none of them were ever allowed to return to Japan.[31] The South Korean government believes that since the end of the Korean War, 3,795 South Koreans, mostly fishermen, have been abducted by the North and that over five hundred Korean War POWs (out of perhaps an initial twenty thousand) are still alive in prison camps.[32] And then there are the occasional foreigners who imprudently choose to live as independent contractors in North Korea and run afoul of the regime. In 1967 the DPRK Ministry of Foreign Affairs hired two foreigners, Ali Lamada and Jacques Sedillot, to come to North Korea to translate the writings of Kim Il-sung into Spanish and French. Both were subsequently accused of spying and sent to prison camps. Thanks to the intervention of the Venezuelan and Romanian governments, the two were released in 1974. Lamada returned to tell his story, but Sedillot died before he could leave Pyongyang.[33]

Gwalliso facilities are much like the village *gyohwaso* prisons, with each political camp, of which there are about a half dozen, housing anywhere from five to fifty thousand inmates deep in mountain valleys. Since agents of the SSD rather than the MPS run the political prison system, inmates and their families are often committed without formal arrest, trial, conviction, or sentencing. Security agents suddenly appear and abduct political suspects from their homes, often in the middle of the night. Neighbors, friends, colleagues, and relatives are never told what happened to the missing, and anyone foolish enough to ask risks investigation. The North Koreans have a saying: "They die without the birds [in the daytime] or the mice [at night] knowing." Almost the only way out of political prison camps is suicide, which is a serious crime: families of prisoners who commit suicide are treated even worse than families of other prisoners, and prisoners who fail in their suicide attempts are tortured. Occasionally, a prisoner is released from a political camp, often for unknown reasons, and anyone who has sufficient money to bribe the right officials has a good chance of being released, or at least moved to a reeducation camp.

Because entire families are sometimes incarcerated, prison camps have schools where the young convicts are taught their lessons, including the all-important political lesson of worshipping the Kim family. Prisoners have no rights. Many die of beatings, starvation, and illness, but so far as we know, there is no accounting of their fates. Surviving for longer than a few months in a political prison requires a strong constitution, a certain amount of luck, and/or a family able to send food into the prison, some of which must be given to the guards. Some inmates survive for many years, but others, especially the young and the old, die within a year.

A typical prison day begins at 5 a.m. and ends at 7 or 8 p.m., with half-hour breaks for breakfast, lunch, and dinner.[34] Like inmates at reeducation camps, political prisoners work seven days a week at the same kinds of jobs. After completing their workday, they attend political study sessions until 10 p.m. The daily food ration is typically a palm-size ball of cornmeal with watered-down cabbage soup or just a handful of raw corn that prisoners can cook. It is impossible to survive for long on such rations, especially while engaging in hard labor, and those prisoners who do survive have learned how to forage for food and bribe the guards.

Prisoners live several to a room in unheated wooden barracks. If an entire family is incarcerated, they may be permitted to build a little hut from scraps of wood with a straw roof and a dirt floor. In winter, prisoners keep warm by huddling together; frostbite is common, resulting in amputated fingers, toes, and limbs. Some camps supply enough electricity to light a single bulb for an hour or two a day, but at other camps wooden torches provide the only illumination. Prisoners get a chance to wash their faces only a few times a month. They go to the bathroom in a hole in the ground; in prison cells, some of which are located underground, they use a can. They wear the same clothes they came into the camp with, and when these wear out, they appropriate the clothing of dead prisoners.

When approached by a guard, political prisoners must bow down to the ground or, in some prisons, get down on their knees. Infractions of camp rules, failure to complete work quotas, and similar offenses are punished by a reduction of food rations, which is an immediate threat to health because most prisoners live on the edge of starvation. Prisoners will do almost anything for a scrap of food, including stealing from other prisoners and failing to notify the guards when a fellow prisoner dies in order to eat his or her food ration for a day or two. Prisoners are also routinely enlisted to spy on each other, and as a consequence they are very careful when talking among themselves.

Prisoners are beaten by guards and by other inmates on the guards' orders. A popular torture, especially during interrogations, is to force prisoners to kneel motionless for hours at a time, sometimes day after day. The slightest movement or utterance results in a beating. Women prisoners are sometimes forced to stand and squat repeatedly until they collapse. Every prison has its special detention cell where prisoners are beaten and starved more severely. Few survive the experience, which is used as a warning to others. One of the cruelest punishments involves locking a prisoner in a windowless box four feet on a side, too small for the prisoner to lie down or stand up in. Prisoners kept in the box for several weeks are permanently crippled if they survive the experience.

Explanations for the North Korean prison system's pervasive cruelty can be found on several levels. At the cultural level, it should be remembered that North Korea is a collectivist society that values the community over the individual. Acting on behalf of the state, prison guards seem to have few misgivings about beating, torturing, and starving prisoners, who are seen as threats to the regime and the social system. Ostensibly for this reason, prison-camp inmates are not supposed to have sexual relations, and pregnant inmates are usually forced to have abortions.

To understand the brutal treatment of prisoners at the level of personal relations, consider that even under the best of conditions, prison guards can be cruel. In the famous Stanford Prison Experiment, a sample of normal American college students was randomly separated into guards and prisoners and then placed in a realistic replica of a prison; within days those students assigned to be guards took on some of the worst characteristics of real prison guards.[35] North Korean prison guards are taught to look upon prisoners as animals. Prisoners are sometimes addressed by their first names, but male prisoners are more frequently addressed as "this son of a bitch" (*ee ssaekkee*) and "this bastard" (*ee nom*) and female prisoners as "this low-class bitch" (*ee jaabnyon*) and "this bastard" (*ee nyon*). It probably does not help that the gaunt, crippled, dirty prisoners come to look like wild animals. Guards who are too kind to prisoners are themselves punished.

One might ask why prisoners who recognize that they are slowly and painfully dying do not fight back. North Koreans in general—and this applies to prisoners—remind foreigners that any resistance to the regime meets not only with more punishment but brings punishment on the rest of the family, whether they are already in prison or not. Consequently, most prisoners see no way out and simply work until they die. According to defectors, occasionally a prisoner will attack a guard or go crazy from hunger and is then beaten and killed. Ahn Myong-chol, a former prison guard, says that he heard of a mass uprising of prisoners at the Onsong Camp in 1987. A prisoner turned on a guard who was beating him, and about two hundred other prisoners joined in, killing another guard and attacking the guard headquarters at the camp. Ahn, who was working at another prison camp, was told that when military reinforcements arrived, they surrounded the camp and killed about one-third of the estimated fifteen thousand inmates.[36]

Human Rights

The North Korean regime has been justly criticized for violating its citizens' human rights. Yet, it is difficult to find a way to change the regime's human rights policies because they are embedded in the structure of its dictatorial rule. Until the 1990s, little specific information was available to outsiders about human rights practices in North Korea, although the broad outlines of the situation were well-known. Inquisitive foreigners could not get into the country, and North Koreans could not get out. However, in response to the famine of the mid-1990s, defectors began to flee the country, bringing with them first-hand accounts of human rights violations. Despite this new information, foreign governments have put little pressure on the Kim regime to improve its human rights practices.

In a dictatorial communist society such as North Korea's, the health, welfare, and security of the majority is supposed to take precedence over the rights of individuals, although in practice individual rights are curtailed to protect the leaders and the ruling party. According to the Leninist-Stalinist model, as adopted by North Korea, human rights policies are rooted in the contest between political classes, giving the revolutionary working class, as represented by the regime, the right and the duty to suppress and eventually eliminate the other classes. As *Nodong Sinmun* puts it, "We do not hide our class character in the human rights issue just as we do not conceal our loyalty to the party. It is our human right to provide workers, farmers, intellectuals, and the people of other strata with freedom and rights and to crack down upon a handful of class enemies violating the human rights of the popular masses. . . . We declare with pride that human rights can be ensured when we consolidate the socio-political organism in which the leader, the party, and the masses share life and death."[37]

When criticized by foreign governments and international organizations for its human rights policies, the Kim regime has responded with a number of arguments. For example, it has asserted that human rights standards are culture specific: "All the countries of the world differ from each other in traditions, nationality, culture, history of social development; and human rights standards and ways of ensuring them vary according to specific conditions of each country. . . . The human rights standards in the DPRK are precisely what the Korean people like and what is in accordance with their requirement and interests."[38] The regime also insists that the most important right any people can enjoy is national sovereignty: "Today [2005], the lesson we once again learn from the United States' atrocious human rights commotions is that human rights is precisely sovereignty, and the protection of human rights is precisely the defense of sovereignty."[39]

North Korea even warned that the passage of the 2004 North Korean Human Rights Act in the United States was a hostile act and virtual declaration of war. The North Korean media have sought to invalidate American criticisms of the Kim regime's human rights practices by claiming that the United States is the world's foremost violator of human rights, although another country can hardly use the U.S. record on human rights, which is by no means perfect, as an excuse for its own human rights failings.[40]

Some people find it odd that the South Korean government has not pressed North Korea harder on the human rights issue or done more to work for the return of POWs and abducted South Korean citizens. After all, the South Korean constitution regards all Koreans, regardless of which side of the Demilitarized Zone they live on, as South Korean citizens, so there would seem to be a strong legal basis for taking an interest in the human rights of North Koreans. However, neither of the two South Korean presidents in office between 1998 and 2007 was willing to make an issue of North Korea's human rights violations. In a 2000 BBC interview, several months after the inter-Korean summit, President Kim Dae-jung explained that he "would not press the issues of human rights and democracy at this early stage as it could be detrimental to building trust" between the two Koreas.[41] In a 2003 interview with the *Washington Post*, Kim Dae-jung's successor, Roh Moo-hyun said, "Rather than confronting the Kim Jong-il regime over human rights of a small number of people, I think it is better for us to open up the regime through dialogue. I think this will ultimately bring broader protection of human rights for North Korean people as a whole."[42]

In recent years, the United Nations has become more vocal in expressing its concern about human rights abuses in North Korea. In September 1981 the DPRK joined Covenant A, the International Covenant on Economic, Social, and Cultural Rights, and Covenant B, the International Covenant on Civil and Political Rights. After submitting its first periodic report to the UN Commission on Human Rights in 1984, the DPRK delayed submitting its next report until 2000. In 2003, the commission adopted its first resolution citing the DPRK for human rights violations on a broad range of issues. A second resolution, passed in 2004, requested the appointment of a special rapporteur to monitor the DPRK's human rights situation, and beginning in 2005 this individual began making a series of reports, citing shortcomings in the following areas: "The right to food and the right to life; the right to security of the person, humane treatment, non-discrimination and access to justice; the right to freedom of movement and protection of persons linked with displacement; the right to the highest attainable standard of health and the right to education; the right to self-determination/political participation, access to information, freedom of expression/belief/opinion, association and religion; and the rights of specific persons/groups, including women and children."[43]

A third commission resolution on North Korea passed in April 2005 recommended that the issue be taken up by the General Assembly, which adopted its first resolution concerning North Korean human rights (as part of a package of resolutions also concerning the Congo, Iran, Turkmenistan, and Uzbekistan) in December 2005. The draft resolution was supported by eighty-eight countries and opposed by twenty-one, with sixty abstentions (including the ROK) and twenty-two absentees. Virtually all the world's developed countries supported the resolution, whereas most of the countries that opposed the resolution had their own serious human rights problems, including Belarus, China, Cuba, Egypt, Indonesia, Iran, Russia, Sudan, Syria, Tajikistan, Turkmenistan, Uzbekistan, Venezuela, Vietnam, and Zimbabwe. Most African countries either abstained or were absent. Since 2005, the United Nations has continued to pass resolutions disapproving North Korea's human rights policies. In 2006, the ROK voted in favor of the annual resolution, perhaps in part because its former foreign minister had just been elected as the incoming UN secretary-general and in part because North Korea had recently staged its first nuclear test. South Korea abstained in 2007, but under the new Lee Myung-bak administration, it not only voted for the resolution in 2008 but cosponsored it. The North Korean government has vigorously rejected all these UN resolutions, claiming that they are initiated by the United States "and its followers." However, given the critical attention the North Korean media have shown these resolutions, the Kim regime is apparently concerned about the bad publicity the country is receiving in the international arena.

Every March, the U.S. State Department issues its annual Country Reports on Human Rights Practices, and every year it singles out North Korea as one of the countries with an especially poor human rights record. Adding to the pressure put on North Korea by international organizations like Human Rights Watch, Amnesty International, and Refugees International, various American groups, such as the U.S. Committee for Human Rights in North Korea and Freedom House, have lobbied for a stronger U.S. government response to human rights abuses. In 2004 the U.S. Congress passed the North Korean Human Rights Act, which was signed by the president. The act focused on three major issues: promoting human rights in the DPRK, establishing a framework to assist North Koreans inside and outside their country, and establishing a framework for protecting North Korean refugees. The act also called for the appointment of a special envoy on human rights in North Korea and authorized (but did not appropriate) $24 million to be used each year between 2005 and 2008 to support the act's agenda. Unfortunately, the implementation of the act became caught up in political and bureaucratic squabbles, and it appears that none of the authorized money was ever appropriated. By 2007, the Bush administration was pushing harder for a negotiated solution to the North Korean nuclear issue, which required North Korea's cooperation in the Six-Party Talks, and the U.S. government's North Korean human rights campaign faltered.

Little Progress, Little Hope

No significant improvement in human rights can be expected under a dictatorial regime such as North Korea's. Extralegal social-control mechanisms are a part of North Korea's totalitarian society, fitting in with all the other parts, such as leadership style, ideology, economic practices, and military dominance. Nor can one expect that other governments will vigorously press North Korea on this issue. China is governed by a communist party that sympathizes with the North Korean Workers' Party's desire to hold on to power. In recent years, South Korea has extended economic and moral support to the Kim regime and, in any case, has no desire to welcome millions of North Koreans. Japan's poor relations with both Koreas force it to keep its distance. The countries of the European Union are far away. The United States is preoccupied with fighting terrorism and ending the Kim regime's nuclear weapons program. And the United Nations cannot take decisive action because most of its members agree with the Kim regime's argument that the first principle of international relations is sovereignty. It is therefore up to the North Korean people to help themselves, if only by employing the "weapons of the weak" outlined at the end of chapter 6.

CHAPTER EIGHT

Defectors

The escape of hundreds of thousands of North Koreans to China and the arrival of over fifteen thousand of them in South Korea (by 2009) is an indictment of the Kim regime's policies as well as a test for the South Korean government. Their disappearance from North Korean society and the information they take out with them are also threats to the Kim regime.

In *Exit, Voice, and Loyalty*, economist Albert O. Hirschman observes that when people are discontented with a situation that cannot easily be changed, their options are to voice a complaint or leave.[1] Wise leaders prefer that discontented followers exercise their voice so that matters can perhaps be adjusted, although hearing bad news is never pleasant, and it is true that complaints can multiply among the discontented and cause their own organizational problems. Dictators rarely countenance complaints, and so far as we know, Kim Jong-il has never considered emulating Chairman Mao, who in a momentary lapse of political judgment proclaimed, "Let a hundred flowers bloom, let a hundred schools of thought contend." The hundred-flowers policy was reversed within a few weeks, and Mao is better known for the Great Proletarian Cultural Revolution of the 1960s that attempted to impose his thought on a half-billion Chinese. In any case, Kim Jong-il has neither the economic nor political resources to satisfy his people, so letting them complain might not be such a good idea after all. Better to be the leader of a sick society than not a leader at all.

Discontented North Koreans try to leave—either physically or psychologically. Earlier chapters have described how North Koreans psychologically escape socialism by ignoring the Kim regime's political and economic teachings. Tens of thousands of others have taken the more extreme step of fleeing the country, a course of action that is dangerous, but not as dangerous as voicing complaints.

Only a few thousand of the twenty-three million North Korean people have ever been allowed to legally emigrate or travel to another country. To protect the image that the country is a worker's paradise, the regime has made it a treasonous offense to leave without permission. Only diplomats, contract workers, and foreign-currency-earning business agents are issued passports. Obtaining a permit to travel across the border into China is somewhat easier than getting a passport but still involves months of waiting and the payment of fees that are beyond the resources of most North Koreans.[2] The only other alternative is to leave the country illegally.

Escape by sea is dangerous and rarely attempted. Trying to cross the Demilitarized Zone (DMZ) into South Korea is suicidal. The least dangerous means of escape is to sneak into China or Russia, which merely involves eluding or bribing North Korean border guards and crossing the Yalu River (forming the western half of the border with China) or the Tumen River (forming the eastern half of the border with China and the short border with Russia). Thousands of North Koreans do this every year, but most border crossers spend only a few days or weeks in China trading goods before bribing the border guards again and returning home. Some choose to stay in China indefinitely, either living an underground existence as unregistered aliens among the two million Koreans who are legal residents of the Chinese border provinces or working their way on to a third country. Estimates of the number of North Koreans living illegally in China range between thirty and one hundred thousand, although during the 1990s famine, the number may have been as high as three hundred thousand.

The most common term in English for a person who does not return to his or her country is *defector*, which first came into use after World War II to distinguish Soviet soldiers who took up residence in the West from the millions of refugees who did so. In this sense, *defector*, which the dictionary defines as one who leaves his or her country for political reasons, is not an appropriate term for the majority of North Korea border crossers because they are fleeing primarily for economic reasons—although by the very act of fleeing they are committing a political crime in the eyes of their government.

Until about 1997, South Koreans usually referred to defectors as *gwisun*, meaning "someone who has surrendered after seeing the light." Beginning in the mid-1990s, *talbukja*, meaning "a person who has left the North," became popular. *Tal* does not imply any motivation or value judgment for leaving; it simply expresses a change in one's location. More recently, the term favored by the government of the Republic of Korea (ROK) is *saetomin* ("new settler"). Some defectors prefer to be called by other expressions, such as *jokugul ttonan saram* ("person who left the motherland"), *kohyangul dengjin saram* ("person who deserted his hometown"), *silhyangmin* ("person who lost his hometown"), or *monjo ttonan saram* ("person who departed earlier"). In English, defectors are also referred to as escapees, refugees, asylum seekers, migrants, deserters, border crossers, and displaced persons. The majority of those leaving North Korea would prefer to return to their homeland if economic and political conditions improved, so in this sense they are only sojourners in a foreign land. In the absence of a completely satisfactory term to describe them, these people are referred to in this book as "defectors" or "former North Koreans."

Defectors are a valuable source of information about what is happening in North Korean society, although their testimony must be used judiciously. Because defectors are usually paid for giving interviews, they may be tempted to exaggerate their experiences in North Korea to make their testimony more marketable. More worrisome, their memories of life in North Korea may become confused with information they have obtained since coming to the South. However, when numerous defectors tell similar stories with different details, their testimony becomes quite credible.

Who Defects?

In the years immediately following the liberation of Korea from the Japanese, many Koreans moved between the northern and southern parts of the country. Between 1946 and the beginning of the Korean War, an estimated 580,000 people came down from the North, and another 400,000 to 650,000 came south during the Korean War.[3] After the war, the border between the two Koreas was tightly shut, and not until recent years has an appreciable number of North Koreans tried to defect—by way of China, not through the DMZ. Only 219 North Koreans arrived in South Korea from 1953 to 1959, and 212 came in the 1960s—probably fewer than the number of pro-communist South Koreans who fled to the North. During the entire decade of the 1970s, when economic conditions in North Korea were about the same as in South Korea, fifty-nine defectors arrived in the South. In the 1980s, when North Korea began to show signs of strain but the Great Leader Kim Il-sung was still at the helm, defectors numbered only sixty-three, although the trickle of South Koreans defecting to the North virtually stopped.

In the 1990s, as economic conditions deteriorated in the North and word of South Korea's wealth started reaching the people, defections increased to 533, the number rapidly rising at the end of that decade and into the 2000s:

71 in 1998, 148 in 1999, 312 in 2000, 583 in 2001, and 1,139 in 2002. If hunger was the primary reason for leaving, the number of defections should have declined after the end of the 1995–1998 famine, but according to defectors, by 1998 people were losing hope that the North Korean economy would ever prosper. After 2002, the number of defections continued to increase, although not exponentially. Some 1,281 people defected in 2003, 1,894 in 2004, 1,387 in 2005, 2,019 in 2006, 2,544 in 2007, and 2,809 in 2008.

An important factor contributing to the outflow of defectors in the latter half of the 1990s was the loosening of restrictions on travel within the country and across the border into China. The authorities realized the people needed to go somewhere to get food, and border guards accepted bribes from travelers for permission to cross the river. Those who did not return from China were listed by local authorities as "missing." At the same time, churches and brokers in China became more experienced in helping defectors transit China to South Korea. Since the turn of the century, enforcement along the border has waxed and waned according to the variable policies of the North Korean and Chinese governments.

Before the 1990s, defectors were hailed in South Korea as *yongsa* ("national heroes"), and upon their arrival the government proudly presented them in press conferences during which they praised South Korea and criticized North Korea. When Kim Dae-jung became president in 1998, the welcome mat was withdrawn. His administration's policy goal was to achieve reconciliation with the Kim regime, and to do so he believed South Korea must avoid angering Kim Jong-il. Defectors were kept away from the public for several months after their arrival, during which time they underwent debriefing, training, and indoctrination. Kim Dae-jung's presidential successor, Roh Moo-hyun, adopted the same policy, and defectors continued to be amazed at how supportive their new government was of the Kim regime they had just escaped.

A few defections have warranted front-page news coverage. In the 1950s, 1960s, and 1970s, South Korea collected three MiG-15s from defecting North Korean pilots.[4] In February 1983 a North Korean pilot flew his MiG-19 fighter down to the South, earning a commission in the ROK air force and a substantial monetary reward; another MiG-19 arrived courtesy of a defector in 1996. A handful of North Korean government officials began defecting in the 1990s. For example, in May 1991 Koh Young-hwan, a North Korean diplomat serving in the Congo, defected. Kang Myong-to, the son-in-law of Premier Kang Song-san, North Korea's third-highest government official, arrived in South Korea in May 1994. Hwang Jang-yop, a former cabinet secretary and author of the *Juche* ideology, along with his associate Kim Tuk-hong, the former chairman of a North Korean government trading company, escaped from their minders while on a trip to Beijing in February 1997. In August of that year, the North Korean ambassador to Egypt defected to the United States with his family. Several members of Kim Jong-il's extended family have defected, including his second wife, Song Hye-rim, her older sister, Song Hye-rang, and Song Hye-rang's son and daughter, Yi Han-yong and Yi Nam-ok. Other North Korean elite cadres may have defected to South Korea and other countries and remained out of public view because they are considered prime intelligence assets.

North Koreans sometimes defect in groups. In 1987 a family of eleven reached Taiwan, from where they were sent on to South Korea. In the spring of 1994, the ROK media reported that over one hundred North Korean loggers in Siberia had escaped from their camps and made it to the ROK embassy in Moscow (the North Korean government claimed the loggers had been kidnapped by South Koreans). In 2002, North Koreans began staging group defections into foreign embassies, consulates, and schools in China.

Following prolonged government-level negotiations, 468 refugees who had separately trekked across China and taken refuge in Vietnam were deported in a group to South Korea in two Korean jumbo jets in July 2004. Although it was an open secret that they were arriving from Vietnam, to avoid further provoking the Kim regime, the ROK government asked the media not to disclose this fact. North Korea's Committee for the Peaceful Unification of the Fatherland, a party front organization, charged that the airlift was a "premeditated abduction and terrorism in broad daylight."[5] The committee added that "South Korea should bear the responsibility for the consequences of this mishap, and all concerned parties will also pay for this," presumably referring to the Vietnamese government. Like most North Korean threats, this one came to nothing. After the Vietnam defection, ROK unification minister Chong Tong-yong asked South Korean organizations to stop aiding North Korean defectors in China, and ROK foreign minister Ban Ki-mun, who would go on to become the secretary-general of the United Nations, signaled South Korean government reluctance to accept defectors by saying that "if North Korean defectors in China go to third countries after lengthy travel through China, we would have little opportunity to deal with them. . . . It would also be difficult for us to bear infinite responsibility for the North Korean defectors."[6]

Most early defectors were soldiers or spies—people who knew how to escape and had the special means to do so—but later people from all walks of life found ways to leave. In the 1990s, defectors also included farmers and laborers (44 percent), students and unemployed workers (39 percent), diplomats and international traders (7 percent), and party and government officials (6 percent); only 4 percent were soldiers.[7] More defectors came with their families, which meant that a larger proportion of defectors were women and children. Since 2002, women defectors have outnumbered men by about three to one. Women find it easier than men to defect because they are less likely to have state-assigned jobs, so when they disappear they are not pursued, and the local police simply list them as "missing." Women also have more job opportunities in China—from housekeeping to waitressing to prostitution. The majority of defectors come from the provinces close to the Chinese border, especially North and South Hamgyong provinces and Yanggang Province—all in the poverty-stricken northeast corner of the country and convenient to the narrow and shallow Tumen River.

It might seem surprising that only a few of the several thousand North Korean diplomats and businesspeople who live overseas have ever defected. Of course, the people sent abroad are the most politically trustworthy members of the core class or they would never be issued a passport. Moreover, members of the State Security Department (SSD) accompany them to keep an eye on their movements and report their activities to Pyongyang. Perhaps a more powerful constraining influence is their knowledge that if they defect, family members, friends, and colleagues back home will be punished.

North Koreans who defect while on a foreign assignment usually do so because they have been called home unexpectedly, a sure sign that they are in trouble with the party. A case in point is the 2002 defection of a North Korean official who managed a joint venture company in Eastern Europe.[8] One day he overheard a telephone conversation between Pyongyang and his vice president, who worked for the SSD, complaining that the manager was bringing his wife to business meetings (she served as an unofficial translator) and suggesting this was not a good idea. The manager heard Pyongyang say that he would be recalled immediately, and that was enough for him. On a previous assignment an early recall had resulted in his spending two years at hard labor, and not wanting to go through this again, he secretly purchased a plane ticket to South Korea for himself and his wife. Luckily for him, European immigration officials did not notice that his passport was from North rather than South Korea, and he flew into Seoul, where the Korean immigration officials were so surprised to see a North Korean disembarking from the plane that they at first thought someone was playing a joke on them.

Even when North Koreans return from successful foreign assignments, they are usually sent to a farm or factory to spend a few months doing manual labor, as a reminder to them that in North Korea they are ordinary workers. They are treated well during this "reeducation period," but it is an unpleasant change of status from their relatively luxurious lifestyle abroad.

The decision to defect is not an easy one. Family members must be left behind to the mercy of the North Korean police, who will henceforth classify them as politically disloyal. Until the 1990s most defectors said they left for political reasons, which usually meant that they had run afoul of the North Korean authorities in one way or another, for example, by being overheard criticizing the regime. Other defectors said they had gotten caught up in bureaucratic power struggles and become scapegoats. It is highly likely that some defectors who claimed to be fleeing for political reasons had committed civil crimes instead.

In the latter half of the 1990s, most defectors were motivated by hunger. After watching friends and family members die, they decided that fleeing to China offered the best hope of survival. As the famine subsided in the late 1990s, but with malnutrition still widespread, many North Koreans left for a better economic life, even though they could survive in North Korea. In a 2004 survey of four thousand defectors, 55 percent said they had left North Korea due to economic difficulties, whereas only 9 percent cited political oppression. Another 20 percent said they left in order to reunite with family members who had already defected, an indication of how the number of defectors could cascade in the future.[9]

The knowledge that foreigners, even Chinese, are living a better life than North Koreans is becoming a major impetus for defection. Some defectors don't intend to go to South Korea; they simply cross the border into China to make a living for a few months, and once there watch South Korean television and learn that what they had been told about the South is totally false. At this point, they become curious (and sometimes angry about having been fooled all their lives) and decide to go to South Korea to see for themselves.

One of the first things most defectors do when they arrive in South Korea is to make plans to bring out family members left behind. In 2006, 44 percent of defectors arriving in South Korea said they had defected with the help of family members who had already made the trip.[10] In one highly publicized case, a seventy-five-year-old South Korean prisoner of war succeeded in defecting on his third try after learning that his family in South Korea was still alive. He then contacted his wife back in North Korea and managed to get her out the next year. Later that year, his daughter and her husband defected. Their three-year-old son, whom they had left with relatives, was soon retrieved by his mother, and another daughter and her two-year-old son defected in the following year.[11]

Defectors who have already made it to South Korea entrust the task of rescuing family members to brokers working in China, some of whom are Korean Chinese, while others are North Korean defectors who decided to go into business and live illegally there. To finance the operation, defectors may turn over their bankbooks to the brokers, who then become entitled to with-draw money that the ROK government deposits for the defectors' welfare.

Occasionally a defector returns to North Korea personally to retrieve fam-ily members, although it is a dangerous undertaking. In July 2007 a South Korean newspaper published a report of a man who defected three times.[12] He first defected in 2003 by crossing the Tumen River into China, where he met his mother and older sister, who had previously crossed over, and the three then went to South Korea by way of Mongolia. After settling in the South, the man missed his wife, so he went back to North Korea and lived with her for eight months. He then crossed over to China and returned to the South, but when his wife gave birth to a daughter, he once again returned to his home. The following year he again defected, taking along his wife and child and several neighbors.

Crossing into China

The bare statistics of defection mask the danger, hardship, and suffering that North Koreans experience when they flee their country.[13] Those who are captured in the act of defecting run the risk of arrest, torture, imprisonment, years of hard labor, and in some cases a lingering death in prison camps. Defectors leave family members behind, knowing that they may be banished or sent to prison camps as punishment for the defection. Many spend years hiding out in China and working as virtual slaves. And those who ultimately arrive in South Korea face a life of second-class citizenship in a strange land.

Only one of the three escape routes available to defectors is practical.[14] The most direct, and by far the most difficult, route is through the minefields and fences of the four-kilometer-wide DMZ. Few are known to have made the trip successfully, and they have been North Korean soldiers familiar with the zone. In February 1998 a captain in the Korean People's Army (KPA) crossed the border, and in June 2005 another KPA soldier made the trip and went undetected for several days before South Korean officials found him liv-ing in a stolen car. In separate incidents, two KPA officers made it through the minefields in 2008.

Only slightly less dangerous is an escape by sea, either navigating down the coast directly to South Korea while trying to evade North Korean patrol boats along the maritime border line, or striking out across the West Sea to reach China two hundred miles to the west (but much closer if the boat just crosses the North Korea–China border), or sailing across the East Sea some five to six hundred miles to Japan. Successful sea escapes involve several people because an individual sailor would have great difficulty navigating such distances in a fishing boat.

The first known case of defectors escaping by boat directly from the North to the South (rather than by way of China) was in May 1997, when two families comprising fourteen people left the West Sea city of Sinuiju, just south of the Chinese border, and mingled with a fleet of Chinese fishing boats before heading south. In August 2002, twenty-one North Koreans arrived in South Korea on a fishing boat they had commandeered in North Korea. The boat's engineer claimed he had not been in on the plan, and at his request he was returned to North Korea. In April 2003 three family members in a motorless fishing boat drifted south in the East Sea for five days before being rescued by a South Korean boat. In March 2006 five defectors, including four family members, crossed the maritime border on the East Sea and drifted for two days before reaching South Korea. And in 2008 a family of four made a three-hour trip directly down the West Sea coast into South Korean waters. In light of the fact that thousands of North Korean fishermen go out to sea in boats of all sizes, it may seem surprising that so few have fled to the South by boat. One explanation is that fishermen who work for themselves make more money than most North Koreans.

By far the easiest way to escape North Korea is to cross the border into China, although that leaves the defector a long way from South Korea. A 2003 Korean Workers' Party (KWP) document offering guidelines on how to stop smuggling could be used as an instruction manual for defectors. The document urges officials in border areas to confiscate Chinese cellular phones (with which smugglers and defectors can contact Chinese brokers and guides) and to "reinforce control of passage on the railroad and roads in the areas along the borders," especially "areas where human traffic is scant, the areas with rivers of narrow widths and shallow depths, [and] the areas that are close to residential areas in neighboring countries or that are connected with roads leading to towns." Local officials are also instructed to "properly block train stations in the regions along the borders, roads that are close to shores on the other side, and railway bridges."[15]

A 2002 SSD lecture titled "Let Us Strengthen the Struggle to Deter

Escapees by Enhancing Revolutionary Vigilance" tells border guards stories about the sorry fate that allegedly awaits defectors in China, Russia, and South Korea, where they are said to be tortured "without exception."[16] The lecture also points out that by escaping, defectors bring shame on their homeland. According to the lecture, indications that someone is planning to escape include their selling their homes and appliances, preparing dried food, claiming that they need money to buy medicine for a sick relative, making visits to border areas, and becoming nervous when receiving unexpected visitors.

For those who do not live near the border, domestic travel restrictions complicate escape. To travel outside one's province requires a travel document issued by the county government, which distributes these passes to workplaces for official travel. It is possible, however, to purchase these passes with bribes or simply to counterfeit them. Travel to restricted areas, including the border and the Pyongyang metropolitan district, requires in addition an endorsement number given by the security office at one's point of origin. Travel passes and endorsement numbers are checked at entrances to train stations, on the trains, and at roadside checkpoints, especially on the outskirts of towns and cities. Because most travelers lack the proper documentation to enter the border areas, they disembark from trains about twenty-five miles short of the border and walk or hitchhike the rest of the way. Walking along the road from town to town is not likely to draw attention because that is how most people travel. When travelers without valid documents or sufficient money to pay suitable bribes are stopped at police checkpoints, they can expect to be beaten and have their possessions confiscated, and if they are repeat offenders, they may be jailed until their hometown police can come to retrieve them.

The final obstacle defectors face is the river. The Tumen River marking the eastern border is narrow and shallow except near its mouth along the border with Russia. For several months in winter, the river can be crossed on the ice, and in the summer it can be forded. The Yalu (Amnok) River along the more populated western border is too wide to cross without a boat, and crossing one of the dozen bridges over either of the two rivers is possible only with official passes. North Korean border police are posted in guard shacks every five hundred meters along the river near populated areas and more thinly in the countryside. Defectors stopped at the river are usually allowed to go on their way if they pay a bribe of at least $20, which is more than most people make in a year, although border crossers may be allowed to proceed without paying a bribe if they can convince the guards that they are just going to China on business and will pay them on their return journey.

Surviving in China

Despite the danger and hardships, crossing into China is relatively easy; living in China without being caught is another matter. The Chinese government does not consider defectors legitimate refugees, even if they are starving and face certain punishment on their return home. Defectors are instead considered illegal aliens, just like people who illegally cross the Mexican border into the United States. Both China and Russia have agreements with the North Korean government to return defectors, and the Chinese also tolerate, perhaps even welcome, North Korean security agents who operate on their side of the border. The real challenge then is for defectors to get out of China and into South Korea or another country that will treat them as legitimate economic or political refugees.

Before they can find a way out, however, most defectors end up living in China for years. A 2003 poll of five hundred defectors revealed that they spent an average of almost four years in a second country before arriving in South Korea. Over 25 percent said they had lived as refugees for between five and six years before arriving in South Korea, whereas only 12 percent had reached the South in one year.[17] The best way for defectors to elude the police is to make contact with one of the South Korean religious organizations that operate clandestinely in the border cities or to take refuge in the home of a Christian Chinese Korean.

As mentioned above, more women than men defect. In some cases North Korean marriage brokers arrange for North Korean women to defect and pass them on to Chinese brokers. Other women are lured by agents who hang around train stations and markets looking for attractive women who seem to be on their own. In the best of cases, marriage brokering is a legitimate business proposition that benefits all parties. In the worst of cases, women are traded like a commodity, with price markups at each stage in the distribution chain. The North Korean broker may sell her across the border for as little as $50, the price of a pig, and a Chinese broker may get $1,000 to $2,000 for her on the retail marriage market.[18] The typical customer for a North Korean woman is an older Chinese farmer who has lost his wife or been unable to find a wife because of age, poverty, or personal defect. Many of the North Korean women who go to China to marry are single or widowed, but some are already married and sell themselves in the hope of reducing the economic burden on their families.

It is difficult for North Korean women to gain legal residency in China, even if they marry a Chinese, although local officials are not always strict about enforcing the law. Defectors must be wary of neighbors who might call the police in order to earn a government bounty of $100 or more. For this reason a new wife is likely to be especially accommodating to neighbors and, of course, to her new husband. Cases of physical and sexual abuse are common. Some women quickly tire of their new life and try to escape. Realizing this, many husbands hold their wives as virtual prisoners, harshly punishing any escape attempts.

Korean men who work in China earn their living as laborers, usually on farms, where they may work for little more than room and board. Like women defectors, they are in constant danger of being turned in to the police. Employers of illegal aliens can be fined the equivalent of several thousand dollars, so defectors must keep a low profile. Farmers employing defectors have been known to turn them in as transients to the police right after harvest so they do not have to pay them. Some defectors go into the mountains, even living in small hillside caves they have dug for themselves. The defectors who have the toughest time are the young children, who survive by begging and committing petty crimes. Most of them are caught after only a few days or weeks along the border, but those who are able to make it to a large inland city can elude the authorities for a longer time.

Chinese police keep a sharp eye out for defectors, making sweeps of homes and businesses in border towns to check identity papers. North Korean agents also operate in the border area, looking for specific individuals such as defecting North Korean border guards or members of the North Korean elite class. Female agents of the *Kisaeng Yodan* ("Geisha corps") take jobs in bars and other places where defectors may work or gather in order to intercept them.

The goal of most defectors, other than those who have gone to China to earn money or visit relatives, is to reach South Korea. To do so usually requires the assistance of a professional guide, who is often provided by one of the South Korean religious organizations that help defectors. Transit has become more difficult since the early 2000s as the Chinese government has cracked down on these guides, sentencing them to prison terms of five to ten years.

There are three ways to get out of China.[19] Defectors who can afford to purchase counterfeit identity papers, a forged passport, and a plane or boat ticket can travel in style, but the cost is in the range of $10,000, which is more than most defectors can get their hands on. A less expensive alternative, which became popular in the early 2000s, is to rush through the gates or climb over the walls of a foreign embassy, consulate, or school in a Chinese city, as a number of defectors have done to get into American, South

Korean, Japanese, Spanish, German, and Canadian compounds. In most cases foreign groups or individuals who want to publicize the plight of the refugees organize these attempts. Once inside the foreign compounds, the refugees often have to wait for months until the foreign government is able to negotiate a safe passage out of the country with Chinese authorities, often to an intermediate destination to avoid angering the North Korean government. For example, twenty-five North Koreans made their way into the Spanish embassy in March 2002, from which they were transported first to the Philippines and then on to South Korea.

The Chinese have taken vigorous steps to block intrusions into diplomatic compounds. In 2002 Chinese police even forced their way into the Japanese consulate in Shenyang and dragged out five North Koreans while consular officials looked on, although thanks to the public outcry in Japan, the North Koreans were later released and permitted to go to South Korea.

Some defectors head overland for Mongolia, whose government tries to maintain good relations with South Korea and consequently does not repatriate defectors to North Korea. However, to reach Mongolia a defector must travel almost a thousand miles over open plains. Only one main rail line goes into Mongolia from China, and the Chinese police watch it closely, as they do the border area.

Currently, the longest, but most reliable, route to South Korea is through Southeast Asia, with the most popular destination being Thailand. Typically, groups of five to ten defectors are guided across China in an underground railway that employs trains, buses, and automobiles to cover a distance of some three thousand miles, before they slip across the border into Vietnam, Laos, or Burma and from there cross into Thailand. The cost for this service begins at about $2,000 and can go up to $10,000 or more depending on the escape route and the number of defectors in the party. Some defectors have sought asylum in Vietnam, but since the 2004 mass defector exodus, Vietnamese officials have discouraged defectors from taking refuge there. In 2007, twenty years after North Korean agents embarrassed the Burmese government by killing a visiting delegation of seventeen South Korean government officials, Burma reestablished diplomatic ties with North Korea, thereby reducing the attractiveness of this country as a destination for defectors. The most popular route for defectors heading for Thailand seems to be Laos, which, despite having good relations with the North Korean government, is so poor and corrupt that defectors with money can bribe the police to gain safe passage through the country. Once they reach the banks of the Mekong River, a short ferryboat ride brings them to Thailand.

The Thai government, which has a history of legitimate business dealings with North Korea (especially as an exporter of rice), honors North Koreans' refugee status and permits them to travel on to South Korea. Upon entering the country, defectors are arrested by Thai police and required to pay a fine of about $300 or spend a month in jail before they are eligible for an exit visa. Conditions in Thai jails can be difficult, but living in a hot and crowded jail is better than being sent back to North Korea, and most defectors immediately surrender to the police.

The defectors who have the easiest time getting out of China are those upper-level cadres whom the South Korean government considers a valuable source of information. In one case, for example, a cadre who had a close relative serving in a top military position illegally crossed into China and went into hiding. Because the defector had high party connections, North Korean officials put out an all-points bulletin on him and told the Chinese police he was wanted for murder. One day he was relaxing in a steamy Chinese bath when he heard several North Korean agents talking about his case and the difficulty of finding him. Realizing how close he was to being caught, the defector decided to trust his fate to the South Koreans and made contact with an agent of South Korea's National Intelligence Service (NIS), who provided him with false papers and spirited him out of China within days.[20]

Forced Return to North Korea

Human rights organizations have estimated that every year China forcibly returns about five thousand defectors, whose fate varies from case to case according to the changing policies of the Chinese and North Korean governments.[21] After the number of defectors started growing in the late 1990s, the Chinese government became more active in tracking them down, as it did in the months leading up to the 2008 Beijing Olympic Games.[22]

Chinese police take captured defectors to a neighborhood police station, where they undergo preliminary interrogation before being transported to a larger police station, where their possessions are confiscated and they are put in a holding cell, often without their belt or shoelaces to prevent suicide attempts. Interrogation may last a week or longer and sometimes includes beatings. The police are interested in learning why the defectors are in China and whom they have contacted. When the investigation is completed, defectors are turned over in groups to the North Korean police, who take them back across the border.

Repatriated defectors are imprisoned in a North Korean jail at the closest border town until police from their hometown can come to get them, which can be a matter of weeks. Prison conditions are harsh, and food is scarce, resulting in a few prisoner deaths, which saves the local police the trouble of having to come and pick them up. On the other hand, prison officials hate for too many prisoners to die in their jails, so they urge the local police to come as soon as possible.

Defector interrogations are routinely accompanied by beatings and often torture. Defectors are asked four key questions: Did you meet any South Koreans? Did you meet any members of religious organizations? Did you watch South Korean TV or videotapes or listen to South Korean radio? Were you trying to defect to South Korea? Women are also asked if they had sexual relations with Chinese men. Those defectors who manage to convince their interrogators that the answer to every question is no will receive only a few months of hard labor as punishment. A yes answer to any one of them generally earns the defector a sentence in a political prison camp for one or more years on the charge of being a traitor or a spy. Interrogators are lenient with those they believe crossed the border simply to get food or earn a little money, as long as the border crossing is not frequently repeated.

The applicable laws on defection provide authorities with considerable latitude in meting out punishment. The mildest punishment for defection is stipulated by Article 233 of the 2004 revision of North Korea's Criminal Code: "Whoever crosses the border out of or into the country illegally shall be sentenced to two years or less of labor discipline." Article 62 stipulates the harshest sentence for defectors who have associated with South Koreans or Americans: "In case a citizen commits such traitorous acts as an escape, surrendering to foreign countries, treachery, [or] handing over secrets to them by betraying the fatherland, he shall be sentenced to more than five years of labor correction. In case the circumstances are serious, he shall be sentenced to an indefinite term of labor correction, death, and confiscation of property." If they are so inclined, the authorities can also add a variety of other charges, including smuggling and "bringing in or spreading decadent culture."

A bribe consistent in size with the seriousness of the alleged crime will usually enable a defector to secure release without serving a prison sentence, with the amount ranging from tens to thousands of dollars. Many defectors repatriated from China make one or more subsequent attempts to defect, even though they risk severer punishment if captured after the first escape attempt. Once the crime of defection has been placed in a person's record, he or she is branded for life as politically unreliable and is subject to closer surveillance than ordinary citizens.

Life in South Korea

Against long odds, some defectors finally make it to South Korea, arriving at a rate of about fifty a week (in 2008). It is difficult to imagine what they face in the new society in which they find themselves, where fellow Koreans speak a different dialect and use many foreign words. Even people who grow up in their own culture usually find the first years of adulthood challenging as they search for a job, take on adult responsibilities, and form long-term adult relationships, but they can at least benefit from the examples provided by their parents, older peers, and the media. Coming from a different culture, North Korean defectors have little to guide them.

As soon as they arrive in South Korea, defectors are taken into custody by the NIS and housed in a special facility in Seoul. Over a period of one week to several months, NIS agents conduct an interrogation in which the defectors are required to write out detailed accounts of their lives. The dual purpose of this interrogation is to verify that they are legitimate defectors (rather than North Korean spies or Chinese Koreans) and to gather fresh intelligence about North Korea. During this period the defectors eat well, watch television, and read newspapers, thus beginning their acclimation to South Korean society.

Before the 1990s, the ROK government classified defectors into several categories according to the value of the information and political capital their defection provided. Ironically, this meant that former members of the North Korean ruling class, who were in part responsible for the oppression of the North Korean people, received greater rewards for defecting than those whom they had oppressed. The ROK government provided former secretary Hwang Jang-yop, the architect of North Korea's *Juche* theory, years of special protection and employment after he defected, although he later clashed with the government over its North Korea policy and the restrictions placed on his movements. Today the treatment of defectors is more egalitarian.

When the NIS is convinced that an individual is a genuine defector, he or she is transferred to Hanawon ("one community"), a government halfway house located in the vicinity of Seoul. Established in 1999 and put under the authority of the Ministry of Unification, Hanawon has been expanded as more defectors arrive, and as of 2008 it could accommodate six hundred people for a three-month period of orientation and education. The three broad goals of the Hanawon program are to provide emotional and psychological support for the new arrivals, to teach them about South Korean and Western capitalist culture, and to provide job training and contacts. The task of acculturation is immense, and a few months at Hanawon can hardly counter a lifetime of indoctrination and experience in a totalitarian socialist state. Most North Koreans have never driven a car, used a computer, or made a call on a cell phone. They have never even imagined a supermarket or a Western-style department store. They do not know how to earn, save, or invest money. Defectors who need further assistance can spend a few additional weeks at one of several Hanawon satellite centers located around the country, and school-age defectors can enroll in the unification ministry's Hangyo-reh middle and high schools.

Defectors usually want to live and work in the capital city of Seoul because, in North Korea, the capital of Pyongyang is the city of the privileged class. The unification ministry runs a lottery to determine who gets to live in Seoul and who must begin life in one of the other cities, which, contrary to what most defectors think, may well provide a more pleasant and welcoming environment. To help them get started, defectors receive a grant of $20,000 (the amount changes from year to year) paid in installments over two years; families receive $37,000.[23] Individuals can receive up to $15,000 in additional payments for completing educational and job-training programs, and additional monies are granted for special needs such as medicine and apartment down payments. To help defectors find employment, the government also subsidizes half of their wages for two years. Special monetary compensation and research positions in government think tanks are provided to a few defectors whom the government believes may have something special to offer in terms of intelligence on North Korea.

In most cases a local police officer is assigned as a defector's case officer. In the past, the police officer accompanied the defector almost everywhere, providing both cultural guidance and protection from confidence tricksters and other criminals—and in some cases from North Korean secret agents. These days, a police officer is simply on call, although defectors considered to be at greater risk from North Korean agents receive more protection, and a few are even housed in the NIS compound outside of Seoul. It is not known how many defectors have actually been threatened by North Korean agents, although it is not unusual for them to receive threatening telephone calls, some of which may come from South Koreans who, for one reason or another, object to their presence. The only known case of assassination was the death of Yi Han-yong (mentioned earlier in chapter 2), a distant relative of Kim Jong-il. Yi came to South Korea in 1982 and published his memoirs in Korean (the English title is *Kim Jong-il's Royal Family*). He was murdered in February 1997, presumably by North Korean agents, perhaps as a warning to Secretary Hwang Jang-yop, who had just defected to the South.

After they arrive in South Korea, defectors expect life to get easier, although they do experience some apprehension based on the stories they have been told since childhood about South Korea being a dog-eat-dog world where only the strong survive. They quickly learn that money is a primary value in South Korean society, and their desire to get rich makes them vulnerable to all sorts of swindles. Because their lives in North Korea were so controlled, they look for freedom in their employment, for example, by becoming entrepreneurs, but they do not realize what a high failure rate new businesses face in a capitalist economy. Often their only area of expertise is their knowledge of North Korea (or rather, their own experiences in North Korea), which they can put to use by giving lectures, but with thousands of defectors already in the South, competition on the lecture circuit is stiff, and only a few defectors can make any money from speaking or writing.

As in all Asian cultures, personal and family connections count for a lot in South Korean society, putting North Koreans at a disadvantage, and employment surveys paint a bleak picture of their chances of finding a job. A 2006 survey of 451 defectors found a 67 percent unemployment rate, and those with jobs were earning only about half the legal minimum wage.[24] Part of the employment problem is that defectors do not want to take the more difficult, less desirable jobs, for example, in manual labor, even though they may be the best entry-level jobs for them.

The annual job turnover rate for defectors has been estimated at 60 percent.[25] Low wages seem to be the biggest complaint, with one poll finding that only 17 percent were satisfied with their income.[26] Rather than consider their jobs the first step up the occupational ladder, many defectors feel that they have already paid their vocational dues in North Korea and deserve a job comparable to the one they had there, even if they gained and kept it by the grace of the party rather than through open competition. In South Korea's relatively hierarchical society, defectors' lack of job seniority within a company also works against them. After several job failures, defectors become discouraged; many simply quit looking for work and fall into poverty. A 2004 unification ministry study found that 70 percent of defectors were receiving government welfare payments.[27]

Success on the job requires personal as well as job skills. Defectors often encounter social and job-related situations in which they do not know how to behave, leading to misunderstandings and awkward relations with other workers. A 2005 survey of five hundred defectors found that 67 percent believed they were treated unfairly in their workplaces, and 40 percent said they felt ostracized by their colleagues.[28]

Defectors suffer from a variety of adjustment problems on and off the job. They have a somewhat different dialect and vocabulary from South Koreans. For example, they are not familiar with words borrowed from other languages because the Kim regime has decreed that only "pure" Korean expressions should be used, although the younger generation is beginning to adopt foreign loan words like "menu," "diet," "music video," "single," "wife," and "fast food"—all commonly used in South Korea as well. Reading can also be a problem. Older South Koreans can read several thousand Chinese characters, some of which appear in newspaper and magazine articles and books, but *Juche* theory has banned the use of these characters in North Korea. In public, the defectors' dialect immediately identifies them as North Koreans. South Koreans tend to keep their distance simply because the defectors are considered different—perhaps like poor relatives whom one is not eager to meet. Their complexion is often slightly darker than that of South Korean city dwellers, making them look like country bumpkins. Their clothes may be too flashy, and their body language somewhat diffident. In short, at least in the first years after they arrive, defectors are viewed by many South Koreans as coming from an inferior culture.

Defectors have trouble making new friends. Life in North Korea is lived in groups: work groups, school groups, neighborhood groups, and party-affiliated social and political groups; individuals who spend time alone immediately fall under suspicion. This communitarian culture puts pressure on individuals to conform, but it also provides social support. South Korean society is far more individualistic. With no restrictions on communication or travel, South Koreans have geographically broader friendship networks than North Koreans. Defectors with distant relatives in South Korea are often disappointed that the relatives do not seem interested in them, which is hardly surprising because in most cases they have not met since before the Korean War. When the Southern relatives become aware that some of their kin have come down from the North, they may not want to get too close for fear of incurring a financial responsibility. For lack of friends and relatives, many former North Koreans join a church, which provides the same kind of complete social environment they were accustomed to in North Korea, and the religious teachings are similar in form to the worship of Kim Il-sung, Kim Jong-il, and Kim Jong-suk—the father, son, and mother.

And then there is the problem of marriage. Although the practice of arranged marriages has disappeared in South Korean society, it is still not uncommon in the North, where personal connections are stronger. As outsiders, defectors are somewhat limited in their choice of marriage partners.

Imagine, for example, what South Korean parents would say if their child proposed to marry a defector. Some defectors marry other defectors, but most eventually marry a native South Korean. Once married, the new partners must cope with the difficulties that arise from their different backgrounds and experiences, along with the marital strains caused by defectors' low self-esteem and employment problems.

Finding a spouse is even more difficult for defectors who were married in the North. Because the South Korean government has conferred citizenship on all Koreans who live in the North, if the defector left behind a spouse, his or her marriage is considered legal until the courts determine otherwise. In some cases the defector was escaping from an abusive spouse (North Korea is still a male-dominated society, and poverty can make people mean); in other cases, the spouse was left behind for economic reasons, and there is no news of what became of him or her. In early 2007, the Seoul Family Court ruled that petitions from defectors for divorce can proceed as long as the unification ministry has issued a determination that the missing spouse does not reside in South Korea. Shortly thereafter, the court granted divorces to thirteen defectors—the first of 429 cases that had been filed at that time.[29]

Personality problems make jobs, marriages, and social relationships more difficult. Most defectors have lived a difficult life and faced physical and emotional challenges that few South Koreans can imagine. A lifetime of coping with fear and deprivation leaves emotional scars. Defectors also suffer from strong guilt when they think of the family and friends they have left behind, who may lose their jobs and their homes and, in the worst cases, be sent to a prison camp. Some defectors also feel guilty about having turned their back on their country, and even some South Koreans blame them for having done so.

Defectors who have left members of their immediate family behind suffer the most. One defector we interviewed said that she had voluntarily left her husband and son because her father had recently been branded a member of the hostile class. Although she was not responsible for this misfortune, her in-laws blamed her for jeopardizing her husband's welfare, so she decided to leave for China, where her mother was living. She gave her son a package of candy and kissed him goodbye, saying that she would be gone for a few days. She told her husband she planned to stay in China (although she really intended to go on to South Korea), and she said that if she didn't return in several months, he should divorce her and remarry. After she arrived in South Korea, she heard that her husband had indeed remarried, and she was working to earn money to bring her son out.[30]

A more tragic story involved the loss of a child. The mother and her husband, who was a security official, were fleeing across the border in heavy snow, with border guards in close pursuit. The mother knew that if they captured her husband, he would be tortured and perhaps killed because of his job. Their little boy began crying, and frightened that he would give away their location, the mother buried him in the deep snow in order to save her husband and herself. They escaped to China and then to South Korea, but she never recovered from the horror of having killed her child and ended up in a psychiatric facility.[31]

Although North Koreans exhibit a broad range of personality traits, as do any large group of people, a South Korean psychiatrist who conducted a survey of 528 defectors in 2001 identified several characteristics that they shared widely: passivity, belief in equal distribution of wealth, reluctance to disturb the status quo, reluctance to express thoughts, a tendency to attribute success to special opportunities rather than individual effort, and a strong need to justify their actions.[32] In some respects, North Koreans hold to more traditional values than do South Koreans. The psychiatrist suggests that defectors have more in common with older South Koreans than with the younger generation, which he notes is ironic because the younger generation of South Koreans tends to be more enthusiastic about reunification.

Several surveys conducted in South Korea have attempted to assess defectors' physical and mental health. The most common physical ailments are digestive problems and arthritis, whereas the most common psychological problems are depression and anxiety.[33] Defectors already suffered from most of their physical illnesses before leaving the North, but the trials of defection exacerbate the psychological illnesses.[34] In a mental-health survey of 196 defectors conducted in 2007, 37 percent were found to be suffering from depression serious enough to require treatment, and 30 percent had milder forms of depression.[35]

North Koreans love their homeland, and were it not for the impact of their collapsed economy, most would probably be willing to live under a dictatorial government—at least for the time being. Only when their basic economic needs were met might they turn their thoughts to gaining more freedom. Albert O. Hirschman's exit-voice theory, introduced at the beginning of the chapter, includes a third factor: loyalty. The more loyal people are, the less likely they are to defect (and if given the opportunity, the more likely they are to complain in an attempt to change the organization or state to which they are loyal). The Kim regime has worked mightily to instill loyalty in its people, but its efforts have had only mixed success in the face of

North Korea's failed economy.[36] As a consequence, the regime must depend on its social- and information-control mechanisms to keep more North Koreans from defecting.

Compared to the 4.5 million East Germans who fled to the West between World War II and German unification (about half of them coming before the Berlin Wall went up in 1961), the number of North Koreans reaching the South is a mere trickle. Should that trickle become a flood, it will put severe strains on both North and South Korean society—strains that the South Koreans, at least, are not prepared to cope with.

CHAPTER NINE

~

The End Comes Slowly

North Korea is designed and run for the benefit of the Kim family and their elite supporters. The fact that Kim Il-sung and Kim Jong-il have remained in power for over half a century under difficult circumstances is a testament to their sagacity, and the political edifice they have so painstakingly constructed will not be quickly torn down.

The portrait of North Korea drawn in the preceding chapters looks something like this. Kim Jong-il is not crazy: he is callous of the welfare of his people, distrustful of almost everyone, and sometimes emotional and even impulsive, but he knows what he is doing. The model of government the two Kims have chosen to adopt and perpetuate is totalitarian dictatorship—although government control is not as total as it might at first appear. Once dictatorship has been chosen as a governing style, the social structure is to a large extent determined, thus explaining the marked similarity of dictatorships around the world.

A totalitarian dictator must run a centrally controlled economy in order to regulate the lives of the people, and it helps if the economy is collective in nature, the better to prevent people from going off on their own. An economy of shortages has the virtue that it focuses people's attention on earning a living and prevents them from cultivating other desires, for instance, for political participation. Government control of information is an important lever of power, and the Kim regime has quite successfully kept its people ignorant of both the outside world and their own society, although this ignorance is not as great as it once was. On the other hand, repressive constraints on information flow pose a problem for the regime, creating what Ronald Winetrobe calls the "dictator's dilemma": people are afraid to tell the dictator what they truly think, and as a consequence, the dictator's knowledge is flawed.[1] To stay in power, Kim must be above the law, and the law must serve his interests; consequently, he is the only person in North Korea who enjoys full human rights. To legitimize his extralegal status, Kim has equated himself with the state, saying, "Without me, there can be no North Korea."

While few foreigners would want to live in a country like North Korea, not all North Koreans live a life of misery. The majority are probably sufficiently satisfied with their country that they would not want to leave, even if given a chance. They are devoted to their families, treasure their friendships, find meaning in their lives, and hope for a better future. They have picnics in the park, go to movies, and enjoy parties with friends—just like people everywhere. They do not have access to the variety or quantity of food that South Koreans do, and they are sometimes hungry, but they enjoy a good meal on occasion. Still, their existence is precarious and subject to changing economic and political conditions. According to a World Food Program (WFP) survey conducted in 2004, one-third of the people never have enough to eat, half sometimes do not have enough, and only 10 to 20 percent always have enough to eat.[2] The food situation has not materially improved since then, with the WFP and other organizations reporting in 2008 that North Korea was experiencing its worst food shortages since the mid-1990s.

Regardless of their situation in life, whether they are members of the upper political class whom foreign visitors may come into contact with or are poor people living in the mountains, North Koreans could and should be much healthier, happier, and freer than they are now. Preventing their lives from improving is, to put it simply, the Kim regime.

Prospects for Survival

To adopt a phrase from the American social reformer W. E. B. DuBois, the end is coming slowly for North Korea. The regime is trying to convince its people that by 2012, the centennial of Kim Il-sung's birth, North Korea will have become an economically powerful state, but there is no prospect of this happening. The regime's political decisions have locked the economy into a cycle of failure, and the government's campaign for economic self-sufficiency is self-defeating. The country's isolation, while protecting the regime, has cut it off from the global economy. And the saber rattling of Kim's military-first politics is isolating the country even more.

Ever since Kim Il-sung's death in 1994, North Korea watchers have speculated about the impending collapse of the Kim Jong-il regime. Kim stayed out of the public eye for three years, during which time no meetings of the

Supreme People's Assembly were held. Floods in 1995 and 1996 devastated the countryside and triggered the Arduous March famine. Most concessionary trade with the former Warsaw Pact signatories ended. Bureaucratic corruption continued unabated. The country was drifting. In the late 1990s, top defector Hwang Jang-yop predicted a collapse within five years.

Then the United States and the international community threw the Kim regime a lifeline. Billions of dollars in aid began flowing into the country in 1996, including over $1 billion from the United States, which in 1994 had signed the Agreed Framework between the United States of America and the Democratic People's Republic of Korea, which provided North Korea with an annual delivery of a half million tons of heavy fuel oil and construction of a new light-water nuclear reactor, all in return for a freeze of Pyongyang's aging nuclear facilities. More important than the oil and the reactor construction was the political recognition that the Kim regime received as a dialogue partner with the United States. In October 2000, North Korea's top political military officer, Vice Marshal Jo Myong-rok, received an invitation from President Bill Clinton to visit the White House, and later that month Secretary of State Madeleine Albright visited Pyongyang—two diplomatic firsts for U.S.–North Korean relations. Other countries also engaged the Kim regime at the highest levels. South Korean president Kim Dae-jung visited Pyongyang in June 2000, and his successor, President Roh Moo-hyun, visited in October 2007. Russian president Vladimir Putin paid a visit in July 2000—the first Russian president ever to visit North Korea while in office. Chinese president Jiang Zemin traveled to Pyongyang in September 2001, marking the first presidential visit since China angered North Korea by normalizing relations with South Korea in 1992. In September 2002, Prime Minister Junichiro Koizumi became the first Japanese head of state to go to Pyongyang and paid a return visit two years later. "Why on earth do I have to go visit big countries?" asked Kim Jong-il in August 2000. "Even though I stay in Pyongyang, various powerful countries come visit me, do they not?"[3]

This international recognition, coming at a time when the country was undergoing its greatest domestic trials since the Korean War, could hardly help but impress the North Korean people, despite their bitter disappointment with Kim's domestic leadership. It undoubtedly emboldened Kim, who took it as a sign that his policies were a success.

The Kim regime continues to employ leverage provided by its nuclear and missile programs. At the Six-Party Talks, first convened in 2003 (and further legitimizing the Kim regime), a new denuclearization agreement was reached in principle in September 2005. Unhappy with delays in its implementation,

North Korea detonated its first nuclear device in October 2006, angering the other five parties to the talks. However, no one could think of a better option than continuing to negotiate, and in February and September 2007, steps were taken to implement the October 2006 agreement, including resuming economic aid to North Korea. It is doubtful that this most recent agreement will be any more lasting than previous ones. At the time this book goes to press, six years after the start of the Six-Party Talks, North Korea appears to have more nuclear weapons and more long-range missiles than before the talks began, and the talks themselves are, once again, in jeopardy.

Destabilizing Influences

Although international events seem to favor the continued rule of Kim Jong-il, his health does not. Kim turned sixty-seven in 2009, and years of drinking and smoking have compromised his health. More importantly, he seems to be suffering from the aftereffects of his 2008 stroke. Until he secures some kind of security guarantee from the United States, Kim must worry about the future of his regime. China, although a loyal supporter to date, holds Kim in low regard and seems to be positioning itself to exercise more influence over the Korean Peninsula in the future. North Korea's relations with Japan remain hostile. The South Korean government's support for the northern regime depends on which administration happens to be in office; the Lee Myung-bak administration that took office in early 2008 is much less generous with Kim than were the previous two South Korean administrations.

Among North Korea watchers, economists tend to be the most pessimistic about the country's chances for survival, and indeed, defectors most often cite economic difficulties as their main reason for leaving their country. North Koreans have gotten used to living in an economy of severe shortages, but they do not like it. The daily struggle to eat, keep warm, and get to school and work continues to threaten social stability. Even the fortunate three million living in Pyongyang, who are Kim Jong-il's strongest supporters, are not insulated from economic hardships. North Korea's international businesses are likewise plagued by economic problems. When the George W. Bush administration in late 2005 tried to pressure the Kim regime to end its nuclear program by targeting foreign banks doing business with North Korea, the effect was dramatic. A North Korean government official involved in international transactions said in a private interview, "I have to find money, but it is almost impossible. There is no credit, no trust, no interest in investment in North Korea."[4]

The influx of information into North Korea, especially about how people in other countries live, is opening people's eyes as they have never been opened before. Even so, not until they cross into China do North Koreans begin to understand how other people actually live, and those who only get as far as the Chinese border area still do not see the prosperity that South Koreans enjoy. Information about the outside world makes the pain of economic deprivation all the more difficult to bear. The most damaging comparisons are with life in China and South Korea, two neighboring countries that North Koreans formerly considered poor. In a 2002 defector survey, 83 percent agreed that "North Korea is far poorer than China," and 79 percent agreed that "South Korea is an economically affluent country."[5] The North Korean people have to ask the obvious questions: Why should South Koreans be so rich when we North Koreans, who are supposedly following a more advanced economic model, are so poor? How can the Chinese, whom we have looked down on all these years, have passed us by, even though they also have a socialist system?

Ordinary North Koreans are also comparing themselves with the more affluent living among them—in what is supposed to be an egalitarian society. Kim Jong-il's lifestyle has never been revealed, so most North Koreans are unaware that he lives like a king. Similarly closed to their view are the lives of the top officials, who live in Pyongyang's residential enclaves. They can, however, see how local party cadres live, and while those people do not live in luxury, they do have more than the average North Korean, even though they are supposed to "serve the people." And then there are the newly rich who flaunt their wealth by driving private cars, wearing expensive clothes, and living in illegally purchased apartments and houses. This violation of socialist equality angers ordinary people, but they dare not voice complaints because rich people also have good political connections. A well-dressed person may be rudely jostled on the street or subjected to snide remarks, but that is usually the extent of the complaints. One former member of the Pyongyang elite class relates how he was forced to take a bus to work after Kim Jong-il decreed, for some reason or another, that people should not ride bicycles in the city. A fellow bus rider, probably frustrated because the buses and trolleys are usually overcrowded and people have to wait in long lines to get on, said, "Hey, you seem to be a well-off class guy with such a fine suit and smooth skin, but let us tell you that we are not happy to see you in such a fine condition."[6]

Another potentially destabilizing factor almost unique to North Korea is the fact that the legitimacy of the father-and-son regime is built on lies: that

Kim Il-sung liberated Korea from the Japanese, that South Korea and the United States started the Korean War, that Kim Il-sung won the war, that Kim Jong-il was born on the slopes of Mt. Paektu, and so forth. In the 2002 defector survey cited above, 41 percent said that North Koreans consider Kim Il-sung's greatest alleged accomplishment to be "liberating us from Japan's colonial rule."[7] Dictators, and for that matter most politicians in democracies, rely to some degree on lies and half-truths to elevate themselves above the masses and distinguish themselves from their competitors for power, but the two Kim's have taken lying beyond even what was seen in the days of Mao and Stalin. What will happen when the truth finally comes out is hard to say. In Russia, the truth about Stalin temporarily dimmed his reputation, but many Russians who miss the economic security the state formerly provided now remember him fondly. Perhaps Kim Il-sung will be forgiven for the same reason. Kim Jong-il, who boasts of resisting "imperialistic aggression," may by that means save his reputation as well.

A destabilizing trend particularly worrisome to the regime is the emergence of a Western-oriented youth culture of individualism and consumerism. Young people want to earn money to buy things they have seen in South Korean videos, and they want to sing South Korean pop songs, dance to Western music, and wear jeans and printed T-shirts. They are not interested in socialism. And then there are the truly pernicious influences on society that are not limited to the youth, including crime, alcoholism, and the use of hard drugs.

Any number of structural influences put pressure on North Korean society and contribute to its instability, although these influences are not so easily seen. The economic cost of corruption is staggering. The insistence on running a socialist command economy is suicidal. Kim's military-first policy guarantees that the best of the country's resources will go to the nonproductive military rather than to the civilian sector. Bureaucratic infighting takes a severe toll on managerial resources. Internationally, the U.S. economic embargo on North Korea, including international trading restrictions such as the Wassenaar Arrangement, hinder North Korean commerce.

Stabilizing Influences

And yet, for all its problems, North Korea appears to be a relatively stable society, and the Kim Jong-il regime, incompetent though it may be in running the economy, seems as secure as when Kim Il-sung was overseeing a growing economy in the 1960s. As in any society, the strongest force for stability is simply inertia. People have grown accustomed to Kim family rule. Kim Jong-il is not well liked, but because his highly respected father appointed him successor, the son is politically untouchable. Politically, North Koreans suffer from a kind of tunnel vision resulting from the fact that they do not have contemporary or historical experience with democratic governance. After centuries of living under Korean monarchs and forty years under a Japanese colonial administration, prior to Kim Il-sung's assuming power, the people have low political expectations. They take for granted that they will be ruled by their superiors and simply wish those superiors would do a better job. At least under the Kim regime, they are ruled by Koreans rather than foreigners.

Another source of stability is the excellent social-control mechanisms the regime has put in place, consisting of an overlapping assortment of security forces that includes the Ministry of People's Security, the State Security Department, and the Security Command, backed up by party cells and neighborhood groups. According to testimony from defectors, spies (actually, ordinary people recruited by the police temporarily) have infiltrated the entire population. Because they have the collective power to undermine the regime, the elites are kept under particularly close surveillance. Those few people with telephones in their homes can expect that their lines are tapped. Everyone in the society, from highest to lowest, must attend weekly political-struggle sessions in which they are required to confess a sample of their failings and report on the failings of others. Hundreds and even thousands of people, including party members, are caught up in purges. And to deter the brave and reckless from disobedience, the Kim regime has perfected the practice of *yongoje*, or "family punishment," whereby not only the individual but his or her immediate family, relatives, and even close friends and associates may be arrested.

The members of the privileged class of three million (the upper half of the core class) appear to support the regime actively on the premise that they would not otherwise have as good a life. Compared to the masses, as well as to what their parents and grandparents had before the communists came to power, they are well-off and know that if they stray from the party line, they risk being thrown back into the working class—or even into prison. They also fear that if South Korea should ever take control of the North, they would face discrimination or punishment. To reinforce this fear, the regime distributed videotapes in the 1990s of former Eastern European Communist Party members reduced to selling pencils on the street.

The Kims have never tolerated the existence of any political party or organized group other than the Korean Workers' Party, so even though the regime's hold on the people has weakened, there are no alternative groups or institutions that people can rally to, unlike in Cold War Eastern Europe where churches, trade unions, student groups, and intellectuals provided the nucleus for political dissent. No political factions exist even among the educated elites. Very small opposition groups might secretly exist, but by the time they became known to outside observers, the regime would already have eliminated them. Defectors say that people sometimes mutter about how bad things are, but only among trusted friends and family, and even so, people are occasionally hauled off to prison for voicing an innocent complaint. North Korean propagandists' warnings that "impure, hostile elements are wriggling inside our country" should be interpreted as the regime's attempt to demonstrate its vigilance rather than as a reference to organized opposition.[8]

Some North Korea watchers have speculated about the existence of deeper political fault lines in North Korean society. For example, it has been suggested that there may be tension between political hard-liners, who prefer the status quo, and soft-liners, who favor liberalizing society. North Koreans indeed hold a variety of viewpoints about the merits of change, but these viewpoints represent differences more in individual opinion than among groups or classes. Likewise, some observers see signs that the party and the military are in competition for power, perhaps also with the government bureaucracy, but there is considerable overlap in membership among these three institutions. Members of the younger generation of North Koreans are more liberal in their ideas and tastes than their seniors, but the different generations do not have their own independent political organizations: everyone is a member of one or more party-controlled organizations.

Yet another source of stability is North Koreans' self-image as "Kim Il-sung's people." As a nation, the North Korean people believe they face a hostile world, and this belief contributes to internal cohesion, as outlined in chapter 1. Most importantly, North Korea's long-running disputes with the United States (over weapons of mass destruction and other issues) create tension that the regime employs to keep its people united in the face of a purported foreign threat.

Some of the factors that threaten to destabilize North Korea act at the same time as sources of stability. The most obvious example is the food shortage, a cause of widespread dissatisfaction with the regime that at the same time keeps people preoccupied with hunting for food. Drug and alcohol use increases crime but also provides an escape from daily misery. Widespread corruption is a clear sign that the government is not working properly, but it also provides a practical way to get things done. Loss of faith in the eventual triumph of socialism highlights the futility of years of working within the socialist system but also stifles the false hope that the party's promises will ever be fulfilled. Finally, Kim Jong-il's remoteness as a leader leaves a gaping hole in the lives of those North Koreans who remember his father, but a remote Kim escapes some of the blame for the poor economy.

Change, Not Collapse

Social instability does not necessarily lead to a dramatic collapse. Numerous African countries have been unstable since becoming independent several decades ago; yet, they survive as sovereign states with well-entrenched rulers. North Korea is probably too organized a society to collapse into anarchy like, say, Somalia, and if it did, South Korea and China would quickly step in to provide economic assistance and social order. A collapse of only the North Korean government and party would be less dramatic (and more likely) than a broad-scale social collapse. This is what happened in the former Soviet Union. People's lives would be disrupted, but since they are already gaining economic independence and losing respect for the law, the collapse of their government would simply give them more room for individual action, although that in turn would introduce a measure of chaos into society.

An even more limited kind of collapse would involve the removal of the Kim family from power. This type of collapse is quite common and even includes political-party changes in democracies. Because Kim Jong-il never appears in public except at local events such as military-base or factory inspections, it would be quite possible for the military to rule in his name without the people even noticing. In this case the greatest threat to social stability would be the emergence of factional strife among party and military leaders.

In some respects North Korea has already collapsed, but the collapse has gone unnoticed because it happened gradually and out of view of foreigners, who expected it to be marked by millions of North Koreans swimming across the Yalu River into China, escaping in small boats to Japan, rushing across the minefields of the Demilitarized Zone, or battling police and ransacking government buildings. But collapse need not be that dramatic. The North Korean leadership system has already seriously eroded as people ignore the official ideology and the words of Kim Jong-il. The more often the media claim that Kim is the "respected and beloved general," the more it can be inferred that people still need to be convinced of this. Party officials have less influence on the lives of the people than they used to (although they can still impose their will on individual citizens when they wish). Government officials must be bribed to do their jobs, which is understandable because their salaries are virtually worthless. With few resources to work with, the government can do little for the people anyway, other than irritate them. Rules and laws are not obeyed unless someone is watching, and lawbreakers avoid punishment by bribing the police.

As for signs of economic collapse, foreigners and defectors alike estimate that North Korea's industry has been operating at no more than 25 percent capacity since the early 1990s. The military economy is probably in somewhat better shape than the civilian economy, but not by much to judge from the condition of military equipment. Even North Korea's showpiece nuclear industry is barely able to function—its temporary shutdown under the most recent nuclear agreement is hardly a loss for the economy or the military.

Given the many variables involved, it is futile to predict North Korea's near-term future, although in the long term—twenty to fifty years out—it is a certainty that the political and economic shape of North Korea will have dramatically changed to accommodate international economic practices and social norms. When Kim Il-sung died, we predicted that Kim Jong-il's rule would be short, but we were wrong for several reasons. First, we did not consider the lack of alternatives to Kim. It now appears that the military, which is an important institutional power holder, has no desire to rule North Korea. Apart from their strong loyalty to Kim Il-sung, who personally designated Kim Jong-il as his successor, the senior generals probably do not think they have the talent to govern the country. Second, we could not imagine how generously and patiently the international community would assist North Korea. Most of the food aid goes directly to the government-run Public Distribution System, ensuring that Kim's supporters are first in line for assistance. Nor could we guess that the South Korean government, beginning with the Kim Dae-jung administration in 1998, would provide strong support for the North rather than try to take advantage of its weakness and promote reunification on South Korea's terms.

If the Kim regime was able to make it through the 1990s, in the wake of Kim Il-sung's sudden death and during a time when the bodies of starved people lay in the streets, it is likely to continue for the foreseeable future. Kim himself may not have long to live, but a successor regime very much like his could continue to play his cards. For now, Kim has given absolutely no indication that he is willing to relax his control over the people, transform

North Korea into a market economy, or tolerate any political opposition. He cautiously opens North Korea's door to the outside world when he sees some profit in it for himself and his supporters, but when things begin to look threatening, the door is closed again. His deft handling of foreign policy, especially his skill at playing on the nuclear phobia of the United States, seems likely to guarantee him continued international attention and support. As it turns out, no country, including the United States, wants to see North Korea collapse, so the very threat of it should be sufficient to extract foreign aid and political support for the regime, even without nuclear and missile programs to bargain with.

What could bring an end to the Kim dynasty? Collapse scenarios would include a military coup, an assassination before Kim had prepared a successor, widespread protests in which the military sided with civilians, a natural disaster of unprecedented proportions, or a plague or famine that killed, say, as much as a quarter of the population. External circumstances that could trigger a collapse might include a total cutoff of foreign aid by China or a preemptive attack by the United States. None of these scenarios appears likely at this time.

In an article written back in 1999, we surveyed experts' predictions for North Korea's future.[9] Out of some forty papers and articles, mostly written since 1996, three studies (by a South Korean, a Russian, and a Chinese) predicted that North Korea would adopt reforms and pull out of its downward spiral. This did not happen. Twenty-one experts correctly predicted that North Korea would manage to muddle through for some years without serious reforms, and ten overly pessimistic experts predicted North Korea would collapse within the next few years. Another set of predictions, made by fifty Korean experts on North Korea affairs and published in a South Korean newspaper at about the same time also gave the Kim regime the benefit of the doubt: 16 percent predicted a collapse within five years, 29 percent saw it coming within ten years, and 53 percent believed North Korea would survive longer than ten years.[10] And in a 1997 South Korean survey, two experts predicted collapse by the year 2000, fifteen by the year 2005, seventeen by the year 2010, and six by the year 2020.[11] In light of these predictions, should one conclude ten years later that the regime has run its course, or could it be that its survival to date portends even greater staying power in the future?

The survey conducted in 2006 by the Korea Institute for National Unification, cited in chapter 6,[12] asked defectors to predict how long the Kim regime would survive: 23 percent predicted less than five years, 48 percent between five and ten years, 16 percent between ten and fifteen years, and 14 percent longer than fifteen years.[13] These predictions foresee bleak prospects for the North Korean people, many of whom will never live to see prosperity or reunification. As for those languishing in prison camps, even a few more years of the Kim regime will be too long.

U.S. Policy Options

Should the United States sit back and wait for the Kim regime to run its course, should it offer support and security to the regime in the hope that it will transform itself, or should it take steps to pressure the regime to change its policies and improve the lives of its people? As it stands, the Kim regime essentially holds its people hostage, and accomplishing hostage rescues, especially when the hostage taker is heavily armed, is not easy. In the current case, it can be argued that the United States is much more interested in the hostage taker's weapons of mass destruction than in the fate of his hostages.

North Korea comes to the world's attention only in connection with nuclear and missile programs and its recurring humanitarian crises. The rest of the time, thanks in large part to the Kim regime's policies of secrecy and isolation, North Korea is a hidden country. Kim Jong-il controls the pace of foreign engagement: when the regime wants attention, it creates a disturbance, gets at least some of what it wants, and then goes back into its shell. The 1993–1994 nuclear crisis was virtually identical to that of 2003 (when North Korea withdrew from the Nuclear Nonproliferation Treaty and restarted its nuclear reactors), and in both cases North Korea was compensated for signing a nuclear-freeze agreement. We would not be surprised if more North Korean–provoked crises of a nuclear and nonnuclear nature occur in the future. When Kim is willing, the Six-Party Talks on the nuclear issue go forward. When he is unwilling, the superpowers have to wait him out. Likewise, every few years floods or other natural disasters strike North Korea, and humanitarian aid is rushed to the scene, but the underlying weakness of the country's infrastructure is never addressed.

Americans should be somewhat cautious about offering policy suggestions for dealing with North Korea because the North Korean people and their neighbors will feel the consequences of dramatic changes in the regime more strongly than Americans living thousands of miles away. And yet, we believe policy suggestions should be rooted in principles as well as in practical considerations. Our policy preference, now as it was eight years ago when we wrote our first North Korea book, is based on the idea that it is best to deal as directly as possible with the North Korean people and to bypass the Kim regime because we believe the success of a North Korea policy should not depend on gaining cooperation from a regime whose goals are often diametrically opposed to those of the United States and, indeed, to the best interests of the North Korean people. It might not be too much of an exaggeration even to say that any U.S. policy or initiative approved by the Kim regime will likely be detrimental to the North Korean people, and any policy that the regime opposes will probably benefit them. Needless to say, the preference for dealing with the people rather than the regime seriously complicates policy formulation because policy talks are government to government, not people to people, and in any case, the ordinary North Korean people remain relatively well hidden from us.

More specifically, our favored policy is to target the North Korean people with information about their government and the outside world and to let them choose how to act on that information. This policy places a heavy burden on the people, but it is, after all, their country. In the final analysis, as an eighteenth-century French diplomat observed, every country has the government it deserves. The North Korean people have supported, often reluctantly, the Kim regime for over half a century, and it is for them to withdraw that support or take action against the regime. What information might be communicated to them and how it would be delivered is suggested by the steps that the Kim regime has already taken to block outside information, for example, by outlawing videos and unfixed radio sets and railing against "imperialistic propaganda" transmitted by the Voice of America, Radio Free Asia, and South Korean radio stations.

We suspect, however, that U.S. government policy toward North Korea will continue to focus primarily on reducing or eliminating Pyongyang's weapons of mass destruction—a policy that unfortunately involves communicating with and rewarding the actors who are the very cause of the many problems that the North Korean people face. We also suspect that nonproliferation agreements with the regime will simply encourage it to brandish new threats in the future. The North Korean people are left out of these negotiations, except to the extent that a few of the economic benefits provided to the regime finally reach them. It is this trickle-down theory that provided the rationale for the engagement policy as pursued by South Korea during the Kim Dae-jung and Roh Moo-hyun administrations. That so-called sunshine policy was supposed to melt or soften the regime by providing it with economic and political security. In our opinion, for this approach to succeed, Kim Jong-il must be persuaded to transform his country into a democracy in which the people have the power to vote him and his supporters out of office—just as Communist Party officials were voted out of office in Eastern Europe. We doubt if Kim will be attracted to this option.

How much humanitarian aid to offer North Korea is a tricky issue. Aid organizations such as the United Nations' World Food Program strongly condemn the politicization of humanitarian aid, as do most governments, including the U.S. government. However, it can be argued that when political decisions create humanitarian crises, as they do in North Korea where the regime has devoted its best resources to the military rather than the civilian sector, there is strong justification for including political criteria in decisions about humanitarian aid. We suggest that humanitarian aid be offered to the North Korean government contingent on its acceptance of strict foreign monitoring (by Korean-speaking aid workers) and clear labeling of the aid's origin. In this way the foreign aid will become part of the foreign information program. If the regime objects to the strings attached to foreign aid, as it almost certainly will, then the rejected aid offer should be communicated to the North Korean people so they know that the only thing standing between them and food is their government.

Our policy recommendation of information operations comes up short on at least two accounts. First, it does not take into account the policy preferences of the South Korean government, which will bear the brunt of any chaos created if the North Korean people choose to rise up against their government. We cannot think of a way to please all parties, and the needs of the North Korean people seem to us to outweigh the economic concerns of the relatively prosperous South Koreans, who in any case should not be optimistic about their own future until they resolve the reunification issue. We would hope and expect that a collapse of North Korean society would prompt the United States and international aid and financial organizations to provide robust economic assistance in order to maintain stability in the region and reduce the economic burden on the South Korean government.

Our second reservation is based on the realization that the U.S. government lacks the capability and interest to mount a serious information campaign. The current level of efforts involving Radio Free Asia, Voice of America, and a few surrogate organizations and radio stations are unlikely to enlighten the North Korean people sufficiently to move them to action if they so choose. The U.S. Department of Defense spends hundreds of billions of dollars fighting its wars but only a few million on "information warfare." Considering that individual American companies each spend up to $2 billion a year on advertising, it is naïve to expect that an annual information budget of a few million dollars can successfully introduce the North Korean people to a new way of thinking about their government and their society.

The Kim regime will certainly not like our policy suggestions. The South Korean government and people may not care for them much either. And many members of the international community may look upon our suggestions as yet another attempt by Americans to meddle in other countries' affairs. But this book is about the North Korean people and what would benefit them, and we believe that if we can open their eyes to the world, they, at least, will thank us.

~

Notes

Chapter 1: The Illusion of Unity

1. Chon Song-ho, "Heart of 10 Million Soldiers and People," *Nodong Sinmun* via the Uriminjokkiri website, March 2, 2004, in Korean.

2. Song Yong-sok, "Love for the Fatherland and Love for the Nation Are the Foundation of Great National Unity," *Nodong Sinmun* via the Uriminjokkiri website, August 8, 2007, in Korean.

3. Hyun-sik Kim and Kwang-ju Son, *Documentary Kim Jong Il* [in Korean, with these title words transcribed in the Hangul alphabet] (Seoul: Chonji Media, 1997), 292.

4. "Two Koreas' Top Brass Resort to Racist Mudslinging," *Chosun Ilbo*, May 17, 2006, Internet version, in English.

5. Annette Kuhn interviews photographer Werner Kranwetvogel on his trip to Pyongyang, "The Great Big Show in North Korea," *Die Welt*, January 21, 2008, Internet version, in German.

6. "Further Improve, Strengthen People's Unit Work," *Minju Choson*, January 23, 2007, 1, editorial, in Korean.

7. Phillipe Grangereau, *Au pays du grand mensonge: Voyage en Coree du Nord* (Paris: Payot et Rivages, 2001), in French.

8. "Outline of Free Medical Care," *Korea Today* via the Naenara website, November 7, 2007, in English.

9. Birke Dockhorn, "Adventure on Rails: Pyongyang with and without an Escort (1996)," in *Nordkorea: Einblicke in ein ratselhaftes Land* [North Korea: Glimpses of a Mysterious Land], ed. Christoph Moeskes (Berlin: Christoph Links Verlag, 2004), 41–47, in German.

10. "Notebook" column by Yi Chae-hak, *JoongAng Ilbo*, November 24, 2003, Internet version, in English.

11. Report by Kazuyoshi Nishikura, Kyodo news agency, March 18, 2003, in English.

12. "J-Style" article by Cortlan Bennett, "Beauty Waiting for a Beholder: Astonishing

Sights Await Visitors to North Korea—If They Can Get In," *JoongAng Ilbo*, August 2, 2003, Internet version, in English.

13. "The Tale of the Real DPRK: First of Several Factual Reports on Today's DPRK," Wangyi (a blog in Chinese) at www.163.com, October 29, 2006.

14. Vladimir Vorsobin, "The Long Arms and Keen Ears of Comrade Kim," *Komsomolskaya Pravda* website, October 13, 2004, in Russian.

15. Anne Schneppen, "In the Dim Luster of the Diamond Mountains," *Frankfurter Allgemeine*, October 30, 2006, Internet version, in German.

16. Michael Harrold, *Comrades and Strangers: Behind the Closed Doors of North Korea* (West Sussex: John Wiley and Sons, 2004), 390.

17. Harrold, *Comrades and Strangers*, 370.

18. Andrew Holloway, *A Year in Pyongyang*, unpublished manuscript available on Aidan Foster-Carter's website at www.aidanfc.net/pyongyang.html.

Chapter 2: The Life of the Leader

1. Ronald Winetrobe, *The Political Economy of Dictatorship* (London: Cambridge University Press, 1998), 106.

2. Winetrobe, *The Political Economy*, 342.

3. Adrian Buzo, *The Guerrilla Dynasty* (Boulder, CO: Westview Press, 1999).

4. The standard biography of Kim Il-sung is Dae-sook Suh's *Kim Il Sung: The North Korean Leader* (New York: Columbia University Press, 1988). Much is available about Kim in more recent sources, as indicated in the notes that follow. See also Andrei Lankov, *From Stalin to Kim Il Sung* (London: Hurst & Co., 2002), which provides a concise biography on 49–76. Also see Sydney A. Seiler, *Kim Il-song, 1941–1948: The Creation of a Legend, the Building of a Regime* (Lanham, MD: University Press of America, 1994).

5. Quoted in KCNA, in English, June 4, 2005.

6. The biography of Kim Jong-il is almost as difficult to research as that of his father, thanks to the work of North Korean propagandists, who have largely rewritten it. The only book completely devoted to his life—or devoting at least several chapters—is Michael Breen's insightful *Kim Jong-il: North Korea's Dear Leader* (Singapore: John Wiley & Sons, Asia, 2004). An official North Korean biography of highly dubious veracity is *Kim Jong Il: The Lodestar of the 21st Century*. It was published serially on the KCNA website, in English, in 1999, with the following chapter titles: "The Son of the Nation," "The Leader of the Workers' Party of Korea," "A Paragon of Present-Day Statesman," "The General Leader of Socialist Construction," "The Supreme Commander of the Korean People's Army," "The Savior Star of the Nation," "The Helmsman of the Cause of Making the World Independent," and "A Paragon of Greatness." Kim's later life is covered in a series of articles in Korean by So Song-u, Chon Hyon-chun, and Kim Chong-min, published in Korean, along with an uncredited, extensive resume of Kim, in the February 1994 issue of the South Korean journal *Pukhan*. Also see Osamu Megumiya's "Secret of Kim Chong-il's Birth and Life of His Mother, Kim Jong-suk," *Seikai Orai*

(August 1992): 34–39, in Japanese. Some facts, and perhaps some South Korean propaganda, can be found in a Republic of Korea government publication titled *The True Story of Kim Jong-il* (Seoul: The Institute of South-North Korea Studies, 1993).

7. Andrei Lankov, one of the most astute observers of North Korea, grew up in the Soviet Union and studied for several years at Kim Il-sung University as an exchange student. His collection of essays on North Korean life provides numerous illustrations of how the North Koreans borrowed aspects of Soviet communist culture. See Andrei Lankov, *North of the DMZ: Essays on Daily Life in North Korea* (Jefferson, NC: McFarland & Co., 2007).

8. Andrei Lankov tells the story in his *Crisis in North Korea: The Failure of De-Stalinization, 1956* (Honolulu: University of Hawaii Press, 2005).

9. Buzo, *The Guerrilla Dynasty*, 237.

10. A summary of the behest was published in South Korea's *Chosun Ilbo* newspaper, in Korean, on November 18, 1996, 9. According to the article, the full behest was published by North Korea that year in volume 44 of the *Collection of Kim Il-sung's Works*.

11. Although it is unusual, hereditary succession, especially from father to son, does have much to recommend it. In a 2007 article on the subject, Jason Brownlee found only nine successful cases since 1946. His research supports Gordon Tullock's hypothesis that this form of succession occurs almost exclusively when the leader predates the ruling political party. Among the advantages of father-to-son succession is the avoidance of damaging succession struggles. For the regime's supporters, hereditary succession provides some assurance that the new leader will not jeopardize their privileged positions. See Jason Brownlee, "Hereditary Succession in Modern Autocracies," *World Politics* 59 (July 2007): 595–628.

12. Morgan E. Clippinger, "Kim Chong-il in the North Korean Mass Media: A Study of Semi-Esoteric Communication," *Asian Survey* 21, no. 3 (March 1981): 289–309.

13. Megumiya, "Secret of Kim Chong-il's Birth."

14. Ri Ki-pong, "Immortal Military Achievements Shining on the Pages of History of Military-First Politics: Reminiscing about the History of Shining Victory the Great General Won in Fierce Confrontation with U.S. Imperialists in the 1960s," *Nodong Sinmun* via the KPM website, February 3, 2008, in Korean.

15. Yi Kun, "III. Diplomat Kim Jong-il (1): A Diplomat Who Has Yet to Debut on the International Stage; 'Invention' of Charisma Hidden from Diplomatic Stage," *Chosun Ilbo*, March 17, 2005, Internet version, in Korean.

16. "Great Military Genius, Iron-Willed Commander," KCBS, March 10, 1994, in Korean.

17. Hyun-sik Kim and Kwang-ju Son, *Documentary Kim Jong Il* [in Korean, with these title words transcribed in the Hangul alphabet] (Seoul: Chonji Media, 1997), 202.

18. Hwang Jang-yop has written several books, available only in Korean: *Pukhan-ui Jinsil-gwa Howi* [Truth and Falsehood of North Korea] (Seoul: Institute for National Security and Unification Policy, June 1998); *Nanun Yyoksa-ui Jjilli-rul Poatta* [I Saw the Truth of History], (Hwang's memoirs) (Seoul: Hanul, 1999); *Odum-ui Pyoneedoen Happyossn Odum-ul Palkilsuopta* [Sunshine That Supports the Darkness Cannot Lighten the Dark-

ness] (Hwang's advice on achieving Korean unification) (Seoul: *Monthly Chosun*, 2001), coauthored with Cho Kap-he and Kim Duk-hong; *Hwang Jang-yop-ui Daejollyak: Kim Jong-il-gwa Chonjaeng Hajiankko Iginunbop* [The Grand Strategy of Hwang Jang-yop: How to Win against Kim Jong-il without War] (Seoul: *Monthly Chosun*, 2003).

19. Ryo Hagiwara, "I Will Risk My Life to Fight against Kim Jong-il," December 1998 interview with Hwang Jang-yop, *Bungei Shunju* (February 1999): 324–46, in Japanese.

20. Cho Kap-che, "Recorded Tape of Kim Jong-il's Live Voice—60 Minutes of Astonishing Confessions Similar to That of a Reactionary," *Wolgan Chosun* (October 1995): 104–28, in Korean. The quotations in the following paragraphs are taken from this source. While residing in the United States, film director Sang-ok Shin and his actress wife, Eun-hi Choi, authored a two-volume work (available only in an out-of-print Korean edition) about their experiences in North Korea: *Choguk-un chohanul chomolli* [Diary: The Motherland Is Beyond the Sky and Far Away] (Pacific Palisades, CA: Pacific Artist Corporation, 1988). See also "Table Talk: Hwang Jang Yop and Shin Sang-ok Talk about the Two Homelands They Have Experienced," *Wolgan Chosun* (March 1999), 609–41, in Korean.

21. Cho Tong-ho, "II. CEO Kim Jong-il (1): Reform and Anti-Reform," *Chosun Ilbo*, February 3, 2005, Internet version, in Korean.

22. Cho, "Recorded Tape," electronic version.

23. Cho, "Recorded Tape," electronic version.

24. Song Hye-rang, *Dungnamujip* [Wisteria House] (Seoul: Jisiknara, 2000), in Korean. She also published *Sosik-ul jonhamnida* [Here Are My Greetings] (Seoul: Jisiknara, 1999), in Korean.

25. "'Daughter' on Kim Chong-il's Private Life," *Bungei Shunju* (February 1998): 274–92, in Japanese.

26. "'Daughter' on Kim Chong-il's Private Life."

27. At this time, none of Fujimoto Kenji's books is available in English: *Kim Jong-il-ui yorisa* [Kim Jong-il's Chef], 2003, in Korean (translated from the Japanese edition titled *Kin Seinichi no Ryoryinin*); *Kin Seinichi no Shiseikatsu* [Kim Jong-il's Private Life], 2004, in Japanese; and *Kaku to Onna o Aishita Shogun-Sama* [The General Who Loved Nukes and Women], 2006, in Japanese.

28. Fujimoto, *Kin Seinichi no Ryoryinin*, 8–9.

29. Ermanno Furlanis, "I Made Pizza for Kim Jong-il," in three parts, *Asia Times Online*, August 4–18, 2001, in English.

30. Kim Mi-yong, "President's Cattle Ranch—Ranch for 'Nobility,' Including Kim Jong-il," *Chosun Ilbo*, March 12, 2002, Internet version, in Korean.

31. Han Young Jin, "The Dear Leader's Apples and the No. 8 Farm," *Daily NK* website, May 30, 2005, in English.

32. Cho Myong-yong, "Noble Benevolence for Coming Generations," *Nodong Sinmun*, December 6, 2003, 2, in Korean.

33. Yi Tae-nam, "The Future of a Prosperous and Rich State Lies in Upholding the General," *Nodong Sinmun*, June 28, 2001, 2, in Korean.

34. Fujimoto, *Kin Seinichi no Shiseikatsu*, 18–27 and 32–42; *Kin Seinichi no Ryoryinin*,

74–80. Yi Yong-kuk, *Nanun Kim Jong-il Kyonghowoniotta* [I Was Kim Jong-il's Bodyguard] (Seoul: Sidae Chongsin, 2002).

35. Konstantin Pulikovskiy, *The Oriental Express: Through Russia with Kim Chong-il* (Vladivostok: Gorodets, 2002), in Russian. Obtained in electronic version.

36. Chon Song-ho, "Heart of 10 Million Soldiers and People," *Nodong Sinmun* via the Uriminjokkiri website, March 2, 2004, in Korean.

37. NTV International, in Russian, August 3, 2001.

38. Aleksandr Vladimirovich Lukin, "Why Does Moscow Need Pyongyang? Russia Is Interested in Gradual Transformations in DPRK," *Nezavisimaya Gazeta*, August 1, 2001, 6, in Russian.

39. "Rumor Mill" column, *Moskovskiy Komsomolets*, August 6, 2001, Internet version, in Russian.

40. Mikhail Krasnov, ". . . But It Is Our Armored Train in the Siding," *Rossiyskaya Gazeta*, August 7, 2001, 2, in Russian.

41. Vyacheslav Kostikov, "Visit of Kim Jong-il Is Humiliation of Russians," *Argumenty i Fakty*, August 9, 2001, 2, in Russian.

42. Yuliya Kantor, "Rain Man," *Izvestiya*, August 7, 2001, Internet version, in Russian.

43. Aleksandr Korzun, interviewing Konstantin Pulikovskiy, *Kommersant*, August 15, 2001, 1, 2, in Russian.

44. Interfax, August 7, 2001, in English.

45. Kim In-ku, "Even after Kim Jong-il's Departure, DPRK Media Said, 'He Will Visit Russia in the Near Future,'" *Chosun Ilbo*, August 2, 2001, Internet version, in Korean.

46. KCBS, August 18, 2001, at 0500 GMT, in Korean.

47. Talk: "Shock of a Great Man," KCBS, August 18, 2001, at 1152 GMT, in Korean.

48. "Shock of a Great Man."

49. The edited transcripts from these tapes are found in "Kim Jong-il's 'Monologues'; Top Secret Instructions Given to Association Leaders," *Gendai*, January 1, 2003, 122–34, in Japanese.

50. *Wolgan Chosun* (April 1997): 306–17, in Korean.

51. Information about decision making in North Korea is fragmentary; so far as we know, none of Kim's close associates has defected. Several views of Kim's leadership style can be found in a June 2004 report issued by the Institute for Defense Analyses and titled *North Korean Policy Elites*, coauthored by Kongdan Oh Hassig, Joseph S. Bermudez, Kenneth E. Gause, Ralph C. Hassig, Alexandre Y. Mansourov, and David J. Smith.

52. An Yong-chol, *"The Mystery of the Son's Rivalry to Become Heir and Who Is This No. 2 Man, Kang Sang-chun—Kim Jong-il's Group of Closest Confidants Wrapped in Veil of Secrecy," Gendai*, August 1, 2003, 110–19, in Japanese.

53. Memoir by the defector Im Kyong-su, "The Inside of DPRK Ministry of Public Security: A Prison Empire of Corruption, Conspiracy, and Torture," *Wolgan Chosun* (June 1999): 340–70, in Korean.

54. Michael Breen, in *Kim Jong-il: North Korea's Dear Leader*, 144, reports that a representative of Hennessey confirmed that North Korea, several years ago at least, was the

company's biggest purchaser of its premium "Paradis" cognac, spending up to $700,000 a year on it.

55. Choe Chol-hui, "Jangmadang [Market] Goods Are More Valuable Than the General's Gifts," *Daily NK* website, February 20, 2008, in English.

56. "'On-the-Spot Guidance Tours' by DPRK's Kim Jong-il Explained," *Chosun Ilbo*, February 19, 2001, Internet version, in English. Also see "Number One Events," *Chosun Ilbo*, May 20, 2001, Internet version, in English.

57. Yi Yong-chong and Chong Yong-su, "North Manual Says U.S. Aims at Leaders," *JoongAng Ilbo*, April 8, 2005, Internet version, in English.

58. "DPRK Leader Inspects KPA Unit No. 802," KCBS, November 10, 2005, in Korean.

59. To take one example: "DPRK Leader Inspects KPA Unit 1337," KCBS, November 11, 2005, in Korean.

60. "DPRK Leader Inspects KPA Unit No. 802."

61. "Legend of Love That Blossomed on the Path of On-the-Spot Guidance," Korean Central Television, February 13, 2004, in Korean.

62. Yi Yong-kuk, *Nanun Kim Jong-il Kyonghowoniotta* [I Was Kim Jong-il's Bodyguard] (Seoul: Sidae Chongsin, 2002).

63. KCNA, March 13, 1998, in English.

64. "Let Us Make Harmonious Homes in the Entire Country," KWP Publishing House lecture material, May 1, 2004, in Korean.

65. Kim In-son, "He Continued to Walk the Footpaths between Fields to Guide the Nation's Farming All His Life," *Nodong Sinmun*, May 30, 1999, 2, in Korean.

66. Kang Chol-hwan, "One Must Pass Six Checkpoints to Enter Kim Jong-il's Official Residence—Parodied Songs Satirizing His Habit of Frequently Visiting Military Units Are Popular," *Chosun Ilbo*, January 20, 2005, Internet version, in Korean.

67. Koh Young-hwan, "Specially Attached Interpreter Who Defected Discloses the True Character of Kim Il-sung and His Son," *Bungei Shunju* (August 1994): 94–103, in Japanese.

68. Ryang Sun, "Great Motherly Party," *Nodong Sinmun*, August 22, 2005, 2, in Korean.

69. Kim Kwang-ok, "Brilliant Commander's Field Uniform," *Minju Choson*, August 11, 2004, 2, in Korean.

70. Interview with Dr. Roland Hetzer, Fuji Television, June 20, 2007, in Japanese.

71. "Rumors of North Korean Ruler Kim Jong-il Undergoing Heart Surgery," *Die Welt*, June 23, 2007, 7, in German.

72. "The Enigmatic Kim Jong-il; Leader's Mythical Birth Key to N. Korean Regime," *Daily Yomiuri*, February 24, 2004, Internet version, in English.

73. The cost has been variously estimated at between $100 million and $890 million.

74. KCBS, July 19, 2000, in Korean.

75. KCBS, October 23, 2000, in Korean.

76. "Wonder Takes Place," KCNA, July 8, 2001, in English.

77. "Kimjongilia Estimated As King of Flowers," KCNA, February 2, 2005, in English.

78. KCBS, April 21, 2003, in Korean.

79. "Wonders on February Holiday," KCNA, February 19, 2001, in English.

80. Cho Chong-chol, "Military-First Teleporting Method," *Nodong Sinmun* via the Uriminjokkiri website, December 25, 2006, in Korean.

81. KCBS, on February 16, 2002 (Kim's birthday), in Korean, quoting that day's *Nodong Sinmun* editorial titled "Let Us Brilliantly Realize the Cause of Building a Powerful State under Great Comrade Kim Jong-il's Military-First Leadership."

82. "Comrade Kim Jong-il's Experience of War," KCNA, October 1, 1997, in English.

83. "45th Anniversary of Kim Jong-il's Start of *Songun* Revolutionary Leadership Marked," KCNA, August 24, 2005, in English.

84. "'Moving Story' Associated with Chol Ridge," KCNA, October 6, 1999, in English.

85. "I Will Tell Him Everything," *Korea Today* via Naenara website, June 3, 2006, in English.

86. Choe Chil-nam and Pak Chol, "Sacred Three Years," *Nodong Sinmun*, July 2, 1997, 3–4, in Korean.

87. "For an Invincibly Powerful State," *Nodong Sinmun*, April 7, 2003 via KCNA, on the same date, in English.

88. "Kim Jong-il Authors 1,400-Odd Works during University Days," KCNA, March 18, 2004, in English.

89. "Leader with Marvelous Memory," KCNA, June 18, 2004, in English.

90. Han Song-ki, "Economic Ideology of Great Leader Comrade Kim Jong-il Is That of Juche Era's Original and Scientific Ideology," *Kyongje Yongu*, February 10, 2004, 5–7, in Korean.

91. "Exclamation of Researcher," *Minju Choson*, September 29, 2004, 2, in Korean.

92. "Let Us Struggle Persistently by Taking Our Party's Idea and Line As Faith," *Nodong Sinmun* editorial (via KCNA), December 2, 2004, in Korean. In a 2006 update of the same idea, Kim is said to have been "perfectly on target" in formulating "all the hundreds and thousands" of policy lines. Kim Pyong-chin, "Great Comrade Kim Jong-il's Military-First Revolutionary Chronicles Are Eternal Treasures for the Socialist Victory and Prosperity," *Nodong Sinmun*, February 28, 2006, in Korean.

93. In his classic article on the use of Kim's title "Party Center," Morgan E. Clippinger lists the characteristics noted in the text as being ascribed to Kim in the North Korean press. See Clippinger, "Kim Chong-il in the North Korean Mass Media," 289–309.

94. Early in his political career (by the end of the 1960s), Kim Jong-il was referred to as "Dear Leader Comrade" (*chinaehanun jidoja tongji*). Two days before his father's death, he was referred to for the first time in *Nodong Sinmun* as *Yongdoja* ("leader"). Beginning in January 1995 he began to be referred to as *Widaehan Yongdoja* ("great leader"). See Young Whan Jo, *Maeu Tukpyolhan Inmul Kim Jong Il* [Very Special Person, Kim Jong-il] (Seoul: Jisik Kongjakso, 1996), 220–27, in Korean.

95. Kim Kum-son, "We Cannot Live Apart from the Bosom—Reciting the Epic Poem 'Mother,'" *Nodong Sinmun*, October 9, 2003, 2, in Korean.

96. Toshio Miyatsuka, *Saishin Naibu Bunsho 150 Tsu wo Ura Yomu: Ganbaruzo! Kita*

Chosen [Reading between the Lines of 150 of the Latest Internal Documents: Go! Go! North Korea] (Tokyo: Shogakukan, July 10, 2004), 62–93, in Japanese.

97. "Song of Faith That Will Remain Forever Generation after Generation," KCBS, June 4, 2004, in Korean.

98. "Ri Po-ik," *Korea Today* via the Naenara website, May 2, 2006, in English.

99. Choe Chong-hon, "The Fundamental Requirement of the Do-or-Die Spirit of Defending the Leader," *Minju Choson*, February 20, 2001, 2, in Korean.

100. So Sung-uk, "Content of the Secret 'Study Note' Document," *JoongAng Ilbo*, April 8, 2005, Internet version, in Korean.

101. "Korean People's Noble Spirit of Defending Leader at Yongchon," KCNA, April 28, 2004, in English.

102. Ho Yong-min, "The Spirit of Defending the Nerve Center with a Do-or-Die Spirit Is an Important Characteristic of the North's Military and People," *Nodong Sinmun*, October 23, 2002, 5, in Korean.

103. "Slogans Discovered on Trees Lauding Kim Chong-il," KCNA, February 6, 1998, in English.

104. "The Respected Mother Is the Greatest of All Great Loyalists Infinitely Faithful to Comrade Supreme Commander," lecture material from the KPA Publishing House dated August, *Juche* 91 (2002), obtained from a Japanese source and published in South Korea by *Wolgan Chosun* (March 1, 2003): 120–30, in Korean.

105. "Workers' Party of Korea Central Committee Secretariat Directive No. 0101," September 25, 2005, published by *Wolgan Chosun*, no date available, in Korean.

Chapter 3: The Economic System

1. Song Hyon-chol, "State's Centralized, Unified Leadership Is the Lifeline of Socialist Economy," *Nodong Sinmun*, February 11, 2009, electronic edition, in Korean.

2. Institute for Far East Studies, "DPRK Economic Growth Estimates for 2006," North Korean Economy Watch, August 22, 2007, www.nkeconwatch.com/2007/08/22/dprk-economic-growth-estimates-for -2006. Also see Dick K. Nanto and Emma Chanlett-Avery, "The North Korean Economy: Overview and Policy Analysis," *CRS Report for Congress*, April 18, 2007. Also personal correspondence with Bank of Korea staff.

3. Jo Dong-ho, "Aid Is Not the Same As Investment," *JoongAng Ilbo*, August 21, 2007, Internet version, in English.

4. For a well-structured review of North Korea's economic history into the 1990s, see Doowon Lee, "North Korean Economic Reform: Past Efforts and Future Prospects," in *Reforming Asian Socialism: The Growth of Market Institutions*, ed. John McMillan and Barry Naughton (Ann Arbor, MI: University of Michigan Press, 1996), 317–36.

5. KCBS, January 4, 2001, in Korean, citing a *Nodong Sinmun* editorial of the same date titled "Let Us Glorify This Year As a Year of New Turnaround by Upholding the Joint Editorial."

6. *Nodong Sinmun*, March 29, 2001, 2, in Korean.

7. Kim Myong-chol, "The Central Tasks in This Year's Socialist Economic Construction," *Minju Choson*, February 22, 2001, 2, in Korean.

8. Song Kun-cho, "Modernizing Local Industry Plants with Up-to-Date Technology Is a Major Task Facing the Local Organs of Power," *Minju Choson*, June 10, 2001, 2, in Korean.

9. Yi Tong-hyon, "*JoongAng Ilbo* Exclusive Summary of Kim Jong-il's Instructions—Let Go of Free State Provisions That Need to Go," *JoongAng Ilbo*, August 1, 2002, Internet version, in Korean. Also see "General Secretary Kim Orders Abolition of Principle of Equalization, Gratuitous Systems; Entire Picture of His Instructions Comes to Light," *Kyodo Clue II*, June 27, 2004, Internet version, in Japanese; said to be based on North Korean internal documents.

10. "Glorify This Year That Greets the 90th Birthday of President Kim Il-sung As a Year of a New Surge in the Building of a Powerful Nation," *People's Korea* 1903 (January 12, 2002): 2, in English.

11. "On Correctly Understanding the State Measure That Has Readjusted Overall Prices and Living Expenses," lecture material from the Korean People's Army Publishing House, July 2002, in Korean. For a published version of the document's highlights, see Kim Kwang-in, "Internal Document on the '1 July Measure'; Special Military Allowance Introduced," obtained by *Chosun Ilbo*, October 15, 2002, Internet version, in Korean.

12. Kim Chi-yong, "In Order to Become a Prosperous Country: Expectations and Support for the New Economic Policies," *Choson Sinbo*, July 26, 2002, Internet version, in Japanese.

13. Ryu Kyong-won, "Merchants Spreading Delusions about the Enemy Using South Korean Goods; What Does the 2007 Market Control Particularly Mean?" *Rimjingang*, March 17, 2008, 82–96, in Korean.

14. Cabinet document released by Japanese NGO's Rescue the North Korean People (RENK) website, December 14, 2004, www.bekkoame.ne.jp/ro/renk, in Japanese.

15. Kim Chi-yong, "Interview with Choe Hong-kyu, Director of the State Planning Commission: Achievements by Improving Economic Management," *Choson Sinbo*, April 1, 2003, in Korean.

16. "'Fatherland's Market': Hearing from Chang Tu-kil, Vice Director of the Commercial Department in the Ministry of Commerce—Significance of New Market," *Choguk* (Tokyo), October 19, 2004, in Korean.

17. Kim Chi-yong, "'From the Scene of Reform': Vitality of Improvement Measures That Are Being Verified," *Choson Sinbo*, December 22, 2003, Internet version, in Korean.

18. "KCNA on Japan's False Propaganda," KCNA, September 8, 1999, in English.

19. Chu Song-ha and Sin Sok-ho, "The North Has Implemented a Nationwide Private Cultivation System," *Tong-a Ilbo*, December 6, 2004, Internet version, in English.

20. Report of an interview with Sin Chang-song, vice president of the DPRK Central Bank, broadcast on Korean Central Television, March 30, 2003, in Korean.

21. Report of an interview with Chong Yong-chun of the DPRK finance ministry, *Choson Sinbo*, May 6, 2003, in Korean.

22. Korean Central Television, December 29, 2007, in Korean.

23. "Visit the Najin-Sonbong Economic and Trade Zone to Witness North Korea's Market Opening," *Wen Wei Po*, July 14, 2007, Internet version, in Chinese.

24. "Hyundai Asan Losses from N. Korea Tours Mounting," *Chosun Ilbo*, May 19, 2008, Internet version, in English. For a brighter picture, see Jin Hyun-joo, "Hyundai Asan's 2007 Profit to Pass 10 Billion Won," *Korea Herald*, December 29, 2007, Internet version, in English.

25. "Sinuiju Designated As Hong Kong–Type Special Zone: First Market Economy Experience in DPRK," *People's Korea* 1920 (September 28, 2002): 3–4, in English.

26. "Sinuiju Designated As Hong Kong–Type Special Zone," 4.

27. Mark O'Neill, "From a Great Height," *South China Morning Post*, May 18, 2004, Internet version, in English.

28. Mark O'Neill, "Kim Eyes New Chief Executive," *South China Morning Post*, September 10, 2004, Internet version, in English.

29. City of Fullerton website at www.ci.fullerton.ca.us/depts/mayor_n_city_council/timeline...of_council_members_n_mayor.asp.

30. SBS Television, September 7, 2004, in Korean.

31. "Roh Calls for Increased Inter-Korean Economic Exchanges," Yonhap, April 1, 2006, in English.

32. "Regulations on Advertisement in Kaesong Industrial Zone Adopted," KCNA, March 5, 2004, in English.

33. Ju Tong-chan, chairman of the DPRK's National Economic Cooperation Committee, quoted by *JoongAng Ilbo*, June 21, 2006, Internet version, in English.

34. Ser Myo-ja, "Group: Most Inter-Korean Businesses End Badly," *JoongAng Ilbo*, October 21, 2005, Internet version, in English.

35. Lee Sun-young, "Doing Business in North Korea Still Difficult: Poll," *Korea Herald*, January 29, 2008, Internet version, in English.

36. Jo Dong-ho, "Aid Is Not the Same As Investment," *JoongAng Ilbo*, August 21, 2007, Internet version, in English.

37. Kim Yon-kwang, "Kim Chan-ku's Testimony Looking Back on His 15 Years As President of Pyongyang Sunpyong Toy Factory: The Gangster Culture [ROK] President Roh Vows to Liquidate Is Found in North Korea," *Wolgan Chosun* (July 1, 2004): 170–90, in Korean.

38. Testimony of William Bach to the U.S. Senate Subcommittee on Financial Management, the Budget, and International Security, Washington, D.C., May 20, 2003. Also see Phar Kim Beng, "Shady Business: N. Korea and Crime," *Asia Times Online*, May 31, 2003, www.atimes.com/atimes/Korea/EE31Dg01.html.

39. *"KCNA Dismisses U.S. False Propaganda against DPRK," KCNA, March 13, 2006, in English.*

40. One of the most authoritative treatments of communist economies is Janos Kornai, *The Socialist System: The Political Economy of Communism* (Princeton, NJ: Princeton University Press, 1992).

41. Kornai, *The Socialist System*, 445.

42. Kornai, *The Socialist System*, 379.

43. For recent discussions, see Stephan Haggard and Marcus Noland, *Famine in North Korea: Markets, Aid, and Reform* (New York: Columbia University Press, 2007), and a collection of previously published articles by Nicholas Eberstadt titled *The North Korean Economy: Between Crisis and Catastrophe* (New Brunswick, NJ: Transaction Publishers, 2007).

44. Nicholas Eberstadt, "Economic Implications of a 'Bold Switchover' in DPRK Security Policy," *Korean Journal of Defense Analysis* 17, no. 1 (spring 2005): 53–84; see the list on 61–63. Reprinted in Eberstadt, *The North Korean Economy*, 245–73.

Chapter 4: The Economy of Everyday Life

1. Kim Chin-chun, vice minister of labor, "Organizing Social Labor in a Rational Manner Is Requirement for Managing Socialist Economy," *Minju Choson*, December 4, 2001, 3, in Korean.

2. Yonhap News Agency, *North Korea Handbook* (Armonk, NY: M. E. Sharpe, 2003), 388, in English.

3. Yonhap, *North Korea Handbook*, 389.

4. Choe Il-ho, "Intensive Agitation for Economy Which Sets Hearts Afire—in the Work of the Sinuiju Shoe Factory's Primary Party Committee," *Nodong Sinmun*, October 6, 2003, 3, in Korean.

5. Sim Kwang-chol, battalion political instructor, "We Will Perform New, Heroic Feats in the Construction of the Sacred Land of the Sun with the Might of the Frontline-Style Propaganda and Agitation," *Nodong Sinmun*, February 28, 2004, 3, in Korean.

6. Kim Young Jin, "Modern Version of Slavery at Samsu Power Plant Construction Site," *Daily NK* website, May 18, 2005, in English.

7. KCBS, April 28, 2001, in Korean.

8. "Feats of Young Koreans," KCNA, August 28, 2002, in English.

9. Kim Yong-song, "An Account of My Personal Experience As a Battalion Commander of a Building Workers Shock Regiment for the Construction of Kwangbok Boulevard, Pyongyang," *Wolgan Chosun* (November 1994): 305–17, in Korean.

10. Hwang Chol-u, "Regularization and Standardization of Labor Life," *Minju Choson*, November 27, 2004, 2, in Korean. Also see KCBS, July 18, 2006, in Korean.

11. Kim, "Organizing Social Labor."

12. Chon Chong-ho, "A Guiding Policy That Should Be Maintained in Socialist Construction," *Minju Choson*, June 13, 1997, 2, in Korean.

13. For example, "Let Us Plan Labor Administration Work to Meet the Needs of the Current Situation," *Minju Choson*, July 25, 2006, 1, editorial, in Korean. Also see Chi Tae-hwa, "The Matter of Administering Labor Incentives in Socialist Society and Its Brilliant Resolution," *Kyongje Yongu*, May 20, 2004, 21–23, in Korean.

14. Kim Chong-il, "Social Ownership Is the Socioeconomic Foundation of the Socialist Work System," *Kyongje Yongu*, November 20, 2003, 13–15, in Korean.

15. Kim, "Organizing Social Labor."

16. "Let Us Thoroughly Fulfill the Tasks Set Forth in the New Year's Joint Editorial—an Enlarged Session of the Plenum of the Cabinet Held," *Minju Choson*, January 15, 2000, 1, in Korean.

17. The edited transcripts from these tapes are found in "Kim Jong-il's 'Monologues'; Top Secret Instructions Given to Association Leaders," *Gendai*, January 1, 2003, 122–34, in Japanese.

18. Yi Sung-chin and Yun Il-kon, "The Number of Day Laborers Hired by Private Parties Is Increasing in North Korea," *Daily NK* website, December 11, 2007, in English.

19. Jae Jean Suh, *North Korea's Market Economy Society from Below*, Korea Institute for National Unification, Studies Series 05-44, May 2005.

20. Lee Kwang Baek, "North Korean 'Exported Workers,' New Source of Kim's Hard Currency," *Daily NK* website, August 19, 2007, in English. Also see Barbara Demick, "N. Koreans Toil Abroad under Grim Conditions," *Los Angeles Times* online, December 27, 2005.

21. Yang Moon-soo, "Are N. Korean Workers 'Exploited' in Kaesong Industrial Complex?" *Korea Policy Review* (June 2006): 30–33.

22. Mikolaj Chrzan and Marcin Kowalski, "North Korean Slaves Working for Gdansk Shipyard," *Gazeta Wyborcza*, March 24, 2006, Internet version, in Polish.

23. "Did North Run Labor Racket in Europe?" *Dong-A Ilbo*, December 3, 2006, Internet version, in English.

24. "All Citizens in This Land Are Soldiers," *Nodong Sinmun* via KCNA, April 25, 2003, in Korean.

25. "Love Gun-Barrel Families," a KCBS report on a *Nodong Sinmun* article, January 29, 2004, in Korean.

26. "Educational Reference Material" from the KPA's publishing house, dated 2003, obtained by *Asahi Shimbun*, November 1, 2003, 15, evening edition, in Japanese.

27. "Let Us Thoroughly Stamp Out the Current Problems of People Damaging Farm Produce and Violating Traffic Rules," KPA Publishing House, August 2002. Referred to in an article titled "Information Shows Even Cannibalism Is Practiced in North Korea; a Document Shows How Bad North Korea's Food Situation Is," *Yomiuri Weekly*, December 21, 2003, 24–25, in Japanese.

28. Chu Song-ha, "Content of the Lecture Material of the North Korean Army's General Political Department," *Dong-A Ilbo*, June 3, 2004, Internet version, in Korean.

29. "Haesol Tamhwa Charyo" (Explanatory Statement Collection), issued in January 2002 and published in Japan's *Shukan Bunshun* under the title "We Have Obtained Secret Documents of North Korea That Show Morale of Troops in the Korean People's Army Is Plummeting; Soldiers Are Becoming Rowdy, Selling Military Supplies, Watching Porno Videos," February 6, 2003, 33–35, in Japanese.

30. "Internal Documents of Kim Jong-il's Army, the Korean People's Army," *Bungei Shunju*, November 1, 2002, 262–71, in Japanese.

31. Quoted in "North Korean Military Manpower," chapter 7 of *Pukhan Kunsa Cheje Pyongga-wa Chonmang* [Evaluation and Prospects for North Korea's Military System] (Seoul: Korean Institute for Defense Analyses, July 25, 2006), 157–87, in Korean.

32. Quotations from North Korean military study material from the Publishing House of the Korean People's Army, titled "On Eliminating Illusions about the Enemy and Further Sharpening the Bayonets of Class," obtained by *Wolgan Chosun* (March 1, 2002): 72–81, in Korean.

33. Pyon Sung-ho, "The Basic Direction of Resolving the Food Problem, the Dietary Problem, in Our Own Way," *Kyongje Yongu*, November 15, 2004, 17–19, in Korean.

34. Yi Min-pok, "North Korean Agriculture Ruined by Political Logic," *Sindong-a*, November 1, 2001, 202–9, in Korean.

35. Kang Chol-hwan, "The Fate of Cattle, Pigs, and Dogs in North Korea," *Chosun Ilbo*, May 6, 2001, Internet version, in English.

36. "Let Us Raise Many Rabbits," *Nodong Sinmun*, January 27, 1999, 1, in Korean.

37. Kye Song-nam, "Another Drive with the Force of a Gale: Remarks of a Vice Minister of Agriculture," *Nodong Sinmun*, July 30, 1999, 3, in Korean.

38. "Let Us Raise Many Rabbits As a Mass Campaign," *Nodong Sinmun*, September 2, 2006, 1, in Korean.

39. Craig Whitlock, "A Colossal Leap of Faith in Fight against Famine," *Washington Post*, February 2, 2007, A10.

40. Kyodo World Service, April 7, 2007.

41. Whitlock, "A Colossal Leap of Faith."

42. "Jinxing Company's Otter Rabbit Exports to DPRK Fare Well," U.S. government report of several Chinese-language articles published between December 2007 and February 2008.

43. "New Method of Breeding Terrapins Developed," KCNA, February 28, 2007, in English.

44. Na Jeong-ju, "South Korea to Import North Korean Chicken," *Korea Times*, March 15, 2005, Internet version, in English. Also see "Northern Chicken to Cross DMZ," *Chosun Ilbo*, March 15, 2005, Internet version, in English.

45. "S. Korean Food Wastes More Than Total N. Korean Food," Yonhap, March 4, 2002, in English. Also see "More to Be Done on Food Waste," *JoongAng Ilbo*, January 8, 2005, Internet version, in English.

46. Cho Myong-yong, "Noble Benevolence for Coming Generations," *Nodong Sinmun*, December 6, 2003, 2, in Korean.

47. "*Nodong Sinmun* on Top Priority to Things for People," KCNA, March 7, 2005, in English.

48. Yi Ki-chun and Na Chong-yon, "A Study of North Korean Household Economy and Consumer Behaviors Following the 1 July Economic Management Improvement Measures" (paper presented at the Korean Society of Consumer Studies 2007 Spring Seminar, Seoul, May 12, 2007), in Korean.

49. "DPRK Cabinet Instruction No. 9: On Thoroughly Implementing the Policy Put Forth by the Great Leader Comrade Kim Jong-il to Effectively Make Use of Cultivated Land So That Organizations and Enterprises Will Resolve Food Shortages for Their Employees on Their Own," dated January 31, 2004, in Korean. The document was made

public by the Japanese human rights organization Rescue the North Korean People (RENK) on its website on October 23, 2004.

50. See, for example, Stephan Haggard and Marcus Noland, *Famine in North Korea: Markets, Aid, and Reform* (New York: Columbia University Press, 2007), 35.

51. Estimates of supply and demand are more complicated. See Haggard and Noland, *Famine in North Korea*, especially 41ff.

52. Stephan Haggard and Marcus Noland, *Hunger and Human Rights: The Politics of Famine in North Korea* (Washington, DC: U.S. Committee for Human Rights in North Korea, 2005), 18. See also chapter 3 in Suk Lee, *The DPRK Famine of 1994–2000: Existence and Impact*, Korea Institute for National Unification, Studies Series 05-06, 2006.

53. "Low Productivity Blamed Chiefly for North Korea's Chronic Food Shortage," Yonhap, November 21, 2003, in English.

54. "N. Korean Tractors Running at 60 Percent Capacity: International Food Agencies," Yonhap, January 8, 2005, in English.

55. Cited in Nicholas D. Kristof, "Hunger and Other North Korean Hardships Are Said to Deepen Discontent," *New York Times*, February 18, 1992, A6.

56. *Nutrition Survey of the Democratic People's Republic of Korea*, a report by the EU, UNICEF, and WFP, November 1998. Available on the North Korea page of the WFP website. See also W. Courtland Robinson et al., "Mortality in North Korean Migrant Households: A Retrospective Study," *Lancet* 354, no. 9175 (July 24, 1999): 291–95.

57. *DPRK 2004 Nutrition Assessment, Report of Survey Results*, February 2005. Available on the North Korea page of the WFP website.

58. Robert E. Black, et al., "Maternal and Child Undernutrition 1; Maternal and Child Undernutrition: Global and Regional Exposures and Health Consequences," *Lancet* 371, no. 9608 (January 19, 2008), Internet version.

59. Seung-Ryun Kim, "Behind the Scenes of Im Su-kyung's 1989 Pyongyang Festival Visit," *Dong-A Ilbo*, October 10, 2005, Internet version, in English.

60. Mark E. Manyin, "U.S. Assistance to North Korea: Fact Sheet," *CRS Report for Congress*, updated October 11, 2006, 2.

61. Haggard and Noland, *Hunger and Human Rights*, 28. Also see the authors' *Famine in North Korea: Markets, Aid, and Reform*.

62. Francois Hauter, "Malnutrition and Alcoholism Are Completing the Decline of This Country, Entirely Dedicated to the Cult of Kim Il-sung and His Heir, Kim Jong-il," *Le Figaro*, April 3, 2002, Internet version, in French.

63. "N. K. No Longer Wants Emergency Aid, Claims to Have Enough Food," Yonhap, September 18, 2005, in English.

64. Ser Myo-ja, "Aid Agencies Question North's Food Capability," *JoongAng Ilbo*, November 18, 2005, Internet version, in English.

65. "KCNA Ridicules U.S. 'Advice' over 'Human Rights,'" KCNA, October 10, 2005, in English.

66. See the North Korea page of the WFP website.

67. For example, Pyon Sung-ho, "The Basic Direction of Resolving the Food Problem,

the Dietary Problem, in Our Own Way," *Kyongje Yongu*, November 15, 2004, 17–19, in Korean.

68. "Improvement of Economic Management System Called For," KCNA, March 5, 2005, in English.

69. "Seoul, UN Worlds Apart in Monitoring N. Korea Food Aid," *Chosun Ilbo*, September 10, 2005, Internet version, in English.

70. "Seoul, UN Worlds Apart in Monitoring N. Korea Food Aid."

71. Haggard and Noland, *Hunger and Human Rights*, 16. Also see the authors' *Famine in North Korea: Markets, Aid, and Reform*.

72. "Discussion" with chief functionaries of party and state economic organizations, titled "Effecting a New Transformation in Basic Construction," August 11, 2004, from *Kim Jong-il Songjip* 15 (August 30, 2005): 453–69, in Korean.

73. Sin Chu-hyon, "Latest North Korea Information—Rationing Suspended throughout North Korea Except in Pyongyang," *Wolgan Chosun* (May–June 2006): 362–65, in Korean.

74. Mike Bratzke, "Last Tango in Pyongyang," *Wolgan Chosun* (November 1, 2004): 254–73, in Korean.

75. UNICEF, *Water, Environment and Sanitation*, UNICEF website, DPRK page, www.unicef.org/dprk/reallives_224.html (accessed on December 26, 2006).

76. Central Bureau of Statistics, Institute of Child Nutrition, DPRK, "DPRK 2004 Nutrition Assessment: Report of Survey Results," page 12 of a pdf report retrieved from the Nautilus Institute website in February 2005.

77. "Kim Jong-il Sends Wild Honey to Pyongyang Maternity Hospital," KCNA, July 22, 2004, in English.

78. "Dying Children in North Korea's Hospitals," *JoongAng Ilbo*, February 21, 2001, Internet version, in English.

79. "Produce and Supply Mass Medicines on Their Own," *Nodong Sinmun*, July 17, 2001, 4, in Korean.

80. "Int'l Red Cross to Scale Down Medical Supply Distribution in North Korea," Yonhap, December 18, 2006, in English.

81. Dr. Vollertsen has written extensively on North Korea. This quotation is from "Life under the Red Star," *JoongAng Ilbo*, April 30, 2001, Internet version, in English.

82. Bratzke, "Last Tango in Pyongyang."

83. Haggard and Noland, *Hunger and Human Rights*, 87–88.

84. "Int'l Red Cross to Scale Down Medical Supply Distribution in North Korea."

85. "Medical Report Shows Most N. Koreans Vulnerable to Epidemics: Lawmaker," Yonhap, September 6, 2006, in English.

86. Park Hyun Min, "Critical Gap of Average Life Expectancy between the Two Koreas," *Daily NK* website, September 8, 2006, in English. Also see Namgung Min, "South Korea's Average Life Span 78 Years, North Korea's 64: A 14-Year Difference," *Daily NK* website, October 23, 2007, in English.

87. "Pyongyang Condo Prices Quadruple," *Dong-A Ilbo*, February 3, 2006, Internet version, in English.

88. "DPRK Profiled: Five Years after 'Economic Reform'—Collapse of Government Control, Division of Society into Classes, Increase in Black Market Traders in DPRK," *Mainichi Shimbun*, Nikkei Telecom 21 database version, July 3, 2007, morning edition, in Japanese.

89. "Let Us Thoroughly Eliminate Private Accommodation Facilities and Give No Room for Enemies' Maneuvering," State Security Department Internal Document, published by *Chosun Ilbo*, October 7, 2005, Internet version, in Korean.

90. Interview with a former North Korean who defected in 1996, Seoul, November 1997.

91. The phenomenon of North Koreans learning to become consumers is discussed in Yi Ki-chun and Na chong-yon "A Study of North Korean Household Economy and Consumer Behaviors."

92. Ryu Kyong-won, "Merchants Spreading Delusions about the Enemy Using South Korean Goods? What Does the 2007 Market Control Mean?" *Rimjingang*, March 17, 2008, 82–96, in Korean.

93. An Yong-hyon, "DPRK Markets That Even Kim Jong-il Cannot Hold in Check," chosun.com, January 13, 2009.

Chapter 5: The Information Environment

1. A readable overview of communications theory approaches is Dominic A. Infante, Andrew S. Rancer, and Deanna F. Womack, *Building Communication Theory* (Prospect Heights, IL: Waveland Press, 2003). Another good source is Stephen W. Littlejohn, *Theories of Human Communication* (Belmont, CA: Wadsworth, 2002).

2. A German visitor quotes Kim Il-sung as using this term in regard to the opening of the Najin-Sonbong foreign trade zone. The term occasionally appears in the North Korean press. For Kim's original quote, see Hy-Sang Lee, *North Korea: A Strange Socialist Fortress* (Westport, CT: Praeger, 2001), 178.

3. Yu Chae-chon, "The Nature and Function of the North Korean Media," in *Pukhanui Ollon* [Media in North Korea] (Seoul: Uryumunhwa, 1990), 45–84, in Korean.

4. Quotation from Kim Pyong-ho, vice director general of KCNA, in an interview with No Kil-nam, editor of *Minjok Tongsin* (of Los Angeles), September 8, 2003, in Korean.

5. "Step Up Propaganda by the Press and Publications Dynamically to Spur the Building of a Powerful State," *Nodong Sinmun* via KCNA, February 12, 2004, editorial, in Korean.

6. KCBS, October 21, 2005, in Korean.

7. "Phoenixes Who Overcame Difficulties with Faith," *Nodong Sinmun*, December 2, 2006, 4, in Korean.

8. Yonhap News Agency, *North Korea Handbook* (Armonk, NY: M. E. Sharpe, 2003), 410, in English.

9. The KCNA website at www.kcna.co.jp is run by North Korean loyalists in Japan.

10. Kim Mi-yong, "DPRK Party Mouthpiece *Nodong Sinmun* Introduced," *Chosun Ilbo*, February 27, 2002, Internet version, in English.

11. *Nodong Sinmun* via KCNA, December 18, 2003, in Korean.

12. "One More North Korean 'Surprise,'" *Korea Herald*, October 7, 1997, Internet version, in English.

13. "Relay Party's Ideology and Intention to the Masses in a More Timely, Faster Way," *Nodong Sinmun*, October 6, 2003, 3, in Korean.

14. "Relay Party's Ideology and Intention to the Masses in a More Timely, Faster Way." According to the article, one model functionary, "after he read, first thing in the morning, the editorial that urged a great upsurge in building a powerful state with the pride of having splendidly celebrated the 55th anniversary of the Republic's founding . . . carried out political work by going out to many cooperative farms bustling with corn harvests and letting them know the tasks suggested in the official party newspaper's editorial."

15. KCBS, December 18, 2003, in Korean. KCTV, December 18, 2003, in Korean. KCNA, December 18, 2003, from its website at www.kcna.co.jp, in English.

16. Paek Hyang and Choe Chin-i, "People Are Sick of the No. 3 Broadcast, and the Town Chief Is Frustrated," *Rimjingang*, November 20, 2007, 154–58, in Korean.

17. Song Mi-ran, "Computer 'Mail,'" *Nodong Sinmun*, July 19, 2001, 4, in Korean.

18. Yi Un-yong, "North Korea's Formidable Hacking Capabilities Revealed by a North Korean Hacking Godfather-Escapee," *Sindong-a*, November 1, 2005, 162–73, in Korean.

19. Philippe Grangereau, *Au pays du grand mensonge: Voyage en Coree du Nord* (Paris: Payot, 2003), 185–87.

20. Bernd Girrbach, "The Diplomacy of Images: Notes of a Film Trip (2002)," in *Nordkorea: Einblicke in ein ratselhaftes Land* [North Korea: Glimpses of a Mysterious Land], ed. Christoph Moeskes (Berlin: Christoph Links Verlag, 2004), 101–8.

21. "Kim Jong-il Authors 1,400-Odd Works during University Days," KCNA, March 18, 2004, in English.

22. "New Books off the Press," KCNA, October 22, 2003, in English.

23. "New Novels off the Press," KCNA, November 3, 2003, in English.

24. "New Novels off the Press."

25. The collectivist nature of film production and consumption in North Korea has been noted by Dr. Suk-Young Kim in her lecture "Illusive Utopia: Fifty Years of North Korean Film" (presented at the U.S. Korea Institute at SAIS, Washington, D.C., April 30, 2007).

26. Ron Gluckman, "Behind the Scenes in North Korea," personal website, www.gluckman.com/NKFilmTokion.html. Gluckman cites film statistics from North Korea and from a survey of North Korean defectors.

27. Johannes Schoenherr, "Permanent State of War: The North Korean Cinema," *Nordkorea: Einblicke in ein ratselhaftes Land*, May 1, 2004, 92–100, in German.

28. Karl Malakunas, "It Ain't Hollywood, but North Korean Cinema Only Has Room for One Star," Things Asian website, April 3, 2005, www.thingsasian.com/goto_article/article.3219.html.

29. Malakunas, "It Ain't Hollywood."

30. Kim Jong-il, *On the Art of the Cinema*, April 11, 1973, in English. Published in Pyongyang by the Foreign Languages Publishing House, 1989.

31. Schoenherr, "Permanent State of War."

32. Yonhap, *North Korea Handbook*, 197.

33. Han Yong-chin, "DPRK's Idolization Propaganda 40 Percent of National Budget," *Daily NK* Internet site, January 10, 2007, in English.

34. O Myong-chu, "Rock Writing," *Dong-A Ilbo*, March 9, 2005, Internet version, in English.

35. "Full Text of the Study and Lecture Program 'On Doing Away with Capitalism,'" obtained by and published in South Korea's *Chosun Ilbo*, December 20, 2002, Internet version, in Korean.

36. Rescue the North Korean People (RENK), "Information Has Been Flowing in Steadily from Outside: The Kim Regime's Sense of Crisis over the Diversifying Values of the North Korean People Is Clearly Revealed," Flash Report No. 9, RENK website, July 12, 2005, in Japanese.

37. "Let Us Live and Work According to Our Own Way," KCBS, December 7, 2004, in Korean.

38. "Let Us Vigorously Wage the Struggle against Phenomena to Uproot the Acts of Smuggling," instructions to North Hamgyong Province Committee, published in 2003 by the KWP, obtained by Rescue the North Korean People (RENK) and published on the group's website, November 22, 2004, in English.

39. "Mass Education Material for the Anti-spy Struggle, *Juche* 93, Part 2," originally published by the SSD in June 2004 under the title "Let Us Heighten Revolutionary Vigilance and Thoroughly Smash the Enemies' Maneuvers Aimed at Rupturing the Building of a Powerful State"; later obtained and published by *Chosun Ilbo*, October 19, 2005, Internet version, in Korean.

40. "Explanation of Laws and Regulations: The Education Law," *Minju Choson*, May 9, 2000, 2, in Korean.

41. *Kodung Kyoyuk* [Higher Education], *Juche* 95, no. 4 (August 6–October 6, 2006), in Korean.

42. Yi Pong-hyon, "Kim Il-sung University Gives Capitalism Lectures," *Hangyore Sinmun*, January 17, 1996, 1, in Korean.

43. Yang Jung-A, "North Korean Education from 7 Years Old," *Daily NK* website, August 29, 2006, in English.

44. Jeannette Goddar, "Attentive Care by the 'Great Leader,'" *Spiegel Online*, November 21, 2007, in German.

45. Philo C. Wasburn, *Broadcasting Propaganda: International Radio Broadcasting and the Construction of Political Reality* (Westport, CT: Praeger, 1992), 30. Also see Alvin A. Snyder, *Warriors of Disinformation: American Propaganda, Soviet Lies, and the Winning of the Cold War* (New York: Arcade, 1995), 25, 166.

46. See RFA's home and FAQ pages at www.rfa.org.

47. See the KBS website at www.kbs.co.kr. This policy may change with a change in ROK government administrations.

48. The origin of "gray" propaganda is disguised, but it does not claim to come from the target country, whereas "black" propaganda attempts to disguise its true origin by purporting to originate in the country toward which it is targeted. The Social Education Broadcasting station, operated by the ROK government's KBS network, beams signals into North Korea and China twenty-four hours per day. Echo of Hope Broadcasting transmits for about twelve hours a day, according to the website ClandestineRadio at www.clandestineradio.com). The station claims to be sponsored by Koreans living abroad but is reportedly run by the National Intelligence Service. Voice of the People Broadcasting, transmitting twelve hours a day as well, advertises itself as a service of the Korean Workers' Union but is said to be operated by the Ministry of National Defense.

49. See the Far East Broadcasting website at www.febc.org.

50. Kevin Kane, "Private Citizens Liberating North Korea with Shortwave Radio," *Daily NK* website, March 4, 2007, in English. Also see Kim Song-a, "University Students Take the Lead in Broadcasting to North Korea," *Daily NK* website, May 3, 2007, in English.

51. Francis Uenuma, "Sending Out Signals to Long-Isolated North Koreans," *Washington Post*, December 30, 2007, A27.

52. Paek Sung-ku, "Kim Jong-il Orders to Confiscate Radios; A Conspiracy Is Underway to Abolish the KBS Social Educational Broadcasting to Keep Step with North Korea's Suspension of Anti-North [sic] Propaganda Broadcasts," *Wolgan Chosun* (September 1, 2003): 249–55, in Korean.

53. Kim Yong Hun, "24 Percent of North Korean Defectors Say They Experienced the Southern Media," *Daily NK* website, December 16, 2005, in English.

54. Voice of National Salvation (VNS), July 31, 2003, in Korean.

55. Yi Chong-hun, "NSC, Was It Taken in by North Korea's Psychological Warfare?" *Chugan Tong-a*, July 1, 2004, 322–33, in Korean.

56. "U.S. Imperialists' Sly and Wicked Ideological and Cultural Infiltration Maneuvers," KCBS, May 27, 2003, in Korean.

57. Cho Song-chol, "U.S. Imperialists' Vicious Psychological Warfare via Radio 'Free Asia.'" *Nodong Sinmun*, June 13, 2003, 6, in Korean.

58. Kim Song-a, "North Korea's Demand to Cease Scattering of Flyers Provides Proof of Their Effectiveness," *Daily NK* website, August 2, 2007, in English.

59. "Activists Urged to Stop Dropping Fliers on N. Korea," *Chosun Ilbo*, September 1, 2006, Internet version, in English.

60. "Concern over DPRK Balloon 'Terrorist Attack Experiments,'" *Sankei Shimbun*, January 10, 1997, 1, morning edition, in Japanese.

61. ROK Unification Ministry website; see "Exchanges and Cooperation" at www.unikorea.go.kr/eng/default.jsp?pgname = AFFexchanges_economic.

62. Kim Ji-ho, "Nightmare Haunts Housewife Detained during Kumgang Tour—under Close Scrutiny for Mental Duress, Min Young-mi Says North Korea Used Her to Save Face," *Korea Herald*, July 27, 1999, Internet version, in English.

63. Kang Chol-hwan, "North Korean Security Believes Yongchon Explosion an Assassination Attempt," *Chosun Ilbo*, May 25, 2004, Internet version, in English.

64. Marcus Noland, *Telecommunications in North Korea: Has Orascom Made the Connection?* (paper sponsored by the Peterson Institute for International Economics and the East-West Center, September 8, 2008).

65. For example, see C. Hovland, O. J. Harvey, and M. Sherif, "Assimilation and Contrast Effects in Reaction to Communication and Attitude Change," *Journal of Abnormal and Social Psychology* 55 (1957): 244–52.

66. Interview with a former North Korean who defected in 1996, Seoul, December 1997.

67. Cho Song-chol, "World Unfit for Humans—United States: Corrupt Society Filled with Trash and Deceit," *Nodong Sinmun*, February 8, 2004, 6, in Korean.

68. Cho Song-chol, "World Unfit for Humans—United States: Unfair Society Where Money Is Everything," *Nodong Sinmun*, February 13, 2004, 6, in Korean.

69. Cho, "World Unfit for Humans—United States: Unfair Society."

70. Cho, "World Unfit for Humans—United States: Unfair Society."

71. Paek Mun-kyu, "Fate of an Occupier Who Has Fallen into a Trap from Which There Is No Escape," *Nodong Sinmun*, November 28, 2003, 6, in Korean.

72. Ri Sok-chol, "Anachronistic Ballad about 'Placing Importance on Alliance' Will Not Take Effect," *Nodong Sinmun*, on July 2, 2005, in Korean; read on Pyongyang Broadcasting Station (Voice of Korea), July 2, 2005.

73. KCTV, January 9, 2004, in Korean.

Chapter 6: Hidden Thoughts

1. Choe Kum-nam, "The Four Firsts Are the Ideological and Spiritual Forces for the Construction of a Powerful State." *Minju Choson*, November 18, 2003, 2, in Korean.

2. Chong-pyo Chung, "Our Fatherland Is an Ideological Power," *Nodong Sinmun*, September 10, 1996, 3, in Korean.

3. Kim Il-sung, "On Eliminating Dogmatism and Formalism and Establishing *Juche* in Ideological Work," speech to Party Propaganda and Agitation Workers, December 28, 1955, in *Kim Il Sung Works* (Pyongyang: Foreign Languages Publishing House, 1982), 9:395–417; quote from 9:395–96, in English.

4. Chong Son-chol, "Being Strong-Willed with the Principle of Independence Is a Fundamental Requirement in Our Times' Politics," *Nodong Sinmun*, March 23, 2001, 2, in Korean.

5. Cho Song-chol, "Let Us Heighten Vigilance against U.S. Imperialists' Psychological Smear Campaign: Cunning Stratagem Abusing Humanitarianism," *Nodong Sinmun*, August 14, 2003, 6, in Korean.

6. Mark E. Manyin, "U.S. Assistance to North Korea: Fact Sheet," *CRS Report for Congress*, Document RS21834, January 31, 2006, 2.

7. "On the Glorious Road to Building a *Juche*-Style Party," KCBS, December 31, 2000, in Korean.

8. Kim Jong-il, "Historical Lesson in Building Socialism and the General Line of Our Party," a talk given to senior officials of the Party Central Committee on January 3, 1992; published in *Nodong Sinmun*, February 4, 1992, in Korean, and carried on the same date by KCNA.

9. Kim Jong-il, "Our Socialism for the People Will Not Perish," a talk given to senior officials of the Party Central Committee on May 5, 1991, published in *Nodong Sinmun*, May 27, 1991, in Korean, and republished in *People's Korea* 1517 (June 8, 1991): 2–7; quote from 4, in English.

10. Song-kuk Choe, "Imperialists' Wily Strategy of Disintegration," *Nodong Sinmun*, May 3, 1998, 6, in Korean.

11. Kang Chol-hwan, "Serious Ideological Disturbance within the North; Original Copy of Ideological Indoctrination Material for North Korean People's Army Cadres Obtained," *Chosun Ilbo*, September 4, 2004, Internet version, in Korean. The title of this North Korean document is "On Resolutely Smashing the Strategic Psychological Warfare of the Enemy Who Aims to Cause Our Internal Collapse and Degeneration."

12. Chang-man Hwang, "The Source of Our People's Revolutionary Optimism," *Nodong Sinmun*, June 1, 1997, 2, in Korean.

13. Kim Myong-hui, "The Revolutionary Spirit for Suicidal Explosion," *Nodong Sinmun*, December 29, 1998, 3, in Korean.

14. Pak Nam-chin, "Immortal Course during Which the Military Assurance for the Consummation of the *Juche* Cause Has Been Provided," *Nodong Sinmun*, June 26, 1997, 3, in Korean.

15. "Our Republic Is a Socialist Military Power," KCBS, August 30, 2003, in Korean.

16. KCNA, January 8, 2004, in English.

17. Gen. Eugene E. Habiger, USAF, commander in chief, U.S. Strategic Command, to the Senate Armed Services Committee, March 21, 1996: "At U.S. Strategic Command, peace is still our profession, and the strength of our deterrent forces remains the backbone of that peace." (www.defenselink.mil/speeches/1996/t19960321-habiger.html).

18. Pae Yong-il, "They Should Bow to Military-First Politics," *Tongil Sinbo*, July 22, 2006, 4, in Korean.

19. Song Mi-ran, "For an Invincibly Powerful State," *Nodong Sinmun*, April 7, 2003, 2, in Korean.

20. "All Citizens in This Land Are Soldiers," KCNA, April 25, 2003, in Korean, citing an April 24 *Nodong Sinmun* article titled "Oh, Soldier."

21. Hwang Chang-man and Chong Kwang-pok, "The People's Army Is a College of Revolution Training Fervent Fighters for the Military-First Era," *Nodong Sinmun*, June 13, 2002, 2, in Korean.

22. Chong Kum-chol, "Frontline-Style Political Work and Work with People's Emotions," *Nodong Sinmun* via the Korean Press Media website (http://dprkmedia.com), March 15, 2007.

23. "Love Gun-Barrel Families," KCBS, broadcasting a *Nodong Sinmun* article, January 29, 2004, in Korean.

24. "Inheritance of the Mangyongdae Family," KCBS, April 12, 2007, in Korean.

25. Yang Sun, "The General Adds Luster to the Glory of the Military-First Fatherland," *Nodong Sinmun*, April 2, 2003, 2.

26. Kim Chong-su, "Creative Ideological Theory on the Balance of Social Classes in the Current Era," *Nodong Sinmun*, August 13, 2004, 2, in Korean.

27. Kim Pyong-chin, "Important Requirement for Building a Powerful Socialist State As Elucidated by the Military-First Idea," *Nodong Sinmun*, May 16, 2003, 2, in Korean.

28. Ryang Sun, "It Is Thanks to the General That We Have the Fatherland," *Nodong Sinmun*, March 12, 2005, 2, in Korean.

29. "Let Us See and Solve All Problems from a New Viewpoint and a New Height," *Nodong Sinmun*, January 9, 2001, 1, in Korean.

30. Susan Kitchens and Josephine Lee, "Royal Flush," Forbes.com, March 4, 2002.

31. Chon U-taek, *Saram-ui Tongil, Tang-ui Tongil* [Reunification of the People, Reunification of the Land], August 2007, in Korean.

32. Hyun-Joon Chon et al., *An Assessment of the North Korean System's Durability* (Seoul: Korea Institute for National Unification (KINU), 2007), in English. The survey was modeled on an earlier survey designed by Sung Chull Kim et al., as reported in *The Assessment on the Crisis Level and the Prospect of Durability of North Korean Socialist System* (Seoul: Research Institute of National Unification, 1996).

33. Chon et al., *An Assessment*, 173.

34. Chon et al., *An Assessment*, 12.

35. Chon, *Saram-ui Tongil*, 174.

36. Chon et al., *An Assessment*, 30–35.

37. Chon Song-ho, "Heart of 10 Million Soldiers and People," *Nodong Sinmun* via the Uriminjokkiri website, March 2, 2004, in Korean.

38. Song Hyo-sam, "The Heart of Socialist Korea," *Nodong Sinmun*, June 3, 2002, 2, in Korean, cited by KCNA on June 4, 2002.

39. Chon, *Saram-ui Tongil*, 197.

40. Chon, *Saram-ui Tongil*, 197.

41. Chon, *Saram-ui Tongil*, 196.

42. Chon, *Saram-ui Tongil*, 196.

43. Chon, *Saram-ui Tongil*, 196.

44. Chon, *Saram-ui Tongil*, 173.

45. Chon, *Saram-ui Tongil*, 172.

46. Chon, *Saram-ui Tongil*, 172.

47. Philippe Grangereau, *Au pays du grand mensonge: Voyage en Coree du Nord* (Paris: Payot and Rivages, 2001), 187, in French.

48. Cho Taek-pom, "Must Not Even in the Slightest Tolerate Imperialist Ideological and Cultural Infiltration," *Nodong Sinmun* via the Uriminjokkiri website, November 22, 2004, in Korean.

49. A good English-language survey of religion in North Korea is David Hawk's *Thank You Father Kim Il Sung: Eyewitness Accounts of Severe Violations of Freedom of Thought, Conscience, and Religion in North Korea* (Washington, DC: U.S. Commission on Interna-

tional Freedom, November 2005). Updates on the state of religious freedom in North Korea can be found in the commission's annual reports.

50. Kang In Duk, "North Korea's Policy on Religion," *East Asian Review* 7, no. 3 (autumn 1995): 89–101. The original source of the statistics is the ROK government's annual *White Paper on Human Rights in North Korea*. See Soo-am Kim, Keum-soon Lee, and Soon-hee Lim, *White Paper on Human Rights in North Korea, 2007* (Seoul: [ROK] Korea Institute for National Unification, 2007), 171.

51. Kang, "North Korea's Policy on Religion," 94.

52. Kang, "North Korea's Policy on Religion," 91. Also see Kim, Lee, and Lim, *White Paper on Human Rights in North Korea*, 171.

53. Kim Jong-il, "Giving Priority to Ideological Work Is an Essential Requisite for Accomplishing the Socialist Cause," KCBS, June 20, 1995, in Korean.

54. "Religious Bodies Get Greater Role in N. Korea with Aid from South," Yonhap, June 22, 2006, in English.

55. "Religious Believers Do Exist in N. Korea: Survey," Yonhap, February 26, 2008, in English.

56. Some of the parallels noted here come from Susan Rothbaum, "Between Two Worlds: Issues of Separation and Identity after Leaving a Religious Community," in *Falling from the Faith: Causes and Consequences of Religious Apostasy*, ed. David G. Bromley (Newbury Park, CA: Sage Publications, 1988), 205–28; quotations from 208–10.

57. Kim Myong-chol, "Public Awareness in Military-First Era," *Minju Choson*, September 28, 2003, 2, in Korean.

58. Rothbaum, "Between Two Worlds," 214–16.

59. "34 N. Korean Defectors Left S. Korea for Other Countries: Report," Yonhap, November 13, 2004, in English, citing a recent survey by *Segye Ilbo*.

60. Georgi Shalchnazarov, an aide to Gorbachev, quoted by David Remnick in *Lenin's Tomb: The Last Days of the Soviet Empire* (New York: Random House, 1993), 168.

61. Robert K. Merton, *Social Theory and Social Structure*, rev. ed. (New York: Free Press, 1957).

62. James C. Scott, *Weapons of the Weak: Everyday Forms of Peasant Resistance* (New Haven, CT: Yale University Press, 1985).

Chapter 7: The Law, Political Class, and Human Rights

1. Tai-Uk Chung, "Beyond the Limits of Intervention? The Dilemma of the North Korean Human Rights Act," *East Asian Review* 16, no. 3 (Autumn 2004): 75–86.

2. Marion P. Spina Jr., "Brushes with the Law: North Korea and the Rule of Law," *Korea Economic Institute Academic Paper Series* 2, no. 6 (June 2007): 1. For another discussion of the North Korea case, see Patricia Goedde, "Law of Our Own Style: The Evolution and Challenges of the North Korean Legal System," *Fordham International Law Journal* 27 (April 2004): 1265–88.

3. Several overviews of North Korean law are available in English. See Soo-Am Kim, *The North Korean Penal Code, Criminal Procedures, and Their Actual Applications*, Korea Institute for National Unification, Studies Series 06-01, March 2006. The full text of North Korea's criminal code was published by South Korea's news agency, Yonhap (Internet version) on December 8, 2004, in Korean.

4. *Choson Minjujuui Inmin Konghwaguk Popchon* [DPRK Body of Law] (Pyongyang: DPRK Law Publishing House, August 25, 2004), in Korean.

5. Kim Il-sung, "For the Implementation of the Judicial Policy of Our Party," April 29, 1958. In *Kim Il-sung, Works* (Pyongyang: Foreign Languages Publishing House, 1983), 12:182.

6. Soo-am Kim, Keum-soon Lee, and Soon-hee Lim, *White Paper on Human Rights in North Korea, 2007* (Seoul: [ROK] Korea Institute for National Unification, 2007), 186.

7. Lee Sung Jin, "Increasing 'Deaths' Ahead of SPA Election," *Daily NK* website, March 9, 2009, in English.

8. "Results of Election of Deputies to Local Power Bodies Released," KCNA, July 30, 2007, in English.

9. "*Nodong Sinmun* Calls for Observing Revolutionary Principle," KCNA, December 10, 2006, in English.

10. Kim, Lee, and Lim, *White Paper on Human Rights in North Korea, 2007*, 116–23.

11. Kim, Lee, and Lim, *White Paper on Human Rights in North Korea, 2007*, 119.

12. Adrian Buzo, *The Guerilla Dynasty, Politics and Leadership in North Korea* (Boulder, CO: Westview Press, 1999). See, for example, 241ff.

13. Kim, Lee, and Lim, *White Paper on Human Rights in North Korea, 2007*, 256.

14. Quoted in "North Korea Targeted South's Elite," *Dong-A Ilbo*, August 13, 2006, Internet version, in English.

15. Victor Kuznetsov, "The Economic Factors of the USSR's Disintegration," in *The Fall of the Soviet Empire*, ed. Anne de Tinguy, 264–79 (New York: Columbia University Press, 1997), 270.

16. Interview with a former North Korean who defected in 1996, Seoul, December 1997.

17. Interview with a former North Korean who defected in 2003, Seoul, September 2004.

18. Interview with a former North Korean who defected in 1995, Seoul, December 1997.

19. Interview with a former North Korean who defected in 2003, Seoul, September 2004.

20. Chong-chol Mun, "Disabled Persons Ousted from the Revolutionary Capital of Pyongyang," *Daily NK* website, April 23, 2007, in English.

21. Kim, Lee, and Lim, *White Paper on Human Rights in North Korea, 2007*, 31–42.

22. Kim Min-se, "Summary Execution during Famine Arouses Fear," *Daily NK* website, January 6, 2007, in English.

23. Soon Ok Lee, *Eyes of the Tailless Animals: Prison Memoirs of a North Korean Woman* (Bartlesville, OK: Living Sacrifice Books, 1999).

24. *Sindong-a*, January 1, 2004, Internet version, in Korean.

25. Kim, Lee, and Lim, *White Paper on Human Rights in North Korea, 2007*, 128.

26. A good source on the North Korean prison system is David Hawk and the U.S. Committee for Human Rights in North Korea, *The Hidden Gulag: Exposing North Korea's Prison Camps* (Washington, DC: U.S. Committee for Human Rights in North Korea, 2003). Also see the ROK government's annual *White Paper on Human Rights in North Korea* published by the Korea Institute for National Unification (KINU).

27. Pyongyang Broadcasting Station, January 18, 2002, in Korean.

28. According to Kim, Lee, and Lim, *White Paper on Human Rights in North Korea, 2007*, 73, defectors who worked as prison guards are Kang Chul-hwan, Ahn Hyuk, Ahn Myung-chul, and Choi Dong-chul. Excellent satellite photographs of concentration camps are included in Hawk's *The Hidden Gulag*.

29. For example, Kim, Lee, and Lim, *White Paper on Human Rights in North Korea, 2007*, 81.

30. "North Korea's Concentration Camps for Political Prisoners," *Keys* (winter 2001): 23–44, in English. Also available at www.nknet.org.

31. The interesting story of the Korean-Japanese migration to North Korea is told by Tessa Morris-Suzuki, *Exodus to North Korea: Shadows from Japan's Cold War* (Lanham, MD: Rowman & Littlefield Publishers, 2007).

32. Kim, Lee, and Lim, *White Paper on Human Rights in North Korea, 2007*, 261 and 273.

33. Hawk, *The Hidden Gulag*, 29–30.

34. Detailed daily schedules as reported by various former inmates are reported in Korean Bar Association, *2008 White Paper on Human Rights in North Korea* (Seoul: Lee Jin-kang, 2009), 553–55.

35. A slide show of the Stanford Prison Experiment is available on the web at www.prisonexp.org.

36. Kang Chol-hwan, "5,000 Prisoners Massacred at Onsong Concentration Camp in 1987," *Chosun Ilbo*, December 11, 2002, Internet version, in English.

37. "*Nodong Sinmun* on Defense of True Human Rights," KCNA, June 24, 1995, in English.

38. A spokesman for the DPRK foreign ministry, KCBS, March 1, 2001, in Korean.

39. "The United States' Human Rights Commotions against the Republic, Which Are Becoming More Blatant Than Ever Before," KCBS, December 30, 2005, in Korean.

40. Chong Pong-kil, "Blatant Declaration of Hostility against the DPRK," KCBS commentary, October 7, 2004, in Korean.

41. "ROK President: Too Early to Press DPRK on Human Rights," *Korea Herald*, October 25, 2000, Internet version, in English.

42. Doug Struck, "A Survivor Recounts Horrors of N. Korea's Prison Camps," *Washington Post*, May 3, 2003, A20.

43. DLA Piper and the U.S. Committee for Human Rights in North Korea, *Failure to Protect: A Call for the UN Security Council to Act in North Korea* (Washington, DC: U.S. Committee for Human Rights in North Korea, October 30, 2006), 72.

Chapter 8: Defectors

1. Albert O. Hirschman, *Exit, Voice, and Loyalty: Responses to Declines in Firms, Organizations, and States* (Cambridge, MA: Harvard University Press, 1970).

2. Soo-am Kim, Keum-soon Lee, and Soon-hee Lim, *White Paper on Human Rights in North Korea, 2007* (Seoul: [ROK] Korea Institute for National Unification, 2007), 149.

3. Andrei Lankov, *Crisis in North Korea: The Failure of De-Stalinization, 1956* (Honolulu, University of Hawaii Press, 2005), 214.

4. Andrei Lankov, *North of the DMZ: Essays on Daily Life in North Korea* (Jefferson, NC: McFarland & Co, 2007), 297–98.

5. "Pyongyang Accuses Seoul of Abducting N. Koreans," Yonhap, July 29, 2004, in English.

6. "Government Can't Bear Unlimited Responsibility for North Korean Defectors," Yonhap, August 16, 2004, in English.

7. Kelly Koh and Glenn Baek, "North Korean Defectors: A Window into a Reunified Korea," in *Korea Briefing 2000–2001*, ed. Kongdan Oh and Ralph C. Hassig, 205–25 (Armonk, NY: M. E. Sharpe and the Asia Society, 2002), 211.

8. Interview with a former North Korean who defected in 2002, Seoul, April 2006.

9. Keumsoon Lee, *The Border-Crossing North Koreans: Current Situations and Future Prospects*, Korea Institute for National Unification, Studies Series 06-05, May 2006, 12, in English. Also reported by Yonhap, December 5, 2004.

10. Keum-Soon Lee, "Policy Implications of North Korean Escapees: Protection and Resettlement Assistance," *KINU Insight* (June 2007): 6. *KINU Insight* is a publication of the Korea Institute for National Unification.

11. "Family of POW Escapes North Korea," *Korea Herald*, April 1, 2006, Internet version, in English.

12. Ser Myo-ja, "North Korean Defects Three Times," *JoongAng Ilbo*, July 6, 2007, Internet version, in English.

13. Many accounts of defection have been published over the years. A recent example is Mike Kim, *Escaping North Korea: Defiance and Hope in the World's Most Repressive Country* (Lanham, MD: Rowman & Littlefield, 2008).

14. All aspects of border-crossing North Koreans are well covered by the annual *White Paper on Human Rights in North Korea*. Also see Lee, *The Border-Crossing North Koreans*. See also International Crisis Group, *Perilous Journeys: The Plight of North Koreans in China and Beyond*, Asia report no. 122, October 26, 2006; James D. Seymour, *China: Background Paper on the Situation of North Koreans in China*, Writenet analysis commissioned by the UN High Commissioner for Refugees, January 2005.

15. "Let Us Vigorously Wage the Struggle against Phenomena to Uproot the Acts of Smuggling," instructions to North Hamgyong Province Committee, published in 2003 by the KWP, obtained and published on the website of Rescue the North Korean People (RENK), November 22, 2004, English-language website at www.bekkoame.ne.jp/ro/renk/englishhome.htm.

16. "Mass Education Document for Struggle against Spies," *Chosun Ilbo*, August 26, 2005, Internet version, in Korean.

17. "North Korean Defectors Reside Abroad Longer before Coming to Seoul: Survey," Yonhap, November 4, 2003, in English.

18. International Crisis Group, *Perilous Journeys*, 13. Also see Han Young Jin, "NK Women Sold for the Price of a Pig," *Daily NK* website, August 9, 2005, in English. The $50 price is mentioned in "Human Trafficking Thrives across N. Korea–China Border," *Chosun Ilbo*, March 2, 2008, Internet version, in English.

19. Good coverage of the conditions of defectors in China and their routes to third countries is provided by International Crisis Group, *Perilous Journeys*.

20. Interview with a former North Korean who did not say when he defected, Seoul, March 2005.

21. A South Korean newspaper cites statistics from the Institute of World Economics and Politics for one of China's provinces. "4809 North Korean Defectors in China Were Deported in 2002," *Dong-A Ilbo*, June 8, 2007, Internet version, in English.

22. For good coverage of the repatriation process, see Lee, *The Border-Crossing North Koreans*, 41–52. Also see David Hawk and the U.S. Committee for Human Rights in North Korea, *The Hidden Gulag: Exposing North Korea's Prison Camps* (Washington, DC: U.S. Committee for Human Rights in North Korea, 2003). Also see the annual *White Paper on Human Rights in North Korea*.

23. Lee Jin-woo, "Unemployment Frustrates Defectors in S. Korea," *Korea Times*, November 13, 2006, Internet version, in English.

24. This information is from a study by Professor Park Sang-in, reported in "Almost 70 Percent of N. Korean Defectors in S. Korea Unemployed: Survey," Yonhap, April 16, 2007, in English.

25. Yoon-Hwan Suh, "Suggestions for Building a Social Support System for the Regional Settlement of North Korean Defectors," *Journal of East Asian Affairs* 16, no. 2 (fall/winter 2002): 395.

26. "North Korean Defectors Dissatisfied with Jobs: Survey," Yonhap, February 17, 2004, in English.

27. "Defectors Face Double Standard," *Korea Times*, October 18, 2004, Internet version, in English.

28. "Nearly 70 Percent of North Korean Defectors in South Feel Discrimination: Poll," Yonhap, January 26, 2006, in English.

29. Cho Ji-hyun, "New Divorce Law for N. K. Defectors," *Korea Herald*, March 1, 2007, Internet version, in English. Also see "Court Permits Remarriage of DPRK Defectors in ROK," Yonhap, June 22, 2007, in English.

30. Interview with a former North Korean who defected in 2003, Seoul, September 2004.

31. Episode related to the authors by a South Korean human rights expert, Washington, D.C., January, 2007.

32. Jeon Woo-Taek, "Promoting National Harmony in a Unified Korea," *Korea Focus* 10, no. 1 (January–February 2002): 88–99.

33. "North Korean Defectors' Health Worse Than South Koreans with Illnesses," Yon-

hap, April 9, 2007, in English, reporting on research conducted by a Seoul National University team headed by Dr. Choi Myeong-ae.

34. "Most Common Health Problem among North Korean Defectors Is Arthritis," Yonhap, October 14, 2005, in English, reporting on research conducted by Korea University professor Yoon In-jin.

35. Kim Tae-jong, "Depression Hits 70 Percent of Defectors," *Korea Times*, June 26, 2007, Internet version, in English, reporting on a research report by Chungnam National University professor Kim Hyun-li.

36. Ri Un-chan, "Loyalty to Party and Leader [Suryong] Is Functionaries' Foremost Life," *Nodong Sinmun* (via KPM Internet), August 20, 2007, in Korean.

Chapter 9: The End Comes Slowly

1. Ronald Winetrobe, *The Political Economy of Dictatorship* (London: Cambridge University Press, 1998), 22.

2. "UN: Six Million N. Koreans Chronically Short of Food," AFP, February 24, 2008, in English.

3. "Full Dialogue between DPRK Leader, ROK Media Delegation," Yonhap, August 13, 2000, in Korean.

4. Interview with a North Korean official stationed overseas, June 2006.

5. Chon U-taek, *Saram-ui Tongil, Ttang-ui Tongil* [Reunification of the People, Reunification of the Land], August 2007, in Korean.

6. Interview with a foreign diplomat formerly stationed in Pyongyang, who heard this story from a North Korean associate, Washington, D.C., May 2005.

7. Chon, *Saram-ui Tongil*.

8. According to an internal DPRK document published under the title "Internal Document Obtained—Kim Jong-il Regime Is Making Squeaking Noises," *Tokyo Shimbun*, August 15, 2003, 4, morning edition, in Japanese.

9. Kongdan Oh and Ralph Hassig, "North Korea between Collapse and Reform," *Asian Survey* 34, no. 2 (March/April 1999): 287–309.

10. Cited by Pan Suk Kim, *Prospects for Change of the North Korean Regime* (paper presented at the International Conference on "The Search for Peace and Security in Northeast Asia toward the 21st Century," Institute for Far Eastern Studies, Kyungnam University, and Council on Korea-U.S. Security Studies, Seoul, October 24–25, 1996).

11. Tae Hwan Ok and Soo Am Kim, *The Initial Phase of Unified Korea* (Seoul: Korea Institute for National Unification, 1998), abstract 97-2, in English.

12. See chapter 6, note 32.

13. Hyun-Joon Chon et al., *An Assessment of the North Korean System's Durability* (Seoul: Korea Institute for National Unification, 2007), 106, in English.

~

Further Reading

Leadership

The most authoritative biography of Kim Il-sung is Dae-Sook Suh's *Kim Il Sung: The North Korean Leader* (New York: Columbia University Press, 1988).

No comparable biography is yet available for Kim's son, but Michael Breen, formerly a journalist in Asia, has written a very readable account in *Kim Jong-il: North Korea's Dear Leader* (Singapore: John Wiley & Sons [Asia], 2004).

The Economy

Marcus Noland, an economist at the Peterson Institute for International Economics, has been analyzing the North Korean economy for some years now. See the institute's website for books and reports, including Stephan Haggard and Marcus Noland, *Famine in North Korea: Markets, Aid, and Reform* (New York: Columbia University Press, 2007).

Everyday Economic Life, Information, and Beliefs

Andrei Lankov, at one time a Russian exchange student at Kim Il-sung University and currently an instructor at a South Korean university, frequently publishes insightful articles and reports on the life of the North Korean people. See, for example, his collection of articles in *North of the DMZ: Essays on Daily Life in North Korea* (Jefferson, NC: McFarland & Co., 2007).

The Korea Institute for National Unification (KINU), which is the think tank of the ROK government's Ministry of Unification, publishes the excellent annual *White Paper on Human Rights in North Korea*, which also covers general living conditions. Several months after each edition of *White Paper* is published, it may be downloaded from the English-language pages of KINU's website at www.kinu.or.kr. It is available in a paperback version as well. KINU also publishes excellent surveys of North Korean defectors.

The English-language pages of the website NKnet at http://nknet.org publish highly informative reports on life in North Korea based on the most recent testimony of defectors and other sources. Also invaluable, the *Daily NK* is available on this website.

The international nonprofit organization Good Friends maintains an English-language page on its website at http://goodfriends.or.kr/eng with *North Korea Today*, an informative weekly newsletter that is also available by e-mail.

Human Rights and Defectors

KINU reports, especially the annual *White Paper*, are excellent sources on this topic.

Also, the U.S.-based nonprofit organization Committee for Human Rights in North Korea maintains a website at www.hrnk.org, where human rights reports can be found, such as David Hawk, *The Hidden Gulag: Exposing North Korea's Prison Camps* (Washington, DC: U.S. Committee for Human Rights in North Korea, 2003), and Stephan Haggard and Marcus Noland, *Hunger and Human Rights: The Politics of Famine in North Korea* (Washington, DC: U.S. Committee for Human Rights in North Korea, 2005).

Two first-hand accounts by defectors who escaped from prison camps are Chol-hwan Kang and Pierre Rigoulot, *The Aquariums of Pyongyang: Ten Years in the North Korean Gulag*, trans. Yair Reiner (New York: Basic Books, 2001), and Soon Ok Lee, *Eyes of the Tailless Animals: Prison Memoirs of a North Korean Woman*, trans. Rev. Bahn-Suk Lee and Jin Young Choi (Bartlesville, OK: Living Sacrifice Book Co., 1999).

Index

About the Authors

Ralph Hassig is an independent consultant specializing in North Korean affairs and an adjunct professor of psychology at the University of Maryland University College, where he teaches courses in social psychology, organizational behavior, and consumer psychology. He was educated at Albion College (BA in psychology), the University of California, Los Angeles (MA and PhD in social psychology), and the University of San Francisco (MBA in marketing). He is the author, coauthor, and coeditor (with his wife, Kongdan Oh) of several books and numerous articles on North and South Korea.

Kongdan Oh is a research staff member at the Institute for Defense Analyses in Alexandria, Virginia, and a nonresident senior fellow at the Brookings Institution in Washington, D.C. She received her BA from Korea's Sogang University (in Korean literature and Oriental history), an MA from Seoul National University (in Korean literature), and another MA and a PhD in Asian studies from the University of California, Berkeley. She engages in policy research on Asia and is a widely cited expert on North and South Korean affairs.